Regional Integration and Development

*Maurice Schiff
and L. Alan Winters*

A co-publication of the World Bank and Oxford University Press.

The findings, interpretations, and conclusions expressed here are those of the author(s) and do not necessarily reflect the views of the Board of Executive Directors of the World Bank or the governments they represent.

The World Bank cannot guarantee the accuracy of the data included in this work. The boundaries, colors, denominations, and other information shown on any map in this work do not imply on the part of the World Bank any judgment of the legal status of any territory or the endorsement or acceptance of such boundaries.

Library of Congress Cataloguing-in-Publication Data

Schiff, Maurice W.
  Regional integration and development / Maurice Schiff and L. Alan Winters.
    p. cm.
  Includes bibliographical references and index.
  ISBN 0-8213-5078-1
  1. Trade blocs. 2. Regionalism. 3. Commercial policy. 4. Free trade. 5. International economic relations. I. Winters, L. Alan. II. Title.

F1418.7 .S35 2002
337.1—dc21

                                                                           2002074094

POD by LSI

Contents

LIST OF BOXES

LIST OF FIGURES

LIST OF TABLES

Preface

The growth of regional trading blocs has been one of the major developments in international relations in recent years; virtually all countries are now members of at least one bloc. In addition to the boom in numbers, the past 10 years have also witnessed qualitative changes in regional integration arrangements. Three of these merit special attention:

- The move from a closed to a more open model of regionalism. The new wave of regional integration agreements (which includes the revival of some old agreements) generally exhibits a more outward-looking stance and greater commitment to boosting, rather than controlling, international commerce.
- The recognition that, in addition to reducing tariffs and quotas, effective integration requires the removal of other barriers, or what has come to be known as "deep integration."
- The advent of trade blocs in which high-income countries and developing countries are equal partners—so-called North-South agreements.

This evolution pointed to the need for the World Bank to undertake a new analysis of regional integration agreements with a focus on developing countries. There are two reasons for this emphasis. First, developing countries are turning to regionalism as a tool for development, and the effectiveness of this tool needs to be assessed. Second, regionalism is part of the global economic environment, and its effects on developing countries need to be better understood. It also seemed desirable to ground the new analysis more firmly in empirical results than had been done previously.

The analysis presented in this book assesses the effects of regional integration arrangements (RIAs) on trade and competition (chapter 2); examines how to make the most of RIAs (chapter 3); considers the impact of RIAs on investment and foreign direct investment (chapter 4); carefully examines the dynamic economic effects of integration (chapter 5); assesses the needs and opportunities for deep integration (chapter 6); explores the intersection between the economic and political effects of integration (chapter 7); and examines the relationship between regionalism and multilateralism (chapter 8). Although regionalism is too complex and *sui generis* to generate universal and operational policy rules, the evidence presented in the first eight chapters is reduced in chapter 9 to a set of consistent policy messages that apply to most circumstances. These rules of thumb are not inviolable, but they should not be broken lightly (chapter 9).

The book is the outcome of a research project on regionalism and development, led by the authors and carried out at the World Bank starting in 1996. The main themes of that research were recently presented in a companion volume, the World Bank Policy Research Report *Trade Blocs* (2000). That report was based on the same ideas and research as are described here, but organized differently and presented in a straightforward way for a broad audience. The present book underpins those themes more firmly by going into more detail than could *Trade Blocs* and by placing greater emphasis on the analytical and intellectual structures that can be used for exploring the effects of regionalism. The research project has also generated more than 100 research papers, more than half of which have been published. Most of these papers are available at <http://www.worldbank.org/research/trade/>.

The research project and this book benefited from contributions and comments by Azita Amjadi, Soamiely Andriamananjara, Richard Baldwin, Fred Bergsten, Jagdish Bhagwati, Magnus Blomström, Eric Bond, Won Chang, Paul Collier, Jo-Ann Crawford, Jaime de Melo, Dean DeRosa, Robert Devlin, Simon Evenett, Raquel Fernandez, Michael Finger, Faezeh Foroutan, Jeffrey Frankel, Anju Gupta, Dominique Hachette, Bart Kaminski, Walter Kennes, Moonhui Kim, Ari Kokko, Pravin Krishna, Praveen Kumar, Sam Laird, Philip Levy, Dorsati Madani, Will Martin, Francis Ng, Marcelo Olarreaga, Pier Carlo Padoan, Arvind Panagariya, Joost Polak, Jonathan Portes, Diego Puga, Sherman Robinson, Peter Robson, André Sapir, Jeffrey Schott, Elena Seghezza, Isidro Soloaga, T. N. Srinivasan, Sherry Stephenson, Costas Syropolous, David Tarr, Peter Tulloch, Athanasios Vamvakidis, Tony Venables, Yanling Wang, Shang-Jin Wei, John Whalley, and Alexander Yeats and by three anonymous referees. Special thanks go to Bernard Hoekman, who co-authored chapter 6. Naturally, none of the individuals who contributed to or commented on the book is responsible for its remaining shortcomings.

Melissa Edeburn, the production editor, and Nancy Levine, the copy editor, did outstanding jobs. Excellent assistance was provided by Mary-Ann Arouna, Rosie Bellinger, Janet Ellis, Maria Lourdes Kasilag, Audrey Kitson-Walters, and Rebecca Martin.

Thanks to Lunia, Dominique, Oliver, and Zhen Kun for their love and support throughout a very long project.

Abbreviations and Acronyms

ACP	African, Caribbean, and Pacific (Lomé Convention) countries
AERC	African Economic Research Consortium
AFTA	ASEAN Free Trade Area
APEC	Asia-Pacific Economic Cooperation
ASEAN	Association of Southeast Asian Nations
BIT	bilateral investment treaty
CACM	Central American Common Market
CAP	Common Agricultural Policy (EU)
CARICOM	Caribbean Community and Common Market
CBI	Cross-Border Initiative (Africa)
CEAO	Economic Community of West Africa (became UEMOA)
CEFTA	Central European Free Trade Area
CEMAC	Economic and Monetary Community of Central Africa/ Communauté économique et monétaire d'Afrique Centrale
CEPGL	Economic Community of the Countries of the Great Lakes/Communauté économique des pays des grands lacs
CER	Closer Economic Relations agreement (Australia and New Zealand)
CET	common external tariff
CGE	computable general equilibrium (model)
CMEA	Council for Mutual Economic Assistance
COMESA	Common Market for Eastern and Southern Africa

xv

CRTA	Committee on Regional Trading Agreements (WTO)
CUSFTA	Canada–United States Free Trade Agreement
EAC	East African Cooperation (formerly East African Community)
EC	European Community
ECOWAS	Economic Community of West African States
ECSC	European Coal and Steel Community
EEA	European Economic Area
EEC	European Economic Community
EFTA	European Free Trade Association
EPA	economic partnership agreement
EU	European Union
FDI	foreign direct investment
FTA	free trade agreement; free trade area
FTAA	Free Trade Area of the Americas
G3	Group of Three (Colombia, Mexico, and Venezuela)
GATS	General Agreement on Trade in Services
GATT	General Agreement on Tariffs and Trade
GCC	Gulf Cooperation Council
GDP	gross domestic product
GNP	gross national product
GSP	generalized system of preferences
HS	Harmonized Commodity Description and Coding System
ICSID	International Centre for Settlement of Investment Disputes
IMF	International Monetary Fund
IOC	Indian Ocean Commission
IPRs	intellectual property rights
ITA	Information Technology Agreement
LAFTA	Latin American Free Trade Area
LAIA	Latin American Integration Association
LATN	Latin American Trade Network
MAI	Multilateral Agreement on Investment
MERCOSUR	Common Market of the South/Mercado Común del Sur
MFN	most-favored-nation
MITI	Ministry of International Trade and Industry (Japan)
MRA	mutual recognition agreement
NAFTA	North American Free Trade Agreement

OECD	Organisation for Economic Co-operation and Development
PTA	preferential trade agreement
R&D	research and development
RIA	regional integration agreement
ROW	rest of the world
SAARC	South Asian Association for Regional Cooperation
SACU	Southern African Customs Union
SADC	Southern African Development Community
SADCC	Southern African Development Coordination Conference (renamed SADC)
SAPTA	SAARC Preferential Trading Arrangement
SMP	Single Market Programme (EU)
TFP	total factor productivity
UDEAC	Union douanière et économique de l'Afrique Centrale (renamed CEMAC)
UEMOA	West African Economic and Monetary Union/Union économique et monétaire ouest-africaine
UNCTAD	United Nations Conference on Trade and Development
VAT	value-added tax
WTO	World Trade Organization

Note: The use of the designations EEC, EC, and EU depends on the time period and historical context.

CHAPTER 1

Regional Integration Agreements: An Overview

The growth of regional trade blocs has been one of the major developments in international relations in recent years. Virtually all countries are members of a bloc, and many belong to more than one. Over a third of world trade takes place within such agreements—nearly two-thirds, if Asia-Pacific Economic Cooperation (APEC) is included. Regional agreements vary widely, but all have the objective of reducing barriers to trade between member countries—which implies discrimination against trade with other countries. At their simplest, these agreements merely remove tariffs on intrabloc trade in goods, but many go beyond that to cover nontariff barriers and to extend liberalization to investment and other policies. At their deepest, they have the goal of economic union and involve the construction of shared executive, judicial, and legislative institutions. For want of a better term, we lump them all into the category of regional integration agreements (RIAs), as defined in box 1.1. The appendix to this chapter lists the principal RIAs.

During the past decade, the move toward regionalism became a headlong rush. Figure 1.1 highlights the dramatic increase in agreements notified to the General Agreement on Tariffs and Trade/World Trade Organization (GATT/WTO) in the 1990s.[1] Of the 194 agreements that had been notified by the beginning of 1999, 87 dated from 1990 or after.

The past decade also witnessed qualitative changes in RIAs. There have been three major developments:

1. *The move from "closed regionalism" to a more open model,* in line with prevailing views about national economic policy. Many of the trade blocs that were formed between developing countries in the 1960s and 1970s were based on a model of import-

1

> **Box 1.1 Defining Terms: What's in a Name?**
>
> Who but a staunch protectionist could have anything against a "free trade agreement"? "Preferential trade agreements" sound less benign, while "discriminatory trade agreements," yet another name for the same thing, sound nasty.
>
> Martin Wolf, *Financial Times*, October 28, 1996
>
> This book is primarily about preferential trading agreements between groups of countries. We refer to them neutrally as regional integration agreements (RIAs) to avoid any unsubstantiated pejorative implications and to convey that arrangements can extend well beyond international trade into areas such as investment, domestic regulation, domestic policies, standards, infrastructure, and politics. Indeed, we shall argue that cooperation in these areas is frequently more important than in international trade and that in some cases governments should eschew using trade agreements as a vehicle for cooperation on nontrade issues. We use the shorthand term "regionalism" to cover the process of creating RIAs.
>
> Although most RIAs are between neighboring countries, this is not universally true—as illustrated, for example, by the free trade agreements between the United States and Israel, Chile and Canada, and Mexico and the European Union (EU) and by Greece's accession to the EU. Nor is it required for most of the analytical arguments that we make.
>
> We do not attempt to cover all arrangements between countries. For example, we do not deal with alliances for defense or political cooperation, not because they are not important but because we have no particular expertise—nor the World Bank any particular mandate—in these areas.

substituting development, and regional agreements with high external trade barriers were used as a way of implementing this model.[2] New-wave RIAs (some of which are old agreements resurrected) are generally more outward looking and more committed to boosting rather than controlling international commerce.

2. *The recognition that effective integration requires more than simply reducing tariffs and quotas.* Many other types of barrier have the effect of segmenting markets and impeding the free flow of goods, services, investments, and ideas, and wideranging policy measures—going well beyond traditional trade policies—are needed to remove them. Such "deep integration" was first actively pursued in the Single Market Programme of the European Union (EU), but its elements are now finding their way into the debate on other regional agreements.

3. *The advent of "North-South" trade blocs in which high-income countries and developing countries are equal partners.*[3] Perhaps the most important example is the North American Free Trade Agreement (NAFTA), formed in 1994 when the Canada–United

Figure 1.1 Regional Integration Agreements, Notified and Active, 1948 to April 2002

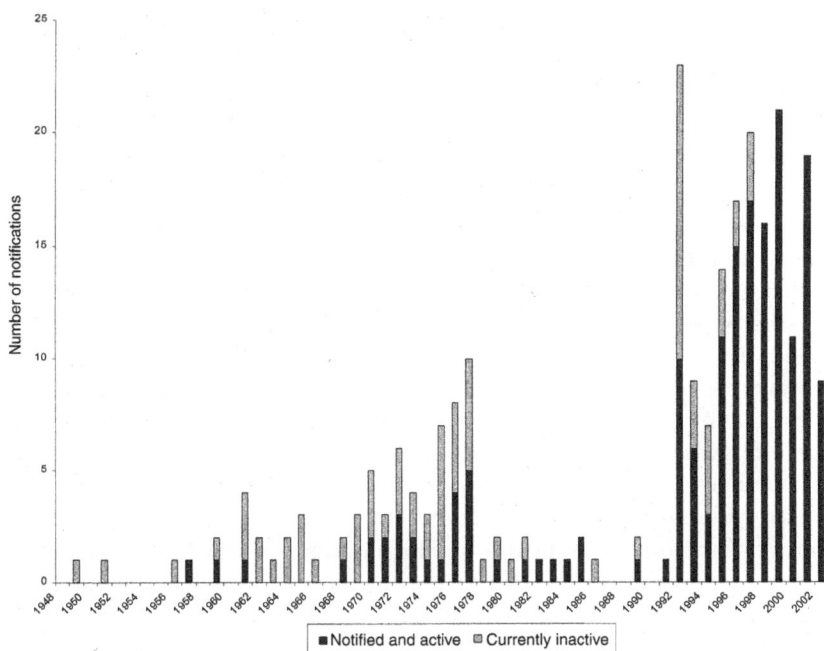

Note: Information on inactive RIAs for 2000–02 is not available.
Source: World Trade Organization data.

States Free Trade Agreement (CUSFTA) was extended to Mexico. The EU also has North-South arrangements, including the Europe Agreements that link the EU with the transition economies of Eastern Europe, a customs union with Turkey, and agreements with many Mediterranean countries. In addition, the EU is committed to negotiating reciprocal trade agreements (economic partnership agreements, or EPAs) with the African, Caribbean, and Pacific (ACP) countries.

These developments have occurred against the backdrop of globalization: new technologies and more liberal trading regimes have led to higher trade volumes, larger investment flows, and increasingly footloose production.

All these considerations reinforced the need for the World Bank to undertake a new analysis of regional integration agreements—one that would take political effects into account, carefully examine dynamic economic effects, assess the needs and opportunities for deep integration, capture the new potentials created by North-South agreements, and be firmly grounded in empirical analysis.

A new analysis would also have to focus on developing countries, for two reasons. First, developing countries are turning to regionalism as a tool for development, and the effectiveness of this strategy needs to be assessed. Second, regionalism is part of the global economic environment and affects developing countries, whether or not they participate in it. Understanding its implications can help them better prepare for and cope with regionalism.

Macroeconomic and exchange rate policies are important for the sustainability of RIAs and affect their perceived or actual desirability. Unsustainable macroeconomic policies may lead to backsliding on countries' commitments to liberalize intrabloc trade or to converge to a common external tariff in a customs union. And unexpected exchange rate changes may affect the short-to-medium-term distribution of the expected gains from an RIA, possibly reducing its attractiveness. For reasons of space and focus, however, we do not deal with these issues, limiting our analysis instead to the real aspects of regional integration. Another consideration is that our interest is in the long-term implications of RIAs, and we view macroeconomic disequilibria as essentially temporary phenomena.

RIAs IN HISTORY

RIAs have been around for hundreds of years. For example, a customs union of the provinces of France was proposed in 1664; Austria signed free trade agreements with five of its neighbors during the 18th and 19th centuries; and the colonial empires were based on preferential trade arrangements. Customs unions were precursors to or were embodied in the creation of new states in, for example, Germany (the *Zollverein*), Italy, and the United States.

The 1930s saw a great fragmentation of the world trading system as governments struggled with the slump in demand without the benefit of global economic institutions to provide liberal focal points. One of the "solutions" adopted was regional preferences. The exact causal relationship between restricted trade and declining incomes during this period is still debated, but fragmentation into closed blocs must have fostered inefficiency and frustrated recovery from the Great Depression.

Partly in response to the experience of the 1930s, and partly under the influence of U.S. idealism and internationalism, the post–World War II system established equal treatment of all partners (nondiscrimination) as a fundamental principle of the trading system. Exceptions were permitted, both on pragmatic grounds and for reasons of principle, and among these exceptions was the ability to create trade blocs—free trade areas (FTAs) and customs unions. Aside from reinforcing existing colonial links, this concession was little used at first, but over its first decade it contributed to the political reconstruction of Europe through the creation of the Benelux customs union in 1947, the European Coal and Steel Community (ECSC) in 1951, and the more far-reaching European Economic Community (EEC) in 1957.

The survival and apparent success of the EEC led to a spurt of regionalism between developing countries in the 1960s. This spurt was mostly driven by the import-substitution creed that protection was required for industrialization—and hence for prosperity—and that this policy would be less costly if extended over a larger economic area. The RIAs were generally very protectionist and interventionist in the sense of trying to determine administratively which industries to have and where they should be located. They involved numerous controls and restrictions on economic activity and, consequently, yielded rather modest economic results. In addition, the degree of implementation was often low, in part because of disagreements on where industries should be located. By the late 1970s, the ineffectiveness of these RIAs had become evident. None seemed to have contributed strongly to development; some had collapsed; and the strains of the debt crisis made those that survived largely moribund.

In the 1980s a huge change in attitudes toward international trade and competition took place. Led by the EU's Single Market Programme, a new wave of apparently more liberal RIAs emerged. These were inspired by a set of hopes and aspirations, the analysis of which is the subject of this report.

The recent growth in regionalism was dominated by the EU's activities: the extension of the Single Market Programme to neighboring countries that were not yet members of the EU, through the European Economic Area; the signing of Europe Agreements with the countries of Eastern Europe; the accession of three new members in 1995; and the development of a more active and formal Mediterranean policy that potentially included RIAs with nearly every Mediterranean country. In fact, of the 87 notifications of RIAs to the WTO since 1990, only 13 had no European partner.

But Europe was not the only continent involved. In the Americas the Canada–United States Free Trade Agreement of 1988 was extended to Mexico in 1994 through NAFTA; Common Market of the South (Mercado Común del Sur–MERCOSUR) was formed in 1991 and the Group of Three (G3) in 1995; and the Andean Pact and the Central American Common Market (CACM) were resurrected in 1991 and 1993, respectively. In 1992 the countries of the Association of Southeast Asian Nations (ASEAN), after 25 years of political cooperation with limited trade cooperation, formed a meaningful FTA, the ASEAN Free Trade Area (AFTA). Since then, additional countries have joined AFTA, which has also started talks with China. The Republic of Korea and Japan, among others, are negotiating an FTA. In West Africa the trade blocs re-formed in more liberal and more tightly organized blocs. The Common Market for Eastern and Southern Africa (COMESA) replaced a preferential trade agreement (PTA), and many of its members also took part in the Cross-Border Initiative (CBI). The Southern African Development Coordination Conference (SADCC) transmogrified into the Southern African Development Community (SADC), which is a trade and economic cooperation association rather than a defense organization. East African Cooperation (EAC) sprang up where the East African Community had failed. In North Africa the Mahgreb and Mashraq groups have renewed their integration efforts.

WHY REGIONALISM?

Many factors lay behind the recent spurt in regionalism. Some were explicitly stated goals, as summarized in boxes 1.2 and 1.3. Other objectives could not be so publicly admitted, and yet others represented more fundamental causes. Among the objectives, stated and implicit, were:

- Governments' wish to bind themselves to better policies— including democracy—and to signal such bindings to domestic and foreign investors
- A desire to obtain more secure access to major markets
- The pressures of globalization, forcing firms and countries to seek efficiency through larger markets, increased competition, and access to foreign technologies and investment
- Governments' desire to maintain sovereignty by pooling it with others in areas of economic management where most nation-states are too small to act alone
- A desire to jog the multilateral system into faster and deeper action in selected areas by showing that the GATT was not the only

Box 1.2 What the Politicians Say: Hopes and Rationales for RIAs

Trade

"The implementation of the Arab Free Trade Agreement will be a major factor that will help the Kingdom expand its export markets."

Hani Mulki, Jordan's minister of industry, trade, and supply, Xinhua News Agency,
September 7, 1998

"The regional integration did not hamper world trade liberalization, but rather was an essential component of it, enabling countries at differing levels of development to participate more effectively in world trade."

Colombia's representative to the meeting of the WTO Working Party on MERCOSUR,
October 10–11, 1995

Investment

"To promote foreign direct investments in ASEAN. The synergies of both [ASEAN and the ASEAN Free Trade Area, AFTA] will ensure that ASEAN remains as a highly attractive and globally competitive investment region."

Datuk Ajit Singh, secretary-general of ASEAN, *Straits Times,*
February 25, 1997

"Such a healthy atmosphere is a major attraction to foreign industrial investment. . . . We encourage Arab investment through which we can find an entry to unify their economies through establishment of free trade markets."

Mohamed Al Amadi, Syria's minister for economy and foreign trade, on the Arab Free
Trade Zone, *Egyptian Gazette,* November 6, 1998

"To clearly regulate the growing trade between our countries, encourage investment and create jobs."

Carlos Salinas de Gortari, president of Mexico, on NAFTA, State of the Nation Address,
November 4, 1994

Security and democracy

"Formation of Euro-Mediterranean forum will give impetus to the partnership at all political, economic, security and development levels."

Ahmed Fathi Sorous, chairman of the Arab Parliamentary Union and speaker of the
Egyptian People's Assembly, interview with Sawt al Arab Radio, October 28, 1998

"NAFTA has contributed to the prosperity and stability of our closest neighbors and two of our most important trading partners. NAFTA aided Mexico's rapid recovery from a severe economic recession, even as that country carried forward a democratic transformation of historic proportions."

William Clinton, president of the United States, letter to the U.S. Congress,
July 1997

Market access

"New Zealand's worst fear is for the world to divide into trading blocs . . . in none of which New Zealand has a home. So we are keen to keep working with ASEAN."

Helen Clark, prime minister of New Zealand, on the New Zealand–Singapore-FTA, *Far
East Economic Review,* August 17, 2000

(Box continues on next page.)

Box 1.2 *(continued)*

Deep integration

"The Europe Agreement with the EC is to provide an appropriate framework for both a political dialogue and a comprehensive cooperation in a broad range of areas and a step towards the Czech Republic's ultimate objective of full membership in the EC."
Representative of the Czech Republic to the WTO Committee on Regional Trade Agreements, May 30, 1997

Growth and development

"Will boost technology transfer from the north to the south Mediterranean countries."
Ahmed Fathi Sorous, chairman of the Arab Parliamentary Union and speaker of the Egyptian People's Assembly, interview with Sawt al Arab Radio, October 28, 1998

"To achieve development and economic growth, alleviate poverty, enhance the standard and quality of life of the peoples of southern Africa, and support the socially disadvantaged through regional integration."
Chris Stals, governor of the South African Reserve Bank, on the SADC, May 1, 1997

Box 1.3 What the Treaties Say: Aims and Objectives

Trade and income

"To enhance the competitiveness of their firms in global markets"
NAFTA, 1992

"To create an expanded and secure market for the goods and services produced in their territories. To reduce distortions to trade"
G3 Treaty (Colombia, Mexico, and Venezuela), 1994

"To modernize their economies in order to expand the supply and improve the quality of available goods and services, with a view to enhancing the living conditions of their populations"
MERCOSUR Agreement, 1991

Investment

"To ensure a predictable commercial framework for production activities and investment"
G3 Treaty, 1994

"Prerequisite for the stimulation of domestic, regional and foreign direct investment and the expansion, growth and the development of the economies of each member state and the region as a whole"
Kinshasa Resolution on the Establishment of COMESA, 1998

"A stimulus to the development of the national economies by expanding investment and production opportunities, trade, and foreign exchange earnings"
Agreement on the Common Effective Preferential Tariff Scheme for the ASEAN Free Trade Area, 1992

Development

"To ensure in particular that these arrangements encourage the development of the less advanced members of the customs union and the diversification of their economies"
Southern African Customs Union (SACU) Agreement, 1969
(Box continues on next page.)

Box 1.3 *(continued)*

Democracy and human rights

"To involve the peoples of the Region centrally in the process of development and integration, particularly through the guarantee of democratic rights, observance of human rights and the rule of law"

SADC Treaty, 1992

"To strengthen democracy and respect for human rights, sustainable and balanced economic and social development, to combat poverty and promote greater understanding between cultures"

Barcelona Declaration adopted at the Euro-Mediterranean Conference, 1995

Regional cooperation and coordination

"To establish a firm foundation for common action to promote regional cooperation in South-East Asia in the spirit of equality and partnership and thereby contribute towards peace, progress and prosperity in the region"

ASEAN Declaration, 1967

"To foster coordinated action by the Parties in international economic fora, particularly in those related to the processes of Latin American integration"

G3 Treaty, 1994

Regional and global integration

"To contribute to the harmonious development and expansion of world trade and provide a catalyst to broader international cooperation"

NAFTA, 1992

"To facilitate the accession of Chile to the North American Free Trade Agreement . . . To contribute to hemispheric integration"

Canada–Chile Free Trade Agreement, 1996

---

game in town and by creating more powerful blocs that would operate within the GATT system

- A desire to help neighboring countries stabilize and prosper, both for altruistic reasons and to avoid spillovers of unrest and population
- The fear of being left out while the rest of the world swept into regionalism, either because this would be actually harmful to excluded countries or just because "if everyone else is doing it, shouldn't we?"

Among the more fundamental causes, we would list the following:

- The collapse of Soviet hegemony, which led the countries of Eastern Europe and the Baltic to embrace democracy and capitalism and those of Western Europe to seek ways of cementing and accelerating their transition.
- The change in understanding of the role of openness in development, coupled with a natural political desire to limit the feared adjustment costs of unilateral nondiscriminatory liberalization.

- The need to create a domestic dynamic for the reforms required to achieve greater openness while at the same time minimizing the political problems of disrupting existing sources of incomes and rents.
- The changed attitude of the United States toward trade blocs, from active hostility to a broadly enthusiastic stance. This shift both fostered RIAs and reduced the diplomatic pressure—overt (through the GATT) and covert—for countries to desist from forming them. It stemmed at least in part from an expressed frustration with the slowness of the multilateral process. Also important, if less public, were the increasing influence of business lobbies in U.S. policymaking, the decreasing competitiveness of U.S. industry, and a lessened willingness to bear the costs of managing the global system without receiving direct payoffs in the form of markets. With the end of the Cold War, the overriding political justification for bearing those costs disappeared, and the debate focused more directly on mercantilist objectives, as it always had in most smaller countries.

This book asks whether the hopes expressed for regionalism are justified, or have been justified by recent evidence, and how their fulfillment might be made more likely. In doing so, it takes the economic arguments summarized above and subjects them to more careful scrutiny than they have usually received.

WHY ANOTHER BOOK ON REGIONALISM?

The literature on regionalism is massive, and a proposal to add to it requires some justification. Our rationale is fourfold:

1. Policymakers need practical advice presented in the form of reasoned argument and evidence. The body of knowledge and analysis that could provide concrete guidance on whether and when to join RIAs, and on how trade groups should be structured to maximize the welfare of the group and its individual members, has not been pulled together before in a single volume. The tradeoffs involved in forming or joining an RIA are complex and difficult to isolate. Although this book provides few universal or easy solutions to these problems, it does attempt to set the issues out clearly and to suggest the analytical paths that policymakers should take in thinking about their own integration arrangements.

2. Regionalism is still a very fertile area for research, with new re-
    sults and interpretations emerging every day. Reading these, let
    alone assessing them, is not the job of policymakers (they have
    better things to do), and so a straightforward presentation of the
    more important recent developments is desirable.

3. World Bank research has yielded new results on regionalism that
    should be made widely available. Among these contributions are:
    • The first coherent discussion of the credibility benefits of RIAs
    • Tests of the role of political factors in setting an RIA's internal
      and external trade policy
    • Analysis of the effects of RIAs on industrialization in develop-
      ing countries
    • A comprehensive assessment of progress on "deep" (policy) in-
      tegration within RIAs
    • Findings on the effects of recent RIAs on members' trade pat-
      terns and trade policies
    • A formal analysis of the economic implications of establishing
      RIAs to promote peace and security
    • Evidence on the growth or nongrowth effects of RIAs
    • A new approach to assessing the effects of RIAs on excluded
      countries.

4. Although the existing literature is huge, there is no consistency in
    the methodologies and intellectual bases of the research or in its
    conclusions. Thus, in addition to summarizing what economists
    think they know and assessing how much confidence to place in
    that knowledge, we also seek to set forth the internal structure of
    the various arguments. The intention is to allow policymakers to
    judge for themselves which results apply to their particular cir-
    cumstances and how well they fit together into a coherent view of
    the RIA under consideration. In particular, we want to help poli-
    cymakers avoid the regrettably common "pick-and-mix" ap-
    proach of selecting a convenient set of results from the literature
    without regard for their mutual consistency.

One consequence of our ambitious agenda is that we are able to resolve fewer issues empirically than we would wish. There are not many
RIAs of sufficient longevity and consistency of application to provide
convincing historical evidence, and each case has so many different characteristics and is so confounded by other factors (such as developments
in national politics, economic policy, and the world economy) that disentangling the various effects becomes difficult. Accordingly, while we report several innovative pieces of empirical analysis—for instance, on the

effects of RIAs on excluded countries and on members' propensities to protectionism—we also rely heavily on examples and on a priori reasoning. We attempt to gauge the plausibility of such pieces of evidence in reaching overall conclusions, but we are conscious that they are more ambiguous than is ideal.

As noted above, developments in the EU and its predecessors have underlain both of the major spurts of regionalism in the postwar era, and Europe has pursued regional integration farther and deeper than any other (voluntary) arrangement outside the historical instances of nation building. Europe has also generated most of the intellectual advances in the field. We draw a great deal on the European experience, but we seek throughout to apply its lessons to developing country issues.

Our approach is essentially economic, reflecting our comparative advantage. Our concern is with whether regionalism aids economic development. We cast the net broadly, however—examining, for example, the implications of the argument that RIAs can be aimed at political objectives, how RIAs affect policy credibility, and the design of institutions for setting trade policy in an RIA. Since these issues hinge on tradeoffs of the sort that economics deals with—how much a reduction of tension is worth in terms of production inefficiency—they fall well within our ambit. We do not, however, give a full account of the political and social aspects of regionalism.

The main themes of World Bank research and policy advice on regionalism were presented in a companion volume, the Policy Research Report *Trade Blocs*, published in July 2000. That report was based on the same ideas and research as are described here, but it was organized differently and was presented in a straightforward way for a broad audience. It had four themes:

- Many RIAs are political in origin.
- Nonetheless, they entail economic costs and benefits, either via their effects on competition or by affecting patterns of trade or of industrial location.
- These economic aspects are important and certainly influence an RIA's chances of survival. Careful design can maximize the net economic benefits of an RIA.
- Regionalism must be viewed in the context of a global trading system that has delivered great benefits to the world over the past 50 years.

This book goes into more detail on the arguments underlying the four themes than could the 2000 report, and it consequently focuses more sharply on the analytical and intellectual structures that have been used for exploring the effects of regionalism. The book is not, however, an academic tome. It is designed for policymakers, and it attempts to lay out the various arguments clearly and accessibly. Its final chapter summarizes as "rules of thumb" the practical lessons that emerge from the analysis.

Regionalism is a complex business and depends heavily on particular features of particular cases. There are no rules for policy toward RIAs that are both universal and operational—the universal rules are so broad as to be nonoperational, and the operational rules are too specific to be universal. The rules of thumb presented in chapter 9 represent our judgment of the general tendencies within good policy advice. Although they are not carved in stone, policymakers should think long and hard before breaking them.

SUMMARY

The remainder of this chapter offers a brief guide to the contents of the book to help readers find their way around the material and to bring the various parts into perspective. Policy conclusions will be evident from the chapter discussions but are brought together in chapter 9.

Regionalism as Trade Policy

Chapter 2 examines the basic economics of tariff preferences—what happens when a country reduces its tariffs on imports from a subset of its partners. Forming an RIA almost always increases trade between members. But does it "create" trade by allowing cheaper products from bloc partners to substitute for more expensive domestic production, or "divert" trade by substituting intrabloc imports for imports from outside the group? The latter can happen when partner goods, because they no longer face tariffs, have a competitive edge over "outside" goods that would otherwise be cheaper. The preference-granting country ends up paying more for the imports, with the increased payments to producers in partner countries being financed by monies that had initially accrued to the government as tariff revenues. Part of this extra cost is a simple transfer from taxpayers in the importing partner to producers in the exporting partner, but because the real cost of imports has risen (the partner is less efficient than outside producers), real resources are wasted by the diversion. If trade diversion predominates across the board, an RIA can reduce the welfare of both partners.

Distinguishing between trade creation and trade diversion is not straightforward empirically, and we discuss some of the difficulties. The deepest of these is deciding what trade would have looked like had no RIA been formed—the counterfactual, or what Europeans refer to as the *anti-monde*. The evidence on the balance between trade creation and diversion in trade blocs is mixed. We offer new research showing that diversion is significant but that for many of the more recent RIAs it has been dominated by the effects of the partners' reductions of barriers to imports from nonpartners that have accompanied the RIA.

The traditional analysis of trade creation and diversion is based on a view of the world in which intercountry trade is driven entirely by differences in productivity and in factor endowments. But trade can also arise from product differentiation and economies of scale, which reduce costs as production grows. Then import barriers become even more costly because competition between firms is weakened and consumers lose from the resulting decreases in output and increases in price. International trade offers an important means of increasing competition by allowing new suppliers to enter markets. RIAs, by fostering trade between members, can generate such benefits because of the combination of larger firm size (which increases economies of scale) and a larger number of firms (which increases competition). When several national markets are merged, the number of producers in each country may fall, while the number of sellers with reasonable access to each market rises because producers from partner countries now have access. For instance, if each country in a two-country RIA starts off with three firms, even if each loses one firm to intra-RIA competition, there will still be four (now larger) firms producing and selling throughout the bloc.

These so-called procompetitive effects are believed to have operated strongly during the course of European economic integration, but there is not yet enough empirical evidence showing that developing countries will be able to benefit greatly from them. The uncertainty partly reflects developing countries' production structure, which is likely to include fewer goods for which differentiation and economies of scale are important, and partly the fact that significant increases in competition eventually depend on far more than merely removing tariffs and import quotas. (See the discussion of policy integration in chapter 6.) And of course, if the aim is to sell in large markets and buy from firms that supply large markets, no market is larger than the world as a whole; there will be greater procompetitive effects from nondiscriminatory trade liberalization than from discriminatory or restricted liberalization.

Making the Most of Regionalism

Why is regionalism so popular if it is just a pale imitation of nondiscriminatory free trade? Chapter 3 describes the basic international trade aspects of the question and goes on to examine how the design features of an RIA might affect its net benefits.

Governments may prefer RIAs to unilateral trade liberalization for several reasons. They may be better able to exploit market power against outsiders by coordinating trade policies. They may place a high value on access to partners' markets and feel that it is better ensured by making access to their own markets conditional on reciprocity. They may prefer preferential to nonpreferential access to partners' markets. And they may want to exploit the regional market as a base for protected industrialization. We do not find the last two arguments convincing.

Clearly, the benefits of regionalism are likely to depend on finding the best partners. The current notion of a "natural" trading partner is not useful in this regard. We show that whether South-South or North-North RIAs generate economic divergence or convergence between member countries depends on the model used and the initial policy stance. We also show that there are several reasons for the obvious tendency for trade blocs to form between neighboring countries, including the desire to reduce trade costs by relaxing or abolishing border formalities and to facilitate the collection of tax revenues.

One of the main themes of this book is our preference for North-South over South-South RIAs for developing countries. If a developing country is going to pursue regionalism, it will almost always do better to sign up with a large rich country than with a small poor one. In trade terms, a large rich country is likely to be a more efficient supplier of most goods and a source of greater competition for local producers. This recommendation is not absolute: several conditions need to be met if North-South RIAs are to be strongly beneficial. Then, too, the North-South option is not open to all developing countries.

Many countries are members of several RIAs. If all these arrangements are compatible, multiple membership may be beneficial—if the RIAs are desirable per se. But there are also dangers. For example, the RIAs may imply conflicting policies vis-à-vis third countries; they may have different regulations governing imports of the same commodity from different sources; or they may have different technical standards—all of which increases the complexity, cost, and uncertainty of trade. There is also a danger in hub-and-spoke arrangements in which one country carries on free trade with many others that do not have free trade between them. In this case, the "hub" country has considerable advantages as a location for economic activity and may suck firms and investment out of the spokes.

An important distinction is that between free trade areas and customs unions. The latter have, in addition to the internal free trade characteristic of FTAs, a common external tariff or, strictly, a common trade policy toward third countries. FTAs are easier to create and can be institutionally very light, whereas customs unions require the negotiation of the common external tariff and coordination of all future trade policy changes. FTAs do face the danger of trade deflection, in which goods enter the member state with the lowest tariff and then move tax free to other members. Except for the extra transport cost, this is efficient economically because it lowers the effective tariff, but it undermines members' own tariff structures. Governments seek to prevent this from happening by imposing rules of origin to ensure that only locally produced goods are exempted from tariffs. Such rules are often cumbersome and protectionist and can greatly reduce the value of the FTA. Customs unions avoid this problem and can induce a greater degree of integration. Finally, FTAs tend to be more liberal than customs unions in their trade policy with respect to nonmembers; they have less market power, and members may compete with one another to reduce tariffs, thus enlarging their own share of the RIA's imports and increasing their tariff revenue.

Lobbying influences tariffs, and it is plain that it will afflict FTAs and customs unions too. For both, there is a presumption that the exceptions to internal free trade negotiated as the RIA is formed will tend to reduce the degree of trade creation and therefore the potential benefits. In the case of customs unions the agreement will change the environment for future lobbying, but whether toward or away from greater protectionism is impossible to say a priori.

The chapter concludes with a discussion of RIAs and tariff revenues. If countries have to use tariffs for revenue purposes, it may appear to pay small developing countries to combine into a single market to reap economies of scale and enhance competition while raising revenue through tariffs on trade with the outside world. In fact, this is far from being a watertight argument. Moreover, there are other potentially complex revenue issues to consider, such as precisely how to replace the revenue lost when tariffs on intrabloc trade are removed and how to avoid reduction of taxes below optimal levels as a result of fiscal competition between members.

Regionalism and Investment

As is clear from boxes 1.2 and 1.3, promoting investment is a prominent objective of many RIAs. The logic is that larger markets, more competition, and improved policy credibility will increase the incentives for investment and so raise incomes. This argument is relevant to all investment but is most explicitly applied to foreign direct investment (FDI). Chapter 4 briefly describes RIAs' policies toward investment and asks whether the arguments advanced for their having positive effects are justified.

Early RIAs were activist and interventionist, coopting regional integration into import substitution at a regional level. Such policies almost completely failed and have been superseded by a much more market-friendly approach that places more emphasis on policies guaranteeing the fair treatment of investment. These guarantees are often embodied in bilateral investment treaties (BITs) or in the investment chapters of RIA agreements. BITs typically contribute to investment by prohibiting certain policies rather than by requiring policies that actively encourage investment, but they may play an important role in facilitating investment flows.

Far more positive in intent is the argument that RIAs add credibility to government policies in general and thus help increase investment and attract FDI. We argue that South-South RIAs are unlikely to do this and may in fact hinder investment if they are not accompanied by liberalization of trade with the rest of the world. North-South RIAs, on the other hand, can enhance a southern country's credibility, but typically only if the RIA is likely to enhance economic performance in its own right and if the northern partner is willing to enforce investment-encouraging "club rules." The latter is more likely to occur if the policies on which a developing country wants to gain credibility are specified explicitly in the agreement and if the northern partner has an identified interest in the southern partner's success—for example, in alleviation of pressures to migrate. In general, this interest will be greater the closer geographically are the northern and southern partners.

Some recent analysis holds that the rate of return on capital (and on investment) could well rise in all members of an RIA regardless of their capital abundance. For example, if tradables are more capital-intensive than nontradables, then opening up boosts the demand for capital; lower tariffs and trading costs for capital equipment might reduce the price of investment goods; and creation of a more efficient financial sector could reduce borrowing costs. Unfortunately, there are few empirical studies of the impact of RIAs on investment; most trade blocs are so new that the data are simply not there. The limited evidence tends to suggest that RIAs have mildly positive effects on investment, but there is no evidence that this translates into increased economic growth. A possible reason is that additional investment may be attracted into inefficient sectors which benefit from the RIA's high external trade barriers. Firmer evidence is available that RIAs boost FDI, especially inflows of investment from nonmember countries.

The real key to investment is the general policy stance in areas such as sound macroeconomic policies, well-defined property rights, and efficient financial and banking sectors. Regional integration may foster investment if it significantly increases policy credibility and market size, but it needs to be accompanied by good policy overall.

Growth and Location

If RIAs can stimulate investment, might they also have a beneficial effect on growth and industrialization? Chapter 5 moves beyond investment to examine the economics of endogenous growth and of agglomeration (or clustering).

Modern growth theory—the theory of endogenous growth—emphasizes the role of knowledge in fostering productivity and growth. Knowledge can be effectively transferred from one country to another through international contacts and trade. Wealthy countries are knowledge rich and so are likely to provide far more access to technology than can poorer trading partners. RIAs that switch imports from richer to poorer sources are therefore likely to have a perverse effect on countries' growth rates. The boost that RIAs can give to members' growth rates by supporting institutional reform also seems likely to be stronger when developing countries join with richer partners than with poorer ones. Developing countries may, of course, increase their access to knowledge and technology through unilateral trade liberalization that does not discriminate against rich countries, and many institutional reforms can also be achieved through the multilateral system.

The direct evidence on RIAs and growth is subject to methodological reservations but is actually pretty consistent. There is some evidence that North-South RIAs can stimulate growth in the southern partner, little evidence that RIAs between developed countries stimulate growth, and no evidence that RIAs between developing countries do so. Casual examination of the recent performances of, say, Mexico, Poland, and Portugal and a formal analysis of NAFTA suggest that serious North-South integration may foster the southern partners' growth, reinforcing our views about the relative merits of the two types of partners for developing countries. The most important message, however, is that the general policy stance of the southern partner is crucial for capturing long-term gains. Broadly speaking, Portugal reformed on joining the EU and benefited; Greece did not reform and did not benefit.

The same preference for North-South over South-South RIAs arises from the discussion of agglomeration. Although economists have long been aware that industry tends to cluster in particular locations, they have only recently learned to model the phenomenon formally and so begin identifying precisely which combinations of conditions must be satisfied for clustering to occur. The theory arose from attempts to understand the possible effects of the enlargement and deepening of the EU (Krugman and Venables 1990) and so is directly applicable to the case of RIAs. The theory is still very young; the models do not yet appear to be very realistic and have to date not been accompanied by much empirical evidence. Thus, they are more parables than forecasts. They do, however, shed light on qualitative factors, and the issues they address are so important for policymakers and publics alike that we think it useful to explore their implications for developing countries.

Creating an RIA is likely to affect the incentives for industry to agglomerate. Usually, it will encourage clustering by increasing market size and allowing more effective exploitation of the links between firms. An RIA may attract industry into member countries at the expense of nonmembers (although if the RIA is small, such effects will also be very small). RIAs also frequently cause industry to relocate from one member to another. For RIAs between poor countries, this seems likely to increase intermember inequalities because under an RIA firms find it easier to agglomerate in the more prosperous countries while still selling in the other member countries. For RIAs involving richer members, the results are less clear-cut, and it is possible that poorer members will experience industrialization as a result of joining an RIA. When agglomeration effects are considered, integration with richer neighbors (in a North-South RIA) looks far better for developing countries than does South-South integration.

Integration of Domestic Policies

As trade barriers have declined, policymakers have come to a better understanding of the importance of domestic regulation for economic integration. The issues surrounding integration of domestic policies are the subject of chapter 6.

Cooperation on domestic policies can substantially increase the gains from forming a trade bloc. It can lift barriers that insulate national markets for similar goods and services and deliver economic benefits many times those available from mere trade agreements. Policy integration—intergovernmental cooperation in designing and applying domestic policies on taxes, health and safety regulations, the environment, standards, and so on—can increase competition in domestic markets by reducing transactions costs and allowing new suppliers to enter markets. Cooperation on domestic policies can also assist in overcoming market failures and can help ensure that trade restrictions are not reimposed through the back door.

Except for the EU, however, RIAs generally have only "shallow" policy integration aims. Their objective is not economic union (which requires institution building of a type we term "deep integration") but an increase in competition through elimination of policy interventions and reduction of market segmentation. A number of recent and pending RIAs—for example, APEC, MERCOSUR, and the proposed Free Trade Area of the Americas (FTAA)—are discussing an intermediate level of integration that entails close governmental cooperation to harmonize domestic regulations and policies, but no supranational authority. Without specific timetables for action and further negotiation, however, neither new nor existing RIAs are likely to make great progress. Experience suggests that such negotiated policy integration is very demanding, both politically and technically. Moreover, RIAs are not the only game in town; indeed, decisions by individual countries to adopt policies employed elsewhere and multilateral efforts to set international technical and regulatory standards have been more common than regional efforts. Developing countries can do much to achieve the benefits of policy integration unilaterally by adopting international standards and by recognizing the regulatory norms of their major markets, such as the EU and the United States.

One puzzle is why governments combine policy integration and trade integration in the same institution. The trade component of an RIA can provide specie to help overcome opposition to institutional and domestic policy reforms, and policy integration can assist the implementation and enforcement of RIA trade policies. Such linkage does not, of course, excuse the selection of suboptimal trade reforms and domestic policies, but if the reforms and policies are desirable in their own right, combining them might be politically efficient.

Wherever possible, policy integration that reduces regulatory costs should extend beyond RIA partners to nonmembers so that the increase in competition is maximized and policy integration benefits all trading partners. Formal intergovernmental agreements such as mutual recognition arrangements for product standards and testing may be necessary for policy integration, but special efforts should be made to ensure that these do not perpetuate or increase discrimination. Explicitly discriminatory policy integration should be resisted.

Competition between regulatory regimes, coupled with mutual recognition, can be a useful route to policy integration. Some element of harmonization may be called for to prevent adverse spillovers—such as a threat that the competitive relaxation of merger regulation will lead to a "race to the bottom"—or to safeguard public health and safety. These measures are generally best limited to minimum standards based on global norms. Regional standards that diverge from global norms will be optimal only if region-specific characteristics exist.

The WTO and other multilateral institutions can play a large role in policy integration. The WTO agenda is as broad as—and often broader than—that of most RIAs, and more can be done in the WTO context than is often recognized by trade bloc proponents. It could help further by adopting rules extending the most-favored-nation (MFN) principle to policy integration initiatives such as customs clearance documentation and procedures that do not require formal intergovernmental equivalency or recognition agreements.

Policy integration proposals are very specific and should be evaluated on their individual merits. Care should be taken that they are for the general good and that, other than as part of a necessary coalition for achieving reform, efforts to link them to trade liberalization are resisted. While integration of domestic policies may sometimes necessitate formal agreements, there is no fundamental reason why it should require trade preferences. The EU and the United States, for instance, have drawn up a series of mutual recognition agreements for sectoral product standards completely outside an RIA context. To date, developing countries have been entirely excluded from such initiatives.

The issue of cooperation in the area of regional public goods such as natural resources, infrastructure, and energy differs from regional integration and is not addressed in this book. Whether and under what circumstances regional integration can help in attaining a cooperative solution regarding regional public goods is examined in Schiff and Winters (2002a).

Regionalism as Politics

Countries often form trade blocs for noneconomic reasons, such as national security, peace, and help in developing political and social institutions. These are public goods and so are unlikely to be efficiently provided in the absence of some form of intervention, such as an RIA. These political objectives can be important for RIAs—sometimes overwhelmingly so—but it is still desirable that they be achieved efficiently and that policymakers pay heed to their economic costs. Chapter 7 examines some of the political objectives of regionalism, discusses their economic implications, and assesses whether trade preferences are necessary for attaining them.

Political benefits such as peace and security can sometimes swamp the simple material considerations that usually determine economic policy. And because such benefits are typically shared by only a limited number of countries—usually, neighbors—it makes sense to pursue them on a regional basis rather than multilaterally. These political concerns are thus relatively more important in analyzing RIAs than for some other international issues. We show that under some circumstances the formation of an RIA may be an effective way to deal with security tensions between neighboring countries; the argument is essentially that mutual trade fosters peace between countries and that regionalism fosters trade. We show that for an RIA designed to enhance security, the optimum external tariff (on imports from nonmembers) declines over time and as integration deepens.

Joining an RIA with large democratic countries can help a developing country achieve or uphold democracy if the RIA imposes "club rules" such as democracy and civil rights on its members. The size and location of the partners matters because larger partners are generally able to impose greater costs on (withdraw greater benefits from) recalcitrants than are smaller ones, and because a democratic partner country is likely to be far more concerned about possible spillovers (such as migration) from events in a sizable and nearby developing country than from elsewhere.

A concern for many RIA members is whether increased regional integration will weaken the nation-state. We argue that for small and even medium-size countries, pooling sovereignty and undertaking collective action can enhance the effectiveness of the state by helping solve economic problems, by strengthening countries against third-country security threats, and by increasing international influence by lowering negotiation costs or increasing bargaining power in dealings with the rest of the world. But, as we argued above, cooperation of this kind does not usually require trade preferences.

Regionalism and the Rest of the World

RIAs are, by nature, exclusive clubs. After all, every country in the world is excluded from nearly every RIA in the world, and every RIA excludes nearly every country. The discrimination by RIAs against excluded countries is real and, according to the latest evidence, can cause significant trade diversion. Trade diversion is mainly a cost to the partners who pay more for their imports, but chapter 8 shows that in two sets of circumstances it can be costly to the excluded countries that lose exports.

First, if exports generate supernormal profits, losing them is costly because the income lost exceeds the value of the resources freed up by not having to produce the exports any more. This can happen, for example, if the exporter is able to charge monopoly prices or (a more important case) where exports are taxed, because the tax-inclusive price received for the exports exceeds the cost of the resources used up in production. Export taxes are rare, but trade theory teaches us that import taxes are export taxes; it is the act of trading (turning exports into imports) that is taxed, and it does not matter which side of the transaction formally faces the tax. Thus, a country with significant tariffs will lose welfare if its exports fall exogenously. Another way of seeing this is that when exports fall, imports must fall as well to maintain the trade balance, and the result is a loss in tariff revenue.

The second case in which trade diversion hurts exporters is when the decline in demand forces down export prices—that is, worsens the exporter's terms of trade. We present new empirical evidence of the significance of this effect from Brazil's experience following the creation of MERCOSUR.

Possibly even more important than the static losses suffered by excluded countries is the issue of whether RIAs are stepping stones toward the ultimate goal of globally freer trade, or millstones around the neck of progress toward this goal. The world of multiple trade blocs is still too new to permit a definitive empirical answer, and economic theory is not completely clear on the matter, but we see significant dangers that regionalism could start to undermine the multilateral trading system. Certainly, regionalism hits at one of the cornerstones of multilateralism as a framework for international affairs—equal treatment for all.

Most analyses of the effects of bloc formation on the tariffs imposed by noncooperating governments suggest that tariffs tend to increase with the spread of regionalism. It is asserted that in some cases regionalism has brought other countries to the negotiating table to agree on new rounds of multilateral trade liberalization; for example, the formation of the EEC is said to have led to the Kennedy Round. We argue that the desired outcome is far from certain and that using such coercive tactics to get others to reduce their tariffs is extremely dangerous. One such act may call forth another, giving rise to "domino regionalism," which seems to lie behind much of the spread of regionalism during the 1980s and 1990s. Under such conditions, one cannot infer that because regionalism is spreading, it is benign. If everyone else is in a gang, you may want to belong to one yourself, but that does not make gangs a good thing.

One of the problems with the theory of domino regionalism is that although enlarging an RIA might increase the incentives for new members to join, it does not necessarily increase the incentives for existing members to let new ones in. Particularly if RIAs discriminate against excluded countries, insiders will want to stop expansion well short of the whole world; there is no point in being inside if there is no one outside to exploit. It is sometimes argued that an alternative would be to insist on open access to all RIAs—any country that could adhere to the rules of an RIA could join it and reap its benefits. In practice, given that accession has to be negotiated (because the rules of nearly all RIAs entail more than just tariff reductions), there is no operational way to insist on such access. We find the concept of "open regionalism" to be more of a slogan than an analytical tool since, depending on the definition used, it either reduces to something else (such as multilateralism) or does not separate "good" from "bad" RIAs.

In time, RIAs will obviously impinge on the trade negotiation process. Some argue that if talks involved a few RIAs rather than many separate countries, they would be simpler and quicker. Possibly so, but this ignores the difficulties caused by having to agree positions within each bloc before and during the negotiations. It is also suggested that RIAs could serve to develop blueprints for technically complex issues before they come to the global level or could provide a means of tackling politically difficult issues that cannot yet be agreed globally. Again, we do not rule out the possibility of benefits through these routes, but they are far from guaranteed.

Chapter 8 concludes with a discussion of how the WTO handles RIAs. While far from perfect, the current rules for developed countries are probably about as good as we can get, but they are currently very poorly enforced. Those for developing countries are looser and make it even easier to create welfare-reducing RIAs. We advocate unifying the rules on the developed country model and enforcing them more actively. The rules, however, cannot guarantee benign regionalism, and responsibility for ensuring that RIAs do not harm their members falls squarely on the governments involved. In this effort, governments would be aided by much clearer analyses of the economic effects of regional blocs than the WTO's current legalistic approach requires.

Rules of Thumb for Regionalism

Chapter 9 summarizes our views on what has been learned from the study. As noted above, regionalism is too complex and sui generis to generate universal operational rules. We believe, however, that there are consistent lessons from the analysis that apply in most circumstances. These are collected as rules of thumb that are not inviolable but should not be violated lightly. The rules are grouped into eight main messages:

- *Use RIAs as a way of fostering competition.* If an RIA is necessary, it should be used as a procompetitive instrument, with a focus on incorporating provisions that will foster greater competition in domestic markets.
- *North-South dominates South-South.* Not all partners are equal. RIAs with high-income countries are more likely to generate significant economic gains than are those with poorer ones.
- *Credibility gains require explicitness.* RIAs can enhance the credibility of economic and political reform programs, but generally only if they explicitly include provisions and mechanisms that directly affect the policies of interest.
- *Only efficient RIAs are likely to help politically.* RIAs can help solve political problems, but if they are economically wasteful or divisive, they could have opposite effects.
- *Regional cooperation does not generally require trade preferences.* The existence of widespread intercountry spillovers calls for cooperation between developing countries in areas other than trade policy, such as regulatory reform and provision of infrastructure. Usually, however, these goals should be pursued independent of trade discrimination.
- *Beware of transactions costs in operating RIAs.* Governments should consider carefully the transactions and implementation costs associated with different types of RIAs.
- *RIAs may have positive or negative fiscal implications.* The fiscal dimensions of RIAs are important for countries in which trade taxes generate a significant share of government revenue.

- *Do not rely on the WTO to ensure that RIAs are beneficial.* Countries should not rely on the WTO to ensure that RIAs are beneficial to members and to outsiders. The WTO forbids some destructive forms of regionalism, but its main contribution toward constraining the potential negative implications of regionalism for nonmembers is as an instrument for pursuing global liberalization on an MFN basis.

APPENDIX. SELECTED REGIONAL INTEGRATION AGREEMENTS WITH DEVELOPING COUNTRY MEMBERS

In this appendix, the name of the agreement is followed by the type of agreement (common market, customs union, FTA, and so on) and by the governing GATT/WTO provision. Article XXIV of the GATT sets out the conditions under which the formation of FTAs or customs unions is permitted. The GATT Enabling Clause, approved in 1971, allows members to "accord differential and more favorable treatment to developing countries without according such treatment to other contracting parties." The years are the dates of notification to the GATT/WTO or, if not notified, of founding.

RIAs between Developed and Developing Economies

European Union (EU), common market, Article XXIV; formerly European Economic Community (EEC), European Community (EC). *1957,* Belgium, France, Germany, Italy, Luxembourg, Netherlands; *1973,* Denmark, Ireland, United Kingdom; *1981,* Greece; *1986,* Portugal, Spain; *1995,* Austria, Finland, Sweden.
European Economic Area (EEA), FTA, Article XXIV. *1994,* EU, Iceland, Liechtenstein, Norway.
Euro-Mediterranean Economic Area (Euro-Maghreb), FTAs, Article XXIV. Bilateral agreements: *1995,* EU and Tunisia; *1996,* EU and Morocco.
EU bilateral agreements with Eastern Europe, FTAs, Article XXIV. *1994,* with Hungary, Poland; *1995,* with Bulgaria, Czech Republic, Estonia, Latvia, Lithuania, Romania, Slovak Republic, Slovenia.
North American Free Trade Agreement (NAFTA), FTA, Article XXIV; extension of *1989* Canada–United States Free Trade Agreement (CUSF-TA), Article XXIV. *1994,* Canada, Mexico, United States.

Asia-Pacific Economic Cooperation (APEC), regional but not preferential agreement; not notified to the WTO. *1989*, Australia, Brunei Darussalam, Canada, Indonesia, Japan, Republic of Korea, Malaysia, New Zealand, Philippines, Singapore, Thailand, United States; *1991*, China, Hong Kong (China), Taiwan (China); *1993*, Mexico, Papua New Guinea; *1994*, Chile; *1998*, Peru, Russian Federation, Vietnam.

Latin America and the Caribbean

Andean Pact, customs union, Enabling Clause. *1969* (revived in *1991*), Bolivia, Colombia, Ecuador, Peru, Venezuela.

Central American Common Market (CACM), customs union, Article XXIV. *1960* (revived in *1993*), El Salvador, Guatemala, Honduras, Nicaragua; *1962*, Costa Rica.

Common Market of the South/Mercado Común del Sur (MERCOSUR), customs union, Enabling Clause. *1991*, Argentina, Brazil, Paraguay, Uruguay.

Group of Three (G3), FTA, Enabling Clause. *1995*, Colombia, Mexico, Venezuela.

Latin American Integration Association (LAIA), Enabling Clause; formerly Latin American Free Trade Area (LAFTA), Article XXIV, *1960*. Revived as LAIA, *1980*, Argentina, Bolivia, Brazil, Chile, Colombia, Ecuador, Mexico, Paraguay, Peru, Uruguay, Venezuela.

Caribbean Community and Common Market (CARICOM), customs union, Article XXIV. *1973*, Antigua and Barbuda, Barbados, Jamaica, St. Kitts and Nevis, Trinidad and Tobago; *1974*, Belize, Dominica, Grenada, Montserrat, St. Lucia, St. Vincent and the Grenadines; *1983*, The Bahamas (part of the Caribbean Community but not of the Common Market).

Africa

Cross-Border Initiative (CBI), common policy framework, with the support of the International Monetary Fund (IMF), the World Bank, the EU, and the African Development Bank; not notified to the WTO. *1992*, Burundi, Comoros, Kenya, Madagascar, Malawi, Mauritius, Namibia, Rwanda, Seychelles, Swaziland, Tanzania, Uganda, Zambia, Zimbabwe.

East African Cooperation (EAC), other, Enabling Clause; formerly East African Community, *1967*, broke up in 1977. Revived *1996*, Kenya, Tanzania, Uganda.

Economic and Monetary Community of Central Africa/Communauté économique et monétaire d'Afrique Centrale (CEMAC), customs union, Enabling Clause, *1999*. Formerly Union douanière et économique de l'Afrique Centrale (UDEAC);*1966*, Cameroon, Central African Republic, Chad, Republic of Congo, Gabon; *1989*, Equatorial Guinea.

Economic Community of West African States (ECOWAS), FTA, Enabling Clause. *1975*, Benin, Burkina Faso, Cape Verde, Côte d'Ivoire, The Gambia, Ghana, Guinea, Guinea-Bissau, Liberia, Mali, Mauritania, Niger, Nigeria, Senegal, Sierra Leone, Togo.

Common Market for Eastern and Southern Africa (COMESA), FTA, Enabling Clause. *1993*, Angola, Burundi, Comoros, Djibouti, Arab Republic of Egypt, Ethiopia, Kenya, Lesotho, Malawi, Mauritius, Mozambique, Rwanda, Somalia, Sudan, Swaziland, Tanzania, Uganda, Zambia, Zimbabwe.

Indian Ocean Commission (IOC), integrated regional program for development of trade; not notified to the WTO. *1982*, Comoros, Madagascar, Mauritius, Seychelles.

Southern African Development Community (SADC), FTA, Enabling Clause; formerly known as the Southern African Development Coordination Conference (SADCC). *1980*, Angola, Botswana, Lesotho, Malawi, Mozambique, Swaziland, Tanzania, Zambia, Zimbabwe; *1990*, Namibia; *1994*, South Africa; *1995*, Mauritius; *1998*, Democratic Republic of the Congo, Seychelles.

West African Economic and Monetary Union/Union économique et monétaire ouest-africaine (UEMOA), customs union, Enabling Clause; formerly Economic Community of West Africa (CEAO), *1973*. *1994*, Benin, Burkina Faso, Côte d'Ivoire, Mali, Niger, Senegal, Togo; *1997*, Guinea-Bissau.

Southern African Customs Union (SACU), customs union. *1910*, Botswana, Lesotho, Namibia, South Africa, Swaziland.

Economic Community of the Countries of the Great Lakes/Communauté économique des pays des grands lacs (CEPGL), to promote regional economic cooperation and integration; not notified to the WTO. *1976*, Burundi, Democratic Republic of the Congo, Rwanda.

Europe

Central European Free Trade Area (CEFTA). *1993*. *1996*, Czech Republic, Hungary, Poland, Slovak Republic, Slovenia; *1997*, Romania; *1999*, Bulgaria.

Committee for Mutual Economic Assistance (CMEA, also known as COMECON). *1949,* Bulgaria, Czechoslovakia, Hungary, Poland, Romania, Soviet Union; *1949,* Albania; *1950,* Democratic Republic of Germany; *1962,* Mongolia; *1972,* Cuba; *1978,* Vietnam. China attended meetings as an observer between the late 1950s and 1961. The Federal Republic of Yugoslavia negotiated a form of associate status in 1964.
Bilateral agreements between individual CEFTA members and individual Baltic countries.

Middle East and Asia

Association of Southeast Asian Nations (ASEAN), *1967. 1977,* ASEAN Preferential Trading Arrangement, Enabling Clause; *1992,* ASEAN Free Trade Area (AFTA), Enabling Clause, Indonesia, Malaysia, Philippines, Singapore, Thailand; *1994,* Brunei Darussalam; *1995,* Vietnam; *1997,* Lao People's Democratic Republic, Myanmar; *1999,* Cambodia.
Arab Common Market, long-term aim is customs union, Article XXIV. *1964,* Agreement for Economic Unity among Arab League States.
Gulf Cooperation Council (GCC), other, Enabling Clause. *1981,* Bahrain, Kuwait, Oman, Qatar, Saudi Arabia, United Arab Emirates.
South Asian Association for Regional Cooperation (SAARC) Preferential Trading Arrangement (SAPTA), preferential trading agreement, Enabling Clause. *1995,* Bangladesh, Bhutan, India, Maldives, Nepal, Pakistan, Sri Lanka.

NOTES

1. The General Agreement on Tariffs and Trade (GATT) was succeeded in 1994 by the World Trade Organization (WTO).

2. "Closed" regionalism was widespread, especially in Sub-Saharan Africa and Latin America. Examples in Africa included the CEAO (created in 1973), ECOWAS (1975), the CEPGL (1976), and the EAC (1967). In Latin America they included the CACM (1960), LAFTA (1960), the Andean Pact (1969), and CARICOM (1973). See the Abbreviations and Acronyms list for full names and the appendix to this chapter for further information on these agreements.

3. These North-South agreements are to be distinguished from the preferential trade agreements implied by colonial preferences.

CHAPTER 2

How Trade Blocs Increase Trade and Competition

Awell-crafted trade bloc can raise efficiency—and economic welfare—in its member countries by facilitating consumer choice and increasing the competition that producers face. Dropping tariff barriers enlarges markets and gives more efficient producers entry into countries where their prices had been inflated by duties and other trade barriers. But trade blocs can easily end up adding, rather than removing, distortions to trade and efficiency. This chapter looks at the basic structure and economics of free trade agreements (FTAs), whose members do away with tariffs between themselves, and customs unions, which, in addition, maintain a common external tariff against nonmembers.

A trade bloc usually increases trade between its members. An important issue, however, is whether it "creates" trade (by allowing cheaper products from other bloc members to substitute for more expensive domestic production) or "diverts" it (by substituting intrabloc imports for imports from outside the group that were cheaper when both faced equal tariffs).[1] Although the evidence on the balance between trade creation and diversion in trade blocs is mixed, we offer some new research findings showing that diversion must be recognized as a serious possibility.

The balance between trade creation and diversion is an important determinant of the overall benefits of an RIA. It is, however, based on a view of the world in which intercountry trade is driven entirely by differences in productivity and factor endowments. But in fact, trade can also arise from product differentiation and from economies of scale that reduce costs as production grows. In these circumstances competition between firms is weakened, and consumers lose. International trade then offers an important means of increasing competition by allowing new suppliers to enter markets. RIAs can generate such benefits by fostering trade between members, although there is not yet sufficient empirical evidence to show that developing countries will be able to reap large gains from this source.

INCREASED TRADE BETWEEN MEMBERS OF TRADE BLOCS

Reducing trade barriers between two countries is likely to increase their trade with each other. Indeed, in many cases, as in CEFTA and the Arab Free Trade Agreement, this is an explicit objective in the treaties establishing the RIAs. Figure 2.1 reports simple "before" (one year before implementation) and "after" (five years after implementation) import statistics to see what happened as nine RIAs between developing countries came into operation. In seven of the nine RIAs, intrabloc trade shares increased, some very strongly. The exceptions, CARICOM and the GCC, were among the slowest to implement internal tariff cuts. Overall, the intrabloc share increased by nearly half.

These results appear to be cause for celebration, since strong international trade performance is now generally accepted as one of the main

Figure 2.1 Share of Imports from Partners in Selected RIAs, One Year before and Five Years after Implementation

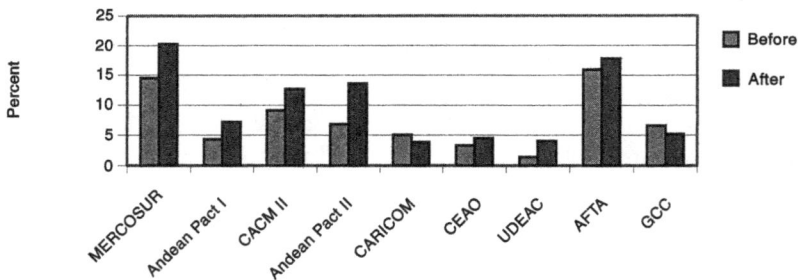

Note: For MERCOSUR, "before" is 1991 and "after" is 1996; for Andean Pact I, 1968 and 1974; for Andean Pact II, 1990 and 1996; for CACM II, 1990 and 1996; for CARICOM, 1972 and 1978; for the CEAO, 1965 and 1971; for UDEAC, 1965 and 1971; for AFTA, 1991 and 1996; and for the GCC, 1980 and 1986. Andean Pact I refers to the original 1969 agreement and Andean Pact II to the revived agreement (1991); CACM II refers to the Central American Common Market (revived). Other abbreviations used are MERCOSUR, Common Market of the South; CARICOM, Caribbean Community and Common Market; CEAO, Economic Community of West Africa; UDEAC, Union douanière et économique de l'Afrique Centrale (now CEMAC); AFTA, ASEAN Free Trade Area; GCC, Gulf Cooperation Council.
Source: United Nations COMTRADE.

determinants of economic prosperity. But before breaking out the champagne, we need to ask whether every increase in trade is desirable and whether these increases are actually attributable to regionalism.[2] To answer these questions, we need both economic theory and a closer look at the trade numbers.

IS MORE TRADE GOOD, OR BAD? TRADE CREATION AND TRADE DIVERSION

The classical reason for gains from trade is that global free trade allows consumers and firms to purchase from the cheapest source of supply, ensuring that production is located according to comparative advantage. In contrast, trade barriers discriminate against foreign producers in favor of domestic suppliers. Domestic import-competing producers are induced to expand even though their costs are higher than the cost of imports. This misallocation starves domestic export sectors of resources, raises their costs, and causes these sectors to be smaller than they otherwise would be. Switching production from goods that a country can produce efficiently to those it cannot reduces real incomes.

Since an RIA liberalizes trade, lowering at least some of the barriers, does it not follow that it too will generate gains from trade? Unfortunately, the answer is, not necessarily. The "gains from trade" argument tells us what happens if all trade barriers are reduced, but it need not apply to a partial and discriminatory reduction in barriers, as in an RIA. The reason is that discrimination between sources of supply is merely shifted, not eliminated. If partner country production displaces higher-cost domestic production, there will be gains—trade creation. But it is also possible that partner country production may displace lower-cost imports from the rest of the world, resulting in trade diversion.

When partner supplies—now facing no tariffs and therefore cheaper—displace sales of local output, the two classical sources of gains from trade apply: real resources are saved by shifting production in the direction of comparative advantage, and consumers benefit from facing lower (undistorted) prices. Such trade creation unambiguously increases economic welfare in the importing country. But RIAs can also divert trade by allowing imports from partners to displace goods from outside the bloc that were cheaper when both faced equal tariffs. Diverting trade from cheaper to more expensive suppliers means that more resources are used up to purchase the same output, which is clearly costly. Under some circumstances, trade diversion also reduces consumer prices because consumers no longer pay tariffs on their purchases; the benefits that this generates help to offset the additional cost of imports—conceivably, even completely.

To see the effects of discrimination, it is helpful to think through a simple example. Suppose that a country can import a good from a potential partner country at $105 per unit and from the rest of the world at $100 and that each pays $10 in duty, making the prices paid by consumers $115 and $110, respectively. In this situation consumers obviously purchase from the rest of the world and pay $110. If the country joins an RIA with the partner, the partner's imports come in duty free. The price consumers pay for imports from the partner country then falls to $105, while imports from the rest of the world still cost $110. The consumers' response is obvious: they switch to the partner country, buying the $105 good and saving $5. But because the government now loses $10 per unit (the revenue it was getting on each unit of imports from the rest of the world), the net effect for the country is a loss of $5, and the RIA has reduced real income. Another way of putting it is that the country (not the consumers) used to pay $100 per imported unit and now pays $105. This is the deleterious welfare effect of trade diversion.

This is just an example, and such circumstances clearly will not apply in all sectors; there are sectors in which partner country costs are less than those in the rest of the world and others in which the country under study is an exporter. The next question is how to identify the circumstances in which trade diversion is more, or less, likely to be a problem.

First, notice that trade diversion can occur only if the country has a tariff on imports from the rest of the world. The cost of trade diversion cannot exceed the height of this external tariff. In our example, if the external tariff is initially low, there is not much tariff revenue to be lost, and reducing the external tariff would not induce a switch in source of supply. One clear policy implication is that the traditional advice to countries to lower external tariffs applies as much to those inside RIAs as to those outside.

Second, trade diversion arises only if partner country costs are out of line with costs and prices in the rest of the world, and this will not be the case if the partner itself has low trade barriers. For example, if the partner had a duty of just $2 per unit, prices and costs in the partner country could not exceed $102 (the price at which imports from the rest of the world would be sold in the partner country). Preferential liberalization would then cost the government $10 but would save consumers in the importing country $8, creating a net loss of just $2 per unit and mitigating the cost of trade diversion. But, as discussed in the next chapter, countries with high trade barriers usually impose rules of origin to prevent trade deflection (reexport of imported goods from the low-tariff to the high-tariff country), and prices could still differ by more than $2.

Third, our example assumes a rather artificial and "frictionless" trade. In reality, products from different countries are not perfect substitutes, and trade faces transport costs and other barriers apart from tariffs. These factors will tend to make the change in the sourcing of imports less sharp than in the example, again mitigating the costs of trade diversion but also reducing the benefits of trade creation.

Finally, note that an RIA between two small developing countries is likely to generate only trade diversion and no trade creation. This can be seen most clearly in the case of homogeneous goods. Since small countries will typically not be able to supply all of their partners' needs for imports, each member will continue to import some quantity of most goods from the rest of the world. For these goods, domestic consumer prices will continue to be fixed at the world price plus the import tariff. Since neither of these changes with integration, consumption does not change. Production, however, increases because each country can now sell to the partner without paying the tariff. Thus, each member country replaces cheaper imports from the rest of the world with more expensive partner imports. The outcome is trade diversion and a loss for both countries (Schiff 1997).

The welfare effect of an RIA on the bloc members as a group depends on the balance between trade creation and diversion. Real resources are saved if inefficient production is cut through trade creation but are lost if imports are switched from low-cost to high-cost partner sources through trade diversion. At the level of the individual country, how the RIA shifts economic welfare between members is also important. It is therefore necessary to consider effects felt via exports, as well as those stemming from imports and tariff revenue.

The preceding discussion of trade diversion focused on imports, but of course, at the same time as the home country is losing through trade diversion, the partner country is increasing its exports. Is not the former's loss just balanced by the latter's gain, so that, allowing for some trade creation, the RIA as a whole is better off? The answer is that there may be an exporter country gain, but it is less, per unit, than the importer country loss.

Recall that in our example consumers switch to imports from the partner country. Partner country export sales expand, but how much of a gain is this for the partner country? If exports are just selling at cost ($105 in the example), selling more units does not raise income in the partner country (because some other sector must contract to release resources for the expansion). If they are selling above cost, there will be a real income gain. But how much higher than cost can the price go? The answer is that the price cannot go above $110 (if it did, consumers would switch back to buying from the rest of the world), so the exporter country gain per unit cannot exceed the gap between the price of imports from the rest of the world and costs ($110 − $105 = a maximum of $5).

This line of reasoning suggests another way of thinking about trade diversion. To return to our example (for the last time), the government has given up $10 of tariff revenue per unit. We can see where this has gone; $5 per unit goes to the higher cost of producing partner country imports compared with the cost of imports from the rest of the world, and the other $5 is divided between domestic consumers and partner country firms. The shares depend on whether these firms are able to raise their prices in response to having preferential access to the domestic market. It is often argued that an advantage of an RIA over unilateral liberalization is that firms benefit from preferential access to partner markets. This is true, but we now see that the gain comes only at the expense of consumers and government revenue. The RIA acts as an inefficient way of transferring some of the country's tariff revenue either to domestic consumers or to partner country producers. These transfers can be very large, depending as they do on the total level of trade in the affected commodities, not just on the amounts created or diverted by the RIA. Thus, they figure prominently in the incentives that different groups have to lobby for RIAs (see chapter 3).

Transfers can also matter greatly in North-South RIAs because developing countries risk losing from an RIA with the North. First, developing countries typically have higher imports from their partners than exports to them and so the flows on which they lose revenue are larger than those on which they gain. Second, they almost always have higher tariffs than developed countries, and developed country firms are consequently likely to gain more from increased access to the developing country's market than vice versa. The developing countries can solve this problem quite simply, however, by lowering their tariffs unilaterally.

GROWTH OF TRADE OVER TIME

The problem with looking just at the changes in trade shares in figure 2.1 is that they do not distinguish trade creation from trade diversion, both of which increase the partner share. To separate these two phenomena, we can examine shares in apparent consumption—the sum of all expenditures in the domestic economy. At an aggregate level, shares in apparent consumption are often approximated by corresponding changes in shares in gross domestic product (GDP). If the share of imports in GDP increases, the economy has become more open and there has been net trade creation. If the share of nonpartner imports in GDP falls, trade has been diverted. Figures 2.2 and 2.3 plot the changes in partner and non-partner imports in GDP for our set of RIAs. Changes in overall openness are the sums of these two figures and are given in Appendix table 2A.1.

The strongest increase in openness associated with an RIA is for MERCOSUR, where imports more than doubled between 1990 and 1996, from 3.9 to 8.1 percent of GDP. CARICOM, the CEAO, and the GCC also performed strongly. Over the periods examined, these blocs display strong trade creation, albeit often from very low initial levels of trade. Their shares of nonpartner imports in GDP also show the strongest increases, the very opposite of trade diversion. If this were all attributable to regionalism—and if this outcome were all that there were to regionalism—figures 2.2 and 2.3 would indeed be an endorsement of this approach to trade policy.

This is, however, not the whole story: we need to know whether the changes would have occurred anyway. That is, we need to identify what would have happened in the absence of the RIA—what students of the economics of integration call the anti-monde, or the counterfactual.

First, a simple numerical adjustment to the trade shares is necessary. Countries that are growing faster will automatically tend to absorb more

Figure 2.2 Intrabloc Imports as a Share of GDP, Selected RIAs, One Year before and Five Years after Implementation

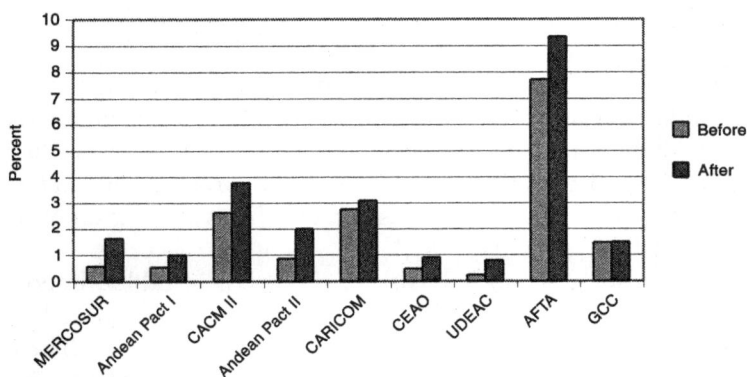

Note: For MERCOSUR, "before" is 1991 and "after" is 1996; for Andean Pact I, 1968 and 1974; for Andean Pact II, 1990 and 1996; for CACM II, 1990 and 1996; for CARICOM, 1972 and 1978; for the CEAO, 1965 and 1971; for UDEAC, 1965 and 1971; for AFTA, 1991 and 1996; and for the GCC, 1980 and 1986. For the full names of the RIAs, see the note to figure 2.1.
Source: World Bank data.

Figure 2.3 Extrabloc Imports as a Share of GDP, Selected RIAs, One Year before and Five Years after Implementation

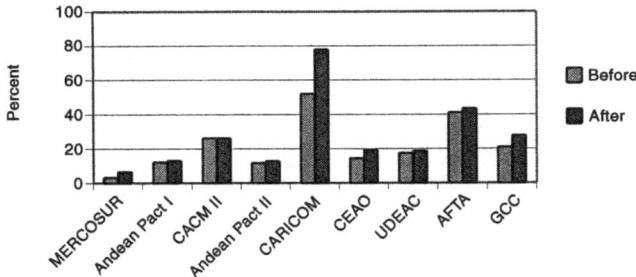

Note: For MERCOSUR, "before" is 1991 and "after" is 1996; for Andean Pact I, 1968 and 1974; for Andean Pact II, 1990 and 1996; for CACM II, 1990 and 1996; for CARICOM, 1972 and 1978; for the CEAO, 1965 and 1971; for UDEAC, 1965 and 1971; for AFTA, 1991 and 1996; and for the GCC, 1980 and 1986. For the full names of the RIAs, see the note to figure 2.1.
Source: World Bank data.

of everyone's trade. Trade intensity indices allow for this by comparing country A's share of B's total imports with A's share of all other countries' imports.[3] If A's share is higher in B than elsewhere, B's imports are biased toward A. Such bias might exist for any of several reasons—for example, commodity composition or geographic proximity. But because factors of this sort tend to evolve relatively slowly, if sharp changes in trade intensity are observed to accompany the creation of an RIA, we might infer a causal relationship. As reported in appendix table 2A.1, intrabloc trade intensities have increased in six of our nine RIAs, and extrabloc trade intensities have declined in seven of the nine.

Next, we have to make allowance for domestic sales, using trade propensity indices, which compare the share of imports from country A in B's GDP with A's share of world trade. Trade propensity is the product of trade intensity and openness (the ratio of B's imports to GDP) and so reflects both the biases in trade patterns and the effects of RIAs on overall trade volumes.

Figure 2.4 shows a strong increase in the mean intrabloc import propensity of our sample RIAs—120 percent over the six-year periods—with notable increases in MERCOSUR, the GCC, and UDEAC. There are declines for three blocs: CACM II, CARICOM, and AFTA. For CARICOM, which has liberalized its internal trade very cautiously, intrabloc trade did not increase strongly; for the other two, the strong increases in their members' shares of world trade make the increases in intrabloc trade look less impressive.

Figure 2.4 Intrabloc Import Propensities, Selected RIAs, One Year before and Five Years after Implementation

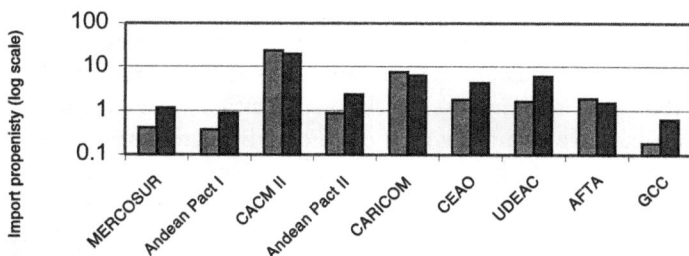

Note: For MERCOSUR, "before" is 1991 and "after" is 1996; for Andean Pact I, 1968 and 1974; for Andean Pact II, 1990 and 1996; for CACM II, 1990 and 1996; for CARICOM, 1972 and 1978; for the CEAO, 1965 and 1971; for UDEAC, 1965 and 1971; for AFTA, 1991 and 1996; and for the GCC, 1980 and 1986. For the full names of the RIAs, see the note to figure 2.1.
Source: World Bank data.

The extrabloc import propensities (figure 2.5) all show modest increases, with a mean increase of 30 percent. That is, in each of our sample RIAs the first five-year period is associated with an increase in the share of GDP spent on imports from nonmembers that is larger than the increase in nonmember shares of world trade. Again, this suggests a good deal of progress toward opening members' economies and indicates that regionalism has been associated with net improvements in economic management.

Figure 2.5 Extrabloc Import Propensities, Selected RIAs, One Year before and Five Years after Implementation

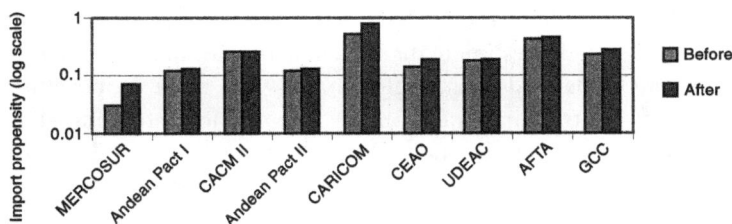

Note: For MERCOSUR, "before" is 1991 and "after" is 1996; for Andean Pact I, 1968 and 1974; for Andean Pact II, 1990 and 1996; for CACM II, 1990 and 1996; for CARICOM, 1972 and 1978; for the CEAO, 1965 and 1971; for UDEAC, 1965 and 1971; for AFTA, 1991 and 1996; and for the GCC, 1980 and 1986. For the full names of the RIAs, see the note to figure 2.1.
Source: World Bank data.

NOT ALL CHANGES COME FROM REGIONALISM

Although the trade changes just discussed were undoubtedly of considerable benefit to the economies concerned, the no-change anti-monde (counterfactual) calculations are far too simple to allow us to conclude immediately that regionalism was working. Specifically, we must ask whether the changes are due more to the nondiscriminatory trade liberalizations that many of the members undertook around the same time than to regionalism per se.[4] To answer this question, we need a more sophisticated way of representing the anti-monde. Members of RIAs may improve their trade policies and performance over time (relative to their starting points), but that can be an extremely undemanding benchmark. Once we recognize the possibility of undertaking nondiscriminatory liberalizations, we see that RIAs can still entail large distortions relative to trade patterns elsewhere in the world or relative to the members' own potential in a nondiscriminatory regime.

The most popular of these more sophisticated approaches, the gravity model, explains trade between any two countries as a function of their GDPs (richer economies both export and import more); their populations (larger economies depend proportionately less on trade than smaller ones); the distance between them (as a proxy for transport costs, cultural similarity, and business contacts); and physical factors such as sharing a land border or being landlocked or an island. To these factors, economists add variables to represent the additional trade that occurs if both countries are members of a given RIA and, sometimes, the ways in which RIA members' imports from and exports to the rest of the world differ from the trade patterns of countries with no effective regional ties.

Gravity models are estimated on the basis of data from many countries. They assume that in the absence of an RIA, member trade bears the same relationship to GDP, population, distance, and so on as does the "arm's-length" trade of the sample countries. This clearly depends on the set of countries and years used to estimate the model. Estimates of trade creation and diversion can be derived for a single year. As with trade propensities, however, pairs of countries may trade heavily for extraneous reasons—cultural similarities, compatible commodity compositions, and the like—and so more convincing results are derived by looking not at snapshots but at *changes* over the period during which the RIAs are being formed.

One of the first gravity models for RIAs (Aitken 1973) examined the effect of the EEC and the European Free Trade Association (EFTA) on European trade. Starting in 1951 (to obtain a picture of pre-EEC forces at work), he estimated gravity models for a number of years and investigated how the coefficients on intra-EEC and intra-EFTA trade evolved. Both the EEC and EFTA substantially increased their intrabloc trade as they reduced internal barriers, starting in 1961 and 1964, respectively. By 1967, Aitken estimated, intra-EEC trade was 80 percent higher than it would otherwise have been, and intra-EFTA trade was 50 percent higher. Bayoumi and Eichengreen (1997) found similar results for 1952–92: the effects on intrabloc trade were concentrated in the early years of EFTA and the EEC, and whereas EFTA was predominantly trade creating, the EEC displayed both trade creation and diversion.

In the first gravity study of developing country RIAs, Aitken and Obutelewicz (1976) found that the 1959–71 association agreements between 18 African countries and the EEC significantly increased mutual trade, with the effect increasing progressively through the period of association.

Frankel, Stein, and Wei (1997) examined intra- and extrabloc trade for eight RIAs—the EC, EFTA, NAFTA, MERCOSUR, the Andean Pact, AFTA, the CER (the Closer Economic Relations agreement between Australia and New Zealand), and the East Asian Economic Caucus—for the period 1970–92. Their results for individual years show that increases in intrabloc trade are generally accompanied by significant drops in trade with the rest of the world (trade diversion).[5]

Finally, to explore the "new wave" of regionalism, a recent World Bank study estimates trade effects for every year during the period 1980–96 (Soloaga and Winters 2001). It explicitly tests whether the changes in the effects are statistically significant and extends the gravity approach by looking for three separate effects on the trade of each RIA: the effects on intrabloc trade, on extrabloc imports, and, uniquely, on extrabloc exports.[6] It considers nine major blocs, comparing members' performance both between blocs and with the performance of 17 countries that were not members of significant arrangements at the time.

They find that in Europe, where further integration was not accompanied by the major liberalization of external trade, trade diversion is evident in the form of increased intrabloc trade and reduced extrabloc trade (relative to expected values). In RIAs between developing countries, on the other hand, the evolution of trade over the period appears to have been dominated by external liberalizations. All trade increased over the period (relative to expectations), but the increases in intratrade were statistically no larger than those in extratrade.

Figure 2.6 summarizes the results for the EU for the period. During those years, the EU experienced significant deepening (the Single Market Programme [SMP]) and enlargement (to Portugal and Spain), and so we might expect to find integration effects. In 1980 the EU shows unusually strong trade with nonmember countries, which is not unusual for gravity models based on large samples of countries. Its substantially lower-than-expected trade between members is also not unusual, but the effect looks particularly large because of the way Soloaga and Winters measure intrabloc effects. They assume that in the absence of an RIA, trade between members would be subject to the same forces as extrabloc imports and exports, and so to capture the effects of the RIA they subtract from the "gross" intrabloc trade coefficients the two extrabloc trade coefficients. Thus, in 1980 EU extrabloc imports were higher than gravity model predictions by 1.86, and extrabloc exports by 0.55.[7] Intra-EU trade was higher than gravity model predictions by 0.63, but in the absence of the RIA, trade between members would presumably have been subject to the same forces as other (extrabloc) trade; that is, imports and exports would have been higher, by 1.86 and 0.55, respectively. When we allow for these general effects, trade between EU members is seen to be lower than it would have been expected to be given those countries' general trading behavior by 1.78 ($= 0.63 - 1.86 - 0.55$).

As noted above, the best estimate of the effects of integration is the change in the intrabloc and extrabloc trade factors as integration occurs. We therefore need to look at the evolution of the effects, as shown in figure 2.6. Clearly, as integration deepens and Portugal and Spain enter the EU, the trade effects decline absolutely: that is, intrabloc trade grows, and extrabloc trade falls relative to expected values. This is consistent with the existence of trade diversion, as well as possible trade creation.

It is interesting to ask whether these changes are statistically significant or could have arisen by chance. To answer this, Soloaga and Winters conducted a separate exercise pooling observations for three periods, 1980–82, 1986–88, and 1995–96. These broadly capture the before and after movements for the new and revived RIAs of the "new wave."

Figure 2.7 summarizes the results for all nine RIAs considered. The individual graphs are conceptually the same as in figure 2.6 except that they contain estimates for only three periods rather than all 17 years. As in previous studies, all the initial (1980–82) non-European intrabloc trade effects are positive, suggesting that even before the blocs were formed or revived, members traded disproportionately with each other. Subsequently, although the trade effects evolved as RIAs were introduced or revived, none of the changes was statistically significant. That is, after allowing for changes in members' trade policy in general, intrabloc trade has not changed significantly over the period of new-wave regionalism.

There was, however, some evidence of effects on overall trade. The EU's and EFTA's propensities to import were significantly lower relative to ex-

Figure 2.6 EU Trade, 1980–96

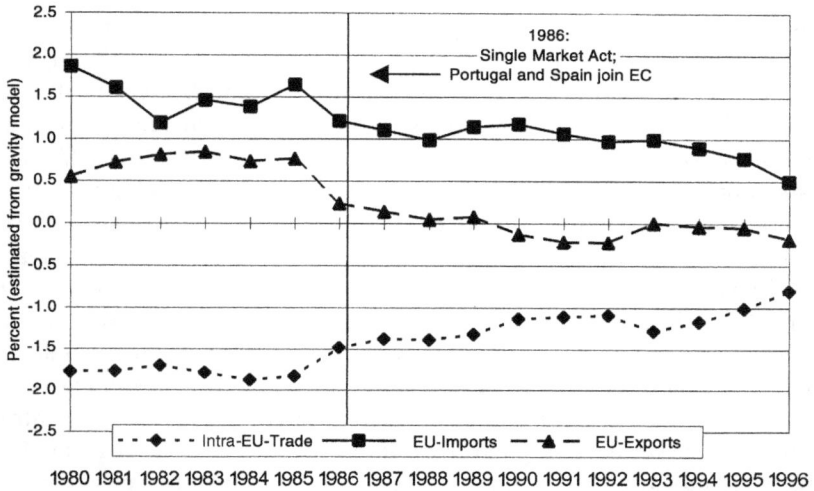

Note: The y-axis shows values of coefficients on RIA dummy variables, in logarithmic equations. A coefficient of b implies that the RIA raised trade by $\{[\exp(b) - 1] * 100\}\%$ above the "expected" value.
Source: Soloaga and Winters (2001).

pected values in 1995–96 than in 1980–82, which is consistent with trade diversion, while the four Latin American RIAs showed positive trends in overall imports; these trends were statistically significantly for the CACM and MERCOSUR. The EU and EFTA appeared to suffer significant declines in their overall exports. NAFTA shows the same patterns as the European blocs, but its changes in trade patterns are not statistically significant.

The conclusion from this work is that regionalism has had a smaller effect on developing countries' recent trade flows than the nondiscriminatory liberalizations that these countries undertook. That is, as Latin American countries, in particular, liberalized their trade in general over the 1990s, we would have expected trade between them to have increased strongly anyway, with stimuli coming as both the exporter and the importer liberalized. Once we allow for this, it appears that members did not increase their trade with each other significantly as a result of their RIAs. By contrast, during the 1980s and 1990s, deepening and enlargement in EFTA and the EU were not accompanied by major external liberalizations (except for the Tokyo Round), and for these blocs, trade diversion is quite evident.

Looking at members' extrabloc trade, it is useful to distinguish the blocs between developing countries that simultaneously liberalized their trade policies in general (ASEAN, LAFTA, the CACM, the Andean Pact, and MERCOSUR in figure 2.7) from the others (the EC/EU, EFTA, the GCC, and NAFTA). Since the mid-1980s, imports from nonmembers have increased relative to expected values (obtained from the gravity model) for the Andean Pact, the CACM, LAFTA, and MERCOSUR (significantly so for the last two). This result reflects their unilateral trade liberalization, which dominated any trade diversion from the RIA. The same applies to ASEAN since 1980. Similarly, with one exception, these liberalizing blocs' exports to the rest of the world have increased relative to expected levels; this is to be expected from a trade liberalization and confirms the dominance of the general liberalization over the discriminatory RIA. The exception is MERCOSUR, where the export and import effects move in opposite directions, suggesting that external trade developments over the 1990s were dominated by competitiveness factors. In this case, given that the export data suggest an increasing focus on intrabloc trade, it would be premature to interpret the strong increases in imports as indicating a sustainable liberalization that outweighs regional biases.

Turning to the cases in which the period since 1980 has not seen a large liberalization, trade diversion is directly evident. Both the EU and EFTA trade more with nonmembers than would be expected from the gravity equations, but the excess has declined significantly since 1980. The same is true for NAFTA since 1986–88, although in this case the estimated changes are not significantly different from zero.

The gravity model compares members' actual trade not with what it was before the RIA—frequently, an undemanding standard—but with what it would have been had members exhibited "average" behavior as defined by the other countries in the sample. A related indicator is a comparison between trade within the RIA and members' export performance in third-country markets, where they receive no preferences. Yeats (1998) found that MERCOSUR members' exports to partners increased most strongly in products where extrabloc exports were weak and protection was relatively high. Since member exports compete with the same third-country suppliers inside the bloc as outside it, Yeats inferred that the greater success of some of the exports within the bloc was attributable to trade preferences. Thus, he concluded, MERCOSUR tariff barriers were diverting trade from cheaper goods made outside the bloc to more expensive internal ones. This is not the same as comparing the RIAs with their members' pre-RIA distorted positions, but it certainly suggests some forgone opportunities from nondiscriminatory trade.

These more sophisticated analyses show a darker side of regionalism. Although RIA partners trade more with each other than objective criteria

Figure 2.7 Effect of RIAs on Trade within and among Blocs, Selected Periods, 1980–96

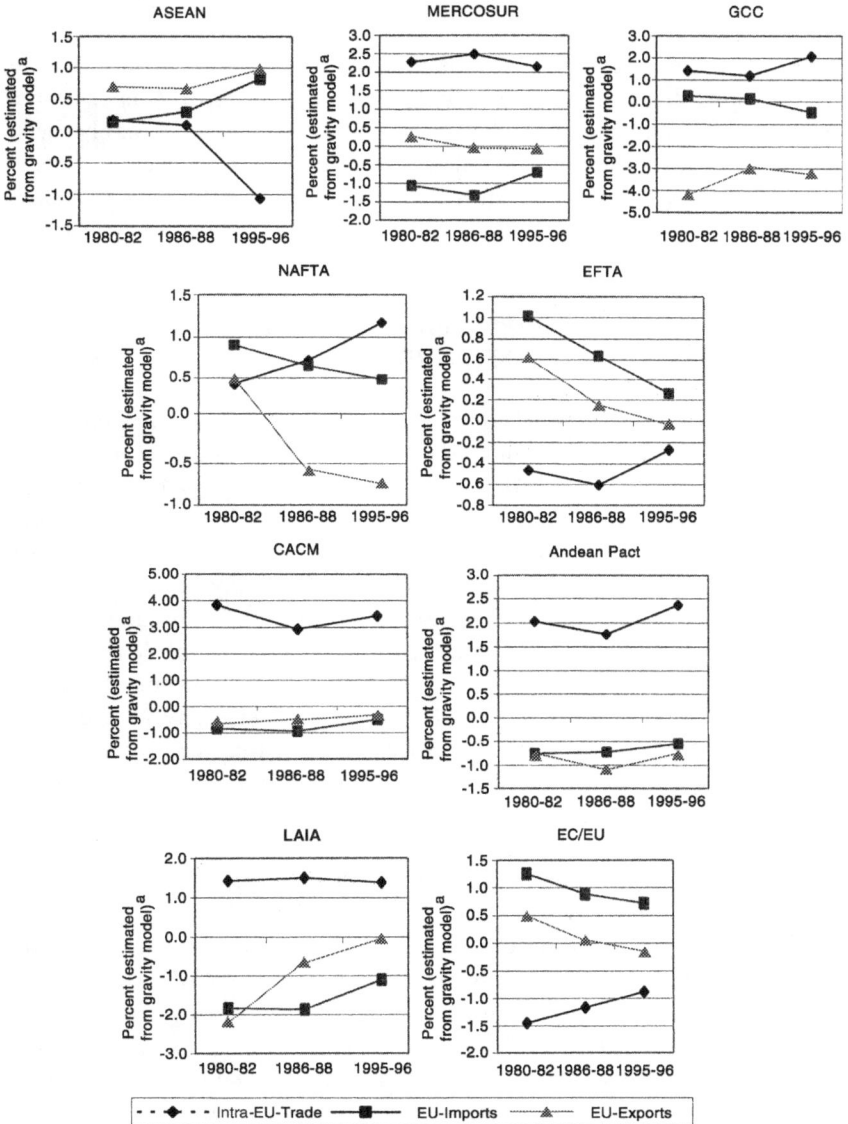

Note: ASEAN, Association of Southeast Asian Nations; CACM, Central American Common Market; EC/EU, European Community/European Union; EFTA, European Free Trade Association; GCC, Gulf Cooperation Council; LAFTA, Latin American Free Trade Area; MERCOSUR, Common Market of the South; NAFTA, North American Free Trade Agreement.
[a] The *y*-axes show values of coefficients on RIA dummy variables, in logarithmic equations. A coefficient of *b* implies that the RIA raised trade by {[exp(*b*) − 1] * 100}% above the "expected" value.
Source: Soloaga and Winters (2001).

would predict, there is little evidence that the excess increases when an RIA is signed or deepened, and there are signs that the degree of openness to the rest of the world can decrease, albeit from levels that exceed normality. One way of reconciling these results with those on trade propensities discussed above is that, over time, the world has become more open. Thus, while RIAs have usually (although not inevitably) been associated with improvements relative to a member's pre-RIA positions, they have not kept up with trends elsewhere, and so members have fallen behind over time.

A CHANGE OF PERSPECTIVE: IMPERFECTLY COMPETITIVE MARKETS

In the analysis above, trade is driven by comparative advantage based on differences in productivity or factor endowments; producers make homogeneous products, and individual firms have no power to influence the prices at which they sell. Economists refer to this situation as "perfect" (in the sense of complete) competition. In the real world, however, competition is often imperfect. In the first place, many products are differentiated, and consumers differ in their preferences for the varieties. This attenuates the effects of price changes on patterns of demand (not everyone wants to switch to a variety that has become cheaper). Producers then acquire a degree of market power; each effectively becomes a monopolist for its own particular variety. Rather than being able to sell only at the exogenously given price determined by an anonymous market, firms can vary their prices and sales according to the demand for their products. Furthermore, individual varieties of goods face not only downward-sloping demand curves but also increasing returns to scale (at least at low levels of output).

These changes in perspective alter economists' views of the returns to regionalism and of how to quantify them and set the scene for a richer menu of integration effects than was found above. Most obviously, they allow us to explain intraindustry trade—the phenomenon in which a country imports and exports different varieties of the same good. Intraindustry trade was hardly acknowledged in economic literature until the 1960s, when empirical studies of Western European RIAs (Verdoorn 1960; Balassa 1974) showed that the bulk of trade expansion within Benelux and the newly established EEC was intraindustry rather than interindustry or intersectoral. Intraindustry trade has subsequently become the leading component of manufactured trade between developed countries, and some studies have suggested a positive link between RIAs and intraindustry trade. For developing countries, however, intraindustry trade seems rather less important, and there is no firm empirical evidence on the connection between it and regionalism.

Product differentiation also changes the analysis of the welfare effects of an RIA. We argued earlier that if two small countries form an RIA, trade diversion inevitably dominates the welfare calculation and that in any market a country can gain only if it ceases to import the good from the rest of the world. (See also the explanation in the appendix to this chapter.) If such imports continue, the country's internal price remains anchored at the world price plus its tariff, and there is no incentive for its domestic behavior to change at all. Displacing all imports from the rest of the world is a very tight condition that makes gains from RIAs seem unlikely. And this tight condition is necessary, but not sufficient, to obtain gains from RIAs.

The critical assumption in the analysis is that the good is homogeneous—every unit is identical regardless of its provenance—so that there is only one price. If, however, domestic, partner, and third-country varieties of the good differ slightly, each has its own price and faces its own demand curve. As partners are exempted from the tariff and supply more goods, the price of the variety they produce will have to fall for them to sell the extra units. This allows at least a chance of domestic consumer and producer effects before third-country trade stops completely. Thus, differentiated goods make gains from RIAs more likely than if goods are homogeneous, although because they weaken the link from reductions in partner prices to reductions in domestic and third-country prices, they tend to reduce the size of the gains when gains are recorded.[8]

Clearly, goods have different degrees of heterogeneity, but unfortunately we have no empirical information about the importance of differentiation in the medium to long run. The ability of firms in most sectors to copy each other in the long run, and the large changes in market shares that are observed over multiyear periods, suggest that the homogeneous goods view is likely to offer reasonably robust predictions of long-run effects. Thus, its basic insight—that if nonmembers face tariffs, member and domestic suppliers of related goods will be able to charge significantly higher prices than if all countries had equal access—will generally be a satisfactory guide to policy.

The most direct application of product differentiation in the analysis of RIAs is in the use of computable general equilibrium (CGE) models. These are fully articulated computer (mathematical) models of the economies under study that include, for example, tariff rates, factor markets, product supplies and demands, and welfare indicators. Using CGE models, researchers can simulate the effects of policy changes associated with RIAs. Because such models typically contain a great deal of microeconomic detail, they can be used to predict changes in production in each sector, as well as changes in factor prices and real incomes.

CGE models have become increasingly sophisticated as researchers have refined the technique.[9] First-generation models assume that all markets are perfectly competitive but that products still differ by country of origin, so that the costs and benefits of RIA membership arise only from trade diversion and trade creation, as discussed above. Second-generation models include increasing returns and imperfect competition and so incorporate the scale and competition effects that are discussed in the next section. Third-generation models contain some dynamics, allowing for capital accumulation and sometimes also technical progress; they are discussed in chapter 4.

The conclusions from these models are, broadly, that there are gains from regional integration but that these gains are small (Francois and Shiells 1994; Harrison, Rutherford, and Tarr 1996). In the first-generation models the interaction between trade diversion and trade creation has effects that are typically only a fraction of 1 percent of GDP. In second-generation models the effect generally increases to around 2–3 percent of GDP, and in third-generation models the gain is approximately 5 percent of GDP.

The strength of these models is that they have sufficient microeconomic structure to allow the effects of a policy change to be traced out in detail and its real income effects to be calculated. Moreover, they are about the only tool available for predicting the likely effects of an RIA

Box 2.1 Computable General Equilibrium (CGE) Modeling: An Explanation and a Health Warning

According to Robinson and Thierfelder, two influential economic modelers, "empirical studies . . . overwhelmingly show that aggregate trade creation dominates trade diversion . . . [and that] in many cases, there is no absolute trade diversion" (Robinson and Thierfelder 1999). This statement is not proved: it relies not on data from actual instances of regionalism but on predictions constructed from CGE models, which tend to emphasize creation over diversion. The reason for this emphasis lies in the models' assumption that products are differentiated, not homogeneous.

The assumption of heterogeneous goods is a major feature of almost all CGE models, which are the workhorses for predicting the effects of RIAs. Partial equilibrium models, such as those in the appendix to this chapter, consider a single market in isolation. General equilibrium recognizes that markets interact in complex ways so that everything depends on everything else. Demand for any one good depends on the prices of all other goods and on income. Income, in turn, depends on wages, profits, and rents, which depend on production, which depends on sales (that is, demand). Prices depend on wages and profits, and vice versa; supply and demand must be equal in all markets, including factor markets; and imports must be paid for by exports plus foreign borrowings. Not only do CGE models allow us to reflect product differentiation, but in the past 10 years they have been extended to incorporate market power, accumulation, and even technical advances.

(Box continues on next page.)

Box 2.1 *(continued)*

CGE models specify all their economic relationships in mathematical terms in a form that allows the model to predict variables such as prices, output, and economic welfare, given information about technology, preferences, and policies. In principle, all the relationships in a model could be estimated from detailed data on the economy over many years. In fact, however, the number and complexity of the relationships far outweigh the data available, and so most CGE models are designed on the basis of theory, intuition, and casual empiricism. Having specified most of the relationships, the modeler manipulates a subset of parameters so that the model will replicate detailed data for one base year. The modeler then re-solves the model, changing a few key features of the base year. For instance, to explore an FTA, tariffs are set to zero on trade flows between the partners; the difference between the base and the new predictions is the predicted effect of the FTA.

CGE modeling is a powerful tool that allows economists to explore numerically a huge range of issues on which econometric estimation would be impossible. One such application is to forecast the effects of RIAs that are yet to be formed. We draw liberally on CGE models in this report—for example, on work by Flores (1997) and by Harrison, Rutherford, and Tarr (1996, 1997, 2002). Although these models embody our best efforts at predicting the effects of future RIAs, it is well to recognize their limitations:

- CGE simulations of an RIA are not unconditional predictions but, rather, "thought experiments" about what the world would be like if the RIA had been in existence and fully operative in the base year.
- Although CGE models are quantitative, they are not empirical. Indeed, they are almost wholly theoretical, with no possibility of rigorous testing against experience. At best, a high proportion of their individual relationships will be based on data and observation, but some components (much less the overall model) can hardly ever be tested. At worst, CGE models represent theory supplemented by incomplete base year data and "guestimated" parameters. In some cases, whole relationships are "guestimated," as in the assumption by Hinojosa-Ojeda, Lewis, and Robinson (1995) that productivity in NAFTA is related to the share of exports in total production.
- Conclusions about trade policy are very sensitive to the values chosen for tariffs and trade restrictions in the base case and simulation experiments. Unfortunately, information on these items—especially on nontariff barriers—is very hard to find and to aggregate satisfactorily to the levels required by the models.
- As noted above, the assumption of heterogeneous goods tips the model toward finding benefits from trade preferences.

before it is implemented. But they have a major weakness: they are not fitted to data as carefully, or subject to the same statistical testing, as econometric models. Critical relationships are often specified with no empirical justification; many crucial variables cannot be measured satisfactorily; the level of sectoral detail is often rather low, which implies a good deal of averaging for the data on important variables; the results are usually very sensitive to measurement error in these hard-to-measure variables; and the specification of the behavioral relationships is usually very simple. These factors probably tend to bias CGE models toward finding benefits from RIAs. The cost of the CGE model's microtheoretic consistency is a complexity that makes it impossible to establish rigorously the relationship between the model and reality. This is not to condemn such models, but it does imply caveats, as noted in box 2.1.

LARGER MARKETS, MORE COMPETITION

The second way in which the existence of imperfect competition changes economists' perceptions of the benefits of RIAs is via economies of scale, which are frequently the cause of imperfect competition. Many countries are too small for activities that are subject to large economies of scale to reach an efficient size. This might be because insufficient quantities of specialized inputs are available or because markets are too small to generate the sales necessary to cover costs. Even if the economy is large enough to support one optimally sized firm, such a firm would be a monopoly, with all the associated drawbacks. Regional integration offers one route for overcoming the disadvantages of smallness: by pooling resources or combining markets, countries can benefit from a combination of scale effects and changes in the intensity of competition. But regionalism is not the only or, indeed, necessarily the most effective way of overcoming the handicap of smallness; unilateral trade liberalization, which shares the markets and resources of the whole world, is likely to be more powerful.

There is plenty of evidence that the number of firms operating in most developing countries is relatively small. Rodrik (1988) reports that measures of concentration (measures of firms' market power) in manufacturing sectors in large developing countries are typically between 50 and 100 percent higher than in developed countries. This is potentially dangerous, although it does not inevitably mean that competition is inadequate; entry costs in developing countries may also be relatively low, which imposes competitive pressure on incumbents because excess profits will be eroded by new entrants.[10]

In principle, an RIA combines markets, making it possible to reduce monopoly power as firms from different countries are brought into more intense competition with each other. This can yield four types of gain. The first is the textbook gain from increased competition: firms are induced to cut prices and to expand sales, benefiting consumers as monopolistic distortion is reduced.[11]

The second source of gain is that market enlargement allows firms to exploit economies of scale more fully. In a market of given size, there is a tradeoff between scale economies and competition: if firms are larger, there are fewer of them, and the market is less competitive. Enlarging the market shifts this tradeoff, as it becomes possible to have both larger firms and more competition. For example, there might be an initial situation in which two economies each have two firms in a particular industry and these firms exploit their duopoly power, setting prices well above marginal cost. After the formation of the RIA, there are four firms in one combined RIA market. This increases the intensity of competition and may induce merger (or bankruptcy) of some firms, perhaps leaving only the three most efficient firms. The net effect is increased competition, larger firm scale, and lower costs. "Triopoly" competition is likely to be more intense than the original duopolies, and the surviving firms, being larger and more efficient, can better exploit economies of scale.

The third source of gain arises if each firm produces a different variety of the product. In the example just given, consumers throughout the RIA now have a choice of three rather than two varieties.

The final source of gain is in the possible reductions in internal inefficiencies that firms are induced to make. If the RIA increases the intensity of competition, it may induce firms to eliminate internal inefficiencies (so-called X-inefficiency) and raise productivity levels (Horn, Lang, and Lundgren 1995). Since competition raises the probability of bankruptcy and hence of layoffs, it also generates stronger incentives for workers to improve productivity and increases labor turnover across firms within sectors (Dickens and Katz 1987).

There is a good deal of evidence that nonpreferential trade liberalizations achieve these gains. A number of studies have found that openness to trade reduces price-cost margins, an indicator of competitive pressure in the industry (Roberts and Tybout 1996).[12] There is also evidence of an association between trade liberalization and increases in efficiency, and between trade liberalization and a reduction in the dispersion of efficiency levels, as low-efficiency firms adapt or are eliminated.[13] Tybout (2000) concludes that most of the efficiency gains from openness come from reductions in inefficiencies rather than from scale effects.

As for regional integration, we have much less direct evidence. The most extensively studied RIA is the EU. Here the static gains from completing the integration of the European market under the Single Market Programme (SMP) were predicted to range up to about 5 percent of GDP, split about equally between the traditional effects described earlier in this chapter and the scale and competition effects just considered (Catinat and Italianer 1988; Emerson 1988).[14] These estimates were based on extrapolations of calculations from a handful of industries and assumed a significant increase in competitive pressure.[15] Indeed, they were characterized as somewhat "heroic" (Winters 1992a).

The ex post evidence available to date is less flattering to the SMP, although, in fairness, it is very provisional. The EU's Single Market Review (CEC 1996) estimated its economic effects at only 1 to 1.25 percent of GDP in 1994.[16] Moreover, there is good evidence that general external trade liberalization has been more important than regional integration in achieving competitive gains. Jacquemin and Sapir (1991) show that the procompetitive effects of trade occur not through high levels of intra-EU trade but only where there is a high degree of import competition from firms outside the EU.

Turning to developing countries, several arguments suggest that the *potential* competitive gains may be larger than for high-income economies. The small size and relatively closed structure of many developing countries mean that there is scope for more fully exploiting economies of scale and for removing local monopoly power. It is often thought that the services sector, with its high levels of restrictions and scope for economies of scale, offers considerable potential gains from opening to competition. That, however, would require the effective integration of services markets within the RIA, which, as shown in chapter 6, is far from common.

A number of studies have calculated the potential (rather than actual) gains that might be expected from the competition and scale effects. Hunter, Markusen, and Rutherford (1992) construct a CGE model of the U.S. and Mexican automobile industries and simulate the possible effects of NAFTA; they predict large increases in output for Mexico, increases in the scale of individual firms, and reductions in price-cost margins. A study of MERCOSUR (Flores 1997) based on a similar methodology suggests GDP gains of 1.8, 1.1, and 2.3 percent for Argentina, Brazil, and Uruguay, respectively, the larger economies gaining less because they are already closer to reaping economies of scale. Flores also uses an interesting decomposition of the sources of welfare gain. As shown in table 2.1, for imperfectly competitive sectors, the most important effects are the direct resource savings from reduced trade and transport costs and the decline in firms' markups. The benefits of increased variety, trade diversion, and changes in export and import prices have only minor effects on welfare.

Quite different results are obtained by Dissou (2002), who uses a similar methodology to examine the effects on Senegal of the West African Economic and Monetary Union (UEMOA), an RIA of small, least-devel-

Table 2.1 Sources of Welfare Benefits in MERCOSUR's Imperfectly Competitive Sectors
(percentage of total)

Sector	Lower Trade Costs	Lower Markups	Diversity	Diversion	Export Prices	Import Prices	Total
Steel	45.2	71.2	−9.2	−3.1	−5.0	0.9	100
Machinery	28.5	82.2	−1.2	−0.4	−9.4	0.3	100
Automobiles	48.5	69.5	0.0	−11.3	−7.2	0.5	100
Other vehicles	50.5	78.1	−2.3	−8.8	−18.0	0.5	100
Chemicals	37.5	73.2	−1.0	−4.4	−6.8	1.5	100

Source: Flores (1997).

Table 2.2 Welfare Effect for Senegal of UEMOA and Unilateral Liberalization
(percentage deviation from base run)

Full Implementation of Customs Union (1)	Elimination of Tariffs on Regional Exports (2)	Improved Access to Regional Markets Only (3)	CET on Nonregional Exports only (4)	Full Unilateral Liberalization (5)
0.57	−0.18	0.15	0.49	1.26

Note: CET, common external tariff; UEMOA, West African Economic and Monetary Union. The import, market access, and CET effects do not add up to the customs union effect, 0.57, because of interaction effects.
Source: Dissou (2002).

oped countries (see table 2.2). UEMOA has a positive effect (0.57 percent, measured as the deviation from the base run) on Senegal's welfare, but on the import side, elimination of tariffs on intra-RIA imports has a negative effect (20.18 percent) because of significant trade diversion. Improved regional market access raises Senegal's welfare by 0.15 percent, which does not offset the welfare loss of 0.18 percent from trade diversion. The small size of the welfare gain, 0.15 percent, is likely to be attributable to the small intrabloc trade flows. UEMOA's common external tariff (CET) is generally lower than Senegal's pre-UEMOA tariffs, resulting in an additional welfare gain of 0.49 percent. Thus, the main benefit from UEMOA for Senegal is the reduction in tariffs with respect to the rest of the world, not the removal of tariffs on intrabloc trade. And the gain from unilateral trade liberalization (1.26 percent) is more than twice the 0.57 percent gain from UEMOA, even though unilateral trade liberalization does not provide the benefit derived from improved market access.

Interesting as the estimates from these studies may be, it should be recalled that since they are based on CGE models, they reflect not actual outcomes but economists' predictions of the likely effects of integration.

There is virtually no direct ex post evidence on the competitive effects of RIAs among developing countries. Indirect evidence, however, shows that these gains depend largely on the existence of complementary production between members and the interpenetration of each other's markets—that is, on intraindustry trade. Although analysis of the importance of intraindustry trade in developing country RIAs is fragmentary and partial, simple statistics show strongly that developing countries, even in the middle-income range, generate far lower levels of such trade than do developed ones.

A well-documented case study of duplication of plant in the tire industry in Central America (Willmore 1974, 1976) illustrates the difficulties developing countries can encounter in reaping economies of scale in practice. A plant in Guatemala had the capacity to meet the entire CACM demand, and there was another sizable plant in Costa Rica. Rationalization did not occur, possibly because the external tariff remained high, enabling the firms and governments (which were generally reluctant to see their firms go under) to collude to impede effective competition. The same occurred with cement plants in the Economic Community of West Africa (CEAO).

So, regional integration schemes may offer developing countries substantial *potential* gains through competition and scale effects. The gains, however, are not automatic, and making sure that they are achieved calls for careful policy design. In particular, it requires easing barriers to entry (for example, for foreign direct investment) and allowing competition free rein even when it hurts. There is much more to competition than the mere removal of tariff barriers. In chapter 6 we return to competitive effects, when we examine policy integration. We show that, to date, few RIAs have been able to advance very far in this direction. It should also be kept in mind that gains from competition and economies of scale may be attainable through unilateral and multilateral trade liberalization.

APPENDIX. THE SIMPLE ANALYTICS OF TRADE CREATION AND TRADE DIVERSION

Appendix figure 2A.1 illustrates the simplest analysis of trade creation and trade diversion, based on the conventional interpretation of Viner (1950). For more detailed analyses, see De Rosa (1998); Robson (1998).

The figure represents the demand for and supply of a good on a market. The good is assumed to be homogeneous across suppliers. We assume that the industry is perfectly competitive and undistorted so that the supply curve faithfully reflects the actual marginal costs of production. It is assumed that the country is small and cannot affect the price of the good on world markets. This implies that the import supply curve is horizontal: no matter how much is demanded by consumers in the country, the world price for the good remains unaffected. Equilibrium requires that demand equal supply. Without trade barriers, consumers will import $Q_6 - Q_1$ from the lowest-cost supplier (country A), with amount Q_1 supplied by local producers. If the government imposes a tariff, the internal cost of imports will rise by the amount of the tariff. In the figure this is represented by an upward shift of the import supply curve, as perceived by domestic purchasers, from p^A to $p^A + T$. The domestic price of imports is now the world price plus the tariff. The total quantity demanded falls from Q_6 to Q_4; sales of domestic industry rise from Q_1 to Q_3; and imports fall to $Q_4 - Q_3$.

Figure 2A.1 The Market for a Single Homogeneous Good

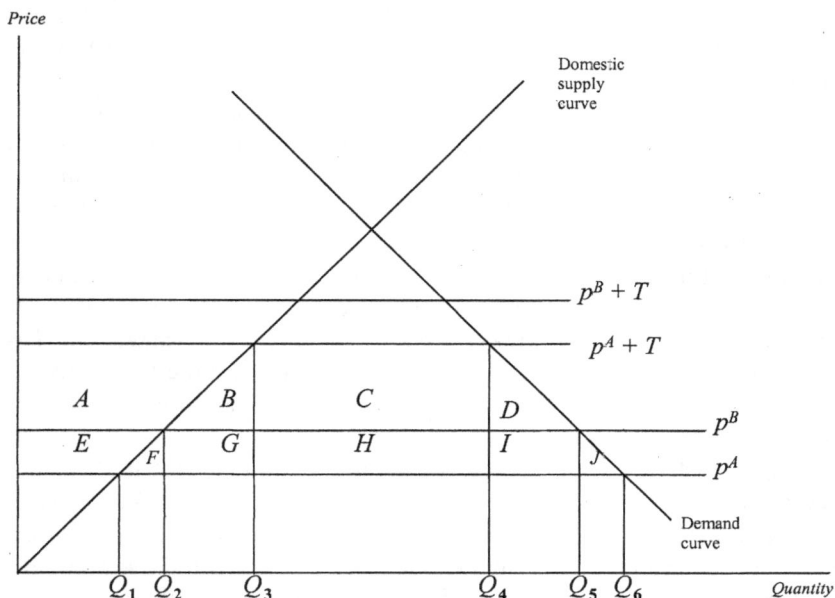

The impact of the tariff on economic welfare is negative. Domestic consumers pay more for the good; they lose the sum of areas $A + B + C + D + E + F + G + H + I + J$. From a national perspective, this is partially offset by the gain that accrues to domestic producers from the higher price (areas $A + E$) and the tariff revenue that is obtained by the government (equal to area $C + H$—the tariff multiplied by the amount imported). The net loss to society due to the tariff is therefore equal to the sum of triangular areas $B + F + G$ and $D + I + J$. These triangles are measures of the distortion in resource allocation that the tariff creates: domestic firms produce too much (relative to free trade), and consumers consume too little.

If it is now assumed that our country concludes an RIA with country A and so eliminates the tariff on imports from A, the same benefits emerge as under general free trade. It is as though country B had never existed—it figures in this commerce neither before nor after the RIA. If, however, the RIA is with B, the higher-cost supplier, the price of imports to domestic buyers falls from $p^A + T$ to p^B. Consumption expands from Q_4 to Q_5; consumers gain $A + B + C + D$; producers lose A; and the government loses revenue $C + H$. The net welfare effect is then $B + D - H$, which could be either positive or negative. Imports from country A cease, replaced entirely by those from B. Of the increase in imports from partner country B, $Q_3 - Q_2$ displaces local sales and constitutes *trade creation* in a pure Vinerian sense, generating welfare gains of area B. $Q_5 - Q_4$ represents the increase in consumption induced by the fall in the internal price; this can also be thought of as *trade creation* and generates welfare gains of D. As in the case of nondiscriminatory tariff cuts, both parts of trade creation are beneficial nationally. The final element of imports from B, however, $Q_4 - Q_3$, is *trade diversion*: imports that initially came from A at price p^A now come from B at price p^B, costing the country welfare equivalent to area H. This is welfare reducing because the country is paying more for its imports: consumers pay less for them, to be sure, but only because the government is no longer collecting a tariff.

Appendix figure 2A.1 illustrates a number of points made in the chapter 2 text. For example, the net effect of the RIA in this market depends on the relative sizes of trade creation and trade diversion; the cost of diversion is determined by how inefficient the partner is relative to world best practice; and the existence of diversion depends on the tariff on A being greater than that cost difference.

For future reference, we observe here that neither A nor B experiences noticeable welfare effects from the RIA. The fact that each is prepared to sell any amount to our country at a fixed price suggests that they would be equally happy selling somewhere else or not producing at all (the price they get from our country just matches the opportunity cost of supplying the good) and that therefore they are indifferent about whether they sell it or not. The most common cause of this outcome in reality is that A and B are very large relative to our market: our demand is just not large enough to matter.

We should also note that it is possible that the barrier to A's and B's exports to us is not a tariff, or indeed any other barrier that produces a revenue (rent) for someone, but a resource-using, or frictional, barrier. For example, it may be that goods have to be extensively tested before admission or that there are large amounts of paperwork to be done. In these cases the positive analysis—what actually happens to quantities and prices—is exactly the same as for the tariff, but the welfare analysis is different. The triangles associated with trade creation remain as before, but with frictional barriers there are no trade diversion losses. Although supply is switched to a higher-cost supplier, there were no rents from trade in the first place, and so there was nothing to lose. The whole of area $C + H$ was just wasted in friction in the first equilibrium. Hence, exempting supplies from B from such barriers represents a real resource saving (at least, provided that doing so does not undermine any other public policy objective achieved through testing or paperwork requirements). Of course, it would be even better to exempt A, as well as B, from the barrier so that imports are available at real cost p^A rather than p^B. This analysis shows that it is better to remove a frictional barrier of x percent than a tariff of x percent: the effects on the private sector are the same, but the first measure entails no loss of government revenue because the government was never getting any.

Appendix figure 2A.2 extends the argument to the case of an RIA between two small countries. This time, we draw the demand curve for imports, representing domestic demand less domestic supply for the good (that is, net demand).[17] We can buy from a small country, or from a large one (the rest of the world). At first, when we impose equal tariffs on each, we divide purchases between them. The small country (supplier B) is able to supply some units very cheaply, but as we demand more, our demand becomes large relative to the small country's capacity to supply, and we drive up its price. The rest of the world (supplier A) is large and can supply effectively any amount we require at a fixed price. Thus, pro-

Figure 2A.2 An RIA with a Small Partner

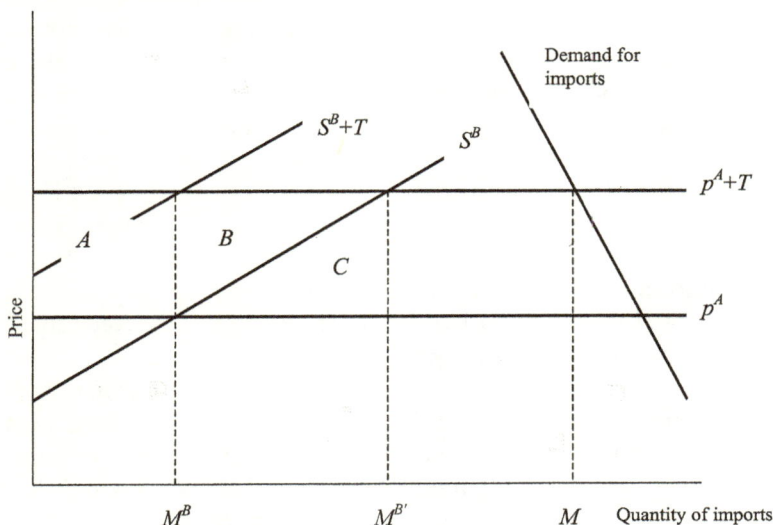

ducers in B are happy to supply us when their costs are below p^A, but beyond that level we buy from A at price p^A. Of course, since we have to buy some units from A, B's firms charge us p^A even though they would supply for less (we have no alternative, so they can collect some rent). Thus, the initial equilibrium involves imports M, of which M^B comes from B and $M - M^B$ from A. The domestic price is $p^A + T$, but of this, only p^A flows to producers overseas; T remains at home with the government.

Now imagine that we join an RIA with B. Now B's producers no longer face the tariff, but if we have to continue to buy some supplies from A at price p^A, the internal price remains $p^A + T$. (A is the marginal supplier and so determines the price.) If the internal price does not change, no domestic behavior changes, and so there is no chance of our gaining anything through production or consumption effects. The sourcing of imports, however, does change because producers in B, exempt from the tariff, can now earn $p^A + T$ from exports rather than just p^A. Naturally they increase their sales, to $M^{B'}$. Moreover, because we are no longer charging tariffs to B, the areas $A + B + C$ in the figure switch from being tariff revenue to being a real cost of imports paid to producers abroad. This is a straight loss for us.

Our country's loss in this case depends on three things: the height of the remaining tariff on A, the initial volume of imports from B, and the extent of trade diversion (the increase in imports from B). Note that we lose the tariff revenue on the initial level of imports from B even if there is no trade diversion! But of course, the extra cost of imports to us represents a gain for B's producers—they get higher prices—so would not all these effects cancel out for the RIA as a whole? The answer is, no, if there is any trade diversion. B's producers get a straight transfer on the initial level of exports, which does cancel out (area A), but as they expand their sales, their real costs rise and so between M^B and $M^{B'}$ the costs of production exceed those that would apply if we bought from A. Of their earnings on the increased level of exports, C is absorbed by extra costs and B is surplus. Thus, overall, B's producers gain by $A + B$, while our government loses $A + B + C$. Given that there is no possibility of trade creation, we can be certain that in this simple case an RIA between small countries will be welfare worsening.

A real RIA covers many goods, and so we would expect to gain export revenue on some to compensate for the losses on others. The calculations above show that the RIA will lose overall, but it is possible that one or the other partner will be a net gainer. This is more likely if a country initially has lower tariffs or smaller imports from its partner.

Table 2A.1 Trade Effects of RIAs between Developing Countries, One Year before and Five Years after Implementation of Internal Preferences
(percent)

	Import Shares		Trade Intensity		Import/GDP Ratio			Trade Propensity	
RIA	Intra-bloc	Extra-bloc	Intra-bloc	Extra-bloc	Intra-bloc	Extra-bloc	Total Imports	Intra-bloc	Extra-bloc
MERCOSUR									
1990	14.5	85.5	10.52	0.87	0.57	3.34	3.91	0.41	0.03
1996	20.2	79.8	14.12	0.81	1.64	6.48	8.10	1.15	0.07
Andean Pact I									
1968	4.3	95.7	2.90	0.97	0.54	12.15	12.69	0.37	0.12
1974	7.2	92.8	6.16	0.94	1.01	13.14	14.15	0.87	0.13
CACM II									
1990	9.1	90.9	81.19	0.91	2.63	26.22	28.85	23.42	0.26
1996	12.6	87.4	64.33	0.88	3.78	26.29	30.07	19.34	0.26
Andean Pact II									
1990	6.8	93.2	6.84	0.94	0.86	11.77	12.63	0.86	0.12
1996	13.6	86.4	15.55	0.87	2.01	12.80	14.81	2.30	0.13
CARICOM									
1972	5.0	95.0	13.59	0.95	2.76	52.05	54.81	7.45	0.52
1978	3.8	96.2	7.66	0.97	3.10	78.01	81.11	6.21	0.78
CEAO									
1965	3.3	96.7	11.68	0.97	0.48	14.39	14.87	1.74	0.14
1971	4.5	95.5	20.78	0.96	0.91	19.28	20.19	4.20	0.19
UDEAC									
1965	1.4	98.6	8.92	0.99	0.24	17.59	17.83	1.59	0.18
1971	4.0	96.0	30.09	0.96	0.79	18.82	19.61	5.90	0.19
AFTA									
1991	15.9	84.1	3.80	0.88	7.73	40.99	48.72	1.85	0.43
1996	17.7	82.3	2.82	0.88	9.34	43.40	52.74	1.49	0.46
GCC									
1980	6.6	93.4	0.81	1.02	1.47	20.96	22.43	0.18	0.23
1986	5.2	94.8	2.15	0.97	1.50	27.71	29.21	0.63	0.28

Note: The dates given for each RIA are the respective "before" and "after" implementation dates. Andean Pact I refers to the original 1969 agreement and Andean Pact II to the revived agreement (1991); CACM II refers to the Central American Common Market. CARICOM, Caribbean Community and Common Market; CEAO, Economic Community of West Africa; UDEAC, Union douanière et économique de l'Afrique Centrale (now CEMAC); AFTA, ASEAN Free Trade Area; GCC, Gulf Cooperation Council.
Source: World Bank data.

NOTES

1. The concepts of trade creation and trade diversion, first formulated by Jacob Viner, continue to dominate the discussion of RIAs (see Viner 1950).

2. It should also be recognized that RIAs take different lengths of time to become fully operational, so that the period chosen here (one year before the RIA to five years after) is only a crude indicator of their effects.

3. Trade intensity and propensity indices are discussed in Anderson and Norheim (1993).

4. Debate rages as to whether nondiscriminatory liberalizations should be attributed to the process of regionalism. This makes a huge difference to how one appraises certain RIAs. The issue is taken up in chapter 3, where we consider the effect of RIAs on trade policy making.

5. The model that Frankel, Stein, and Wei (1997) prefer (they do not say why) estimates a single effect for each RIA, applying equally to 1970, 1980, 1990, and 1992. This suggests that RIAs had positive impacts on all trade flows except for the EC's intrabloc trade and EFTA's and NAFTA's trade with nonmembers. The authors conclude that there is little trade diversion. But estimating a constant effect over 1970–92 seems inappropriate, given the changes that were occurring in RIAs at that time.

Frankel and Rose (2000) use a gravity model to examine the effect of currency unions and FTAs on trade and find strong intraunion and intra-FTA effects, with the latter equal to between 70 and 100 percent of the former.

6. Statistically, this is equivalent to estimating effects on extrabloc imports, extrabloc exports, and intrabloc trade. What Soloaga and Winters refer to as an overall import effect is numerically the same as an extrabloc import effect, and similarly for exports. The size of the intrabloc trade effect differs between the two parameterizations, however. The effect in the (alternative) version of this endnote would equal that of the text model plus the two extrabloc effects (see the example in the text).

Statistically Soloaga and Winters actually proceed by estimating effects on total imports, total exports, and intrabloc trade, but they show that their estimates may be simply translated into statements about extrabloc imports, extrabloc exports, and intrabloc trade of the sort made in the text.

7. In the gravity model these coefficients are added to the logarithm of trade; the effect is obtained by multiplying trade by $\exp(1.86)$ and $\exp(0.55)$, respectively.

8. As shown in appendix figures 2A.1 and 2A.2, although triangle gains are obtained from the reduction in the price of imports from partner countries, the RIA generates rectangles of losses because of a reduction in imports of substitute products from excluded countries. In other words, trade diversion results in a loss in tariff revenues and welfare, and the net impact of the RIA on welfare is ambiguous.

9. The classification of CGE models is taken from Baldwin and Venables (1995), which surveys some of these studies in greater detail.

10. Tybout (2000) finds no evidence that price-cost margins are systematically higher in developing than in developed countries, although he reports a number of instances where this is so.

11. Djankov and Hoekman (1997) report the positive effects of trade reform on competition in Bulgaria.

12. See also Levinsohn (1993); Harrison (1994); Foroutan (1996); Krishna and Mitra (1998).

13. See Nishimizu and Page (1982); Tybout, de Melo, and Corbo (1991); Haddad and Harrison (1993); Tybout and Westbrook (1995); Harrison (1996).

14. Later research added, even more speculatively, dynamic growth effects on top of these estimates (Baldwin 1989; McKibbin 1994). These effects are considered in chapter 4.

15. The original industry studies in this area were undertaken by Smith and Venables (1988).

16. This is not an easy calculation because many of the measures of the SMP were not adopted until late in the process, EU data were available only until 1994, and several other shocks such as recession and German reunification clouded the picture.

17. An alternative assumption is that there is no domestic production, so that all consumption has to be met from imports.

CHAPTER 3

Making the Most of Regional Integration

One important message that emerges from the analysis in chapter 2 is that, in purely trading terms, an RIA cannot provide any benefits that member countries cannot attain through nondiscriminatory tariff reductions. When we look at the effects of RIAs on reallocation of factors of production (assuming that their quantity and productivity are not affected by regional integration) or on patterns of consumption, there appears to be no economic rationale for forming trade blocs. Nondiscriminatory tariff reductions would bring a country all the gains of trade creation without the costs of trade diversion and would thus be a superior option. When transfers between government revenue and producers are taken into account, one member might do better in an RIA than under nondiscrimination, but only by driving the other partner even farther below that level. Thus, the arguments in chapter 2 cannot explain why *both* members would agree to an RIA.

Then why are RIAs so popular? Several explanations are offered in later chapters—for example, that regionalism helps reduce the chances of conflict with neighbors or facilitates the negotiation of agreements to share regional resources—but here we consider whether extending the analysis of purely trade or border factors could explain this popularity. We find that trade-based factors offer little justification for preferring RIAs to free trade, although we do find reasons why RIAs formed with other motivations tend to be between neighbors and, more controversially, why developing countries will generally gain more from RIAs with developed countries than with other developing countries.

The judgments behind these conclusions are necessarily empirical and pragmatic. Although economic theory suggests that RIAs can always be designed to be welfare improving, in practice the necessary information, the incentives, and the legal rights to manipulate the instruments of trade policy to guarantee such outcomes are missing. Ultimately, it is not theoretical possibilities or empirical generalities that define the appropriateness of an RIA but practical issues such as which partners are actually chosen and the level of tariffs against the rest of the world. These are the subject of this chapter.

FREE TRADE WITH WHOM?

One of the rare questions on which trade bloc economists agree is the commonsense proposition that an RIA between any set of countries could be designed to leave the rest of the world indifferent, at least one of the members better off, and the rest no worse off (Kemp and Wan 1976; Panagariya and Krishna 2002). Unfortunately, this result requires that external tariffs be set so that members' total trade with the rest of the world (commodity by commodity) is maintained at preunion levels and that lump-sum taxes and transfers take place between partners. The required external tariffs are almost impossible to calculate—and might conflict with WTO obligations—while the transfers are never feasible in practice.[1]

Given these practical constraints on ensuring that any given RIA is welfare improving, and the reality that forming an RIA with one set of partners precludes or at least complicates creating one with others, the question of why an RIA might be attractive cannot be divorced from the question of who belongs to it. We therefore consider in this section both rather generic arguments in favor of discrimination and rather specific ones about the particular attractions of RIAs with certain types of partner.

Why Not with Everyone?

One argument for preferring an RIA—specifically, a customs union—to free trade is that if a trade bloc's joint economy is large, coordinating its international trade policies will allow it to strike better bargains with trading partners.[2] That is, it can reap terms-of-trade benefits not available to its members acting independently. This rationale is examined in chapter 8, where we consider the effects of RIAs on the rest of the world, for such gains are necessarily at the latter's expense. There is very little research on such benefits, but Chang and Winters (2002) suggest that they may have been important for MERCOSUR. In general, however, improving the terms of trade is not commonly believed to be a big motivator of trade policy stances, and besides, most RIAs, especially among developing countries, are pretty small.

A second argument concerns market access. An RIA not only affects imports but also promises the benefits of duty-free access for exports to partner markets. This is an important consideration for a country that is considering joining an RIA, but the benefits the country derives from such market access can only come at the expense of its partner—which, for its part, would be better off if it were to eliminate its tariff. The benefits are the exact counterpart of the tariff revenue losses discussed in chapter 2. Both parties cannot gain simultaneously from such transfers.

Another aspect of the same argument is that countries may feel better able to liberalize their own trade if others are doing so at the same time. If improved access to another market depends on opening one's own, a new constituency for trade reform may be created among exporters. If countries simultaneously reduce tariffs on each other's exports, adverse terms-of-trade changes are less likely than if only one party liberalizes (Bagwell and Staiger 1999), and if several liberalize together, the need for any one of them to devalue its currency to maintain its foreign balance is reduced. Also, adjustment might be easier if export sectors are expanding as import-competing sectors contract. These are all reasons for coordinating trade reforms across countries, and RIAs provide one way of doing this. But concerted unilateralism, under which several countries introduce MFN liberalization together, would also fit the bill, as several APEC member countries argued in the early days of that agreement.

A third reason for favoring RIAs over MFN free trade arises if member countries wish to industrialize behind protective barriers. Forming a group that provides scope for intrabloc industrial specialization reduces the cost of protection and can generate welfare gains that would not be open to members through unilateral tariff liberalization (Cooper and Massell 1965). The first wave of RIAs among developing countries in the 1960s and 1970s set import substitution as a major policy objective, and a number of RIAs, including LAFTA and ASEAN, appear to have been explicitly motivated by gains from pursuing industrialization on a regional basis. But these policies must be based on noneconomic governmental objectives or public-goods arguments, given that there are few grounds for concluding that economic gains can be derived from protected industrial development.

If industries can be rendered competitive at higher levels of output when preferential markets are available, it might appear that an RIA could be justified. But it has then to be explained why the industry would need the support of a protected regional market if mere expansion of output (perhaps through scale economies) suffices to make its costs competitive. The issues surrounding the dynamics of industrialization and long-term comparative advantage are addressed in more detail in chapters 4 and 5.

Choosing Partners: The "Natural Trading Partners" Fallacy

Ever since customs theory began, with Viner (1950), economists have puzzled about who the perfect partners would be. For many years, this proved to be a sterile debate, with every proposal turning out to be, at best, a restricted and special case. (Panagariya 1997 lists the most important contributions to the discussion.) Recently, World Bank research has yielded new findings which, if they do not close the book on the controversy, at least shine a brighter light on the question.

Early research focused on whether potential RIA members were complementary in their production and consumption patterns and whether they were already major trading partners. The first criterion proved very difficult to pin down. In the early 1990s the second appeared to gain considerable currency, along with the notion that countries close enough to each other to reap savings on transport costs were natural partners (Wonnacott and Lutz 1989; Summers 1991).

Before assessing the validity of the argument that countries which already trade disproportionately with each other are ideal partners for an RIA, we examine whether this has been the case for most RIAs. The left-hand side of table 3.1 shows, for a sample of RIAs, the share of intrabloc trade in partner countries' total trade at the time of bloc formation. The right-hand side shows the share of an individual country's total trade that is carried out with a bloc it is joining. It is clear that the intrabloc share of trade is much larger in North-North RIAs (EEC, 38.6 percent; CUSFTA, 30.2 percent) and in North-South RIA's (NAFTA, 42.1 percent) than in South-South RIAs. The largest intrabloc share in South-South RIAs is in ASEAN (16.7 percent), followed by MERCOSUR (12.9 percent), the EAC (12.8 percent), and CEFTA (10.3 percent). The other RIAs have much smaller intrabloc trade shares: below 1 percent for three Sub-Saharan African RIAs (UDEAC, the SADC, and the CEAO), 1.0 percent for the CACM, 2.3 percent for the Andean Pact, 3.2 percent for SAARC, 3.3 percent for the G3, and 4.2 percent for the GCC. This

Table 3.1 Trade Shares, Selected RIAs
(percent)

RIA and Year Formed	Share of Intrabloc Trade in Total Trade	Country, RIA, and Year Joined	Country's Trade with EU (or CACM) as Share of Country's Total Trade
Andean Pact (1969)	2.3	Costa Rica-CACM (1962)	2.5
ASEAN (1967)	16.7	Czech Rep.-EU (1995)	46.7
CACM (1962)	1.0	Estonia-EU (1995)	16.7
CEAO (1973)	0.9	Hungary-EU (1994)	41.5
CEFTA (1993)	10.3	Iceland-EU (1994)	60.0
CUSFTA (1989)	30.2	Latvia-EU (1995)	21.7
EAC (1996)	12.8	Lithuania-EU (1995)	23.0
EEC (1962)[a]	38.6	Morocco-EU (1996)	74.4
G3 (1995)	3.3	Norway-EU (1994)	61.3
GCC (1981)	4.2	Poland-EU (1994)	49.4
MERCOSUR (1991)	12.9	Romania-EU (1995)	41.8
NAFTA (1994)	42.1	Slovak Rep.-EU (1995)	26.4
SAARC (1985)	3.2	Slovenia-EU (1995)	53.7
SADC (1980)	0.1	Tunisia-EU (1995)	56.8
UDEAC (1966)	0.9		

Note: ASEAN, Association of Southeast Asian Nations; CACM, Central American Common Market; CEAO, Economic Community of West Africa (became the Western African Economic and Monetary Union, UEMOA); CEFTA, Central European Free Trade Area; CUSFTA, Canada–United States Free Trade Agreement; EAC, East African Cooperation; EEC, European Economic Community; EU, European Union; G3, Group of Three (Colombia, Mexico, and Venezuela); GCC, Gulf Cooperation Council; MERCOSUR, Common Market of the South; NAFTA, North American Free Trade Agreement; SAARC, South Asian Association for Regional Cooperation; SADC, Southern African Development Community; UDEAC, Union douanière et économique de l'Afrique Centrale (became the Economic and Monetary Community of Central Africa, CEMAC).
a. The EEC was formed in 1957, but the earliest bilateral trade data obtained are for 1962.
Source: World Bank data.

evidence leads us to conclude that RIAs are typically formed between neighboring countries but not necessarily between countries that are already major trading partners.

As the table shows, except for Costa Rica and the CACM, the countries that signed FTAs with the EU were major trading partners with it. As more countries joined the EU, staying on the outside became ever more costly, and the incentive to join increased. This phenomenon of "domino regionalism" is examined in more detail in chapter 8.

Attractive though it would be to have a shortcut to assessing RIAs, the concept of "natural trading partners" has little or no operational content. To be useful, it would have to be easily applied and to identify trade that we wish to stimulate artificially by means of preferences. That a trade flow is already large says nothing about the need to stimulate it: the advantages of proximity and conformable commodity composition are already reflected in its size. In fact, some flows are large because of existing distortions and need to be curtailed rather than boosted.

The argument on transport costs is more sophisticated but is ultimately of little more practical use. RIAs can be advantageous if they allow two countries to trade a good with each other that, previously, one exported to the rest of the world and the other imported at a higher price. This situation could arise either because the rest of the world levies tariffs or export taxes on its trade or because of transport costs (Wonnacott and Wonnacott 1981). By trading together and so reducing the margin between the buying and selling prices, the RIA improves one or both countries' terms of trade, but only if at least one of them ceases its trade with the rest of the world. Amjadi and Winters (1999) show that although for MERCOSUR high transport costs on trade with the rest of the world offer scope for large terms of trade gains, very few goods seem likely to experience the required change in trade patterns. Similarly, with the advent of NAFTA, Mexico reduced rather than expanded the set of goods (defined at the six-digit level of the Harmonized Commodity Description and Coding System trade classification) for which the United States or Canada, or both, were its only suppliers.

Schiff (2001), revisiting the natural trading partners debate, argues that both advocates and detractors of the hypothesis have largely missed the point because, although they have analyzed the target country's relationships with its potential partners and with the rest of the world, they have failed to consider relationships between the last two. This is important because it constrains the patterns of trade and prices that could actually rule in the world prior to the formation of the RIA. Once this is taken into account, the size of the preexisting trade flow is no guide to "naturalness"—the relationship is neither necessarily positive (as advocates claim) nor necessarily negative (as detractors claim). Schiff does, however, argue that for a given target country, larger partners are better than smaller ones because they are more likely to satisfy the target country's import demand without increasing prices, and they are less likely to cease importing the target's export goods from the rest of the world and hence to reduce their internal price of these goods below the world price plus their tariff on third countries. He also argues that the RIA is likely to be better off if its members are complementary in the sense that under nondiscriminatory trade policies, each would import what the other exports rather than what the other imports.

In a recent paper, Krishna (forthcoming a) estimates the welfare effect of a U.S. reduction in its preferential tariffs with respect to the imports of various trading partners and examines the relationship between these welfare effects and the distance, as well as the volume of trade, between the United States and its trading partners. He finds no correlation between geographic proximity and the welfare effect of these RIAs or between trade volume and welfare effect. Thus, he obtains no support for the natural trading partners hypothesis.

Choosing Partners: Comparative Advantage

The second line of inquiry in the question of choosing partners is pursued by Venables (2000, 2002), who considers the comparative advantage of RIA members relative to each other and to the rest of the world. For several special models, comparative advantage is important in defining a country's ideal partners and helps to determine whether RIA members' incomes converge or diverge—a topic we discuss more fully in chapter 5.

Suppose that two developing economies both have a comparative disadvantage in manufactures relative to the rest of the world but that for one the disadvantage is less than for the other. Kenya and Uganda can serve as examples. Their comparative disadvantage in manufactures could stem from many alternative sources—technological, geographic, or institutional differences. Let us assume that it is because of different endowments of capital: Kenya has little capital per worker relative to the world average, but Uganda has even less. The initial position is one in which each country has some manufacturing that serves local consumers and survives because of relatively high tariff protection.

Now suppose that, starting from a position in which they levy identical tariffs on all imports, these two countries form a customs union. Since Kenya has a comparative advantage in manufacturing relative to Uganda (although not relative to the rest of the world), it will expand manufacturing output to supply the whole customs union, or at least move in that direction, while Uganda's manufacturing sector will contract. These developments move Kenya's production structure farther away from its true comparative advantage while moving Uganda's closer. Surprisingly, however, Kenya gains from the reallocation, while Uganda may lose and will certainly do less well than Kenya. The reason is that Uganda suffers trade diversion: some manufactures that were previously imported from the rest of the world are now imported at greater cost from Kenya. For Kenya, by contrast, there are gains from being able to supply manufactures in the Ugandan market, protected from competition with the rest of the world.

The implication is that countries with comparative advantage closer to the world average do better in an RIA than do countries with more extreme comparative advantage. Interposing the "intermediate" country between the "extreme" one and the rest of the world distorts the extreme country's trade, causing a switch in import supplier. But the intermediate country does not experience this switch in supply; its trade with the extreme country and its trade with the rest of the world are less close substitutes and therefore less vulnerable to trade diversion. This, in turn, implies that a customs union between two poor countries will tend to cause divergence (the richer country—Kenya in this case—gains, while the poorer country, Uganda, loses) but that a customs union between two rich countries will tend to cause convergence (the poorer country is closer to the world average and gains more than its partner). The same basic forces therefore mean that regional integration between rich countries causes their incomes to converge, whereas integration between poor ones causes divergence.

What if the countries lie on opposite sides of the world average and form North-South RIAs? The model is, unfortunately, ambiguous (Venables 2002: figures 4–6). If the developing (southern) partner is not too far from the world average, it will almost certainly gain, but if it is very poor (that is, very poorly endowed with capital or skills), it is likely to lose unless its partner is correspondingly very rich (very well endowed).

Venables shows that for these results to hold, trade patterns must be very particular. If goods are homogeneous (as in the Ricardian and Heckscher-Ohlin models), the partners must not trade prior to the formation of the customs union and must trade afterward ("corner solutions"). Alternatively, products may be differentiated by origin (the Armington assumption) such that every country is the sole supplier of its own particular varieties of each good, which is another form of corner solution.[3]

But the results do not hold in general. In particular, if both partners are small and trade with the rest of the world both before and after formation of the customs union, we are back in the world described in the chapter 2 discussion of trade creation and diversion, in which integration can have no beneficial effects. To see this, keep the assumption of equal tariffs and assume a Heckscher-Ohlin model with homogeneous goods, where both Kenya and Uganda initially import manufactures and export agriculture. Before the customs union is formed, producers of manufactures obtain the world price plus the tariff by selling at home but receive only the world price by selling to their prospective partner. Thus, they sell only at home, and they import the excess demand from the rest of the world (ROW). With equal domestic prices in the two countries, marginal costs are the same as well. Of course, given that Kenya has relatively more capital, it produces more manufactures than Uganda, but that is immaterial as long as it imports from the ROW. After the customs union is formed, both countries can get the same price at home and in the partner's market. But since marginal costs were already equal to the domestic price before the RIA was formed, the RIA has no effect on prices or trade flows; neither Kenya nor Uganda gains or loses.

In fact, if Kenya had the higher tariff on manufactures initially and the customs union adopted that tariff unionwide, we would see convergence, not divergence. Provided that both countries imported manufactures from the ROW initially, the marginal cost of producing manufactures would be lower in Uganda because its tariff is lower. Thus, once the customs union was formed, Uganda would export manufactures to Kenya (until marginal costs were equalized), while Kenya would reduce its imports from the ROW; Uganda would gain, Kenya would lose, and South-South integration would result in convergence. This should not come as a surprise: since countries would already have exploited or arbitraged away their comparative advantage positions by trading on the world market, the only thing left to exploit once the RIA was formed would be trade policy differences.

Another restriction in this model is the number of potential partners and goods (Krishna forthcoming b). Once we assume several potential partners in the North that are producing differentiated products, North-South RIAs may result in welfare losses because the high substitution between northern goods may result in large amounts of trade diversion. As discussed in chapter 2, the southern partner can minimize the costs of trade diversion by reducing tariffs unilaterally.

Neighborhood RIAs

One of the most striking features of international economic integration is that the great majority of RIAs involves neighboring countries (hence the term "regional"!). The main exceptions are APEC (if it can be considered a RIA), the Group of Three (Mexico does not border either Colombia or Venezuela), various plurilateral FTAs (the EU with South Africa, with Mexico, and with Chile), and bilateral FTAs such as those between Canada and Chile, Chile and Mexico, and Israel and the United States. The possible benefit of regionalism in reducing the chances of conflict with neighbors might explain some of this, as might its role in helping them negotiate agreements to share regional resources. Other possible reasons include a history of cooperation with, and better knowledge of, neighboring countries and a desire to replace past tensions with an institutional framework that promotes cooperation.

One pure trade possibility is that neighbors together constitute a regional market for certain goods that, for reasons of taste or excessive transport costs, are not tradable with the rest of the world. If an RIA includes all potential suppliers of such a good, it is equivalent to multilateral free trade and hence, for small countries, is bound to be welfare improving. This is a more demanding criterion than simply observing that members do not import this good from the rest of the world, which might just reflect existing tariffs. The situation is also relatively rare; in 1993, for example, out of a total of 4,858 types of goods, the four MERCOSUR countries imported only 124 types exclusively from each other (Amjadi and Winters 1999). These "local" markets were concentrated in agriculture and accounted for just half of 1 percent of total imports. Enlarging the criterion to goods for which over 95 percent of imports comes from other members adds only 155 types, or 2.2 percent of total imports. Poorer countries may well have higher proportions of their trade in such local markets, but even so, this does not seem likely to be a significant potential benefit of regionalism. Moreover, even if trade were restricted to close neighbors, that is not an argument for forming an RIA: nondiscriminatory liberalization would have the same beneficial effect.

Another important reason for forming a customs union between neighbors is to reduce the transactions costs involved in border formalities. These are often more important hindrances to trade than customs duties and are far more likely to be avoidable between contiguous than between distant countries. Even for neighbors, however, eliminating these costs can be a complex process; the EU took from 1957 until the mid-1990s to get close to having "invisible borders" between even a subset of its members.

A third incentive for neighborhood customs unions is to ensure that countries get their proper shares of tariff and other fiscal revenues when goods are in transit or are transferred. (That is, the customs union contains agreements to transfer tariff revenues from the country of collection to the country of final destination. Such agreements can be contentious if the partners do not trust each other fully.) These administrative considerations, which are particularly important for landlocked countries, played a major role in the origins of four long-standing African RIAs: UDEAC, the CEAO, the EAC, and SACU. A customs union can also help avoid the costs of smuggling or tax competition. Senegal has long sought to form a customs union with The Gambia to remove the incentive for its citizens to smuggle in imported manufactures from that country. Robson (1998) estimates that for many years such smuggling generated a significant proportion (an estimated 25 percent in 1980) of The Gambia's revenues from import duties—at Senegal's expense.

North-South or South-South RIAs

North-South RIAs mostly involve arrangements between developing countries and the EU or, more recently, North America. Those two trading areas include a high proportion of the world's most efficient producers of many products, operate behind relatively low tariffs for manufactures, and are capable of supplying the bulk of the needs of the southern economies. To see the advantages this has for RIA formation, consider the polar case of a good for which domestic supplies and imports from partners and nonpartners are perfect substitutes.

The southern partner in a North-South RIA reduces its tariffs on imports from a supplier large enough to satisfy many of its needs at little more than the prevailing international cost. If it imports only from the northern partner after the bloc is formed, its domestic prices fall to northern levels and it benefits from increased consumption and reduced production of high-cost domestic substitutes. In effect, in the commodities for which this is true, the South can enjoy gains from a North-South RIA much like those from unilateral liberalization on an MFN basis. In the language of appendix figure 2A.1 in the previous chapter, it is as if p^A and p^B were very close together, so that losses from diversion (area H) are small.

There are two critical issues here. First, how frequently and by how much do the northern partner's costs exceed international minima? Although the EU and the United States are generally efficient producers and are subject to international competitive pressures, there are still plenty of products for which they are not least-cost producers. Even if their cost disadvantage were only, say, 5 percent, it would apply to a high proportion of imports and so would represent a significant loss of income relative to multilateral free trade. As early as 1977, Roemer identified the tendency for metropolitan countries to sell far broader ranges of goods in their colonies and former colonies than they were able to do on world markets. This is the direct analogue of the 5 percent margins.

Second, one needs to be confident that prices would actually fall to the internal levels of the northern partner. The story above implicitly assumes that the partner becomes the only supplier, but as we saw in chapter 2, if imports do continue from third countries which continue to face the tariff, domestic prices will not fall, and there will be no gains. The southern country will just lose tariff revenue. But even if third-county imports do cease, what makes northern firms cut their prices to their domestic levels? The answer is, competition, and if anything occurs to curtail competition between northern firms in the southern market, the price cuts will be curtailed or wholly absent. Among the things that could curtail competition are collusion (tacit or otherwise) not to compete in these "captive" markets; economies of scale in selling (for example, consignment size) so that it is not worthwhile for more than one or two firms to sell in the southern market; and product differentiation. The last increases the chances that the posttariff prices of northern goods will fall somewhat, but it curtails the effects of such price decreases on competing domestic suppliers.

The southern government would, of course, lose tariff revenues—to domestic consumers to the extent that consumer prices fell, and partly to northern producers if their prices exceeded those at which imports occurred before the RIA. As we saw in chapter 2, the former is just a transfer within the southern country, but the latter represents a transfer of income to the northern partner.

The most striking example of trade dependence between developing and developed partners is probably NAFTA. In 1991, before NAFTA was a real possibility, 70 percent of Mexico's imports came from the United States, and for 614 out of the 4,854 trade headings in which imports occurred, the United States or Canada was the only source. By 1996 the share of imports from the United States had risen to 78 percent, but, in line with the general liberalization of the economy accompanying NAFTA, the number of imports bought only from NAFTA partners had decreased to 296. Without information on prices, it is impossible to quantify the effects, but Mexico's continuing extensive imports from nonpreferred suppliers makes it likely that its internal prices are significantly influenced by the remaining tariffs against them. Moreover, because Mexico's tariffs are typically well above U.S. tariffs, Mexico's losses of tariff revenue on imports are likely to far exceed its gains on its exports to the United States. Thus, Mexico's gains from NAFTA in the simple trade dimension are likely to be considerably less than those possible if tariffs were removed from all import sources.

North-South RIAs such as NAFTA and the Euro-Mediterranean agreements are typically FTAs rather than customs unions. When these RIAs do involve customs unions, as in the Turkey-EU agreement, the southern partner is effectively obliged to adopt the lower northern tariff, implying a substantial measure of trade liberalization. This is a further source of gain.

HOW MANY RIAs?

For an individual country, an attractive strategy may be to maintain many RIAs simultaneously, especially with its main trading partners. This would combine duty-free access to multiple markets with zero tariffs on imports from multiple sources. Such a strategy, pursued by several countries in a given region, can result in overlapping RIAs and in what is known as "spaghetti-bowl regionalism." We return to this at the end of the section. Putting aside the complications associated with overlapping RIAs and the very real danger that different FTAs have different administrative requirements such as rules of origin (as discussed in the next section), combining a number of RIAs could effectively substitute for free trade. Several countries now pursue essentially this strategy. For example, Chile is party to 12 trade agreements (APEC and LAIA, plus bilateral links with Argentina, Bolivia, Canada, Colombia, Ecuador, the EU, MERCOSUR, Mexico, Peru, and Venezuela). Panama belongs to nine; Mexico to eight (with eight more under negotiation); Bolivia, Costa Rica, and Nicaragua to five each; and El Salvador, Guatemala, and Honduras to four each. The picture is equally complex for Eastern Europe: the Slovak Republic belongs to nine RIAs, the Czech Republic and Slovenia to eight, Estonia to six, and Hungary, Latvia, Poland, and Romania to five each. RIA memberships in Africa are shown in figure 3.1, which reveals a pattern of overlapping blocs.

The EU has a wide range of RIAs with European and Mediterranean partners and, counting its nonreciprocal trade agreements, actually offers tariff preferences to all but 10 of its trading partners (Winters 2000).

The results for Chile from a multiregional CGE model suggest strong benefits from such "additive regionalism" (figure 3.2). Chile's current agreement with MERCOSUR appears to have a potential welfare-reducing effect, at least on the simple trade criteria applied here. An FTA with NAFTA would be more attractive because of the better market access. Indeed, all of the positive benefits from NAFTA are attributable to the gaining of tariff-free access to the U.S. market for nongrain crops; without this, Chile would lose. Joining both MERCOSUR and NAFTA offers overall gains of 1.48 percent of GDP. This exceeds the sum from the two separate FTAs by 0.87 percent, which is broadly a measure of the extent to which liberalizing two sources of imports simultaneously reduces trade diversion.[4] Adding the EU and the rest of Latin America to the cocktail adds value strongly, both through further reductions in trade diversion and by increasing Chile's access to export markets. These estimates should not be taken too seriously as absolute values, but the basic

Figure 3.1 Overlapping Blocs in Africa

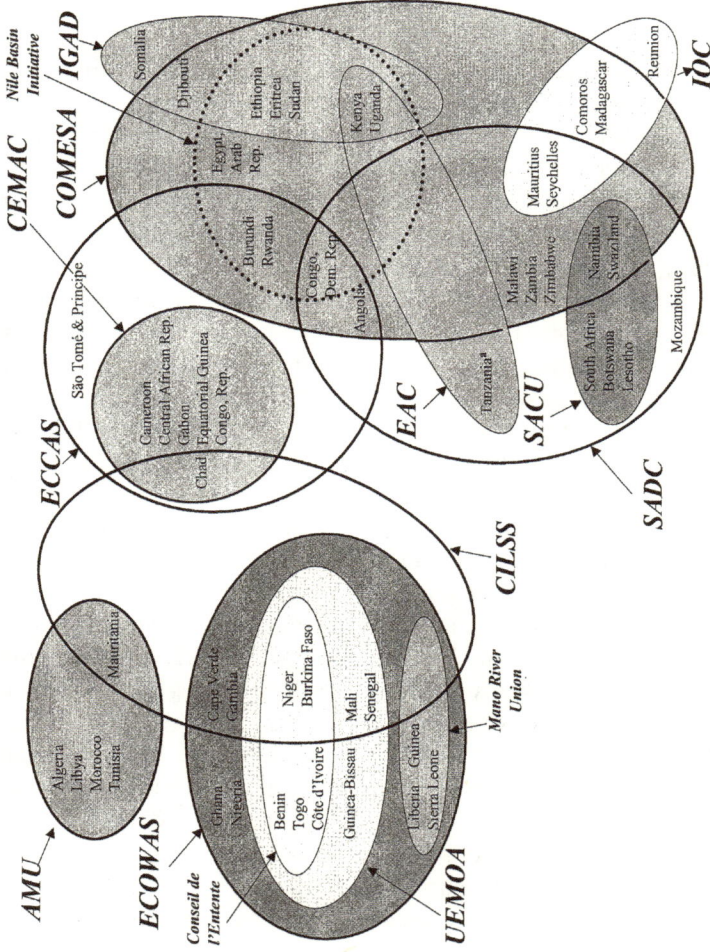

Note: AMU, Arab-Maghreb Union; CBI, Cross-Border Initiative; CEMAC, Economic and Monetary Community of Southern Africa; CILSS, Permanent Interstate Committee on Drought Control in the Sahel; COMESA, Common Market for Eastern and Southern Africa; EAC, East African Cooperation; ECCA, Economic Community of Central African States; ECOWAS, Economic Community of West African States; IGAD, Intergovernmental Authority on Development; IOC, Indian Ocean Commission; SACU, Southern African Customs Union; SADC, Southern African Development Community; UEMOA, West African Economic and Monetary Union.

insight that—provided it is administratively straightforward—additive regionalism could generate benefits is worth noting.

One problem with the incremental approach is that Chile's early partners thought they were negotiating access to a market that was effectively protected by 11 percent tariffs against everyone else, and they were prepared to "pay" for that privilege with their own concessions. Then they discovered that Chile was selling essentially the same deal to other partners. In two cases this led to protests, which Chile addressed by accelerating tariff reductions on the complainers' exports. The solution to partner complaints about unforeseen liberalization was yet more liberalization. This was a good outcome for Chile, but it is evident that the threat of this kind of problem could undermine the whole approach. Managing multiple RIAs is clearly not easy. However, if credibility and administrative skills are high, if one's country is an attractive partner, if the FTAs cover the bulk of trade, and if the cost of trade diversion incurred before a large number of FTAs is in place is not high, it could be a useful strategy.

Figure 3.2 Potential Gains from Additive Regionalism for Chile from Joining Additional RIAs

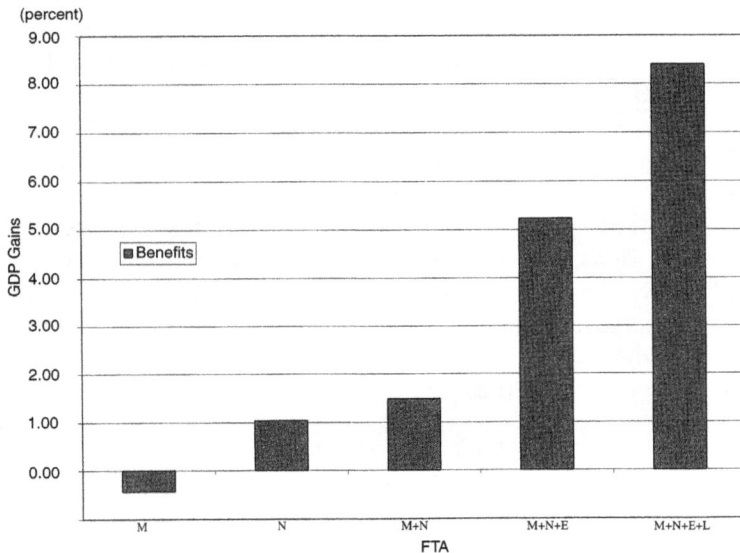

Note: E = EU, European Union; L = Latin America; M = MERCOSUR, Common Market of the South; N = NAFTA, North American Free Trade Agreement.
Source: Harrison, Rutherford, and Tarr (2002).

Moreover when, in chapter 4, we look at the dynamic effects of RIAs, we shall see that such effects might also arise from multiple RIAs. The best example is "hub-and-spoke" regionalism. If one country (or group of countries) has RIAs with a number of countries that maintain barriers between each other, then this hub country becomes the preferred location for investment—firms can reach more markets tariff free than they can from any of the other locations—and this will tend to bid up factor prices and raise real income in the hub. The world's largest hub is the EU, which has separate RIAs with nearly all other European and many Mediterranean countries, most of which do not grant each other free trade.

A quite different situation arises if a country's multiple RIAs conflict. All members of a customs union must set the same external tariffs. Yet Bolivia, Colombia, Ecuador, Peru, and Venezuela are in the Andean Pact (a customs union), while Colombia and Venezuela are also in the Group of Three (an FTA with Mexico), and Bolivia has formed an FTA with MERCOSUR. Similarly, as was shown in figure 3.1, Namibia and Swaziland belong to COMESA while also belonging to SACU, a customs union with South Africa and Botswana, and Tanzania belongs both to the SADC and to the EAC, a customs union with Kenya and Uganda. Since these obligations are formally contradictory, it may be unclear which will prevail in practice, and special conditions and exclusions may have to be formulated. In addition, the administrative aspects of the various agreements tend to differ, notably as concerns rules of origin. The outcome is a mass of complex rules that traders have to cope with (and frequently seek to avoid).

Sub-Saharan Africa seems to combine the worst of the various elements examined. As shown in figure 3.1, most of its RIAs overlap with others, and a number of countries belong to RIAs with contradictory obligations. Expending the region's scarce administrative resources on negotiating and managing multiple and complex RIAs is unlikely to be efficient. Finally, the host of regional RIAs is unlikely to provide a significant increase in market access or in trade liberalization for the countries in the region, most of whose trade is with Organisation for Economic Co-operation and Development (OECD) countries.

FREE TRADE AREAS AND CUSTOMS UNIONS

A central issue for countries planning to integrate their trade is whether to choose a free trade agreement or a customs union. Of the 162 RIAs notified to the GATT/WTO as of August 1998, 143 were FTAs, which have zero internal tariffs but no harmonization of external tariffs, and 19 were customs unions, which have a common external tariff as well as internal free trade.[5] Under most circumstances, customs unions are more efficient than FTAs and allow greater market integration, but they also require more coordination and place tighter constraints on individual member policies and sovereignty.

Trade Deflection and Rules of Origin: More Protection

A major worry for FTA members is trade deflection, the redirection of imports from third countries through the FTA member with the lowest external tariff. If unconstrained, this device reduces the effective tariff of every member to that of the lowest plus the transport cost involved in indirect importing, which is wasted. The usual solution is rules of origin, the apparently reasonable requirement that goods qualifying for tariff-free trade should be produced in a member country rather than just pass through member countries. In practice, rules of origin often become instruments of protection.

Rules of origin can lead to trade diversion when exportables between FTA members are not wholly produced within a partner country but rely partly on inputs imported from nonmember countries. Under rules of origin, exports have to derive a certain proportion of their value from local content or undergo certain production processes within the FTA to obtain duty-free treatment. Trade diversion will result if the rules of origin create an incentive for producers in one partner to purchase higher-cost inputs from another even though cheaper inputs can be had from the rest of the world. Rules of origin can also artificially increase domestic sales if the favored input is domestically produced.

Although trade between Canada, Mexico, and the United States had a high regional content even before the three countries formed NAFTA (Cordoba 1996), NAFTA's rules of origin have serious protective effects in certain sectors, shifting their trade and investment patterns from lower-cost to higher-cost sources. Most clothing produced in Mexico gains tariff-free access to the North American market only if its inputs are virtually 100 percent sourced in North America (WTO 1995). In the automobile industry the origin requirement of 62.5 percent local content has induced Japanese automobile manufacturers with plants in Canada to invest to produce components in the United States rather than import cheaper components from Japan. The rules of origin also require the tubes in color televisions to be of North American origin if the televisions are to receive duty-free treatment. Since the inception of NAFTA in

1994, five television tube factories have been planned or established in North America by Japanese or Korean firms, probably at the expense of expansion in Southeast Asia (Stephenson 1996). Even tomato catsup is affected (box 3.1).

Rules of origin effectively allow protection to be "exported" from one member to another even if each country maintains its preintegration structure of external tariffs. The more restrictive the rules of origin, the greater the scope for trade diversion on intermediate products. At some point, however, the rules become so restrictive that producers opt to source inputs from outside the free trade area and forgo duty-free access.

Rules of origin also pose governance problems for developing countries. They take considerable effort to negotiate and are opaque and complex to operate.[6] The EU's agreement with Poland has 81 pages of small print in its rules-of-origin section, and NAFTA has about 200 (Krueger 1997). FTAs require controls on products crossing internal frontiers to ensure compliance with rules of origin and the payment of customs duties for noncomplying imports, and this can pose significant administrative costs. Herin (1986) estimated these costs at 3 to 5 percent of f.o.b. (free on board) prices for EFTA-EC trade. Documentation and verification—and their costs—must be a continuing part of FTA arrangements in order for importing countries to avoid tariff revenue losses and keep the protection system effective. Finally, rules of origin allow customs authorities—and individual customs officers—a good deal of discretion. The administrative cost of ensuring that this discretion is not abused is considerable, and the cost of failing to do so is even higher.

Box 3.1 Rules of Origin Are Protectionist

To Chile's dismay, the rules for tomato catsup changed when the Canada–United States Free Trade Agreement (CUSFTA) evolved into NAFTA. Under CUSFTA, catsup processed from imported tomato paste qualified for duty-free treatment in internal trade, but under NAFTA rules the tomato paste itself must be produced within a NAFTA member in order for the catsup to qualify for free entry. In 1992 Chile was the leading foreign supplier of tomato paste to the United States, and the catsup produced from the tomato paste enjoyed free entry under CUSFTA. Mexico and Chile together accounted for over 80 percent of U.S. tomato paste imports, in roughly equal quantities. Under NAFTA, catsup made out of Chilean paste can no longer circulate duty-free, and Chile's share dropped to 5 percent, while Mexico's share rose to 75 percent.

Source: Palmeter (1993).

Indirect Trade Deflection: Exporting Protection

Rules of origin may prevent the FTA member with the lowest tariff rate from importing goods and sending them on duty free to another. But they do not prevent a low-tariff partner from meeting its own requirements for a product from the rest of the world and then transferring a corresponding amount (or all) of its own production to its partners. This is termed indirect trade deflection, and its consequences for efficiency depend on the capacity of the low-tariff country to supply all its partner's needs. If it can meet the partner's entire import requirements at its own tariff-inclusive price out of its own production, it will render the partner's high tariffs ineffective and at the same time earn additional rents. In the limiting case that every good fell into this class, indirect trade deflection would render a free trade area equivalent to a customs union that takes the lowest preunion tariff as the basis for the CET (Robson 1998).

If, however, the low-tariff country cannot meet the full import needs of its partner, the latter continues to import its marginal requirements from the rest of the world, and the domestic price remains anchored to the world market price plus its unchanged tariff. Then, although the exporter enjoys additional rents—the high-tariff country's forgone duties—there would be no beneficial effects on resource allocation in the high-tariff partner, and real resources would be wasted as trade was diverted from third-country to partner suppliers.

Unfortunately, there has been no empirical investigation of indirect trade deflection within RIAs, but it has been observed working across trade blocs. Trade deflection through the EU and thence into the United States has modified, or even nullified, the effect of increased U.S. nontariff barriers for textiles and clothing (Hamilton 1988).

Customs Unions Offer Lower Trading Costs and Greater Integration

Customs unions have common external tariffs and so do not formally need rules of origin. Provided that they also define and enforce any nontariff protection measures at the bloc level, they can, at one stroke, avoid all the administrative costs and distortions associated with rules of origin. Harmonizing nontariff barriers, however, is a demanding requirement; for example, throughout its first 30 years the EU allowed members to maintain their own quotas on certain third-country imports such as clothing, footwear, and steel and to use border measures to prevent those goods from crossing internal borders (Winters 1993). The EU-Turkey customs union allows the parties to impose antidumping duties on each other, which automatically requires the presence of border formalities and rules of origin to define partner goods. Similarly, if, say, industrial or safety standards differ between members, border controls or their equivalent will be necessary for enforcing them.

In effect, a customs union needs to have not only a common external tariff but also a trade policy that is common in all respects. Customs unions are thus a good deal more complex to create than FTAs. Although they offer greater market integration and lower costs, they also require more ongoing coordination. Adopting a CET means reconciling the interests of member states and then establishing continuing political arrangements to deal with subsequent adjustments—for example, modifications stemming from global trade talks, or the imposition of temporary safeguards, antidumping duties, or antisubsidy duties. Those arrangements may imply substantial loss of sovereignty over trade policy instruments and revenue sources. FTAs also need an initial reconciliation of interests, effected through the character and restrictiveness of the rules of origin that are adopted, but once these are settled, only relatively light institutional arrangements are needed.

EXTERNAL TRADE POLICY

The net benefits of RIA membership depend directly on the external trade policy stance. There are strong arguments for pursuing a policy of external openness in conjunction with regional integration.

To begin with, trade diversion is more likely, and more costly should it occur, the higher are external trade barriers. It is more likely because the relative price differences created by preferential liberalization will be greater with a higher external tariff, inducing trade diversion in more sectors. And it is more costly, since a higher external tariff will provide greater incentives for inefficient sectors to expand. Producers are able to charge high prices (because the tariff protects them from world competition) and capture what was previously tariff revenue on trade between members. Fundamentally, and just as for individual countries, the gains from competition with low-cost suppliers—gains to consumers, gains from developing an efficient industrial structure, and competition-induced efficiency gains at the firm level—may be forgone if tariffs inhibit such competition. These are arguments both for low tariffs, on average, and for tariff schedules that are relatively uniform, avoiding peaks. Very high rates in particular sectors are almost certain to produce diversion, as in EU agriculture.

A common complaint about such advice is that forming or deepening an RIA causes adjustment costs and that simultaneous external liberalization magnifies these costs to an unacceptable level. The problem with this argument is that adjustment costs are only worth paying at all if the adjustment is in the right direction. High tariffs or tariff peaks might induce costly economic changes that move the country away from economic efficiency. Besides, simulation studies of regional integration involving developing countries and large high-income nations or blocs (such as the EU) suggest that the adjustment costs associated with RIA implementation are as high as those that would arise if trade liberalization were implemented on a nondiscriminatory basis (Rutherford, Rutstrom, and Tarr 2000).

These are compelling arguments for a genuinely liberal external policy to accompany RIAs—but "should" does not always determine policy. An important question is whether RIAs change the balance of incentives and forces for external liberalism. If so, one could start to answer the question of whether regionalism is a stepping stone to multilateralism or a millstone around its neck. In part, the answer is determined by the interactions between the RIA and outside countries (as discussed in chapter 8), but it also depends on the RIA's internal incentives and constraints on trade policy.

As so often, there is no simple empirical regularity that would allow us to resolve these questions. In 1994—15 years later than originally intended—the Andean Pact finally set a common external tariff (which neither Bolivia nor Peru accepted). An average CET of 12.8 percent replaced average tariffs of 11.1 percent in Colombia, 10.2 percent in Ecuador, and 11.8 percent in Venezuela (Echavarria 1998). Under NAFTA, Canada reduced tariffs on around 1,500 items imported from nonmember countries, while Mexico raised tariffs on 503. Since the founding of the EEC in 1957, the average common external tariff on manufactures has fallen from about 13 percent to about 3 percent in 2001 (following the Uruguay Round). Clearly, it is necessary to consider the parts of the argument separately and in more detail.

Setting External Tariffs in an FTA: A Race to the Bottom?

FTA members decide their own tariff policies while keeping intrabloc tariffs at zero. The interactions between members may reduce external tariffs for three reasons. First, if tariffs on fellow members are constrained to zero, the optimal level on closely competitive goods from third countries will be relatively low, to reduce trade diversion. Second, if there is trade deflection, high-tariff countries lose tariff revenue. If they reduce their tariffs to just below the level of their partners, they can recapture the revenue without affecting internal prices or resource allocation. A series of such moves in a competition between members will tend to lower external tariffs (Richardson 1995). Third, if duties on inputs used to produce exports to other members cannot be rebated, high-import tariffs render exporters of final goods uncompetitive. This concern apparently lay behind Canada's decision to reduce 1,500 tariffs on inputs in 1995, shortly after the establishment of NAFTA.

There are, however, three counteracting forces that can increase protection. First, rules of origin essentially export protection, allowing producers in one country to benefit from protection in another. Second, the result of fierce FTA competition in the intra-FTA segment of their business might lead firms to seek protection against third-country imports in another segment. This requires the firm to provide different goods or different varieties in the two segments, but that is not unusual. And it might be reinforced by the third force for protection: as tariffs on partners are fixed rigidly at zero, resources for lobbying against third-country imports become more plentiful. The balance between these pro- and anti-protection forces will vary from case to case, but there is at least something in the view that an FTA could encourage liberalism.

Trade Policy Institutions in Customs Unions Can Increase Protection

The situation in customs unions is quite different. Creating a customs union provides an (unavoidable) opportunity to review tariff structures and create new institutions for determining trade policy. National tariffs must be harmonized at some agreed level, and in the process international obligations—notably those toward the WTO—must be respected. As explained in chapter 8, WTO rules are not a particularly good guide to economic policy, and customs unions are best served by using the domestic advantages of a liberal unilateral trade policy as their guidebook. Tariffs should be low, and the number of rates very few. Nonuniformity across products tends to increase administrative costs and encourage discretion and corruption, so if the CET is more uniform than the rates it replaces, there will be an additional benefit to RIA members.

Unfortunately, the forces created by a customs union do not lead in particularly liberal directions, although care in establishing the union and its institutions can help. By coordinating their trade policies, members of a customs union may be able to increase their negotiating power against the rest of the world. If they are able to negotiate effectively as a bloc (which does not always happen), this will change the nature of world trade talks, probably in the direction of greater protection (see chapter 8).

In the most hegemonic of customs unions, SACU, South Africa simply decided trade policy and compensated the smaller countries for the costs it imposed on them. Similarly, Brazil dominated the determination of MERCOSUR's external tariff (Olarreaga and Soloaga 1998). Large countries are generally less dependent on international trade and more prone to protection than smaller ones.

Even in more evenly balanced customs unions such as the EU, it may pay to allow one member disproportionate power over certain negotiations. If tariffs in the customs union and the rest of the world are strategic substitutes (that is, if as one bloc increases its tariff, the optimal response of the other is to lower its own), letting the more aggressive member "lead" negotiations with the rest of the world on an issue will result in higher customs union tariffs and lower tariffs abroad than if the union negotiated collectively. In this outcome, the lower tariff in the rest of the world increases welfare in the customs union, possibly by enough to offset the costs of the union's own tariff. If, however, tariffs are strategic complements, the customs union would gain by letting its less aggressive member lead, resulting in lower tariffs and higher welfare all round (Gatsios and Karp 1991, 1995). Unfortunately, there are no general rules for determining which tariffs are complements or substitutes (even in simple models), so it is not clear whether delegation within the customs union would lead to higher or lower external tariffs.

Moreover, once one recognizes that tariff setting is a continuing process (a repeated game, in economic jargon), the situation becomes even more complex. A more aggressive leader will be able to extract a more favorable deal because its threats to retaliate (with the whole of the customs union's resources) will be more credible. Whether this leads to lower protection overall depends on whether a more aggressive customs union can achieve a more liberal outcome by virtue of its readiness to retaliate or whether it actually has to use its retaliatory muscle. The smaller the union, the less likely it is to achieve a liberal outcome overall.

By convention, the EU allows countries disproportionate influence, up to and including veto power, over policy in areas in which they claim vital interests. Given that a country's interest in a sector is commonly related to that sector's share in its GDP, it is easy to imagine this feature enhancing the interests of producers. The effect on a customs union's trade policy depends in part on whether a sector's having a high share of a member's GDP reflects comparative advantage or past policy distortions. If the former, one might expect relatively liberal stances; if the latter, protection will be strongly defended.[7] One encouraging aspect of this situation is that because any trade creation will tend to relocate production in a sector toward relatively more efficient members, over time this could reduce protectionist pressure.

Even with genuinely intergovernmental decisionmaking in a customs union, several features can lead to protectionist biases in the process of aggregating individual members' preferences into a common policy. Policy will generally be made by bureaucrats and ministers representing their own governments, and this can create a protectionist bias. The incentives for bureaucrats, who can reap no direct reward from the profits they create, tend toward the protectionist (Messerlin 1983), and adding layers of intergovernmental decisionmaking tends to swing influence away from voters and toward official preferences for administrative convenience and a quiet life (Scharpf 1988). If there is no single political location at which the costs and benefits of protection come together—such as the presidency in the United States—the costs, which are usually spread thinly and widely, will tend to be dominated by the more concentrated and obvious benefits, and a bias toward producers and protection will be introduced. If policies are enshrined in the customs union's constitution, as in the EU's Treaty of Rome, which defines the need for and objectives of the Common Agricultural Policy, or if they acquire their own bureaucracies—again, as in the case of EU agricultural policy—interventions are legitimized and defended from within, and reform can become very difficult (Winters 1997b).

Problems can also arise if the costs of policies are allocated across countries in proportions different from their benefits. If a government wishes to minimize the danger of its nationals having to bear the costs of protection (consumer costs and higher factor prices) with no payoff for its own producers, and if it believes that it may not be able to defeat the calls for protection, it will tend to join protectionist coalitions and seek protection for its own industries. The solution is to ensure that some institution at the level of the customs union (a hegemony or a central body) takes responsibility for all the costs and benefits of the whole package (see box 3.2).

Institutional responsibility for policies must be clear. In the EU the struggle between the European Commission, representing the center, and the national capitals for control of nontariff barriers to imports arguably resulted in more active use of those instruments than the parties might

---

Box 3.2 Restaurant Bills, Universalism, and Protection

Institutions for making decisions about protection can impart a protectionist bias to the outcome. Two simple but instructive models of institutional failure are the restaurant bill problem and universalism.

The restaurant bill problem

Four acquaintances go to a restaurant and decide, before ordering, to split the bill four ways. Is it surprising that the bill is higher than when each pays for his own meal?

Similarly, suppose a country's benefits from a policy regarding a product are proportional to its share of the customs union's output of that product, while its costs are proportional to its share of GDP. A production subsidy financed from general taxation will have this characteristic, as will, approximately, a tariff, which benefits producers at the expense of consumers. If each country has a veto, or if consensus is valued highly, countries sitting down to settle on a package of price-increasing policies on several products will press for inclusion of any good for which their share of production exceeds their share of GDP. As each country is likely to have several products for which this is true, the easiest package to build—and to sell at home to local pressure groups—will increase the prices of nearly all products even if, overall, each country would have preferred "no change" to the outcome actually agreed on.

Universalism

Imagine that protection for steel is being discussed and that each of three member states in a customs union produces one type of steel. If any one type is protected, the government of the country in which it is produced receives all the "benefits" (profits, employment, political convenience, and so on), but each member bears some of the costs—which exceed total benefits, since protection is inefficient. Net costs are zero if the measure is rejected (Shepsle and Weingast 1981).

The difficulty facing a government in deciding how to vote is expressed in the position, "We oppose this measure in principle, but if it passes, we want our share of the spoils." The worst outcome is that protection passes but the country's producers are on the outside. Thus, if governments fear that they might not be able to stop a protectionist measure, they will vote for it, but on the condition that it cover their own producers.

Simple arithmetic (Winters 1994) shows that this situation is quite likely to arise in small groups of decisionmakers, and experience confirms this insight. Universalism drove the introduction of the U.S. Smoot-Hawley tariff of 1929, with individual congressmen acquiescing to protection for their fellows' "pet" industries in return for reciprocal treatment for their own (Schattschneider 1935). In the EU, the United Kingdom opposed the inadequate McSharry agricultural reforms in 1992 but, instead of being adamant, used most of its influence to ensure that large farms (of which it has relatively many) were not excluded from income support mechanisms (as McSharry had originally proposed). In 1995 the EU Council of Ministers passed 92 of its 94 common trade policy decisions unanimously. Given that trade policy typically redistributes real income from one member to another, this suggests that something like universalism was going on (Bilal 1998).

---

otherwise have wished. The commission had to prove that it could use nontariff barriers to meet national objectives in order to win control of them; although its measures were possibly less restrictive than national ones would have been, they applied to all members rather than just one (Winters 1993).

Lobbies Bias RIAs toward Trade Diversion

Lobbying is a fact of life for trade policymakers, and creating an RIA gives interest groups new threats to manage and new opportunities to influence policy. When industrial associations were asked for their views on the FTAA, the Florida Citrus Mutual said that the proposed RIA would "mean the end of the U.S. industry" and that "citrus products must be exempted from further tariff cuts." The Rubber and Plastic Footwear Manufacturers Association asserted that eliminating duties would "cause havoc" and spell the death of that industry. Exempting footwear "would have virtually no impact on any country's balance of trade figures and would in no sense violate the [WTO requirement that the FTAA cover] substantially all trade."[8] When NAFTA was signed, some U.S. industries were granted 15 years to adjust to free trade; they included industries such as citrus that already had the highest protection. In addition, new and more protective rules of origin were formulated for textiles and clothing and for autos.

In 1998 UEMOA debated the details of its CET within a previously agreed tariff structure of 5 percent on intermediate goods, 10 percent on capital goods, and 20 percent on consumer goods. Aside from the addition of some temporary surcharges, one of the notable features of this debate was the conclusion that cement was a consumer good worthy of 20 percent protection. In 1997 private sector protests led Madagascar to postpone tariff cuts promised under the IOC (Lecomte 1998: 5). The Andean Pact allows members to charge tariffs below the agreed CET level—provided that there is no local producer of the good concerned (Echavarria 1998).

One does not need much experience of the world to recognize the fingerprints of lobbyists on these stories, and in fact, lobbying is a particular problem when forming an RIA. Not only does it lead to resistance to internal free trade and liberal external policies, but it does so in ways that make trade diversion more likely.

Governments respond to pressures from domestic interest groups to increase popular support and their chances of reelection. Lobbying for a sector or an interest provides a "public good" in the economist's sense that the policies sought apply to all group members regardless of how much they contribute to the lobbying effort. The larger the group of beneficiaries, the more difficult it is to prevent people from free-riding (benefiting without contributing), and the smaller the benefit that any individual receives, the less likely he is to take the trouble to enter the debate. For these reasons, consumers find it very hard to organize a lobby, and lobbying is dominated by producers, who typically organize along sectoral lines. This effectively gives profits a double weight in the government's calculations: once as a source of income in the traditional assessment of national economic welfare and again as a source of lobbying support, which governments value in its own right. The heavy private sector involvement in current regional plans—APEC and the FTAA—shows how seriously firms take the opportunity to influence this element of the business environment. RIAs are undoubtedly better for being business friendly, but lobbying can bias an RIA too far toward producer objectives.

Trade creation can be a mixed blessing for a negotiating government: it generates surpluses for consumers at home and for exporters in the partner country but reduces them for one of the main lobbying groups—domestic import-competing producers. Trade diversion generates no such reduction in profits, and although it yields fewer consumer gains, that may matter less to governments concerned about reelection or about keeping the support of business elites. If two governments can exchange trade-diverting concessions, trade diversion becomes attractive politics even if it is bad economics.

This bias toward trade diversion has two major implications. First, regionalism may be attractive where multilateral liberalization is not. Farmers and policymakers in the EU accept internal free trade as managed through the Common Agricultural Policy but are not ardent supporters of global trade talks on agriculture. Brazil is keen to see MERCOSUR have internal free trade in information technology products, but it was the main holdout on the (nearly) global Information Technology Agreement of 1996. Second, exceptions or delays in achieving free trade tend to be concentrated in sectors with strong trade creation potential—the very sectors that promise economic gains (Viner 1950; Grossman and Helpman 1995). If the creation of RIAs is driven primarily by the industrial attractions of trade diversion, regional liberalization cannot continue all the way to global free trade because the last step in that direction would necessarily generate only trade creation.

These dangers are elegantly demonstrated by Krishna (1998) for a simple three-country world in which policy is determined solely by its effects on profits. He shows that, taking just two of the countries, the more trade diverting is an FTA between them, the stronger its backing and hence the more likely it is to come about. He then shows that following the formation of such a two-country RIA, the backing for further (multilateral) liberalization with the third country is reduced. An implication of this outcome is that a multilateral liberalization which was feasible before the FTA might cease to be feasible afterward. Very simply, an exporter might find any liberalization of foreign markets worth lobbying for, but having once achieved a regional liberalization, he might find that the (possibly negative) incremental returns to lobbying for global liberalization did not warrant the effort. Thus, if the world should attempt to achieve multilateral free trade via regionalism, progress would stop at the intermediate stage: regional stepping stones would leave us stranded in midstream.[9]

Another factor favoring lobbying for an RIA rather than for MFN free trade is uncertainty. A country's exporters can be confident that they will benefit from an RIA partner's tariff concessions if the latter are restricted to RIA members, even if they are inefficient. If the market is opened to all comers, these exporters can be much less confident that they will be the beneficiaries. Hence, although global negotiations will open more markets than regional negotiations, for any given market exporters are likely to lobby harder for regional than for MFN liberalization.

It is sometimes argued that multinational companies are a bulwark against protectionism because they operate on both sides of tariff borders. Multinationals do frequently seek lower barriers to their imported inputs, and this can effectively discipline local pressures for protection. But multinationals also frequently show strong protectionist instincts. In the early 1990s, when the Europe Agreements were under negotiation, West European motor vehicle producers penetrated Eastern European markets in a fairly noncompetitive way, with one firm setting up in each market. Their entry encouraged (and was allegedly conditional on) fierce import restrictions. Similarly, as Brazil raised barriers to nonregional production, world auto producers expanded their capacity there. Box 3.3 provides further evidence of the role of pressure groups in defining MERCOSUR's CET and in obtaining exceptions both to it and to internal free trade.

RIAs Open a New Environment for Lobbying

Besides providing an opportunity to influence the new tariff structure itself, the creation of an RIA also alters the environment in which pressure groups seek changes in trade policy. Unfortunately, we do not have much of an idea about the direction in which this factor will push.

Some scholars argue that lobbying pressure is diluted by customs unions. It costs more to lobby for a 1 percent increase in one's own tariff in a customs union than in a single country because there is more opposition to overcome (de Melo, Panagariya, and Rodrik 1993; Panagariya and Findlay 1996) or a larger number of representatives to influence

Box 3.3 Pressure Groups and MERCOSUR

A highly nonuniform common external tariff (CET), with its numerous exceptions, makes MERCOSUR an ideal case study of the role of pressure groups in RIAs (Olarreaga and Soloaga 1998). Negotiation of the CET culminated in the Ouro Preto Protocol of December 1994. Each member was allowed an exceptions list. As shown in the table, the initial CET applied only to about 75 percent of the universe of 9,119 tariff lines. Left out were capital goods, computer and telecommunication equipment, automobiles, and sugar. Convergence to the CET is to be achieved for most goods by 2006, but there is no agreement on convergence dates for sugar and automobiles. The Ouro Preto Protocol also established a list of deviations from intra-MERCOSUR free trade. These were scheduled to disappear by 2000.

Olarreaga and Soloaga set about to explain variations and deviations from the CET across 27 industries, using measures of political and interest group activity such as wages, industrial concentration indices, labor-capital ratios, import penetration, intraindustry trade, and trade creation. Among their findings were the following:

- Sectors where significant trade creation is likely tend to be exempted from internal free trade. Internal free trade is also resisted more successfully by sectors with high employment shares. This reflects government desire to avoid large-scale labor adjustments, as well as the voting strength and trade union presence of large sectors. High third-country import penetration, which puts competitive pressure on domestic firms, also leads to high protection.
- Political considerations explain 58 percent of the variation in the CET across industries. The negotiated CET in any sector is correlated with the share of capital remuneration in value added in that sector and with the share of sector-specific capital in total inputs. If labor is fairly mobile and new firm entry is difficult, existing capital receives most of the benefits of protection. The researchers also found a positive correlation with industry concentration: more concentrated industries find it easier to organize lobbying efforts and are thus more effective lobbyists.
- The CET in a given sector mainly reflects the preferences of the member country that has the greatest production in that sector. Thus, Brazil's preferences are the main determinants of the structure of the CET, as that country represents at least 70 percent of MERCOSUR production in each of the 27 sectors considered.

Deviation from the CET and from Internal Free Trade among MERCOSUR Members

	Deviation from the CET		Deviation from internal free trade	
	Number of tariff lines	Share of total tariff lines (percent)	Number of tariff lines	Share of total tariff lines (percent)
Argentina	1,540	17	231	2.5
Brazil	1,605	18	17	0.2
Paraguay	2,101	23	293	3.2
Uruguay	1,961	22	407	4.4

Note: Several other deviations from the CET are not shown here; they include preexisting special promotion regimes and the tax-free areas of Manaus, in Brazil, and Tierra del Fuego.

(Richardson 1994). Given the lower individual returns and the greater difficulty of controlling free-riding in a larger, more diverse group, the sum of member lobbying activity falls as a result of integration. The lobby from, say, Senegal does not wish to devote resources to lobbying for protection for producers in Togo. Such spillovers will probably reduce average protection, even if some members succeed in gaining higher tariffs on some goods than they would individually.

All these analyses presuppose, however, that fragmented lobbies face a unified customs union government, whereas the reality might be exactly the opposite. The RIA's governments might be fragmented, while some lobbies' power may be enhanced by integration (Winters 1993; Bandyopadhyay and Wall 1999). For example, each member might start with a lobbying game in which industry and agriculture more or less cancel each other out. But if integration enables agriculture lobbies to cooperate (because they produce the same things) while industry lobbies compete (because they produce different things), the customs union may end up with agricultural protection. Overall, therefore, although dilution effects will undoubtedly be present, they will not always predominate.

An RIA that generates trade creation can create a liberalizing momentum, and this will reinforce dilution effects. Industries that shrink because of lost protection eventually lose lobbying power. By squeezing relatively inefficient sectors and promoting more efficient ones, regionalism might ease future liberalization. Hathaway (1998) attributes the decline in U.S. footwear protection since the 1970s to the sector's declining ability to lobby effectively as it contracted from 216,000 employees in 1960 to 58,000 in 1990. The industry association found it ever harder to obtain import restrictions and instead started to focus on helping firms adopt new technologies. In 1990 its president decided to "stop spending one more penny or one more minute . . . on import restrictions," and the association began admitting importers into its ranks. In 1991 it decided not to oppose tariff cuts on footwear under the U.S. Caribbean Basin Initiative. Its reaction to the FTAA, however (cited above), suggests that seeking special protection is a hard habit to kick.

Furthermore, an RIA may well concentrate lobbying activity against outside countries. Once an RIA has been firmly agreed, there is no point in lobbying for protection against partner suppliers. This may well turn attention to third-country suppliers, and it also means that lobbying resources will be released to make lobbying against those suppliers cheaper than before. The result is likely to be greater pressure on external tariffs (Panagariya and Findlay 1996).

It is certainly the case that lobbying activity has increased hugely in Europe since the advent of the EU and that it has become much more intensely focused on Brussels. The number of lobbying organizations in Brussels grew from 300 in 1970 to about 3,000 in 1990 (Anderson and Eliassen 1993). Expenditure on lobbying was approximately $150 million in 1990 and was rising rapidly. By 1998, there were 13,000 professional lobbyists in Brussels, approaching one for every European Commission staff member (*The Economist,* August 14, 1998). Magee and Lee (1997) offer one of the few formal attempts to quantify their effects, by analyzing external protection in France and Italy as the EC widened and deepened between 1968 and 1983. The main effect was the supposedly exogenous liberalization trend throughout the OECD countries, which broadly halved average tariffs, from 15 to 7.5 percent. In addition, however, Magee and Lee identified a 1.7 percentage point increase in the average due to greater pressure from industries suffering from trade creation and where mergers had increased concentration. This rise was partly offset by a 1.1 percentage point decrease attributable to the dilution of lobbying efforts as the political arena enlarged from the national to the EU scale and as some industries grew rapidly as a result of increased market size and efficiency gains.

It is not possible to say a priori whether, once it is formed, a customs union will be more or less vulnerable to lobbying. Much will depend on the institutions it adopts.

RIAs and Protection: Summing Up

Unfortunately there is too little empirical evidence to balance the arguments on RIAs and protection accurately; whether RIAs will increase or decrease protection remains an empirical matter. Foroutan (1998) suggests that RIAs have not increased their protection levels recently, but the evidence is not particularly strong. (These results are discussed in box 8.3 in chapter 8, when we examine external pressures on RIA trade restrictions.) Whatever the net effect, there are likely to be benefits from establishing good trade policy institutions at the customs union level.

Members should avoid excessively bureaucratic decisionmaking methods, ensure that a single institution takes responsibility for the whole package of measures, and refrain from writing protectionist policies into an RIA's basic documents. Even where members opt for an explicitly intergovernmental approach and eschew a central authority for the customs union, they should establish a central body that is responsible for analyzing the collective interest in trade policy and widely disseminating the results. This body should be so composed and constituted that it will avoid equating benefits solely with production or identifying high intrabloc trade shares with the collective interest.

INTEGRATION AND TAXES

Many developing countries are heavily dependent on trade taxes as a source of revenue; some African countries raise as much as half of government revenues this way.[10] Membership in an RIA erodes these revenues—directly, as tariffs on intra-RIA trade are reduced, and indirectly, when trade diversion occurs, as importers switch away from external imports subject to tariffs. Revenue loss can also arise if a customs union sets tariffs below a country's pre-RIA levels. As we saw above, the loss of government revenue lies at the heart of the trade diversion argument: a consequence of trade diversion is that revenue is transferred to partner producers, causing a direct loss to the given country. If the government has difficulty in mobilizing alternative revenue sources and is already spending its revenue efficiently, then even losses that are transferred to domestic consumers (as when tariffs on nonmembers fall), could be costly. Formation of an RIA may therefore need to be accompanied by steps to improve the take from domestic excise, sales, or value-added taxes (VATs).[11]

How much revenue has typically been lost as a result of RIA formation? In practice, countries that are less dependent on trade taxes often end up losing larger amounts of revenue. This paradox arises because intra-RIA trade volumes are typically high in RIAs in which dependency on trade taxes has been quite low, such as the EU, while countries with higher trade tax dependency have tended to form RIAs with countries with which they have relatively little trade.

There are, however, exceptions to this. Cambodia derived 56 percent of its total tax revenues from customs duties prior to its entry into AFTA (the ASEAN Free Trade Area), with two-thirds of these duties levied on imports from ASEAN countries (Fukase and Martin 2000). Entry into ASEAN provided a powerful stimulus for the introduction of a VAT in early 1999. Turning to Africa, it is estimated that when UEMOA is fully operational, it will roughly halve Senegal's tariff take, from CFA 100 billion to between CFA 39 billion and CFA 63 billion. Of this, the bulk is attributable to reductions in external protection, with intrabloc trade preferences accounting for no more than CFA 5 billion.[12] In the SADC, some of whose countries are heavily dependent on trade with South Africa, substantial amounts of revenue are involved. Table 3.2 provides estimates of the revenue cost of moving to free internal trade, which would approximately halve customs revenue in Zambia and Zimbabwe, costing the governments 5.6 and 9.8 percent in government revenue, respectively. These are substantial revenue losses and point to the need to

Table 3.2 Revenue Implications of a Free Trade Area: Customs Duties before and after Formation of the Southern African Development Community (SADC)
(percent)

Member Country	Customs Duty as Share of Total Tax Revenue	Estimated change	
		In Customs Duty	In Total Tax Revenue
Malawi	14.3	−36.7	−5.3
Mauritius	29.8	−18.2	−5.4
South Africa	3.6	4.9	0.2
Tanzania	24.0	−8.3	−2.0
Zambia	12.3	−45.3	−5.6
Zimbabwe	18.4	−53.3	−9.8

Note: There are discrepancies between the customs duty revenues reported by customs departments and those reported in budget numbers. For example, Malawi reported duty revenues for fiscal 1996 of 1,505.2 million and 2,028.7 million kwacha, but its customs department reported 615 million kwacha. For consistency, we have used the numbers reported by customs. The projections assume that each country's average tariff rates against SADC members are zero.
Source: IMF staff calculations.

ensure that alternative tax systems are in place before eliminating sources of trade tax revenue.

It is important to inquire what form revenue replacement takes, not only because inefficient taxation reduces economic welfare but also because the net benefits of signing an RIA can depend critically on how distortionary taxes are. Under Chile's FTA with MERCOSUR, it is predicted that VAT rates will need to be increased by half—from an average of 7.9 percent to around 12 percent—to maintain revenue neutrality (Harrison, Rutherford, and Tarr 1997). But in fact, Chile's VAT is fairly distortionary. If Chile were to improve collection and eliminate ad hoc exemptions to create a fully uniform VAT, it could halve the nominal average rate and increase real incomes by 0.3 percent while at the same time making tariff revenue replacement cheaper and trade reform more attractive. Rather different results apply to the Egypt-EU FTA (Konan and Maskus 2000). If lost revenue is replaced by current discriminatory taxation on capital, Egypt gains about 0.3 percent of GDP under the FTA. Cleaning up the tax system, however, would yield total gains of 1.4 percent, and the marginal effect of the FTA is then to reduce welfare by 0.2 percent. So, an FTA may be better than current policy, but once the gains from tax reform are reaped, it is actually harmful.

For poor economies, import tariffs represent one of the cheapest and easiest ways of collecting government revenue, especially if the country has only a few well-defined outlets for international trade. The observation above that in most cases RIAs between such countries pose few threats to revenue raises another intriguing possibility: perhaps small countries can obtain a given tariff revenue at lower economic cost by combining in an RIA than by acting independently. The tradeoff is straightforward to describe (if not to quantify). An RIA between small countries may offer benefits in terms of larger markets and more competition than nondistortionary tariff policy but at the same time will require higher taxes on imports from third countries.[13] If the former gains outweigh the latter losses (plus, of course, the trade diversion to which small-country RIAs are condemned), the FTA will help revenue-constrained countries.

There are several caveats to this argument, however. First, if an RIA is better than nondistortionary tariff policy and yet still entails an increase in tariffs against the rest of the world, there are clearly significant gains to be had by developing other sources of revenue, and this course should receive high priority. Second, revenue tariffs, whether discriminatory or not, should have different patterns from protective tariffs. If varied across commodities, they will be high on those with inelastic demand for imports and will have no correlation with whether there is local production. Probably better from a practical perspective would be a single tariff rate that is uniform across commodities. Uniform tariffs eliminate distortions between different imports, significantly reduce administrative costs (which were, after all, the reason for using tariffs to raise revenue in the first place), and substantially reduce the scope for lobbying or corruption. Third, when there is no domestic production, a tariff is equivalent to an excise tax (which is levied on all sources of a good, including domestic sources). Then it is better to call the measure an excise tax to make clear that should domestic production grow up behind the tariff wall, it will be taxed at the same rate as imports. This will prevent the emergence of inefficient domestic activity in response to the side-effect protection associated with a revenue tariff. Fourth, as we have argued extensively, even without revenue considerations there is no presumption that an RIA between small countries will improve economic welfare; indeed, the balance of the argument is to the contrary.

Fiscal Compensation

A problem for many trade blocs among developing countries is that some members account for disproportionate shares of the bloc's import-competing production and hence of the tariff-free trade within the bloc. This problem was evident in the CACM, where El Salvador and

Guatemala accounted for the bulk of industrial production; the CEAO (where Côte d'Ivoire is in this position); the East African Community (Kenya); and SACU (South Africa). The other members, whose losses of tariff revenues were translated into higher prices for industrial imports from the more industrialized countries (that is, who suffered trade diversion), felt that they needed compensation.

These concerns are magnified if trade policies, not just trade, are unbalanced. An extreme example is the Lebanon-EU FTA, currently under negotiation. In 1995 Lebanon's imports from the EU were 3,547 billion Lebanese pounds, with an average tariff rate of about 15 percent, and its exports were 143 billion pounds, with an average tariff of perhaps 4 percent.[14] Potential revenue losses from the FTA are about 532 billion pounds, or approximately one-sixth of government revenue, but the gains on exports come to only about 5 billion pounds. Arguments for similar discrepancies have been made for Mexico in NAFTA (Bhagwati and Panagariya 1996) and for the South Africa-EU agreement (Teljeur 1998).

In some RIAs, such as NAFTA, compensation is explicitly ruled out in the negotiation process. Where it is not, the only practical way to estimate the warranted compensation in an existing RIA is to compare actual revenue with what would be collected if members imposed the external tariff on all their imports, including those from other members. This is essentially how the SACU agreement handles compensation for Botswana, Lesotho, Namibia, and Swaziland (the BLNS countries). But such estimates are essentially accounting exercises that make no allowance for the fact that the quantities and pretax prices of tradable goods change as a result of an RIA—as does welfare. Compensation based on forgone revenues represents a political settlement to allow for the most obvious sources of disparity in the costs and benefits of RIAs, using a transparent and analytically plausible formula. But no simple formula can provide more than a crude approximation for offsetting the disparities in costs and benefits in a broader appraisal of an RIA. Nor, in the face of economic change, can any such formulas maintain the balance of advantage initially agreed by political negotiation.

One broader argument that governments sometimes make in assessing an RIA is that protection helps maintain value added and employment in manufacturing and thus that imports from partners are economically costly even when they displace higher-cost domestic output. This was among the arguments that led to SACU's inclusion of an enhancement factor in its revenue distribution formula, which initially increased compensation about 40 percent above estimated revenue losses.[15] The plausibility of such development benefits and the role of RIAs in achieving or frustrating them are examined in the next chapter.

Two major problems beset such compensation arrangements and make it difficult to devise mutually acceptable compensation formulas. First, although the transfer benefits accrue to the private sector (which may be partly foreign owned), compensation has to be provided out of public revenues by authorities who often face practical constraints on revenue raising. Second, the costs that are compensated are direct, immediate, and obvious, while any wider benefits from integration tend to be diffuse and uncertain and accrue only in the longer term. The failure of compensation has often been accompanied by failure of the RIA itself, as happened to the East African Community and the CEAO, or by the withdrawal of members—Chad from UDEAC and Honduras from the CACM. In the light of this experience, unless prospective partners are structurally balanced, both actually and potentially, the formation of an RIA is highly risky without the simultaneous adoption of low external tariffs to minimize the transfers implied in duty-free intra-RIA trade. Low external tariffs, of course, also increase economic efficiency.

Tax Competition

Except for the very largest countries, RIAs constrain members' fiscal discretion and sovereignty. This is most obvious for customs unions, where the CET transparently removes tariffs from the policy domain of any single country. But there will also be constraints on a wider set of instruments in both customs unions and FTAs. Measures to minimize transactions costs, maximize the tax base, and avoid smuggling will all create pressures for a degree of indirect tax harmonization.

We have already seen how these factors have stimulated the formation of some RIAs as countries have sought to manage their neighbors' tax policies and halt smuggling by eliminating fiscal borders. Here we consider the opposite side of the coin, in which constraints are unwelcome side effects of RIAs signed for other reasons.

If goods flow unimpeded across an RIA's internal borders, governments may be tempted to lower indirect tax rates to capture revenue from cross-border shopping. This tax competition could lead to a widespread reduction in indirect tax rates. Such an outcome could be welcome in that it brings about a downward convergence of effective tax rates and leads to efficiency gains by reducing consumption distortions. An alternative view, however, is that disregarding such fiscal spillovers leads to a welfare loss for the RIA as a whole because tax receipts and total expenditure fall below optimal levels. This view is frequently argued by the larger continental members of the EU; box 3.4 gives an illustration of the same problem in classical times.

Tax harmonization has been a major issue within the EU over many years, generating fierce controversy and even at times threatening to derail the Single Market Programme. Recognizing that some harmonization is indispensable to the operation of a single market, members have agreed to adopt a minimum standard VAT rate of 15 percent, with no more than two reduced rates. No agreement, however, was reached on precisely which goods and services fall into which tax bracket or on the use of higher than standard rates. Efforts to harmonize excise taxes on, for example, alcohol or gasoline have formally been even less successful, although tax competition driven by demands from users or producers has induced a measure of de facto harmonization.

Fiscal discretion has long been an issue in SACU, whose smaller members have virtually no role in determining tariffs or other indirect taxes in the customs union area. But even where they formally retain the power to set rates in a closely integrated customs area, the pressures to harmonize VAT rates at or close to South African levels are so strong that the BLNS countries still have little control over their indirect tax regimes.

Outside the EU and SACU—for instance, in UEMOA and UDEAC (now CEMAC)—tax harmonization has not been successful. For developing countries, the moral is to not underestimate the political difficulties of tax harmonization—and to recognize that trying to eliminate mild differences across borders may be more trouble than it is worth. In the United States and Canada, for example, differences in state and provincial sales taxes of the order of 5 percentage points are an irritant rather than a major problem.

Box 3.4 Taxes: A Race to the Bottom

Taxes can be a battleground for countries—and for traders. In the fourth century B.C.E., Rhodes, with control of the sea-lanes and with a vibrant port, was a key commercial power in the eastern Mediterranean Sea. Rhodes charged a 2 percent tax on the value of cargo carried on all ships entering its harbor, including transit cargo. To escape the tax, Roman traders lobbied for the creation of a free port in Delos. Once that port was established, trade rapidly shifted away from Rhodes, which lost most of its harbor tax revenues. But this tax competition shortly proved costly to shippers: Rhodes had used part of its tax proceeds to police the sea-lanes and prevent piracy. Without the revenue, these activities declined, piracy increased significantly, and trade became more costly (Adams 1993: 83–84).

NOTES

1. Srinivasan (1997) attempts to calculate such external tariffs, but under very restrictive circumstances.

2. Recall that free trade agreements have internal free trade, while customs unions have both internal free trade and a common external tariff (trade policy) against nonmembers. The section "Free Trade Areas and Customs Unions" in this chapter contains a fuller discussion.

3. Note that these corner solutions are a necessary but not sufficient condition for the results to hold.

4. The benefits of access to MERCOSUR and to NAFTA markets are basically independent of each other, hence the change in the overall benefits must reflect the combination of the import effects.

5. Of course, many RIAs contain other elements as well; this classification refers only to their policies on trade in goods.

6. Agreement on the rules for clothing and autos was a major issue in NAFTA (Krueger 1997).

7. A sector with comparative advantage may prefer high protection so that it can reap high rents on sales within the customs union, but at least it could survive with lower protection. It may also seek liberalization in other import sectors to reciprocate for any liberalization that it seeks in its export markets.

8. *International Trade Reporter* 15 (31, August 5), 1998.

9. Models in which citizens vote directly on their own interests can generate a similar outcome (Levy 1997), especially if the partners are similar and relatively capital abundant compared with the rest of the world (for example, the EU).

10. Trade taxes include export and import taxes, trade monopoly profits remitted to governments, and taxes and official profits on foreign exchange transactions.

11. Not every MFN tariff cut reduces tariff collections. The initial duty may be above the revenue-maximizing rate, especially when exemptions and evasion are taken into account. Thus, revenue replacement is not always as daunting as may at first appear.

12. These estimates, from a CGE model, are made as though UEMOA had been fully operational in 1996. They vary according to whether quantities of trade are allowed to change in response to the RIA and, if so, according to what assumptions (Ng and Winters 1998).

13. Relative to the pre-RIA position, the partners import less from third countries (trade diversion) and need to make up the revenue that is forgone by raising tariffs on third countries.

14. Data are from Martin (1996); Fuleihan (1997); and Moukarbel (1997).

15. A further argument was that SACU lacks any institutional arrangements for controlling administrative interventions by South Africa that hinder the industrial development of the smaller member countries, or for adjudicating disputes relating to the operation of the customs union.

CHAPTER 4

Stimulating Investment

Investment is a key component in economic development and has become one of the main objectives of countries pursuing regional economic integration. The logic is that larger markets, more competition,
and improved policy credibility will increase the incentives for investment
and by that means raise incomes both directly, by increasing the capital intensity of production, and indirectly, by encouraging technical progress.
These arguments are relevant to investment from all sources, but they are
applied particularly often to regionalism as a means of attracting foreign
direct investment (FDI). In NAFTA, for example, stimulating FDI flows is
an explicit objective. This chapter briefly describes the policies of trade
blocs toward investment and asks whether the arguments advanced for
such policies having positive effects are justified.

The first section explores explicit investment policies. In early RIAs,
these policies were almost always activist and interventionist, coopting
regional integration into regionwide import substitution. Such policies
almost completely failed and have been superseded by a much more
market-friendly approach that places more emphasis on policies guaranteeing the fair treatment of investment. These guarantees are often embodied in bilateral investment treaties or, where there are trade and other
links, investment chapters in RIA agreements. They typically foster negative integration—that is, they preclude certain policies rather than require policies that actively encourage investment—but they may play an
important role in facilitating investment flows.

We then examine the common argument that RIAs add credibility to
government policies other than investment rules and thus help increase

investment and attract FDI. We argue that South-South RIAs are unlikely to provide much added credibility and may in fact have the opposite effect, especially if they are not accompanied by liberalization of trade with the rest of the world. North-South RIAs, by contrast, can enhance a southern country's credibility, but typically only if the RIA is likely to improve economic performance in its own right and if the large northern partner is willing to enforce investment-encouraging "club rules." The latter is more likely to be true if the policies on which a developing country wants to gain credibility are specified explicitly in the agreement.

Of course, investment does not depend only on explicit policies. An RIA will stimulate investment if it raises expected returns or lowers costs. Classic economic analysis predicts that a South-South RIA should have no impact on returns to capital but that a North-South RIA will increase the relative price of exportables in both countries, thus raising wages and decreasing the return to capital in the South and causing investment there to fall. More recent analysis holds that the rate of return on capital (and investment) could well rise in both countries regardless of capital abundance. RIAs typically reduce the transactions costs of tradables more than those of nontradables, so if tradables are more capital-intensive than nontradables, RIAs will increase the demand for capital and raise its rate of return. Lower tariffs and trading costs for capital equipment can also reduce the price of investment goods, increasing the rates of return and accumulation. Furthermore, integration may result in a more efficient financial sector, especially for a southern member of a North-South RIA, reducing lending margins and the cost of funds and increasing investment.

Unfortunately, few empirical studies of the impact of RIAs on investment are available; most trade blocs are so new that the data are simply not there. Ex ante simulations show, however, that increased investment is most likely in North-North RIAs, somewhat less likely in North-South RIAs, and least likely in South-South RIAs. Where we do have ex post evidence on investment, it tends to suggest mildly positive effects, but there seems to be no evidence that this translates into higher economic growth. Firmer evidence is available for FDI, which seems frequently to boom after an RIA is signed. We explore this and explain why it is likely that RIAs stimulate inflows of investment from nonmember countries but have ambiguous effects on intrabloc flows.

Throughout the chapter, we argue that general policy reforms such as sound macroeconomic policies, well-defined property rights, and efficient financial and banking sectors are likely to be far more important in influencing investment and FDI than merely joining an RIA. Reforms such as macroeconomic stabilization, market liberalization, and privatization should raise the returns to all factors and foster investment. Regional integration will promote investment if it significantly enhances policy credibility and increases market size, but only if it is accompanied by good policy overall.

The discussion of investment leads naturally to questions about the location of industry and economic growth. These topics are dealt with in chapter 5.

INVESTMENT POLICIES

This section traces the evolution of investment policies in RIAs since the early days and discusses current policies embodied in bilateral and multilateral agreements.

Investment Planning: A Dead End

Until about 1980, theories of economic development placed great store on the stimulation of investment and on the role of the public sector in directing it (and often financing it). The prevailing theories of import substitution called for governments to plan industrial structure carefully and to ensure that the untoward effects of competition did not disrupt the search for economies of scale. Naturally, regional economic integration was seen as a potential tool for this endeavor. Recognizing that individual national markets were too small to support large-scale industries, policymakers planned to meet regional demand through one or a few large regional projects instead of numerous smaller national ones. Thus, for example, the 1982 Preferential Trade Agreement, an RIA of eastern and southern African countries (and the predecessor of COMESA, which was created in 1993), called for member states to cooperate to promote collective self-reliance and complementary industrial development and to expand trade in industrial products.

The idea was that if countries desired a given level of industrial activity but were indifferent about its precise composition, an RIA would reduce the cost of achieving it. The RIA would allow each member to specialize in particular industries and reap the economies of scale associated with supplying the whole RIA rather than have to maintain a wider set of smaller industries to serve just their national markets (Cooper and Massell 1965; Johnson 1965). As we saw above, there is nothing wrong with the logic that larger markets allow greater efficiency, but application of the theory proved top-heavy. Planners looked to intraregional specialization to support their comprehensive regional development plans, which typically put the pursuit of scale economies above all other objectives. National industrial development plans restricted entry and were coordinated across countries to avoid duplication and the underutilization of industrial capacity. This regional "rationalization" of industry was, effectively, just infant industry protection and import substitution on a regional level.

These policies were almost universally failures. RIA members were often unable to agree on industry location.[1] In one of the most notorious examples, Côte d'Ivoire, Ghana, and Togo agreed in 1976 that they could reap economies of scale if Togo built a single cement plant to serve the region. The countries disagreed, however, on how to manage the industry, and each country ended up with its own cement plant supplying its own domestic needs (Robson 1998). Agreeing to forgo industrial sectors so that partner countries can establish them imposes tangible and immediate costs on governments in return for uncertain benefits in the future, when some other project is assigned to them in turn. Understandably, without a history of trust and experience in working together, and without any great confidence in the market mechanism, governments were reluctant to do this.

The sorry experience of managed industrialization, the evolution of economic orthodoxy toward reliance on markets, and the increasing mobility of international capital have combined to move most recent RIAs (and reincarnations of old ones) away from outright industrial planning. Instead, countries have looked at integration as a means of generating investment by making the market more attractive and by improving policy credibility. In addition, many have sought to alter the environment for FDI directly by changing the regulations governing it, either on an MFN basis or just within the bloc. In fact, many countries have signed bilateral investment treaties independent of trade agreements.

Bilateral Investment Treaties

Bilateral investment treaties (BITs) have become an important part of the regulation of worldwide investment flows.[2] There are now well over 2 thousand BITs linking countries on all continents and at all levels of development. They are important in their own right and as models for and precursors to regional investment treaties, most of which are part of broader RIAs. BITs are generally short agreements that provide "shallow" or "negative" integration for investment—that is, they seek to remove barriers and alleviate uncertainty affecting investment rather than stipulate positive actions to encourage it.[3] They are almost always reciprocal and typically contain sections dealing with their scope of application (definitions of investment, nationality, and so on), the admission of investment, general standards for the treatment of investment once it has arrived, and dispute settlement. Most also contain a number of specific provisions.

Most BITs explicitly defer to domestic law on the admission of investment; governments retain almost complete discretion to manage the sectors in which FDI occurs and the shares of ownership that foreigners may hold. The United States has generally been more progressive, insisting, in most of its BITs, on national treatment on the admission of investment (no less favorable treatment for U.S. residents than for domestic residents), subject only to explicit specific exceptions. During the 1990s, when FDI assumed a much more prominent role in development thinking, this approach began to find favor elsewhere, as well.

On standards of treatment once investment has arrived within the host country, virtually all BITs call for fair and equitable treatment, security of ownership, and freedom from unreasonable or discriminatory restrictions on the operation of investments. Nearly all guarantee MFN treatment (the principle that no foreigner should be treated more favorably than the partner country's residents), although, as with trade, this is subject to exceptions permitting even more favorable treatment of partners in an RIA. Most BITs also specify national treatment, and, in fact, the treatment of foreigners is often more favorable than for domestic residents—for example, where domestic residents face foreign exchange restrictions but foreign firms effectively do not. Nearly all BITs contain provisions on the transfer of funds associated with FDI and on expropriation. Here, too, the United States has led the way in introducing provisions that restrict the imposition of performance requirements and permit the international mobility of key personnel.

Dispute settlement provisions vary but usually define arbitration procedures that in recent BITs are often based on international standards such those of the World Bank Group's International Centre for Settlement of Investment Disputes (ICSID). An interesting aspect of the provisions is that they sometimes provide for private entities in one partner country to take action against the government of the other.

Treatment of Investment in Current Regional Arrangements

At the regional level, some treaties are just multicountry extensions of BITs—that is, freestanding investment agreements. These include, for example, the 1970 Agreement on Investment and Free Movement of Arab Capital among Arab Countries, and the 1993 Colonia Protocol on the

Promotion and Reciprocal Protection of Investment within MERCOSUR. Others, of more interest to us, form part of broader RIAs that include trade and sometimes other provisions. For example, the EU, the Andean Pact, LAIA, NAFTA, and COMESA all have investment provisions.

The most far-reaching investment provisions are those of the EU, where the objective has been to create a common market with a single market for capital and investment. Restrictions on investment and the movement of people are long gone, and the remaining frictions are in areas such as differences in taxation and company law. The European Single Market Programme sought to address some of these issues, but the process is not yet complete. An important part of the integration of capital markets in the EU is its common competition policy, which restricts the worst excesses of investment incentives (known as state aids).

Just as it has been very progressive in its BITs, the United States has been instrumental in advancing the treatment of investment in RIAs. NAFTA contains a deep and innovative investment chapter, especially considering that it is only a free trade agreement rather than a customs union. It has become a model for other associations such as the Group of Three and for APEC, with respect to its nonbinding investment principles.

NAFTA provides for national treatment in establishment; MFN treatment in establishment and operation; a ban on new performance requirements and a phaseout of old ones; guarantees of convertibility at market-exchange rates of funds for repatriating profits, disinvestments, and so on; and a ban on expropriations except for public policy reasons on a nondiscriminatory basis and with full compensation. This is a far-reaching menu, even though the signatories made a number of exceptions in the annex to the investment chapter, including general national security exceptions and sector- and country-specific ones. NAFTA also has extensive dispute settlement provisions that permit private action against governments.

In 1994 APEC members agreed on an even more extensive set of principles governing investment but were able to do so only on a nonbinding basis. These principles basically represent a goal toward which national regimes might seek to evolve in the fullness of time. They offer no concrete protections at present and so probably have only a very slight (psychological) effect on intra-APEC investment flows.

Multilateral Investment Agreements

Many bilateral and multinational agreements other than RIAs embody national treatment. Prominent among them are the OECD's Codes on

Liberalization of Capital Movements and Current Invisible Operations, and its National Treatment Instrument, which requires that nonresident enterprises which have been permitted to establish in host countries be treated in the same manner as domestic firms. A number of developing countries have agreed to sign these codes. Recently, the OECD tried to liberalize investment further and establish binding dispute settlement procedures in the Multilateral Agreement on Investment (MAI). This initiative failed both because the OECD countries turned out not to be ready for such a step and because, for a variety of reasons, the MAI aroused substantial opposition among nongovernmental organizations (Henderson 1999). Investment policy has also been proposed as a subject for future WTO negotiations under the Doha Development Agenda, but only if all members first explicitly agree on the form and content of those talks at the WTO ministerial meeting in 2003.

INTEGRATION AS AN AID TO CREDIBILITY—NOT AN AUTOMATIC EFFECT

A country intent on restoring or accelerating growth must improve its economic management, but this may not be enough if it suffers from low credibility as a result of, say, a history of bad policies. Potential investors, domestic or foreign, are likely to be suspicious of the government's stated intentions if they have been burned in the past by sudden tariff changes, tax increases, or nationalizations. Thus, the benefits of economic reform will be slow to arrive if credibility has to be built up over time. In fact, reform may well fail without credibility: investors may not respond, may respond perversely because they anticipate reversal, or may launch speculative attacks against the reforms, and interest groups that lose under the reform may attempt to reverse it.

In developing countries, poor credibility can stem from a number of factors. Governments driven by interest groups or reelection pressures may be tempted to reverse reforms, or elections may bring a party opposed to the reforms into power. Kleptocratic regimes can make opportunistic raids on investors, and ethnically riven societies may pursue destructive redistributions. Unless governments can make a convincing case that they will refrain from such actions, investment is likely to remain low.

But it is difficult—and takes a long time—for a country to raise its standing by itself. When reform is hampered by a lack of faith, governments must try to reduce uncertainty, and one way of doing this is to anchor reforms through a credible binding commitment. Estonia, for example, with no track record to appeal to, established a currency board to take monetary policy out of the government's hands.

RIAs Allow Bad Policy to Be Punished

Another route might be to sign an RIA that locks in reforms by changing the incentives for bad policy. Such an outcome may come about either because the RIA increases the rewards for good policy or the costs of a bad policy directly or because it permits "punishment" by other RIA members if the country breaks "club rules" (Fernandez and Portes 1998). In the latter case the partners must have the power and commitment to enforce the necessary reforms. The partners need to be large and stable enough, and to have a sufficiently strong interest in the RIA, to make it worth their while to discipline the target country. This is a difficult combination to achieve, for the larger and more stable a country is, the less likely it is to depend on any particular RIA for its prosperity.

A partner country is likely to be more concerned about a neighbor than about a distant partner, and more willing to serve as a policy anchor for it. Mexico's economic performance is more important to the United States than Argentina's because Mexico is a more important trading partner and Mexican social and political instability can affect perceived U.S. welfare directly, especially via migration (see Francois 1997 and box 4.1). Similarly, the EU is likely to be more concerned about Poland or Hungary than about Pakistan or Zimbabwe.

A large country can also support integration among its former colonies. French sponsorship gave the two African monetary unions in the CFA zone, which have survived for more than four decades, enough credibility to resist a needed devaluation for many years. Similarly, the British Colonial Office gave SACU, which goes back over 80 years, credibility for its first half-century; later SACU became a kind of North-South RIA dominated by a hegemonic power, South Africa.

If reforms are clearly stipulated in an RIA treaty and a clear and credible punishment incentive exists, a North-South RIA can provide a strong commitment mechanism and raise the credibility of the reforms. By writing the reforms into an RIA agreement, subsequent punishment is given a formal legal basis, and if the reforms also affect the partner countries' welfare, their imposition of punishments is legitimized politically.[4] The obvious cases in which treaties define policies include trade policies between the partner countries in an FTA, external trade policies in a customs union, and perhaps aspects of investment policy such as

Box 4.1 NAFTA and the Credibility of Mexico's Policy Reforms

Did NAFTA increase the credibility of Mexico's policy reforms? One way to check is to look at Mexico's behavior following its 1982 and 1994 debt crises. The 1982 debt crisis led to an enormous increase in economic intervention by the government, which nationalized the banking system and put in place foreign exchange controls, a universal regime of import-licensing requirements, and controls on foreign investment.

Mexico started to liberalize its economy around 1985, dismantling its import-licensing regime and reforming its foreign exchange restrictions and its laws on foreign investment and intellectual property. It acceded to the GATT in 1986, and it established formal consultation mechanisms on trade and investment with the United States well before the establishment of NAFTA.

In 1985 Mexico's average tariff was 18.5 percent (100 percent for some products), and its average tariff on consumer goods was 45 percent. After it joined the GATT, its bound tariff rates fell significantly, and its applied average tariffs by sector fell to between 4 and 13.1 percent. Tariffs were further capped by Mexico's entry into NAFTA in 1994. Thus, through NAFTA and the GATT, Mexico's government severely limited its ability to raise tariffs and to dismantle its trade and investment reforms.

Whereas the debt crisis of 1982 led to nationalizations, exchange controls, and a dramatic increase in protection to deal with the balance of payments crisis, the same did not occur in 1994. With the support of multilateral agencies and the United States—Mexico's largest trading partner by far—intervention was aimed at stabilizing the economy without closing it. And although protection did increase on some non-NAFTA imports, the general thrust toward openness was not heavily compromised.

What explains the different reactions to the two crises? Some have argued that the shift in the prevailing intellectual climate toward liberalization was sufficient (Bhagwati and Panagariya 1996). This was clearly important, and possibly necessary, but equally plausible is that Mexico had locked in its policies through accession to the GATT and to NAFTA in a way that made reversal very costly.

national treatment. Agreements might also include various deep integration measures and so generate credibility in these areas, as well (see box 4.2).

What RIA treaties typically do not include is macroeconomic and general domestic policy constraints. Whalley (1998b) argues that a desire to increase the credibility of domestic reforms was central to Mexico's negotiations on NAFTA. "Mexican negotiators were less concerned to secure an exchange of concessions. . . . The idea was clearly to help lock in domestic policy reform through this process" (71–72). But, in fact, NAFTA covered neither macroeconomic policies (which got completely out of hand in the run-up to the implementation of the agreement in 1994) nor privatization and deregulation, which actually have moved rather slowly in Mexico. Indeed, one might argue that the intense focus on NAFTA in the early 1990s encouraged an overoptimistic view of Mexico's economic prospects, diverted attention from macroeconomic management, and discouraged macrostabilization for

Box 4.2 Credibility on Deep Integration: The European Single Market Programme

Holmes and Smith (1998) argue that one effect of the removal of intraregional trade barriers under the European Single Market Programme (SMP) was a reduction of the risk premium on investment. In their view, trade policy commitments by EC (now EU) governments lessened future uncertainty and induced additional investment and growth. Had these commitments merely covered reductions in tariffs, it is not clear that they would have had to be implemented regionally rather than multilaterally. But they went much deeper, to issues such as standards, customs formalities, and domestic regulation in which EU institutions are critical and over which the new power of enforcement granted to central bodies—the European Commission and the European Court of Justice—added considerable leverage. Baldwin, Francois, and Portes (1997) forecast a similar reduction in risk premiums for the Eastern European countries as they accede to the EU over the next decade.

fear of puncturing the political enthusiasm for NAFTA on either side of the border. By contrast, the Europe Agreements between the EU and the transition economies of Central and Eastern Europe do cover certain domestic policy reforms (for example, on competition policy), as do the RIAs between Australia and New Zealand and between Iceland and the EU.

RIAs Can Affect the Incentives for Good Policies

An RIA may increase the returns to investment-friendly policies by enlarging the potential market. Similarly it may increase the costs of "anti-investment" policies or fiscal laxity because the domestic market is more exposed to competition. It will be clear from this that genuinely liberal RIAs can increase the credibility of promises of good policy, whereas RIAs that do little to increase competition and exposure will not do much for credibility, either. That is, direct credibility effects will tend to magnify the static effects discussed in chapter 2. They are the icing on the procompetitive cake of an RIA, but no cake means no icing.

An RIA can also help lock in the larger partner's trade policies. Most RIAs have dispute settlement mechanisms, which can improve the security of market access by providing a forum for dealing with disputes. Such mechanisms, however, are frequently very political and smack of managed trade. A small country may have little power to resist effectively if its larger partner reneges on an agreement by, for example, applying antidumping measures incorrectly to help some domestic interest group. Moreover, even where the small partners can insist on addressing the problem, solutions frequently take the form of guaranteed access for politically determined quantities rather than restoration of free competition. Security of access can be particularly attractive if trade wars are feared. In the early stages of negotiating NAFTA, the president of Mexico at the time, Carlos Salinas de Gortari, declared, "what we want is closer commercial ties with Canada and the United States, especially in a world of big regional markets being created. We don't want to be left out of any of those regional markets" (cited in Perroni and Whalley 1994).

RIAs Can Signal Government's Reform Intentions—If Genuine

Closely related to the incentives to pursue good policy is the use of an RIA to signal that a government has changed its spots. If entering an RIA entails (political) sunk costs in terms of challenging interest groups that will lose from increased competition, and if it requires liberal or sound policies to make sense, entry provides the government with a signaling device, for only a government with genuinely liberal intentions would sign. So, in the presence of asymmetric information about the type of government, an RIA could improve credibility.

This argument is a persuasive explanation for some developing country governments' recent interest in RIAs. There has been a shift in perceptions of the policy requirements for economic growth, and after several decades of pursuing inward-looking policies, governments clearly require a means of signaling genuine changes in their attitudes. What is less evident is whether RIAs are the best means of signaling and whether signaling is sufficient to justify RIAs. First, there is the "icing on the cake" argument mentioned above. If an RIA is genuinely liberal—that is, if it increases domestic competition and creates trade—it is beneficial (relative to the status quo) in those terms alone, and credibility is an extra, albeit one that may be more valuable than the fundamental static gains. Second, there are other means of signaling and winning credibility: trade policy binding at the WTO; acceptance of the IMF's Article VIII; domestic rhetoric; and constitutional limitations, for example.[5] These measures do not carry the trade-diverting risks of RIAs.

Moreover, a country's policy credibility will not benefit from entering an RIA if its government is not already heavily committed to reform. Compare Greece, which did not undertake much-needed macroeconomic reforms after joining the EU, with Portugal and Spain, which did. Portugal and Spain gained credibility and benefited from increased FDI; Greece's credibility—and FDI performance—remained low. This example confirms that even strong, deep North-South RIAs are not sufficient to ensure good policy or credibility. Indeed, Alogoskoufis (1995) suggests that accession to the EC actually exacerbated Greece's policy problems by providing transfers which enabled the country to postpone needed reforms. A further disappointment of this kind is likely to be the economic partnership agreements (EPAs) between the EU and the ACP countries (see box 4.3).

Box 4.3 Will RIAs Enhance Credibility in Africa?

African countries desperately need policy credibility. An influx of investment and technology would assist the growth strategies that are absolutely fundamental for alleviating poverty successfully. Unfortunately, RIAs are unlikely to help in this regard, and if they divert attention from more important domestic issues that might enhance credibility, they will be positively harmful.

We have already argued that even if combining small poor economies into a trade bloc has attractions, enhancing credibility is not one of them. Thus, only North-South RIAs are of direct interest here, and, of these, only those with the EU are likely to be significant. (U.S. trade with Africa is small and is dominated by oil; the EU is far more important for Africa in terms of traditional links, location, and the depth of trading and investment flows.) In the Cotonou Agreement of 2000, the EU and the African, Caribbean, and Pacific (ACP) states agreed to turn their nonreciprocal trading agreement, the Lomé Convention, into fully reciprocal North-South RIAs, in the form of economic partnership agreements (EPAs). Prominent among the reasons for this step was the ACP states' desire for credibility, using the EU as an external agent of restraint (Collier 1996). Our analysis suggests that they are unlikely to succeed in this. (Several other reservations are stated in Winters 2000 and Schiff and Winters 2002b.)

Even on the narrow issue of the instruments negotiated under the RIA, such as tariffs on intrabloc trade, the incentives for the EU to discipline a small African country have to be considered. The EU clearly has the necessary market power, but does it have the will? Its traditions on trade policy, even between its own members, are fairly pragmatic, and since the EPAs use high-level political bodies to manage intrabloc relations, it is easy to imagine managed trade solutions and temporary derogations emerging, rather than punishment. The internal politics and public relations associated with the EU's excluding a traditional supplier from its market because, as the press might put it, "it just happened to need to raise tariffs to close a fiscal deficit," would be very difficult—the more so because most of the ACP countries are former colonies of EU members. Finally, ACP countries are so small and so distant that EU governments have no significant material interest in their success or their markets.

Even if the EPAs enhance the credibility of the ACP countries' low barriers to EU imports, they will have little effect on their trade policy toward third parties, which is at least as important because of the potential losses from trade diversion. FTA members set their own trade policies, so there is no formal discipline and not much of a political, moral, or legal case for the EU to press ACP partners to be liberal in this respect. There are incentives such that when tariffs on imports from the EU are fixed at zero, those on the other suppliers will be lowered, but these are not guaranteed to prevail (see the discussion in chapter 3). Similarly, although the EU is trying to induce some of its other association partners to liberalize their mutual trade (for example, within the Central European Free Trade Area and in the Mediterranean area), it has not pressed for liberalization of these partners' third-country trade, which would entail a loss for the EU.

The EPAs are not strong devices for signaling ACP countries' liberal intentions, simply because these countries generally appear to have few such designs. In the extended negotiations, ACP countries resisted having to open their markets to EU imports, demanded very long adjustment periods, and initially sought to obtain a waiver in the WTO to permit the current (WTO-inconsistent) Lomé arrangements to continue indefinitely. (The actual waiver obtained in 2001 covered the period to 2008.)

Regional versus Multilateral Routes to Credibility

There are several reasons why RIAs might provide better or more credibility than can multilateral agreements, specifically the WTO. First, many countries have bound their tariffs at the WTO at levels significantly higher than their applied tariffs and can raise them without violating their WTO commitments. Given the weakness of the lock-in mechanism, domestic and foreign investors will remain hesitant to commit resources.

Second, RIAs allow countries to make commitments on matters that are difficult to negotiate multilaterally, including aspects of deep integration, such as harmonization of investment codes. Thus, not only are more policies explicitly constrained, but there are more areas in which punishment can be exercised.

Third, for commitments to be credible, there must be a high degree of certainty that retaliation will follow violations. More countries are affected by a country's actions at the WTO than in an RIA, which by definition has few members. RIA members therefore internalize a larger share of the total loss from any violation—100 percent in a two-country RIA—and have a stronger incentive to retaliate than countries at the WTO. In addition, RIA members have less scope for free-riding on the punishment (that is, for letting others take action) and more direct returns to making the agreement credible overall (Fernandez and Portes 1998).

The WTO, however, does have proven enforcement procedures; it brings major trading powers into the frame; and it is less subject to renegotiations and internal political pressures. Also, as noted above, only "good" RIAs will have any credibility effects. Thus, even if a developing country has entered a North-South RIA, it is also likely to gain by acceding to the WTO. Mexico used both the GATT and an RIA to lock in its reforms (see box 4.1), as have the Eastern European countries, which have sought WTO membership as well as Europe Agreements over the past decade.

RIAs AS INVESTMENT STIMULI

More than trade policy is needed to attract investment; the climate for investment also matters. This section looks at how policy integration within RIAs can influence investors' decisions and at whether integration has a positive effect on growth.

Integration Affects Incentives to Invest

For policy changes to have a positive impact on investment, they must raise expected returns or lower costs. Recent analyses (for example,

Baldwin and Forslid 1996; Baldwin and Seghezza 1996; Baldwin, Forslid, and Haaland 1996) suggest that the rate of return on capital (and on investment) can rise in all integrating countries regardless of capital abundance.[6] The researchers note that regional integration typically reduces the transactions costs of tradables more than those of nontradables, shifting both demand and supply toward tradables. If, as is commonly believed, tradables are more capital-intensive than nontradables, trade liberalization will raise the relative demand for capital and hence its rate of return. The higher rate of return then increases the amount of capital that people wish to use and so increases investment. (Extra investment is required to boost the capital stock, but even after the desired levels are reached, investment will not fall back to its original level because the greater amount of stock requires more servicing and replacement.) Moreover, increased competition in tradable goods sectors may induce improvements in efficiency, lower markups, and a larger demand for inputs in those sectors, further increasing the relative demand for capital. Integration may also affect the prices of capital goods. Lower tariffs and trading costs on imports of capital equipment may reduce the price of investment goods, raising the rates of return and accumulation. Increased competition from capital goods imports could also stimulate the domestic capital goods industry to greater efficiency.

These arguments are less forceful in low-income than in middle-income countries because low-income countries' capital goods already generally enter with low or zero tariffs and there is no indigenous capital goods industry before integration. Developing countries have often given their industries high rates of effective protection by imposing zero or low tariffs on capital goods and high tariffs on final goods. This policy gives capital-intensive industries the highest effective protection, so that if those industries lose most with integration (as they well might in a North-South RIA), the result will be a reduction in the demand for capital and in investment. Additionally, of course, for a small country that continues to import capital goods from the rest of the world, prices will not change, as was explained in chapter 2.

Regional integration that goes beyond tariff reduction may raise the efficiency of the financial sector, reducing lending margins and the cost of funds and leading to higher investment. This is likely to provide some benefits for developing countries. Two small developing countries may gain by integrating their financial sectors because of the increased competitiveness and because integration may allow them to diversify their portfolios better and reduce their risk premia. These benefits will, however, be small if the countries have similar endowments and production structures and thus highly correlated shocks. The benefits of increased competitiveness are likely to be more important in an RIA with a large partner that has a well-developed financial sector than in an RIA between developing countries—and the gains from nondiscriminatory liberalization will be even larger. Financial integration is, however, difficult; even the EU needed several decades to achieve it. And, as discussed in chapter 6, the deeper integration needed to capture these benefits has been mostly absent in South-South RIAs.

Overall, the theoretical arguments that an RIA will raise returns and investment in developing countries are more persuasive for North-South RIAs than for South-South ones. Furthermore, increased investment must not be equated with increased economic welfare: investment that is not well conceived can diminish welfare. The conditional nature of the arguments made must also be kept in mind. RIAs may raise investment, but to be certain, one must be sure that the conditions actually apply. Whether an RIA will raise the return to capital depends on the capital intensities in the various sectors and on the initial tariff structure. Opening up the financial sector under unstable macroeconomic (fiscal and exchange rate) policies is likely to hurt more than help.

Finally, RIAs are not *necessary* for inducing investment. General reforms such as stabilization, market liberalization, and privatization should raise the returns to all factors and are likely to be more than enough to increase private investment. In the mid-1970s Chile began a profound process of unilateral economic reform that led to a significant increase in its savings and investment rates, approaching those of the East Asian "tigers." (In fact, Chile *left* the Andean Pact to gain more freedom for undertaking its reforms.) Neither is an RIA *sufficient* to induce investment, as we saw with Greece. What seems to matter most is the quality of domestic policies. A country suffering from low credibility (say, as a consequence of a long history of illiberal policies and failed reforms) may be able to use a North-South RIA to raise its investment level if it first undertakes serious reforms and then uses the RIA to give the reforms credibility.

Investment Does Not Necessarily Mean Growth in RIAs

Baldwin (1989, 1992), in a major ex ante analytical study of investment effects in an RIA, postulates a positive investment effect from the European Single Market Programme (SMP). Early estimates placed the static gains from the SMP at around 5 percent of GDP (CEC 1988). Treating these as pure gains in productivity that raise rates of return, Baldwin argues that investment will also increase as a result. Considering the investment increases in the context of a Solow (1956) growth model, in which the steady-state (long-term) growth rate of the economy is given exogenously and is independent of government policy, Baldwin argues that as capital accumulates, the economy can support a higher level of income, and thus growth will increase temporarily as it approaches this level. Baldwin terms this additional medium-term income effect, which adds perhaps another 5 percent to GDP, the "medium-term growth bonus." But whereas the static income effect of the SMP is essentially free (setting aside temporary adjustment costs) and so constitutes a pure welfare gain, the medium-term income effect must be paid for by increasing investment—sacrificing present consumption for higher future consumption. Thus the welfare gain associated with the medium-term income effect is only about 0.5 percent of GDP—only one-tenth of the income effect itself (Baldwin 1993). The static effect would be spread over, say, 5 to 7 years following completion of the internal EC market, while it would take about 10 years for half of the medium-term effect to be realized.

Integration in the EU seems likely to have a greater impact on investment and growth than will RIAs involving only developing countries. The SMP not only deals with border measures such as tariffs and nontariff barriers but also entails "deep integration," which aims to eliminate all barriers to the movement of goods, services, people, and capital and pertains to a much larger market. Thus, it should have a greater impact on contestability of markets and competitiveness of firms than would the simple removal of trade barriers within a smaller bloc, such as is found in most South-South RIAs.

The evidence on the impact on investment of RIAs involving developing countries is scarce and ambiguous. Brada and Mendez (1988) estimate the effects of integration on capital formation in RIAs involving developed and developing countries (EFTA, the EEC, CMEA, LAFTA, and the EAC) and find that except in the CMEA, investment increased but that the effect on growth was very small. They conclude that the "dynamic effects of integration can neither explain the rapid growth of West European countries in the 1960s nor serve as a strong justification for encouraging nonmember countries to join existing schemes or to organize new ones" (167).

De Melo, Montenegro, and Panagariya (1993), by contrast, report that African RIAs such as the CEAO and UDEAC experienced increased investment rates following integration. In the CEAO, created in 1974, the investment rate in member countries increased from 6.8 percent of GDP in 1960–72 to 8.6 percent in 1973–85. The corresponding increases for UDEAC, created in 1973, are from 15.9 to 18.3 percent, and for the Andean Pact (1969), from 18.3 to 19 percent.

Such stimuli, however, are not unambiguously desirable when external trade barriers are high; with high barriers, investment is likely to go to the highly protected capital-intensive sector, where the private rate of return on capital is high but the social rate of return is low or negative. Hence, the higher rate of investment need not raise economic growth or improve welfare. De Melo, Montenegro, and Panagariya (1993) find no significant differences in growth rates for members of RIAs compared with other countries, and, in a multivariate regression analysis, they find no effect of membership in an RIA on growth in developing countries. Despite rising investment rates in the CEAO, UDEAC, and the Andean Pact, income growth fell in all three. The declines in growth rates are not necessarily attributable to the formation of the RIAs, since the growth rates both of developing countries as a whole (78 countries) and of OECD countries also fell in this period, probably because of the 1973 oil shock. Still, the declines certainly do not support the view that regionalism boosts growth—a subject to which we return in chapter 5.

An important lesson from these results is that the current sacrifice which additional investment entails need not result in additional future benefits if investment occurs in a distorted environment. By contrast, in a liberal policy environment where domestic relative prices reflect world prices and private rates of return approximate social ones, additional investment is likely to be productive. This is another reason for lowering external trade barriers as countries form RIAs.

REGIONAL INTEGRATION AND FOREIGN DIRECT INVESTMENT

The formation of an RIA affects investors' decisions about where and how to invest. The motives behind these decisions, and the evidence that an RIA attracts investment, are examined in this section.

Motives for FDI

Although FDI is subject to the same forces that influence total investment, it also responds to various specific determinants. One common motive for FDI is to boost local sales and market access. Access to large or rich markets can be an important factor in attracting FDI into a country. In a survey conducted by Japan's Ministry of International Trade and

Industry (MITI) on the motives behind Japanese manufacturing FDI in Asia, North America, and Europe, 70 percent of respondents cited local sales as a major factor (Kawai and Urata 1996). Similarly, the spurt of FDI in ASEAN countries in the late 1980s is usually attributed to those countries' rapid growth (Alburo, Bautista, and Gochoco 1992).[7] A necessary condition for this sort of investment is that the market not be as readily accessible from outside the bloc. That is, FDI motivated by market access is of the "tariff-jumping" variety. FDI for automobiles and automobile parts in ASEAN economies increased partly because these were highly protected sectors and FDI was the only way to gain a foothold (Bhalla and Bhalla 1997). The same happened in MERCOSUR. It is important to note that tariff-jumping FDI can be immiserizing—that is, it can reduce domestic economic welfare. The tariff directs capital into sectors in which the RIA does not have comparative advantage, and by causing other factors of production to flow into those sectors, it reduces output in those in which it does.[8]

These factors are more likely to stimulate FDI flows from outside the RIA than between members. Firms originally located in a member country receive access to the whole market without relocation and so have less incentive to invest in other members. Firms located in third countries, on the other hand, will have more incentive to locate new production facilities in a member country and to service the other members of the bloc through intra-RIA (preferential) exports. Such "platform investment" is particularly likely if there are increasing returns to scale in production, making for lumpy investments that are viable only above a certain size. The integrated market may become large enough to bear the fixed costs of the establishment of new foreign affiliates. Thus, RIAs might attract more foreign investment (for example, in the production of consumer durables) into developing regions as a whole than can fragmented national markets. Whether these effects are more likely for RIAs between larger countries or between smaller ones depends on the relative sizes of the blocs' demands for a product and the minimum efficient scale of production. Combining several small economies may make new FDI attractive in small-scale industries, but these same industries may already be present in larger countries even without an RIA. And it is not likely that any developing country RIA could stimulate FDI in, say, the production of large airliners.

A second important set of motives behind FDI is to take advantage of local factors of production (such as local labor) and to set up export platforms. In the MITI survey mentioned above, 44 percent of the Japanese firms surveyed indicated that use of local labor was one of their motives.

These motives can be enhanced if a developing country forms an RIA with a developed country, as a firm located in the developing country can then take advantage of cheap inputs while obtaining free access to the large developed economy. Although Mexico had long been used as an export platform to the United States, after 1994 NAFTA had a profound impact on FDI into Mexico from countries outside the bloc, as this investment became a way to guarantee market access to Mexico's northern partners (Blomström and Kokko 1997; Fernandez and Portes 1998). About 80 percent of the vehicles produced by U.S. auto manufacturers in Mexico in 1997 were for export, compared with 48 percent in 1994 (USITC 1997). Following the creation of NAFTA, Japan redirected part of its FDI from the United States and Canada toward Mexico. Whereas Japanese investments in the United States are geared primarily for the local market (and are mainly directed toward manufacturing, commerce, and banking and finance), those in Mexico, particularly in the automobile industry, are intended more for the NAFTA continental market.

A third factor may be that the removal of internal barriers in the RIA allows firms to allocate operations across member countries more efficiently. Thus, if RIA members differ in their endowments, the RIA may stimulate vertical FDI. This potentially important aspect of North-South arrangements lies at the heart of Ethier's (1998) theoretical exploration of the benefits of regionalism. With guaranteed preferential access to the northern market, the southern country becomes an attractive location for labor-intensive activities. Knowing this, it is more confident of receiving inflows of investment and is hence more comfortable with liberalizing than it would be under multilateral liberalization, where it would face fiercer competition for inflows. This argument is equally applicable to intrabloc FDI and to that from outside.

Evidence of the Positive Effects of Integration

There is strong circumstantial evidence that creating or deepening an RIA stimulates FDI. For example, between 1946 and 1970, the number of manufacturing subsidiaries of EC-member multinationals located in other EC countries increased more than sixfold, from 68 to 434, while those located in non-EC European countries increased only from 95 to 311 (Yannopoulos 1990). Similarly, the European Commission (1998) found that intra-EU FDI rose more rapidly than investment outside the EU following the introduction of the SMP. Germany and the United Kingdom, in particular, switched their investment from the United States to the EU beginning in the late 1980s.

It has also been widely documented that European integration has made member countries more attractive to U.S., Japanese, and other third-country firms. The creation of the single market in 1992 had a significant impact on decisions by Japanese, Korean, and Taiwanese (China) companies to establish operations in the EU (Motta and Norman 1996).[9] Total inflows of FDI into member countries expanded from ECU 10 billion in 1984 to ECU 63 billion in 1989. During this period, inflows into the United States also increased, but at a significantly lower rate (WTO 1995). The European Commission (1998) found that the EU's share of worldwide inward FDI flows increased from 28 to 33 percent during 1982–93.

Turning to North-South RIAs, the data show that FDI to Mexico rose from $4.3 billion in 1993 to $11 billion in 1994, the year NAFTA came into force (figure 4.1). The experience of RIAs between middle-income countries is similar: for example, following the signature in 1991 of the Treaty of Asunción that established MERCOSUR, FDI in member countries increased from $3.5 billion in 1991 to $18 billion in 1996 and to $38 billion in 1998. With nearly $11 billion in FDI in 1996 (up dramatically from $1.1 billion in 1991), Brazil surpassed Mexico as the largest FDI recipient in Latin America (table 4.1). A qualification to these figures is that one cannot know for sure that it was the RIA per se rather than better policy in general that boosted FDI; in the case of MERCOSUR, the two occurred more or less simultaneously. And the welfare implications are ambiguous because some of the boost in FDI, as in the automobile sector, was caused by trade and industrial policy distortions such as very high tariffs.

Figure 4.1 Net Inflows of Foreign Direct Investment, Mexico, 1985–96

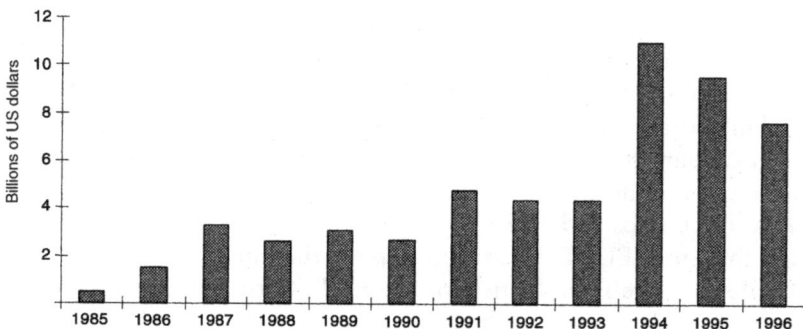

Source: World Bank, *World Development Indicators,* various years.

Table 4.1 Net Inflows of Foreign Direct Investment, MERCOSUR, 1991–98
(millions of current U.S. dollars)

Country	1991	1992	1993	1994	1995	1996	1997	1998
Argentina	2,439	4,384	2,763	3,432	5,279	6,513	8,094	6,150
Brazil	1,103	2,061	1,292	3,072	4,859	11,200	19,652	31,913
Paraguay	84	137	111	180	184	246	270	256
Uruguay	0	1	102	155	157	137	126	164

Source: World Bank, World Development Indicators, various years.

Although we have some evidence of the impact on investment of North-North and North-South RIAs and of South-South RIAs among large middle-income countries, no such evidence is available for South-South RIAs among small low-income countries. Furthermore, all the cases cited in the literature indicate anticipation of the RIA followed by something of a decline. This strongly suggests that RIAs change firms' views of the optimal stock of investment in member countries. Thus, we observe a big step-up during the adjustment period but only a small permanent increase in the flow commensurate with maintaining the higher stock. There is no evidence to date that steady-state flows of FDI increase.

One area not examined here is the potential of FDI to generate technological knowledge spillovers. This question is examined in chapter 5.

NOTES

1. Such pacts can also fail because the country assigned to produce certain products lacks the capacity to do so. The Andean Pact assigned exclusive production rights to different countries by sector in 1970. The program failed when Bolivia produced only 2 of the 10 products assigned to it and Venezuela violated the agreement and started making the products (Echavarria 1997). In other cases the more industrialized member countries (for example, Kenya in the EAC and El Salvador in the CACM) refused to accept constraints on the expansion of their manufacturing sectors.

2. This section draws on the discussion in WTO (1996).

3. The terms "shallow" and "narrow" integration are discussed in chapter 6.

4. In the 21st century, a northern government that imposes punishments which are neither legally based nor politically imperative is likely to stir up a storm of protest about neocolonialism and interference.

5. Article VIII of the IMF's Articles of Agreement deals with the general obligations of members, including avoidance of restrictions on current payments, avoidance of discriminatory currency practices, convertibility of foreign-held

balances, information provision, consultation regarding existing international agreements, and collaboration regarding policies on reserve assets.

6. These studies were developed mainly with the European Single Market Programme in mind but may also apply to RIAs that involve developing countries.

7. The share of ASEAN in world inward FDI increased from 2.5 percent in 1985 to 4.3 percent in 1990.

8. Bhagwati (1987) has proposed another trade-oriented explanation for FDI, which is grounded in the political economy of protection. In this interpretation, "quid pro quo" FDI is made not to circumvent tariffs but to defuse the threat of protection. Unlike the tariff-jumping kind, this type of investment occurs in anticipation of the imposition of protection, in which case FDI that transfers technology and promotes employment is in the nature of a bribe paid to the host country in return for allowing free access to the investor country's exports. This may be significant in the EU.

9. Motta and Norman (1996) argue that this may have been a consequence of the stricter application of antidumping legislation in the EU beginning about 1985.

CHAPTER 5

Growth and Location

Economic growth lies at the heart of economic development, and for many countries growth must be driven by industrialization. This chapter considers two of the main concerns of developing country policymakers, and ultimate justifications of regional integration agreements: economic growth, and location of industries.

We ask, first, how RIAs affect long-run growth, and we find that the preference for North-South over South-South RIAs based on the analysis of static effects holds for dynamic effects as well. Modern growth theory—the theory of endogenous growth—emphasizes the role of knowledge in fostering productivity and growth. It stresses that knowledge can be effectively transferred from one country to another through international contacts and trade. Wealthy countries are knowledge rich and so are likely to provide far more access to technology than are poorer trading partners. RIAs that switch imports from richer to poorer sources are thus likely to have a perverse effect on members' growth rates. RIAs might also help countries boost their growth rates by supporting institutional reform, and this effect too seems likely to be stronger when developing countries join with richer partners than when they form an RIA with poorer ones.

The direct evidence on RIAs and growth is subject to some methodological reservations but is actually pretty consistent. There is little evidence that RIAs between developed countries stimulate growth, some recent evidence that North-South RIAs may affect growth, and none that RIAs between developing countries do so. Casual examination of the recent performances of, say, Mexico, Poland, and Portugal and a formal analysis of the effects of North-South versus South-South RIAs suggest that serious North-South integration may foster growth, reinforcing the earlier conclusions about the relative merits of the two types of partner for developing countries.

Second, how do RIAs affect the development and location of industry in developing countries, and can they materially affect countries' growth prospects? The discussion of investment in chapter 4 suggested that RIAs can stimulate investment and thus might have a beneficial effect on either industrialization or growth. In this chapter we move beyond investment to consider the economics of agglomeration (or clustering).

Although economists have long been aware that industry tends to cluster at particular locations, they have only recently learned to model this agglomeration formally, allowing them to begin identifying precisely the combinations of conditions that must be satisfied for it to occur. The theory arose from attempts to understand the possible effects of the en-largement and deepening of the European Union (Krugman and Venables 1990) and so is directly applicable to the case of RIAs. The theory is, however, very young; the models do not yet appear to be very realistic and have to date not been accompanied by much empirical evidence. They are more parables than forecasts, but they do offer considerable insight into qualitative factors, and they address such a major concern of policymakers and publics alike that we need to explore their implications for developing countries.

Creating an RIA is likely to affect the incentives for industry to agglomerate. Usually, it will encourage clustering because the RIA increases market size and allows more effective exploitation of the links between firms. An RIA may attract industry into member countries at the expense of nonmembers, although if it is small, this effect will also be very small. RIAs also frequently lead industries to relocate from one member to another. For RIAs between poor countries, this seems likely to increase intermember inequalities because under an RIA firms find it easier to agglomerate in the more prosperous countries while still selling in the other member countries. For RIAs involving richer members, the results are less clear-cut, and it is possible that poorer members will experience strong industrialization after joining an RIA. For developing countries, integration with richer neighbors (North-South RIAs) looks better from an agglomeration point of view than does South-South integration.

SOUTH-SOUTH AND NORTH-SOUTH REGIONALISM AS STIMULANTS TO GROWTH

In the final analysis, the principal objective of trade policy is economic growth. Any change that generated even a small increase in the long-term rate of economic growth would result in cumulative gains that would easily swamp any static and medium-term benefits of the sort discussed so far. If openness stimulates growth, as is often claimed, is it not reasonable to expect that partial openness (regionalism) would at least partially stimulate growth—especially since it frequently appears to affect investment rates? The remainder of this chapter examines these claims and finds little evidence for them for South-South RIAs but some evidence for North-South RIAs. It should be kept in mind, though, that even when regionalism does have beneficial effects, nondiscriminatory openness typically offers them as well.

A well-structured RIA might increase a member country's underlying growth rate, raising its development trajectory by, for example, increasing credibility (as we saw in chapter 4) or reducing tensions between countries (see chapter 7). These, in turn, could raise capital and labor productivity, lead to additional flows of investment and knowledge, and push an economy several notches up on the development path.

The scope for policy-driven growth is a contentious issue among economists. The traditional (neoclassical) view of economic growth admits no means of influencing the long-term growth rate, which is set exogenously according to rates of population growth and technical progress (Solow 1956). Even if policy can influence the rate of capital accumulation, it can affect the growth rate only temporarily. As capital accumulates faster, it runs into diminishing returns, so that, in time, the additional investment is completely absorbed by the additional depreciation associated with having extra capital stock, and the capital-output ratio eventually stops increasing. Hence, although the level of income increases, and so does the medium-term growth rate as the economy approaches its new growth path, the long-term growth rate does not increase.

More recent endogenous (self-generated) growth theory, however, holds that the returns to capital—especially human capital (Lucas 1988) and knowledge capital (Romer 1986, 1990)—do not diminish at the aggregate level because of positive spillover effects. Thus, policies that affect the accumulation of these factors can permanently raise the long-term growth rates of output and income.

The theoretical literature on openness and growth has not generated robust findings on the link between RIAs and growth. Although openness is typically positively associated with growth, especially where trade or FDI is a medium for transferring knowledge, this is not necessarily true for regional integration. Recent empirical work, however, indicates that North-South RIAs are likely to generate productivity gains to the developing partner (see "Trade, Convergence, and Spillovers," below).

Knowledge and Institutions as Keys

Accumulation of physical capital can have little effect on long-term growth because physical capital eventually encounters diminishing returns. Human capital is different. Although individual human capital is also expected to run into diminishing returns, one person's return can be positively affected by the average level of available human capital through positive spillover effects. For instance, an engineer is likely to be more productive if she can interact with and learn from other qualified engineers than if she cannot. Thus, the average level of human capital may rise without running into diminishing returns and can have an impact on long-term growth (Lucas 1988).

Knowledge is given the primary role in endogenous growth theory—increases in knowledge capital are expected to have a permanent positive impact on the rate of growth. Knowledge, once produced, has the public-good characteristic that its use by one user does not prevent its use by another. Creation of knowledge has large spillover effects to others and is therefore likely to display increasing rather than diminishing returns.

Another important factor is the legal, institutional, and regulatory framework, which includes the quality and stability of the political process, de facto property rights, and other institutional aspects. Olson (1996: 7) reviews the factors determining per capita income and growth and concludes that "the most important explanation of the differences in incomes across countries is the difference in their economic policies and institutions." Hall and Jones (1999) find that most of the variation in output per worker across countries cannot be explained by endowments. They conclude that a country's long-run economic performance is determined primarily by the institutions and policies that make up the economic environment within which individuals and firms make investments, create and transfer ideas, and produce goods and services. Recent studies by Acemoglu, Johnson, and Robinson (2001) and by Engerman and Sokoloff (1997) find that institutions have had a fundamental role in explaining growth in the last few centuries.

Given this general framework, how can policy affect long-term economic growth? First, a government can promote investment in education and other forms of human capital. Second, it can improve its political and legal institutions so as to enhance incentives to accumulate and innovate. Regional integration may be able to help, in terms of both policy integration (chapter 6) and international politics (chapter 7). If, by joining an RIA and taking policy integration measures, a country improves its legal and regulatory framework, it may obtain a growth benefit. (There are, however, few examples outside the EU of countries actually engaging in policy integration.) Joining an RIA may also help a country improve its political system if this is a condition for membership (chapter 7).

Trade policy can play a major role in knowledge accumulation. Knowledge has international public-good characteristics, with cross-border spillovers through trade, FDI, scientific exchanges, and the like. Since most developing countries are not major producers of scientific or technical knowledge, it is important that they pursue foreign trade policies which enhance the acquisition of knowledge from abroad. If openness helps, what sort of openness? Is general opening up of the economy the best way to absorb foreign knowledge? Or can developing countries do better through preferential trade liberalization?

Trade, Convergence, and Spillovers

Ben-David (1993) offers convincing evidence that increasing mutual trade among affluent countries leads to upward convergence in per capita incomes. He shows that in Europe, the strong increases in trade associated with increased integration coincided with a dramatic narrowing of per capita incomes across countries. As shown in figure 5.1, there was an almost continuous convergence in per capita incomes in Europe as integration proceeded, from 1947, when the Benelux customs union was created, through 1981. Stages along the way included the creation of the ECSC in 1951 and of the EEC in 1957, elimination of quotas in 1962, and removal of internal tariffs in 1968. Income differences narrowed by about two-thirds over the period, and the convergence was upward, with the poorer countries experiencing faster growth than previously.

Do these results imply that a developing country has only to increase its trade with affluent countries to raise its growth? Not according to this approach (but see below). Ben-David (1994) finds benign convergence among developed countries, with the poorer catching up with the richer; no convergence between middle-income countries or between them and other countries (including rich ones); and a malign convergence among poorer countries. He also finds that convergence is common between countries that are major trading partners (known as convergence clubs) but not among random groups of countries (Ben-David 1998). This reinforces the view that trade is the mechanism through which convergence occurs, although the underlying cause might be some other aspects of openness, such as FDI, that are strongly correlated with trade. Ben-David (1996) finds that the existence of convergence clubs is attributable more to convergence in rates of total factor productivity (TFP) growth than in investment rates; Henrekson, Torstensson, and Torstensson (1997) de-

Figure 5.1 Equalizing Exchange: Trade Liberalization and Income Convergence, 1947–81

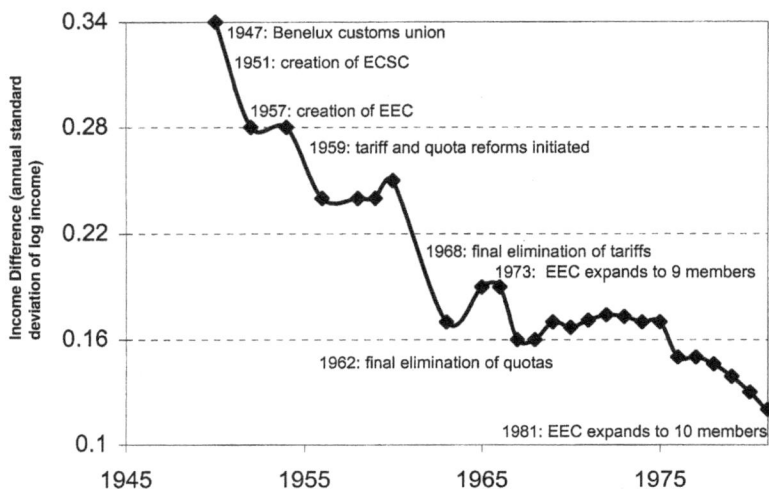

Note: ECSC, European Coal and Steel Community; EEC, European Economic Community.
Source: Ben-David (1993).

rived similar findings for the EC and EFTA. These results suggest that (as predicted by endogenous growth theory) convergence arises from the contacts and information—the knowledge—generated by trade and FDI, rather than from incentives to accumulate physical capital.

Karras (1997) examines whether integration facilitates convergence in the per capita incomes of member countries by investigating convergence during the period 1960–90 in three RIAs: ASEAN (5 countries), the EU (15 countries), and LAFTA (7 countries). Three empirical tests all reveal strong convergence in the EU (the initially poorer countries grow more quickly), somewhat weaker convergence in LAFTA, and absence of convergence, or even divergence, in ASEAN. Karras concludes that regional integration does not guarantee convergence in the standards of living of member countries but that convergence may be associated with the degree of economic integration (as manifested in reduction of protection, enhanced internal trade, and increased policy coordination), which is highest in the EU and weakest in ASEAN. Another possibility is that convergence is more likely in North-North RIAs (the EU) than in South-South ones (LAFTA and ASEAN).

A more formal stream of work on trade and productivity is that by Coe and Helpman (1995) and Coe, Helpman, and Hoffmaister (1997), who seek to explain TFP levels in OECD countries and developing countries, respectively. The authors construct an index of total knowledge capital, measured by accumulated investment in research and development (R&D), for each developed country. They assume that trading partners obtain access to a country's stock of knowledge in proportion to their imports from that country—total imports, in the 1995 paper, and imports of machinery and transport equipment in the 1997 study.

In both exercises, access to foreign knowledge has a statistically significant effect on productivity. For developing countries, Coe, Helpman, and Hoffmaister find that TFP is related both to the openness of the economy (the ratio of imports to GDP) and to the interaction of the latter with the access to foreign knowledge that foreign trade provides. An economy benefits from foreign knowledge, first, according to how open it is in general and, second, according to whether it imports mainly from those countries that have the largest knowledge stocks. These results are intuitively very attractive and suggest, again, that trade is a major conduit for spillovers between countries.

Lumenga-Neso, Olarreaga, and Schiff (2001) argue that the new approach developed by Coe and Helpman (1995) has not been carried through to its logical conclusion because countries also obtain "indirect" knowledge spillovers through trade. That is, France (say) obtains knowledge spillovers from trading with other OECD countries, which means that it can draw on more knowledge than it alone produces. Therefore, any country (say, Belgium) that trades with France will obtain not just direct knowledge spillovers from the knowledge France produces but also indirect spillovers from the knowledge France acquires through its trade with other countries. The authors find that these indirect spillovers are larger than the direct ones and that both have a significant impact on TFP. They also perform various tests and obtain results that are statistically superior to those obtained by Coe and Helpman.[1]

Coe and Helpman's approach has been extended in recent work focusing on developing countries. In an industry-level analysis, Schiff, Wang, and Olarreaga (2002) show that southern countries' TFP responds more strongly to North-South trade than to South-South trade. Another finding is that R&D-intensive industries in the South learn mainly from trade with the North and that industries with low R&D intensities learn mainly from trade within the South. Thus, North-South RIAs tend to favor the development of R&D-intensive industries, while South-South RIAs tend to favor the development of low-R&D-intensity industries. The authors conclude that forming a South-South RIA may delay the transformation of member countries to a high-R&D economy by reducing technology spillovers from the North.

Work on Latin America (Schiff and Wang 2002a) shows that the interaction between education and OECD knowledge spillovers has a positive effect on TFP in R&D-intensive industries. The implication is that there are virtuous growth cycles, with increases in education resulting in increases in the TFP of R&D-intensive industries, greater demand for skilled labor (which is typically complementary with technology), increased demand for education, and so on. Moreover, given that OECD R&D stocks grow continuously over time, the interaction effect between education and OECD knowledge spillovers implies that education has permanent effects on productivity growth in R&D-intensive industries. Since these industries benefit mainly from spillovers from the North, the interaction effects provide another argument for North-South rather than South-South RIAs in Latin America. The FTAA and the Chile-EU FTA, as well as prospective North-South RIAs such as the EU-MERCOSUR FTA, should help in this regard.

Keller (2002) shows that the impact of technological knowledge on TFP diminishes as the distance between the knowledge-exporting and knowledge-importing countries increases. Although he does not specify the channel of knowledge diffusion, this effect appears likely to apply to trade. This would seem to suggest that in choosing a partner in the North, a developing country is better off, other things being equal, choosing a close rather than a distant one. According to this view, Mexico is better off selecting Canada and the United States as trading partners than Japan or the EU. This is supported by the findings of Schiff and Wang (2002b) showing that the impact of foreign knowledge from the United States and Canada on TFP in Mexico is several times larger than that from the rest of the OECD.

Choosing the Wrong Partners Can Harm Growth

An important implication of Coe, Helpman, and Hoffmaister's (1997) work is that any trade policy—including formation of an RIA—that switches a developing country's imports of machinery and equipment from countries with high stocks of knowledge to countries with lower stocks may harm growth. Conversely, an increase in openness is likely to result in faster TFP growth. Thus, countries seeking to accelerate TFP growth should pursue trade policies that increase openness and avoid switching trade from countries with high knowledge stocks to countries with lower stocks.

The corollary is that a developing country contemplating forming an RIA is usually better off choosing a partner with a high—and quickly growing—stock of knowledge. If an RIA among developing countries results in trade being diverted away from more to less knowledge-intensive suppliers—say, if Argentina switches from U.S. and Japanese to Brazilian capital goods—it may harm TFP growth. The static analysis of RIAs has long observed that trade diversion is potentially harmful. Dynamic analysis suggests that trade diversion may be harmful if the diversion is from a source with a large stock of knowledge to one with a smaller stock but beneficial if it is from a small knowledge source to one with a larger stock of knowledge.

To give one illustration, Winters (1997a) applies the Coe, Helpman, and Hoffmaister approach to simulate the impact on TFP growth of an FTA between Lebanon and the EU. He conservatively assumes that signing a Euro-Mediterranean Agreement shifts 4 percent of Lebanese imports from the United States and Japan to the four large EU economies, which have smaller R&D stocks. This lowers the R&D capital stock to which Lebanon has access by 12.5 percent, causing a 1 percent reduction in Lebanon's TFP. But the agreement will also probably result in an increase in the openness of the Lebanese economy, and this will offset the dynamic diversion effect. Provided that the increase in openness is more than 2.5 percent (from 8.5 to 8.7 percent), Lebanon would show a net increase in TFP. Even so, the analysis raises the question as to whether the EU is the best partner for Mediterranean or Eastern European countries from the viewpoint of knowledge spillovers, as other areas, such as the United States and Japan, have typically generated more knowledge.[2]

Spillovers, however, are also affected by closeness in geography, language, and history (Keller 2002), which may lower the cost of absorbing and adapting knowledge from European sources. For example, importers in Morocco may find it easier to learn how a machine operates if it is imported from France rather than from Japan because of the language bond and because Moroccans often have long-standing relationships with French traders.

Schiff and Wang (2002b) show that in the case of NAFTA, trade diversion in Mexico is dynamically beneficial because the diversion takes place from a source (the OECD countries outside North America) with a small effect on TFP to one with a larger impact—the United States and Canada. The authors estimate elasticities of TFP with respect to foreign knowledge of 0.36 for the United States and Canada and 0.04 for the rest of the OECD. They then simulate the effect of NAFTA and find that it raises TFP in Mexico by 5.5 to 7.5 percent, 0.5 percent of which is attributable to trade diversion and the rest to trade creation.[3]

Although this analysis indicates that an RIA with a country or region that has a large or fast-growing stock of knowledge may lead to dynamic gains, such gains might not last forever. The regions that generate the most knowledge today may not do so in the future. For instance, the United Kingdom was the leader during the Industrial Revolution, and Japan led in various industries in recent decades. A country that had RIAs with Japan and East Asia might have obtained significant dynamic benefits before 1990 but, given the present crisis in that region, might now be losing relative to one that had a nonpreferential trade policy. From a long-term viewpoint, nondiscriminatory trade liberalization is probably the optimal policy in a world where it is hard to predict which region will generate the most knowledge in the future, and where it is difficult to join and leave RIAs. That is, unilateral free trade may be optimal from a long-run dynamic perspective, as well as a static viewpoint.

Another reason why unilateral MFN liberalization may be optimal is that knowledge travels not only from North to South (through trade and FDI) but also between northern countries through licensing mechanisms, trade, and FDI. Hence, the level of knowledge of a northern country depends not only on its own production of knowledge but also on how much knowledge it acquires from other northern countries. An OECD country may produce relatively little knowledge itself but may have access to additional knowledge through trade. This is likely to reduce the cross-country variation in knowledge stocks in the North. Lumenga-Neso, Olarreaga, and Schiff (2001) show that although the cross-country coefficient of variation of *produced* technological knowledge stocks is 0.70 for OECD countries, it is only 0.29 with respect to *available* knowledge stocks, where available stocks include spillovers from trade with other OECD countries. Thus, a developing country may benefit from trading with a northern country that generates little knowledge indigenously because the latter has acquired knowledge from other northern countries. Given the present level of understanding of how knowledge transfers are generated, nonpreferential trade liberalization seems likely to be the more robust policy recommendation. For a few countries, however, North-South integration may make sense; Mexico is an example. If the preferential route is chosen, a robust result seems to be that a poor country will gain little or nothing from an RIA with another poor country and that a North-South agreement is preferable.

The theory of endogenous (self-sustaining) growth is predicated on the assumption that knowledge spills over from one enterprise to another without the receiving enterprise having to purchase it; it is an externality. This is what reconciles decreasing returns at the firm level with constant or even increasing returns at the industry or economy level.

Such externalities provide a justification for policy intervention, for, as is well known, in the presence of externalities, market outcomes are not optimal. The work of Coe, Helpman, and Hoffmaister is perfectly consistent with this view, which suggests benefits to an activist policy that shifts imports toward high-knowledge suppliers.

In fact, however, the model also works in the absence of such externalities, that is, with developing country importers paying for and internalizing all the knowledge they receive through trade. They could then be expected to choose their trade patterns correctly, and even if they could raise growth rates by choosing a different pattern of supply, they are rational in not doing so because of the cost involved. In these circumstances there is no case for intervention to stimulate growth, and an RIA that artificially disturbed the pattern of trade would be distortionary. We do not claim that there are no spillovers in knowledge diffusion through international trade, but we do want to caution against the view that there definitely are. And even in the presence of knowledge spillovers, unilateral MFN liberalization may be optimal because knowledge advantages may not last.

FDI and Knowledge Spillovers

Blomström and Kokko (1998) describe three forms of knowledge spillovers from the presence of FDI: (a) local firms improve their productivity by copying some technology used by affiliates of foreign firms operating in the local market; (b) the entry of an affiliate leads to more severe competition in the host economy, so that local firms are forced to use existing technology and resources more efficiently; and (c) competition forces local firms to search for new, more efficient technologies. Although these potential spillover effects seem analytically plausible, results from the empirical literature are mixed, at best. One reason is that foreign firms may take action to limit spillovers to the host country's domestic firms.

A fourth form of knowledge spillover is the effect on domestic upstream firms that sell to affiliates of foreign firms or on domestic downstream firms that buy from these affiliates—"backward" and "forward" linkages. The effect of spillovers on the productivity of upstream and downstream firms is empirically more promising because foreign firms typically procure domestic inputs of better quality than do domestic firms, produce better intermediate products to be used by downstream firms, or require downstream firms to improve the marketing and distribution of their final products.

Studies on FDI and productivity of domestic firms typically find no positive intraindustry spillover effects and may even find negative ones. Aitken and Harrison (1999) use data from Venezuela to study whether domestic firms benefit from FDI and find (a) a positive relationship between increased foreign equity participation and plant performance, suggesting that individual plants do benefit from foreign investment, and (b) a decline in the productivity of domestically owned plants when foreign investment increases, suggesting a negative spillover from foreign to domestic enterprises. A possible explanation is that FDI reduces the share of the market left for domestic firms and that under economies of scale, a smaller output implies a higher average cost. Another is that foreign firms typically select the best workers, leaving less productive workers for the domestic firms. One issue left unresolved, which may affect Aitken and Harrison's results, is causality: that is, does plant performance improve because of FDI, or does FDI go to better-performing plants? Kokko (1996) uses Mexican data to examine whether there are significant spillovers associated with competition effects from foreign presence and finds no significant competition effect.

Haddad and Harrison (1993) find, for Morocco, no significant relationship between higher productivity growth in domestic firms and greater foreign presence in the sector. Djankov and Hoekman (2000) study the effects of FDI on Czech firms and find that foreign investment has the predicted positive impact on local TFP growth of recipient firms but that joint ventures and FDI appear to have a negative spillover effect on firms that do not have foreign partnerships.

Empirical studies have found, however, that FDI generates interindustry spillovers through backward and forward linkages. A foreign firm buying local inputs is likely to help the local upstream firm ensure that these inputs possess some required characteristics or are of a minimum quality. Similarly, the foreign firm may sell inputs that are tailored to the downstream firms and raise their productivity. Kugler (2001) has found this to be the case for Colombian firms, and similar evidence has been found for other developing countries, including Indonesia.

Smarzynska (2000) shows, for transition economies in the early 1990s, that within high- and medium-technology sectors, foreign investors who are leaders in technology and marketing techniques tend to engage in wholly owned projects rather than share ownership, in order to minimize leakage. This result, however, does not hold in low-R&D industries. Smarzynska (2002) also finds for Eastern Europe and the former Soviet Union that weak protection of intellectual property rights (IPRs) deters investors in high-R&D sectors that rely heavily on IPRs and encourages projects that focus on distribution rather than production. A conclusion that can be drawn from this work is that IPR protection is an important component of measures for attracting technology-intensive FDI. We saw in chapter 4 that domestic policy reforms are essential to attract FDI; it would seem that to attract R&D-intensive FDI, RIAs may require good IPR laws.

FDI in the export sector can be expected to be more attractive than in the import-competing sector. First, it is less likely to result in static welfare losses (see chapter 4). Second, it is likely to be internationally competitive, since it exports to the world market, or to benefit from preferential access to partners' markets. The formation of NAFTA has had the effect of attracting FDI in export-oriented activities and is likely to result in a "quality-ladder" phenomenon over time and in increased productivity. MERCOSUR, by contrast, has led to some tariff-jumping FDI, as in the automobile sector, with production of goods that are mainly exported to Brazil and are typically not competitive in OECD countries. These conclusions are supported by the work of Balasubramanyam, Salisu, and Sapsford (1996), who find that the growth effect of FDI is stronger in countries which pursue export-promotion rather than import-substitution policies. The likelihood of FDI going to the export sector can be increased by reducing protection to import-competing sectors.

Cross-Country Evidence on Openness and Growth

Despite the well-known shortcomings of cross-country regression as a research technique—for example, its almost complete inability to establish causation—huge use has been made of it as a tool for exploring the determinants of economic growth. We review here some of the main studies on trade and growth based on cross-country regressions. Many of them have included openness in one form or another, and nearly all have identified a positive relationship between openness and growth. Several of the earlier works in this genre (Dollar 1992; Sachs and Warner 1995a; Edwards 1998) have received rather rough treatment recently at the hands of Rodriguez and Rodrik (2001). The latter argue that these studies' measures of openness are so flawed that the relationship remains unproved, especially as it pertains to the trade dimension of openness as opposed to the macroeconomic (exchange rate) dimension.[4] It is important to note that Rodriguez and Rodrik do not argue that openness hinders growth—there is no general evidence for this proposition—but merely that the positive relationship is not yet fully established. Rodriguez and Rodrik's views have been challenged by Bhagwati and Srinivasan (1999), who argue that since the case for openness was based on far more than cross-country regressions, losing that strand of evidence should not have a great effect on the overall conclusion. Commenting on Rodriguez and Rodrik, Jones (2001) estimates some 100 specifications; he concludes that trade restrictions are harmful to long-run income and that the effects are potentially large, although there is a great deal of uncertainty regarding the magnitude of the effects. He also points out that cross-country growth regressions are a coarse tool for addressing this question.

In an influential study, Frankel and Romer (1999) go to great lengths to sort out the causation between trade and growth. They show that the part of trade attributable to purely exogenous factors such as population size, land area, and distance seems to generate improved growth rates—that large countries close to large markets grow faster. From this, they tentatively infer that other aspects of trade—those attributable to policy—will also boost growth. The latter conclusion seems quite reasonable, since many of the trade barriers that countries impose appear to be analytically equivalent to transport costs, which Frankel and Romer have shown to be inimical to growth.

All the studies mentioned above refer to nondiscriminatory liberalization. The direct evidence that RIAs stimulate growth is weak. Henrekson, Torstensson, and Torstensson (1997) use a cross-sectional regression to suggest that European integration enhanced members' growth rates during the period 1976–85, possibly by as much as 0.6–0.8 percent per year, and that the influence operated through technology transfer rather than through investment. Other commentators have failed to replicate these results, and Baldwin and Venables (1995) state that no study has identified positive growth effects for non-European RIAs. Vamvakidis (1998) shows that the EU's marginally significant positive impact disappears once one has taken the openness of individual member countries into account. Vamvakidis' results are probably more reliable than those of Henrekson, Torstensson, and Torstensson because of his longer time period and because the latter sought to capture general openness via a price distortion index based on Dollar (1992), which Rodriguez and Rodrik (2001) argue is flawed. Vamvakidis does find beneficial effects on a country's growth rate from having large, rich, open neighbors, but this is quite independent of participation in RIAs. Cross-country growth regressions by de Melo, Montenegro, and Panagariya (1993) and by Brada and Mendez (1988) similarly find no growth effects from RIAs over the 1960s to 1980s.

The strongest and most direct approach to identifying the growth effects of non-European RIAs is that of Vamvakidis (1999), who uses panel data to explore whether countries' growth rates changed when they liberalized their trade and compares the 10 years before liberalization with the 10 years after. Vamvakidis finds strong evidence that nondiscriminatory liberalizations boosted growth and that discriminatory ones (that is, RIAs) did not. He did not explore the effects of the RIAs created or revived in the 1990s because data for 10 years after liberalization were not yet available. Leaving aside the possibility that new data would show an improvement, Vamvakidis has provided strong evidence that RIAs are neither good nor bad for growth. His results differ from those based on the technology diffusion model, which indicate that the southern member can gain from a North-South RIA.

AGGLOMERATION AND INDUSTRIALIZATION

Comparative advantage is not the only force that influences the location of activity in an RIA. As economic centers start to develop, cumulative causation mechanisms come into effect, leading to clustering (or agglomeration) of economic activity and extending the advantage of locations that have a head start.[5]

Spatial clustering of economic activities is pervasive. Cities exist because businesses, workers, and consumers benefit from being close together. Particular types of activity are frequently clustered, the most spectacular examples being the concentrations of electronics industries in Silicon Valley, cinema in Hollywood, and banking activities in the world's financial districts. Clustering also occurs in many manufacturing industries—for example, U.S. automobile manufacturing in the Detroit area, and the medical equipment, printing machinery, and other industries studied by Porter (1998).

The Balance between Centripetal and Centrifugal Forces

Clustering or agglomeration typically arises from the interaction between centripetal forces, which encourage firms to locate close to each other, and centrifugal forces, which encourage them to spread out. The centripetal forces are usually classified in three groups (Marshall 1920):

- Knowledge spillovers or other beneficial technological externalities that make it attractive for firms to locate close to each other—in Marshall's phrase, "the mysteries of the trade become no mysteries, but are, as it were, in the air."
- Various labor market–pooling effects, which encourage firms to locate where they can benefit from readily available labor skills.

- Linkages between buyers and sellers. Firms will, other things being equal, want to locate where their customers are, and customers will want to locate close to their suppliers. These linkages are simply Hirschman's (1958) backward (demand) and forward (supply) linkages. They create a positive interdependence between the locational decisions of different firms that can give rise to a process of cumulative causation, creating agglomerations of activity.[6]

These centripetal, or agglomeration, forces can operate at an aggregate level or can be much more narrowly focused. For example, aggregate demand creates a backward linkage, drawing firms from all sectors into locations with large markets. Other forces affect broad classes of business activity: these include availability of basic industrial labor skills and access to business services such as finance and telecommunications. By contrast, knowledge spillovers affecting particular technologies, or the availability of highly specialized inputs, might operate at an industry level. In this case the forces work for clustering of the narrowly defined sector rather than for clustering of manufacturing as a whole.

Pulling in the opposite direction are centrifugal forces, which include congestion, pollution, and other negative externalities that might be associated with concentrations of economic activity. Perhaps the most obvious indicator is the very high rents in major cities. Competition for immobile factors will deter agglomeration, as the price of land (and perhaps also of labor) is bid up in centers of activity. Similarly, the presence of many firms in core areas increases competition and drives down margins. Finally, there are the demands of consumers who are not located in the centers of activity; dispersed consumers will encourage dispersion of producers, particularly if trade barriers or transport costs are high.

Trade Liberalization Can Aid Industrialization

Trade liberalization affects the balance of the centripetal and centrifugal forces through at least three mechanisms (Puga and Venables 1997, 1998; see also box 5.1): (a) reductions in a country's import barriers improve the market access of firms located in its partner countries; (b) opening a country's markets to increased product market competition from foreign firms reduces the profitability of local firms; (c) lower import barriers mean cheaper imported intermediate goods and hence higher local profitability. The mix of these effects depends on the type and extent of liberalization—unilateral, multilateral, or regional—and on the relative strengths of the centrifugal and centripetal forces.

Box 5.1 Modeling the Agglomeration Effects of RIAs

Puga and Venables (1998) outline a new approach for studying the effects of different types of trade liberalization (multilateral, unilateral, regional, and so forth) on the industrialization process in developing countries. Although their model is highly stylized, it provides the first formalization of phenomena that have long been discussed at an intuitive level.

The authors consider a three-country model containing a large northern country and two small southern ones. Each country has two sectors: a perfectly competitive homogeneous commodity sector ("agriculture") and a monopolistically competitive industry ("manufactures") in which firms produce several varieties of differentiated products. In addition to real trade costs, ad valorem tariffs are imposed on all trade flows in manufactures; trade in agricultural produce is free. For simplicity, Puga and Venables choose their initial parameter values such that at the status quo ante equilibrium, the two southern countries produce only agricultural products and no manufactures. From that starting point, they solve the model for progressively lower tariff barriers. Trade liberalization always attracts industry to the South, but the timing and magnitude of industrialization differ depending on the type of liberalization and on the centripetal and centrifugal forces.

Under multilateral trade liberalization, industry initially starts up in only one of the two southern economies; agglomeration economies make it unprofitable to maintain two new locations before one has achieved a reasonable size. As trade barriers continue to decline, it becomes profitable for manufacturing to set up in the other southern country as well, partly at the expense of the first, which suffers a small fall in its share of world industry. At tariffs below that point, the southern economies are identical, and further reductions in tariffs bring a steady relocation of industry from the North to both economies. Unilateral liberalization by the developing countries also promotes their industrialization because it makes for cheaper intermediate inputs from the North, but its effects are weaker than those of multilateral liberalization because the market access dimension is lacking.

Membership in an RIA may or may not be better than unilateral reform. South-South RIAs will be sensitive to the market size of member states, but above a critical level, industry establishes in both partners because of the effective enlargement induced by the reciprocal reduction in intra-South barriers. The spread of industry is uneven, however, with industry initially developing in one of the countries and spreading to the second only when trade barriers are lower. The southern economies attract less industry than they would under multilateral liberalization because they do not benefit from greater access to the northern market or to intermediate goods produced in the North.

Compared with a South-South arrangement, a North-South RIA offers better prospects for the participating southern country. Industry spreads more quickly and to a larger extent because the southern economy benefits from both improved access to the northern market and the low cost of intermediates. In this model, with only one northern market or supplier, the participating southern country is better off in a North-South RIA than under multilateral liberalization. Both deliver the same market access and cheap intermediates, but under the RIA, competition is weaker because the excluded southern country is presumed to receive neither advantage. And even if the participating country is better off than under multilateral liberalization, the South as a whole is worse off because the excluded South does not receive any industry.

Multilateral reduction of trade barriers can increase the profitability of industrial location in developing countries by decreasing the price of imported intermediate goods and offering firms better access to larger developed country markets. It can, however, also reduce profitability by making markets more competitive. The first two effects, combined with large wage differences between northern and southern countries, can dominate and cause industry to move to the South. As the world trading system has become more open, industrial production has gradually moved from the United States, Western Europe, and Japan to developing countries in Latin America, Southeast Asia, and Eastern Europe. The spread has been quite uneven across developing countries, since the stronger centripetal forces in middle-income countries make them more attractive as industrial locations. For example, in 1995 Asia, with 33 percent of the developing world's total income, received 65 percent of all FDI flows to developing countries, while Latin America (with 31 percent of total income) got 27 percent and Africa (8 percent of total income) only 5 percent.

Unilateral trade liberalization by one developing country can attract industry and bring real income gains, despite more intense import competition, if the availability of cheaper imported intermediate goods becomes a dominant force. Industry will develop sooner, and on a larger scale, the greater is the share of intermediates in production and the larger is the market in the liberalizing economy. The spread of industry to the South, however, is likely to be slower than under multilateral liberalization, as unilateral liberalization does not improve developing countries' access to large northern markets.[7]

Preferential trade liberalization affects both the locational attractiveness of the bloc relative to the rest of the world and the relative attractiveness of individual bloc members. An RIA increases the locational advantage of its members at the expense of the excluded countries; it allows member country firms to sell their output and buy their inputs on larger markets, setting off beneficial centripetal forces and pulling production and industry into the bloc and away from countries outside the RIA (Puga and Venables 1997, 1998).[8] The strength of these effects will depend on the size and nature of the integrated market (that is, its combined income and output and the depth of its integration), and many developing country RIAs will be too small to have significant locational effects. For example, none of the active African RIAs has a GDP larger than Belgium's; UEMOA's GDP is less than 10 percent of Belgium's GDP, CEMAC's is less than 4 percent, and even the SADC's is less than 65 percent. Recalling the economies of scale arguments that are commonly made for European integration, it is plain that for many industries, such groups are well below the necessary size for attracting industry.

Moreover, even for industries where scale requirements are low, many South-South RIAs have failed to attract activity because, at least until recently, they have lacked the institutional preconditions. In most African RIAs, not only are markets too small but, in addition, infrastructure is poor, a sound legal framework is lacking, progress in economic reform has been slow, there is heavy government intervention, the private sector is small and fragile, and economic and political instability are common. We argued in the preceding chapter that addressing these matters is the key to investment, and the same is true for industrial agglomeration. Unilateral reforms to achieve a sound business environment are the sine qua non of industrial development and are far more important than regional integration issues of any hue.

Intermember Distribution: Divergence Is Likely in South-South RIAs

Turning to the internal distribution of industry, we need to ask how regional integration affects the balance between centripetal and centrifugal forces. Can membership bring about or amplify the clustering of economic activity, and if so, might it widen income differentials between partner countries?

By reducing trade barriers, membership in an RIA makes it easier to supply customers from a few locations. This suggests that the balance of forces may be tipped in favor of agglomeration, although the ensuing relocation of industry could develop in several different ways.

One possibility is that particular sectors become more spatially concentrated. This is likely if the centripetal forces act at a narrow sectoral level. For example, industries in the United States are much more spatially concentrated than in Europe, even controlling for the distribution of population and of manufacturing as a whole. This difference suggests that further regional integration in Europe could cause agglomeration at the sectoral level—for example, Germany gets engineering, financial services cluster in the United Kingdom, and so on. The possibility that this might happen is generating some concern in Europe, although the evidence for it is so far rather weak (see Midelfart Knarvik and others 1999). If it does happen, it will create considerable adjustment costs as the industrial structure of different locations changes, but it will also yield aggregate benefits because of the real efficiency gains from spatial concentration. This sectoral agglomeration need not be associated with increases in intra-RIA inequalities; each country or region may attract activity in some sectors.

An alternative possibility is that instead of there being relatively small sectors, each clustering in different locations, manufacturing as a whole comes to cluster in one or a few locations, leading to deindustrialization of the less favored regions. This outcome is more likely, the smaller is manufacturing as a whole—either because it is a small share of the economies or because the economies are small overall. Small sectors need to concentrate to create critical mass, and if, in addition, the share of manufacturing is small, fitting the whole of manufacturing into one or a few locations is less likely to encounter factor supply constraints and to lead to rising prices of immobile factors such as land. Concentration will also be more likely if linkages are broad, across many industrial sectors, rather than narrowly sector specific. This situation is more apt to occur in early stages of development, when a country's basic industrial infrastructure—transport, telecommunications, and access to financial markets and other business services—is thinly developed and unevenly spread.

This suggests the real possibility that RIA membership could lead to agglomeration and divergence between member countries, reinforcing the effects of comparative advantage discussed in chapter 3. It seems likely that both comparative advantage and agglomeration are at work in some South-South RIAs, with both forces leading industry to agglomerate in the relatively richer and initially more industrialized members. As Nairobi, Abidjan, and Dakar have attracted manufacturing, so they have started to develop business networks and the linkages that tend to lock manufacturing into the location. The process might be further accelerated by the propensity of FDI to cluster in relatively few locations. Agglomeration then accentuates the forces for divergence that we outlined above.

Industry agglomeration in a subset of member countries can create tensions within an RIA. Several South-South RIAs have failed because of disputes over the location of industry and the design of compensation schemes for perceived losers. In the 1950s and 1960s severe frictions between Kenya, Tanzania, and Uganda arose over the benefits from economic integration within the East African Community. Uganda and Tanzania contended that all the gains were going to Kenya, which was steadily enhancing its position as the industrial center of the common market, producing 70 percent of the manufactures and exporting a growing percentage of them to its two relatively less developed partners. By 1958, 404 of the 474 companies registered in East Africa were located in Kenya. By 1960, Kenya's manufacturing sector accounted for 10 percent of its gross national product (GNP); in the other two states the share of manufacturing was 4 percent (Hansen 1969). The community collapsed in 1977, having failed to satisfy the poorer members that they were getting a fair share of the gains.

In other circumstances agglomeration forces can help offset the divergences associated with comparative advantage. For example, firms choosing a location in NAFTA may want both the agglomeration bene-fits of locating in the United States and the factor price advantages of Mexico, but the latter may predominate. Thus, in North-South arrange-ments the South could become a preferred location for assembly indus-tries (for example, automobiles) or subcontracting industries such as textiles, possibly in export-processing zones. This happened with the growth of automotive assembly plants (maquiladoras) south of the U.S.-Mexico border: major investments (exceeding US$500 million) in new capacity and plant expansions in Mexico by Japanese, German, and Ital-ian auto parts producers benefited from NAFTA-related changes in Mex-ico's Auto Decree that liberalized foreign investment restrictions in the sector and provided access to Mexican and Latin American markets (USITC 1997).

These examples suggest that from the point of view of the participat-ing developing economy, North-South arrangements are better than South-South ones because they give a southern economy the benefits of both improved access to a large northern market and low-cost northern intermediates. For the same reasons, southern economies attract more in-dustry under multilateral trade liberalization than under South-South schemes. In fact, it is possible that a North-South RIA will generate more industry for the southern economy than would a multilateral liberaliza-tion, depending, among other things, on how important the northern partner is in the South's total exports. Where this happens, however, it is at the expense of excluded southern countries, which industrialize more slowly because they neither gain market access nor liberalize their own regimes (see box 5.1).

There are also likely to be locational effects within member countries. The strongest example is probably Mexico, where liberalization and ac-cession to NAFTA have shifted the center of economic gravity from Mexico City to the northern border. Krugman and Elizondo (1996) have argued that closed economies such as pre-1986 Mexico are more prone to extreme agglomeration because the only linkages are domestic ones. The Mexican trade liberalization vis-à-vis the rest of the world started to undermine the dominance of Mexico City and to disperse industry to other locations in the country. This was supplemented by the increasing importance of the United States as a trading and production-chain part-ner as it introduced border preferences and subsequently signed NAFTA (see box 5.2).

An important final point is that agglomeration forces will be strongest at intermediate levels of trade barriers (or transport costs). When barri-ers are very high, each country will have its own industry to supply local

---

Box 5.2 The Influence of Regionalism on Within-Country Location: North America

If the main nonpolicy barriers to trade are transport costs, economic integration should increase economic activity in border cities (Hanson 1996). The lure of frontier regions is stronger if production of final goods uses foreign intermediate inputs. After the U.S. Automotive Products Trade Act of 1965 eliminated barriers on motor vehicle trade with Canada, motor vehicle production expanded along the Michigan-Ontario corridor.

Integration with the United States has had strong effects on industrial location in Mexico, where industry has shifted toward states with good access to the U.S. market. This integration has been effectively under way since the mid-1980s, when Mexico removed most barriers to foreign trade and lifted restrictions on foreign ownership. Mexico has developed a large export-manufacturing industry that specializes in the assembly and processing of foreign-made components. A large part of this industry imports most of its inputs from, and ships most of its output back to, U.S. firms. The plants are overwhelmingly concentrated in Mexican cities on or near the U.S.-Mexico border. Employment growth has been higher in regions that have larger agglomerations of industries with buyer-supplier relationships with U.S. firms (Hanson 1998).

The growth of export production in Mexican border cities also makes U.S. border cities natural sites for complementary manufacturing activities, and production activities in the United States are relocating accordingly. U.S. border cities specialize in the industries that produce parts and components for Mexican assembly plants. Hanson (1996) argues that NAFTA, by further lowering trade barriers, is likely to contribute to the further expansion of the binational production centers that are forming along the border. He finds that employment growth in U.S. border cities is positively correlated with employment growth in Mexican export assembly plants.

---

consumers. When they are very low, firms go where labor costs are cheapest because they can bring in their inputs and ship their output at very low cost, as with the production networks described in box 5.1. But where barriers are intermediate, firms are reluctant to move away from suppliers and other agglomeration benefits, yet they are able to supply foreign markets through exports.

NOTES

1. Coe and Helpman (1995) and Coe, Helpman, and Hoffmaister (1997) assume, rather than ascertain by testing, that imports from industrial countries provide the correct weights with which to combine those countries' stocks of foreign knowledge to reflect importers' access to it. Keller (1998) finds that Coe and Helpman's results are little better than can be obtained through a random weighting. Lumenga-Neso, Olarreaga, and Schiff (2001), who extend the Coe and Helpman approach by taking indirect knowledge spillovers into account, obtain results that strongly dominate those of Coe and Helpman and weakly dominate Keller's. Coe and Hoffmaister (1999) show that the weights used by Keller were not truly random and find that Coe and Helpman's results are superior to

those obtained with random weights, in which case R&D spillover effects are nonexistent. Both sets of results suggest that trade is an important channel for knowledge spillovers, although the testing of alternative hypotheses remains to be conducted.

2. Schiff and Wang (2002c) show that Poland obtains larger TFP gains by trading with the United States and Canada than by trading with the EU.

3. Schiff and Wang (2002b) tested whether the difference in effects was attributable to NAFTA itself by allowing the various parameters to differ in the post-NAFTA period from the pre-NAFTA one. None of the parameters was found to be significantly different in the later period.

4. Commenting on Rodriguez and Rodrik, Hsieh (2001) provides suggestive evidence that restrictions on capital goods imports have important adverse effects on growth, particularly in developing countries. This is consistent with the findings of Coe, Helpman, and Hoffmaister (1997).

5. This section is based on Fujita, Krugman, and Venables (1999).

6. This argument only works if there are increasing returns to scale in production; if there are not, firms can put small plants in many different locations.

7. For many goods, such access is already pretty free, so unilateralism is not completely stymied.

8. Of course, these effects are in addition to the (positive or negative) resource allocation effects analyzed in chapters 2 and 3.

CHAPTER 6

Integrating Domestic Policies*

Cooperation on domestic policies can substantially increase the gains from forming a trade bloc. It can lift barriers that insulate national markets and deliver economic benefits many times those available from preferential trade agreements. Intergovernmental cooperation in designing and applying domestic policies such as taxes, health and safety regulations, environmental standards, and so on—what we call policy integration—can increase competition in domestic markets by reducing transactions costs and allowing new suppliers to enter markets. Cooperation on domestic policies can also help in overcoming market failures and ensuring that trade restrictions are not reimposed through the back door.

Most existing RIAs aim only to reduce market segmentation by constraining the use of national policies rather than by actively integrating them. The main exceptions are the EU and the Closer Economic Relations (CER) agreement between Australia and New Zealand. A number of other RIAs, including some still under construction, are beginning to discuss policy integration. But without specific timetables for action and further negotiation, neither new nor existing RIAs are likely to make great progress. Experience suggests that negotiated policy integration is very demanding, both politically and technically.

An RIA can assist policy integration by providing an institutional framework and by making available sources of gain that may help overcome opposition to policy reforms. Similarly, policy integration can assist the implementation and enforcement of the trade component of an RIA,

* *This chapter was co-authored by Bernard Hoekman.*

147

which (provided that the trade provisions are desirable) could be a major gain. Regulatory policies are even more vulnerable to capture than are trade policies, however. Care is required to prevent such policy-bundling from merely creating rents for the few at the expense of the many.

Competition between regulatory regimes, coupled with partners' mutual recognition of each other's standards or regulations, can be a useful approach to policy integration, but it is not without its challenges. Harmonization may still be called for in some dimensions to avoid adverse spillovers, such as the threat of a "race to the bottom," or threats to public health or safety. Such harmonization is generally best limited to minimum standards based on global norms; idiosyncratic regional standards will be optimal only if region-specific characteristics exist. Mutual recognition agreements, whereby countries agree to treat goods meeting partners' standards as if they met their own, can easily become barriers to trade with nonpartners. Wherever possible, policy integration to reduce regulatory costs should extend beyond RIA partners to nonmembers so as to maximize the increase in competition. Certainly, formal intergovernmental agreements are necessary for some elements of policy integration, but special efforts should be made to avoid perpetuating or increasing de facto discrimination.

Moreover, RIAs are not the only route to policy integration; much can be done to reduce transactions costs and facilitate market access by adopting international standards and best practices unilaterally and by participating in multilateral fora with global membership. Indeed, unilateralism and multilateralism have been more common than regional approaches toward coordinating technical and regulatory standards. Developing countries can achieve many of the benefits of policy integration unilaterally by adopting international standards and recognizing the regulatory norms of their major markets or suppliers such as the EU and the United States.

For this reason, the WTO and other multilateral institutions play a large role in policy integration. The WTO agenda is as broad as, or broader than, that of most RIAs, and more can be done in the WTO context than is sometimes recognized. The WTO could help further by requiring members to apply the MFN principle to policy integration initiatives that do not require formal intergovernmental equivalency or recognition agreements, such as customs clearance documentation and procedures.

Policy integration proposals are very specific and should be evaluated on their individual merits. Care should be taken to ensure that they are for the general good. Except as part of a necessary coalition for achieving reform, efforts to link them to regional trade liberalization should be resisted. While integrating domestic policies may sometimes require formal agreements, there is no fundamental reason why it should require trade preferences. The United States and the EU, for instance, have drawn up a series of mutual recognition agreements for sectoral product standards completely outside an RIA context. To date, however, developing countries have been entirely excluded from such initiatives.

This chapter explores the role that regulatory policy interaction between RIA members could play in developing country RIAs. It draws mainly on EU experience, since that is by far the most advanced example to hand. Its main conclusion is that policy integration offers scope for considerable gains, but only at the expense of very hard political and technical work and at the risk of exacerbating rather than erasing distortions. Because of the difficulties of achieving policy integration, governments should not casually assume that deep integration will automatically make their RIAs welfare-enhancing. They will need to be both determined and well informed if integration is to be turned to good effect. Governments should also be alert to the opportunities for reducing transactions costs and market segmentation held out by multilateral organizations and unilateral action.

DEFINING POLICY INTEGRATION

In this section we define policy integration and discuss the modalities available for pursuing it. We distinguish between agreements that treat foreign goods or firms exactly the same as domestic ones (which is not policy integration) from those that involve negotiating how both sets of goods or firms are treated (which is). We then distinguish between intergovernmental coordination of policies, harmonization of standards across countries, and recognition by governments of each other's standards as approaches to policy integration. We largely ignore the first approach, which is essentially ad hoc and nonbinding, and concentrate on the remaining two. In addition, because our focus is on the international trade dimensions of RIAs, we also ignore government cooperation on nonregulatory matters such as infrastructure and water resource management and on issues of monetary integration. Both are hugely important but lie outside the boundaries of this book.[1]

The Baseline: National Treatment

National treatment requires that foreign products or producers, once they have entered a territory, receive the same treatment as domestic counterparts with respect to taxes, health and safety standards, competition rules, and so on. National treatment has always been a basic building block of international trade treaties. It ensures that liberalization commitments cannot be circumvented by the discriminatory application of domestic policies, such as an excise tax that is higher for foreign than for domestic products.

National treatment does not constrain a government's policy sovereignty per se; it merely precludes discrimination in favor of domestic suppliers and allows foreign goods, services, and factors to compete with domestic ones on an equal basis. It can have particularly far-reaching effects if it is applied to services and factor markets. Although much rarer than preferential agreements in goods, stand-alone agreements have been used to create common markets for factors of production. For example, Denmark, Finland, Iceland, Norway, and Sweden operate a common labor market that has eliminated immigration controls for their residents. Similarly, the 1973 Trans-Tasman Travel Arrangement gives citizens of Australia and New Zealand the right to work and reside in either country. In both instances, the common labor market is underpinned by agreements on health services and social security, illustrating that agreements in the labor area are multidimensional packages.

As we saw in chapter 4, national treatment has also been important for investment flows, assuring investors that governments will not discriminate against them after they have invested. RIAs vary in the extent to which they offer national treatment to investors, with the EU, NAFTA, and the EU's Europe Agreements going farthest toward abolishing performance criteria and related policies such as local content and trade-balancing requirements. Only the EU has completely liberalized market access and entry by foreign firms across the board, although U.S. investment treaties normally seek such pre-establishment rights at a sectoral level and the Doha Development Agenda, agreed on at the WTO ministerial conference in 2001, calls for WTO members to consider extending these rights. As has been noted, however, RIAs are far from necessary for establishing investment agreements. There exist many stand-alone investment agreements and a few multilateral ones.

Beyond National Treatment: Policy Integration

Policy integration involves deliberate actions by governments to go beyond national treatment and seek to reduce the market-segmenting effect of regulatory regimes through coordination, harmonization, or mutual recognition of national policies and enforcement mechanisms (box 6.1).

Box 6.1 Defining Terms: "Deep" and "Shallow" Integration

The term "shallow" integration is sometimes used to describe integration based on national treatment. "Deep" integration (the term favored by Lawrence and Litan 1990) then refers to efforts that go beyond that. Tinbergen (1954) coined the terms "negative" and "positive" integration, which correspond, basically, to shallow and deep integration. Negative integration entails removal and limitation of policies, as distinguished from positive efforts to coordinate them.

The terms "deep" or "positive" are misleading if used to suggest that this type of cooperation is more profound, far-reaching, binding, or beneficial than integration based on national treatment. This is not necessarily so. "Deep" cooperation may be limited to only a few areas of little economic consequence. It may even be welfare reducing for one or more members of an RIA if it involves the adoption of rules that are suboptimal from a national perspective. In this volume we reserve the term "deep integration" for agreements such as the EU that aim at achieving some measure of economic union and that create supranational institutions for pursuing this goal. The more general term "policy integration" is used for less far reaching cooperation on domestic policies and regulations.

It can be pursued unilaterally or cooperatively. International cooperation is generally driven by market access concerns and by recognition that increased competition will bring economic benefits. Experience suggests that a mix of harmonization and mutual recognition is required to achieve policy integration where the underlying regulatory policies have national health, safety, or prudential objectives.

Modes of Policy Integration: Coordination, Harmonization, and Recognition

The principal instruments of policy integration are coordination, harmonization, and acceptance ("recognition") of foreign regulatory regimes. Countries can cooperate on domestic policies through commercial agreements to facilitate trade and investment flows or by pursuing more far-reaching economic unions that require them to cede sovereignty to supranational institutions which develop and enforce rules. With the notable exception of the EU, existing RIAs are primarily commercial instruments that do not aim at economic union. Policy integration, if pursued, is intergovernmental and issue specific, driven by a realization that there are potential gains from cooperation in a particular area.

Coordination of Domestic Policies. Coordination is the least far-reaching type of policy integration. It is limited to efforts by governments or regulatory bodies to cooperate in developing or implementing a norm or rule, and it involves "voluntary and largely unenforceable alignments of national policies and measures in particular fields" (Robson 1998). Coordination may be based on formal agreements on, for example, the use of the principle of positive comity in the application of competition law, or may be ad hoc, as in cooperation on infrastructure projects.[2] We do not discuss coordination further in this book, as it implies no binding commitment on the part of governments.

Harmonization of National Standards and Regulations. Harmonization may involve unilateral adoption by one country (or RIA) of another's set of rules, or negotiation of a common set of disciplines. Examples abound of unilateral harmonization to the standard of another country or RIA. These cases are often driven by market-size disparities. For example, in 1992 Canada adopted U.S. auto emissions standards to ensure that its automakers could realize economies of scale by avoiding separate production lines for its home and U.S. markets. Switzerland, similarly, adopted the EU regime on technical regulations and industrial standards so that Swiss goods could enter and circulate in the EU on the same basis as EU-produced goods (Messerlin 1998).

Many developing countries use legal regimes developed in Europe or the United States, usually maintaining systems inherited from a colonial past or military occupation. Others have deliberately adopted foreign norms. Korea imported many German and U.S. product standards in the 1950s as part of a strategy for upgrading the quality of industrial production and fostering exports.

Harmonization between more equal partners requires a deeper institutional setting. Efforts to set common norms may be limited to intergovernmental cooperation or may involve a decision to cede sovereignty to common or supranational institutions for rule-setting. In the EU the power to propose directives and regulations (that is, to propose rules) has been delegated to the European Commission, and the European Court of Justice has strong supranational powers of enforcement. In NAFTA harmonization is limited to member states' acceptance of binding independent third-party adjudication or arbitration on disputes about rules, which is much less intrusive than the EU arrangements.

Recognition of Foreign Regulatory Regimes and Conformity Assessment Procedures. For a country that sets certain norms for goods and services within its borders, the natural first thought is to test imports on entry. It is, however, potentially very costly to devise and enforce standards, and so there are incentives to cooperate with trading partners. Unilateral recognition of foreign regulatory regimes is the simplest route: a country just adopts international norms or the standards of a trading partner. Thus, a government may decide that the professional qualifications of doctors trained and certified in certain countries are sufficient to allow them to practice in the country (although other constraints may still restrict entry by foreign services providers). Similarly, foreign certification for certain imports may be accepted as proof of safety; the Underwriters Laboratories (UL) mark, for example, is accepted in many countries. The key to unilateral recognition is familiarity with and trust in partner standards and certification systems.

Where familiarity or trust are weaker, or where, for nationalistic or mercantilist reasons, partners are not willing simply to adopt each other's standards, mutual recognition agreements (MRAs) are a possibility. These entail each member's recognizing its partners' standards as acceptable inside its own boundaries, but without applying them to its domestic suppliers. MRAs can cover either the standards themselves or the conformity assessment systems used to establish compliance with standards.

Harmonization as a tool of policy integration and the idea of relying on the principle of mutual recognition to facilitate trade have been pursued most intensively by the EU. MRAs may be required even if a unilateral harmonization strategy is followed, as the trading partner whose standards are emulated may not accept foreign test results or conformity assessment systems as equivalent to its own even if the formal standards are identical. Conversely, European experience suggests that mutual recognition may require some degree of harmonization of either standards or testing procedures to ensure that the underlying norms satisfy basic minimum standards, especially in areas where mandatory standards or regulations apply (see box 6.2).

Mutual recognition has proved a useful tool for increasing competition in European markets, but even there it has turned out to be hard work (see Messerlin 2001), and it may not be viable at all for developing country RIAs. The process relies heavily on mutual trust in the competence and ability of the institutions responsible for enforcing mandatory standards and on a willingness to accept some compromise in setting minimum standards. Even if developing countries adopt EU, U.S., or international standards, significant institutional strengthening is likely to be required before developed country governments will accept "home country supervision." Alternatively, greater reliance could be placed on third-party conformity assessment of goods and services.

Box 6.2 Harmonization and Mutual Recognition as Substitutes or Complements: The EU Experience

Article 36 of the Treaty of Rome permits EU members to maintain domestic policies that restrict trade if necessary for protecting national health, security, or morals or the environment. Virtually all RIAs have similar provisions. Initially, the EU sought to limit the market-segmenting effects of national regulations under Article 36 through a process of harmonization. Many of the early efforts toward harmonization centered on food standards—the first harmonization directive, issued in 1962, dealt with food coloring. Progress toward harmonization was very slow, in part because adoption of an EU-wide norm required unanimity. It took over a decade to reach agreement on the composition of fruit jams and mineral water, and only nine directives on foodstuffs were adopted between 1962 and 1979. Differences in national norms, reflecting national tastes, histories, and legal regimes—and the efforts of producer lobbies seeking to restrict competition from imports—made it difficult to achieve the required consensus. For example, the Germans set great store by their *Reinheitsgebot*, a standard established in 1516 specifying that beer may have only four ingredients: malted barley, hops, yeast, and water. Other countries permit preservatives or additives.

The result of such differences was that little progress was made toward reducing the market-segmenting effects of national standards. Indeed, member states continued to adopt numerous inconsistent and idiosyncratic product regulations. In a landmark 1979 case the European Court of Justice found that a German ban on the sale of a French Cassis de Dijon used to prepare kir, an aperitif, could not be justified on the basis of public safety or health. This established the principle, later incorporated into the 1987 Single European Act, that goods legally introduced into circulation in one member state could not be barred from entering and being sold in another.

The EU's "new approach" to standards, which dates from 1985, differentiates standards that have health and safety (public interest) dimensions from those that do not. For the latter, governments must recognize other members' regulations as equivalent to their own. For the former, rather than full harmonization, members agreed on a process of determining common minimum standards ("essential requirements"). Moreover, as part of the Single Market Programme, standards became subject to qualified majority voting rather than unanimity. Between 1987 and 1995, 28 new-approach directives were adopted specifying essential requirements. Meanwhile, under the old approach, which also became subject to majority voting, adoptions increased from an average of 12.5 a year over 1958–85 to 20.8 a year over 1986–97 (Pelkmans 1990; Neven 1996). Even at these rates, standards are likely to remain a significant barrier for some years.

Clearly, mutual recognition cannot wholly replace harmonization as an approach to standards. In many cases harmonization is required to define "essential requirements," and governments will not agree to mutual recognition if they feel that vital interests are at stake. Moreover, it is not correct to argue, as Torrent (2002) does, that mutual recognition is merely another route to harmonization. Where the differences between standards are minor or concern unimportant dimensions, governments may be prepared to accept other members' standards as long as their own are accepted elsewhere in return, even if in a full harmonization negotiation they would feel obliged to hold out for their own positions.

THE ECONOMICS OF POLICY INTEGRATION

Policy integration can benefit countries by reducing transactions costs. This saves resources from being wasted on unproductive activities, lowers market access barriers, and integrates segmented national markets for similar goods and services, all of which increases the degree of competition. Well-executed policy integration can benefit both RIA partners and, on occasion, producers in the rest of the world. In this section we discuss five elements of the economics of policy integration: transactions costs, increased competition, spillovers (externalities), compensation of losers, and identification of the appropriate geographic level for cooperation. Most candidate policies for integration contain elements of several of these issues.

Transactions Costs

Domestic regulations can segment markets by impeding foreign firms from competing with national ones. This may be deliberate or may simply be a side effect of a policy objective. For example, health and safety standards may entail duplicative testing and conformity assessment in both exporting and importing countries. Customs procedures may also be duplicative or redundant: tax authorities in an exporting country may require data very similar to that demanded by the importer's customs officials, but in a different format. All such administrative requirements impose transactions costs on enterprises that engage in international exchange and raise consumer prices.

Border Formalities. It has been estimated that in the early 1990s the costs of border formalities affecting intra-EU trade (which was already mostly duty free except for some goods originating in Portugal and Spain) were equivalent to more than 1.2 percent of the gross value of internally traded goods (European Commission 1997). And intra-EU trade procedures were efficient compared with those in many other countries. In 1988 the EU had already adopted a Single Administrative Document (the EUR-1 form), and many members had simplified their procedures to reduce customs burdens for large traders. Similarly, in intra-EFTA trade, Herin (1986) estimated that complying with rules of origin cost an average of 3 percent of the value of a transaction, even though for such administrative tasks, EFTA was probably one of the cheapest places in the world.

Standards Certification. Standards represent another potential source of large gains from the reduction of transactions costs. Over 60 percent of U.S. exports are subject to health, safety, and related standards in their destination markets. Government-issued certificates are required for 45 percent of exports to the EU; private third-party certification is accepted for 15 percent; and manufacturers' self-certification suffices for the rest (Wilson 1996: 7). Within the EU, about 75 percent of the value of intra-EU trade in goods is subject to mandatory technical regulations

(European Commission 1996). Certification in regulated sectors can involve frequent and redundant sampling of products—sometimes up to 100 percent of foreign goods—and this can effectively block imports.

Duplicative testing and certification requirements have rapidly become more important as barriers to international trade. Unter (1998) estimates that redundant testing and conformity assessment procedures faced by Hewlett-Packard increased sixfold over 1990–97. The EU now requires third-party testing, certification, or quality system registration for certain regulated sectors. It will accept certification only by organizations that have been approved by the member states as being technically competent and that have been notified as such to the European Commission. This considerably raises the costs for non-EU manufacturers in many sectors. Avoidance of these costs was a prime motivation for the EU-U.S. MRA negotiations.

EU-U.S. trade talks on mutual recognition of conformity assessment began in 1992, with the aim of ensuring that assessments performed by independent entities would be accepted in both markets. The EU sought assurance that U.S. certifiers were competent to test for EU "essential requirements" and that European firms could test and certify to the corresponding U.S. regulatory requirements. On its side, the United States sought to eliminate the costs of exporters' having to obtain certification by EU-approved bodies in addition to meeting U.S. requirements. The EU's increasingly communitywide approach to standardization did, however, mean that U.S. firms now had to seek only one certificate for all EU markets, which greatly increased the returns to negotiating an agreement.

Significant differences in European and U.S. testing and certification systems made agreement difficult. The European system relies less on firms' self-declarations of conformity, and more on mandatory third-party testing and certification, than does the U.S. system. As of 1998, member states had certified only 600 testing bodies to the European Commission out of a total of over 10,000 such bodies in existence, ranging from large multinationals such as SGS, Inchcape, and Bureau Vertitas to small in-house testing facilities. Virtually all those approved were European (Messerlin 1998).

In June 1997 the United States and the EU concluded an MRA that covered conformity requirements in telecommunications equipment, information technology products, medical devices, and pharmaceuticals and that was expected to address acceptance of test data, laboratory accreditation, and final product certification. After a two-year period, certifications performed anywhere by a facility recognized under the MRA in the United States or Europe were to be accepted.

The agreements cover more than $40 billion of bilateral trade. The MRA on telecommunications and information technology products alone could save consumers and manufacturers approximately $1.4 billion, implying that the frictional costs abolished were equivalent to a 5 percent tax on the goods traded (Wilson 1999). Although this is a significant cost reduction, the MRAs are regarded as a second-best solution by U.S. industry, which would prefer to rely much more heavily on supplier self-certification instead of third-party conformity assessment.

MRAs have been a much less satisfactory route for developing and transition countries seeking to reduce standards-related costs in the EU. Their own standards are not acceptable in the EU, and they find it difficult to prove that their testing institutions are reliable. The Europe Agreements, signed from 1992 on between the EU and the Central and East European countries, recognized the possibility of concluding MRAs. By 1995–96, however, the EU had decided to push instead for complete harmonization, at least in part because it felt that recognizing transition economy standards, some of which were suspected of protectionist intent, would cause significant difficulties.[3] Progress on complete harmonization has been very slow.

One transition economy, the Czech Republic, cut through the impasse with respect to its own imports by applying the principle of "one standard, one test, supplier's declaration of conformity" (Unter 1998). Under this approach, goods that satisfy international standards and are accompanied by a supplier's declaration (based on in-house or third-party tests) that the product conforms to the relevant standard may enter the country without additional testing.

Frictional Transactions Costs. A key aspect of many of the procedural and administrative requirements ("red tape") that slow trade and movement across frontiers is that they raise the border prices of goods and services. This distinguishes these "real trade costs" from measures such as import duties and quantitative import restrictions that raise the costs of goods to consumers but do not affect border prices. Duties and quantitative restrictions generate revenue for the state or rents for those who obtain the right to import. No rents or revenues are generated if a measure simply imposes additional costs by requiring firms to spend resources that could otherwise be used productively. As a result, the domestic welfare benefits of eliminating frictional barriers can be significantly higher than those from the abolition of tariffs (see the appendix to chapter 2).

Any determination of the welfare implications of policy integration for RIA members must consider the extent to which the regulatory barriers that are being reduced are frictional. It must also establish whether the reduction in frictional costs applies to all trade. This is difficult to do with precision. Efforts to quantify the effects of differential standardization, duplicative testing requirements, and excessive controls and inefficiencies in customs clearance in the EU suggest that these barriers may easily give rise to a "tax" of up to 2 percent of the value of the goods shipped. In a developing country the figure can be a multiple of this; estimates of the average cost range up to 10 percent of the transaction value (WTO 1998). In Egypt in the early 1990s customs red tape was a significant barrier to trade; redundant testing and idiosyncratic standards alone imposed taxes equivalent to between 5 and 90 percent of the value of specific shipments of goods subject to mandatory standards. Reducing these frictional barriers through an RIA with the EU would give Egypt an estimated welfare gain equal to 4 percent of GDP, compared with no change if the FTA were limited to abolishing tariffs (Hoekman and Konan 1999).

Maximizing the Benefits of Policy Integration through Nondiscrimination. As chapter 2 made clear, lowering tariffs on partner goods can lead to welfare-reducing trade diversion, but if markets are competitive, reducing purely frictional barriers within an RIA cannot reduce welfare. If frictional barriers are reduced on a nondiscriminatory rather than preferential (members-only) basis, the gains will be correspondingly larger because all traders, regardless of location, will benefit from the cost reductions. Many administrative simplification and harmonization measures designed to facilitate customs clearance and trade can be, and generally are, applied to nonmembers as well as members of an RIA. Of course, nondiscrimination will not obtain if the required policy integration can *only* be achieved through formal agreements between governments to accept each other's regulatory regimes and apply common administrative procedures or substantive requirements. In such cases the benefits can be extended by allowing nonmembers to conclude parallel agreements with RIA members—ideally, as a matter of course. Agreements such as MRAs regarding health, safety, and prudential conformity assessment systems can easily be stand-alone; they do not have to include the preferential trade dimensions of the RIA.

Policy Integration to Increase Competition

In addition to reducing transactions costs, policy integration may benefit countries by breaking down barriers to entry (access to markets) and restraining governments from using domestic regulatory policies to protect domestic firms. Both are routes to increased competition in domestic markets and thus are almost bound to increase economic welfare, provided that they do not undermine other policy objectives. The challenge is usually to determine whether the market access effect of a regulation is necessary to achieve its underlying policy objectives; mechanisms for deciding what is legitimate and for resolving disputes can be vital to the stability of an RIA (box 6.3). These issues pervade many aspects of the modern economy. Here, we illustrate them by reference to services, public procurement, and contingent protection.

Services Liberalization. International services transactions frequently require consumers and providers to be at the same place at the same time.[4] Market-access restrictions on services accordingly include not only barriers to cross-border trade in services but also policies affecting the physical entry of services producers into markets. Most countries restrict the access of foreign services, services firms, and services workers to their

---

Box 6.3 When Is Nondiscrimination Discriminatory? The Economic Effects of Recycling Requirements

A number of U.S. states, motivated by a desire to reduce the rate at which dumps and landfills become exhausted, have passed mandatory recycling laws requiring that a minimum percentage of the content of newsprint be recycled material. These laws hurt Canadian producers of pulp and newsprint, who find it prohibitively expensive to import old newsprint to combine with the virgin wood they routinely use. (Forestry products are a major Canadian export and a source of strong comparative advantage.) The result has been a significant reduction in these producers' sales in the United States. During the period 1989–92, the market share of Canadian producers in the United States fell by 10 percent, from 56 to 50 percent (Vogel 1995: 229). The issue, however, has not been brought to either the WTO or NAFTA for dispute settlement.

Similar regulations have been a source of market access disputes in the EU. A 1981 Danish bottle-recycling law required that all beer and soft drinks be packaged in reusable containers and that retailers take back all containers sold. Metal containers were banned. Other EU producers contended that the law imposed discriminatory costs on them. The 1988 Cecchini report argued that although the law was nondiscriminatory de jure, two-way transport costs for bottles were prohibitive beyond a distance of 300 kilometers (Cecchini 1988: 60, cited in Vogel 1995: 84), and the European Commission challenged the law, arguing that instruments less restrictive of trade could be used to attain the government's objectives. The European Court of Justice, however, found the disposal and reuse requirements legal and required only that Denmark accept metal containers, as long as producers met the reuse and recycling requirements.

These examples illustrate that although domestic regulations can restrict market access, other members may tolerate the situation if it is justified by overriding noneconomic objectives. But they also suggest that RIA members may need to develop clear rules of the game and establish credible dispute settlement systems to determine when these rules have been violated.

domestic markets. The restrictions are difficult to quantify, but they are generally thought to be very high in comparison with tariffs on goods (see table 6.1). Clearly, the gains from increasing competition in services are likely to be massive.

The striking thing about services restrictions is their variety. Sometimes trade in services is simply prohibited; markets in domestic trans-

Table 6.1 Tariff Equivalents of Restrictions on Services Trade
(percent)

Economy or Region	Average Tariff[a]		
	Merchandise	Business and Financial Services	Construction
North America[b]	6.0	8.2	9.8
Western Europe	6.0	8.5	18.3
Australia and New Zealand	5.0	6.9	24.4
Japan	6.0	19.7	29.7
China	18.0	18.8	40.9
Taiwan (China)	n.a.	2.6	5.3
Other newly industrializing countries	n.a.	2.1	10.3
Indonesia	13.0	6.8	9.6
Other Southeast Asia	10.0	5.0	17.7
India	30.0	13.1	61.6
Other South Asia[c]	25.0	20.4	46.3
Brazil	15.0	35.7	57.2
Other Latin America	12.0	4.7	26.0
Turkey[c]	13.0	20.4	46.3
Middle East and North Africa	20.0	4.0	9.5
Central and Eastern Europe and Russia	10.0	18.4	51.9
South Africa	6.0	15.7	42.1
Other Sub-Saharan Africa	n.a.	0.3	11.1
Rest of world (ROW)	n.a.	20.4	46.3

n.a. Not available.

Note: The basic methodology is to estimate a gravity equation vis-à-vis U.S. trade, using exports as the dependent variable and per capita income, GDP, and a dummy for Western Hemisphere countries as regressors. Hong Kong (China) and Singapore are used as a free-trade benchmark in the regressions, and deviations from predicted imports relative to this benchmark are taken as an indication of barriers to trade. These are backed out from a constant-elasticity import demand function as follows: $T_1/T_0 = (M_1/M_0) *$ $(1/\varepsilon)$, where T_1 is the power of the tariff equivalent, $T_0 \equiv 1$, the free-trade benchmark, M_1/M_0 is the ratio of actual to predicted imports (normalized relative to the free-trade benchmark ratio for Hong Kong and Singapore), and ε is the demand elasticity (assumed to be -4).

a. Tariff averages are unweighted across all commodities and for the latest available year, which in many cases is 1997 or 1998. Country coverage of regions is not comprehensive. The reported figures should be regarded as indicative of the prevailing order of magnitude only.

b. North American values involve assigning Canadian and Mexican values to the United States.

c. Turkey and Other South Asia are not available separately in the U.S. data and have been assigned ROW values.

Source: Hoekman (2000).

port and basic telecommunications services may be reserved exclusively for domestic suppliers. Many countries also require that activities such as legal, insurance, educational, surveying, and investment advisory services be performed by residents (who may be foreign nationals) or by citizens. Even if there are no formal prohibitions, services suppliers in such fields as law, accountancy, and medicine often must obtain local certification or licensing. The standards are often set by professional bodies, which may also be responsible for licensing procedures—and have a self-interest in limiting competition. Their principal weapon is nonrecognition of foreign qualifications, diplomas, and training programs. This may be justified when training standards differ significantly among countries, but more often, the allegedly key differences are invisible to the disinterested eye.

In many services sectors, suppliers need access to distribution and communications infrastructure, especially telecommunications networks. A dominant telecommunications carrier, whether public or private, may discriminate among users of its network services by imposing restrictions on the ability of new services providers to link to the network or by forcing them to build infrastructure to reach interconnection points. For example, discrimination in ancillary services (such as being listed on computer reservation systems) can substantially reduce the competitiveness of an airline. Limitations on advertising are commonly used to reduce the ability of foreign insurance firms to compete, and restricted distribution arrangements can effectively bar market access for branded products. In all these cases, procompetitive regulatory intervention is required to overcome the barriers—for domestic as well as foreign suppliers.

There is substantial evidence that such restrictive policies reduce competition in services industries and are very costly. Producer services, in particular, play a crucial role in the development and growth prospects of any nation; agricultural output can be lost because of poor transport and storage facilities, and substandard communications networks can raise the costs of doing business. Access to global networks in communications and transport and to competitive support services is vital for international competitiveness in manufacturing. For example, many of the cost-raising effects of Egypt's domestic policies are the result of regulations that restrict competition in services and make Egyptian services industries inefficient. Maritime shipping is a monopoly, and estimates from the mid-1990s show that rates then were 25 percent higher than those in neighboring countries for equivalent routes; fees charged by the public companies that provide port services for the handling and storage of goods were 30 percent higher (Mohieldin 1997). Policy integration that reduced average services prices by 15 percent could lead to estimated welfare gains for Egypt of about 5 percent of GDP, depending on what proportion of nontariff barriers affecting trade in goods is frictional and on whether cost reductions are applied on a nondiscriminatory basis (Hoekman and Konan 1999). Services sector production would double.

Liberalizing services can be a multilayered affair, and if it is to be successful and have a significant effect on competition and welfare, all layers must be considered. Before Portugal's accession to the EU, entry into its insurance markets was effectively prohibited. After accession, many EU firms entered the market, but this had no effect on the conduct of incumbent firms because prices remained regulated (Barros 1995).[5] Similarly, the U.S. federal government deregulated trucking in the 1970s and 1980s, but about two-thirds of truck shipments are intrastate, and many states continue to regulate the sector. Daniel and Kleit (1995) estimate that state-level entry restrictions raise average prices of truck shipments by 20 to 30 percent above what would prevail if entry were unrestricted.

As with tariffs on traded inputs, the higher is the tariff equivalent of distortionary regulatory policies for services, the higher is the tax on industries that use those services as inputs. Given the importance of services in the production process, it is important to take account of the extent to which inappropriate regulatory regimes raise their costs. The exclusion of liberalization commitments on services in the Euro-Mediterranean FTAs implies that many industries in Mediterranean countries will confront negative effective protection in the second half of the transition period to regional free trade. The tariff on their outputs will have fallen to zero, but they will still be paying above world prices for their services inputs. Extending liberalization to services would ease manufacturing's adjustment to the new competitive situation (Hoekman and Djankov 1997).

Public Procurement A second area that is frequently almost devoid of competition is government procurement, where public entities are often permitted or required to discriminate in favor of domestic firms when procuring goods and services. A well-known example is the U.S. "Buy American" laws that apply to all government contracts.[6] Many developing countries have legislation under which contracts can be awarded to a foreign supplier only if the foreign supplier's bid is 15 or 20 percent cheaper than the lowest bid by a domestic supplier. Discrimination can take the form of outright bans, price preferences, local content rules, or residency requirements. In principle, application of the national treatment rule would go far toward eliminating procurement favoritism, but national treatment may need to be complemented by some degree of policy integration if market access opportunities are to be effective. In the EU, for example, common procedural requirements relating to calls for tenders, minimum periods between publication and closure of bids, and so forth have been imposed to ensure transparency and give potential suppliers realistic opportunities to bid for contracts. Only a limited number of RIAs (the EU, NAFTA, and the CER) subject public procurement to national treatment and incorporate additional procedural policy integration. Their rules are very similar to those in the WTO Agreement on Government Procurement (Hoekman and Mavroidis 1997).

It is important to note that there are legitimate reasons for governments to buy goods and services preferentially from local suppliers. Products may be effectively nontradable, or there may be problems of asymmetric information that necessitate active monitoring of suppliers by customers and therefore require geographic proximity (Evenett and Hoekman 1999). In these cases, until the market failures can be addressed RIA-wide, discrimination may be optimal.

Contingent Protection. A third area in which increased competition is vital is contingent protection. Trade policies in this category go beyond tariffs and quotas to include antidumping duties, countervailing duties, and "emergency protection" to address balance of payments disequilibria or to guard an industry from "excessive" import competition. Contingent protection—in particular, antidumping—has become a major market access barrier in many jurisdictions.

Eliminating the possibility of contingent protection is of great importance for enterprises and consumers, as the threat alone can be a barrier to market access. It was this threat that moved Canada to seek an FTA with the United States in the late 1980s and the EFTA countries to negotiate the EEA agreement with the EU (Hindley and Messerlin 1993). A problem is that governments which are unwilling to abolish antidumping policy—which would be the optimal course from an economic perspective—will need to agree how much policy integration is required to make abolition politically feasible. Thus, insofar as instruments of contingent protection respond to industrial policies that are believed to distort international competition, governments will need to agree on what alternative constraints are required on such policies. The most obvious industrial policy that can give rise to competition concerns is subsidies. The WTO Agreement on Subsidies and Countervailing Duties allows members to impose duties on subsidized imports that materially injure domestic competitors. Governments negotiating RIAs may therefore require disciplines on subsidy practices as a condition for abolishing countervailing duties. This need not imply policy integration; members can simply agree to refrain from using certain types of subsidies or to limit their extent.

Much has been written about the absence of an economic rationale for antidumping (Finger 1993a). The only argument that has potential validity is that dumping can be predatory when a foreign firm or cartel seeks to force domestic competitors out of the market by pricing below cost with the intention of raising prices once the competition is gone. But if there is predation, national antitrust laws should be able to address the problem.[7] This can be done unilaterally, without the need for international agreement or for harmonization of competition regimes. If, however, there is a fear that foreign firms will be able to use anticompetitive practices in their home markets to enhance their export competitiveness, governments may condition the abolition of antidumping on agreement regarding specific competition disciplines.

Spillovers

In addition to fostering competition by lowering transactions costs and enhancing market access, policy integration can also improve welfare by "internalizing" externalities—that is, by remedying the problem of one country's actions impinging on another country other than via the price mechanism. A distinction must be drawn between externalities associated with trade and investment liberalization and those with no connection to trade policy, which should be the subject of cooperation quite independent of any RIA. Even for the latter, however, the regular interaction between member governments that comes with an RIA may facilitate communication and create trust such that agreements on domestic policies to improve the joint allocation of resources become possible.[8]

Effects of National Competition Policy on Trading Partners. Domestic competition law and policy raise a combination of externality and market access issues. Foreign antitrust policies may have a negative effect on domestic welfare. A merger between foreign firms that is allowed by the countries' antitrust authorities may increase export prices (Dixit 1984; Ordover and Willig 1986; Graham and Richardson 1997). Similar issues arise with respect to the toleration or encouragement of export cartels. An antitrust authority monitoring an industry that mostly exports may take a permissive attitude toward export cartels which allow the nation to improve its terms of trade. Analysts exploring the question of whether the elimination of trade barriers gives rise to greater incentives to use antitrust strategically have reached conflicting conclusions. Horn and Levinsohn (1996) find that this outcome is not very likely even in areas where it would seem to be most easily applied—merger policies and export cartels. Bond (1997) suggests the opposite, both in theory and on the basis of a study of U.S. merger standards in the late 19th century. He concludes that a "race to the bottom" in policies emerged as states competed to loosen merger policy in an attempt to attract businesses to register—and pay taxes—in their jurisdictions (box 6.4).

Social and Environmental Standards. Concerns that liberalization will force countries to lower domestic standards have led to pressures on governments to make social or environmental commitments when negotiating RIAs. As long as the national standards reflect the preferences and natural conditions prevailing in a country, and as long as the social or environmental consequences of trade do not spill over from one country to another, there is no reason why greater trade should induce trade partners to change their laws. Altering domestic social or environmental standards would entail a move away from what is considered beneficial by the nation's citizens. Attempts to force partners to adopt "higher"

Box 6.4 Antitrust Law Competition by U.S. States in the 19th Century

In the United States in the late 19th and early 20th centuries, technological changes (railways and the telegraph) led to a decline in transport costs and to increased competition, analogous to what would happen in an RIA that abolished trade barriers. Federal law at the time focused on combating the anticompetitive practices of large trusts engaged in interstate commerce, and the 1890 Sherman Act's ban on price fixing gave firms an incentive to merge. State authorities were responsible for approving mergers and granting corporate charters; states that were willing to have lax merger standards could thus pass laws to encourage firms to merge and then incorporate in their jurisdictions. The most liberal state, New Jersey, managed to attract more than half of the corporations with a capitalization of $10 million or more. By 1902, New Jersey was able to pay off the entire state debt from the tax it imposed on the capital stock of merging firms and to abolish property taxes. Other states tried to follow New Jersey's lead, and a race to the bottom ensued. Eventually, 42 states adopted similar laws, but with only limited success—once there, firms tended to stay in New Jersey.

Whether this race to the bottom was harmful is debatable, but it clearly illustrates how reductions in trade barriers can interact with other policies and how competition between rules can have marked effects on policy outcomes. Countries contemplating RIAs need to consider whether those effects are likely to be benign (as the EU has assumed in areas where it has used obligatory mutual recognition to pursue its Single Market Programme objectives) or malign.

Source: Bond (1997).

standards that do not reflect their national preferences and conditions should also be rejected, as they will result in inefficient resource allocation (Bhagwati and Srinivasan 1996). Gains from trade arise in large part because countries differ; national social or environmental policies are simply one determinant of these differences and do not constitute barriers to trade or give rise to "unfair" trade. Of course, if pollution in one country affects a neighbor, there will be gains from cooperation. The vital issue in social and environmental policies is to ensure that there is actually a real economic spillover to be addressed.[9]

There is little evidence of a race to the bottom in social and environmental standards.[10] Thomas Holmes (1998) finds that U.S. manufacturing firms are attracted to states which ban closed shops (a requirement that all employees in a plant belong to a trade union) but that there has been no tendency for states to compete in this dimension (box 6.5).[11] Other experience suggests that, if anything, a "march to the top" is more likely, driven in part by pressure from interest groups that seek to apply uniform "high" standards in all RIA members. An example is the 1970 U.S. Clean Air Act, which allowed California to maintain stricter standards than the national norms embodied in the federal legislation. Over time, the national norms converged to the higher California standard, upon which California further tightened its norms. Other examples of the "California effect"—the ratcheting upward of standards in competing political jurisdictions (Vogel 1995: 259)—include EU standards on auto emissions, packaging, and toxic chemicals. This process may easily be detrimental to developing country members of North-South RIAs. An extreme example is the plight of the former East Germany after unification, when the former West German labor's insistence on equal wages and conditions in both parts of the country led to massive job losses in the east.

Box 6.5 Labor Policies in U.S. States: Spillovers, but No "Race to the Bottom"

A recent empirical analysis of one aspect of the influence of U.S. states' labor policies on the location of manufacturing (T. Holmes 1998) finds that the share of manufacturing in employment in states with "pro-business" regulatory environments is one-third higher than in adjacent states without such policies. This study is noteworthy not only in indicating that state policies appear to matter but also in suggesting that differences across states are stable through time—that there is no race to the bottom. Despite its effects on location, the distribution of the policy studied (whether a state has a law banning a requirement that all employees of a firm join a union) has not changed significantly since 1958; in the past two decades only two states have passed such laws, and none have repealed them.

Regional Free Trade Not Dependent on Policy Integration. The rhetoric of policymakers and their advisers often suggests that policy integration is necessary for attaining free trade. During the period leading to the
creation of the EEC, policymakers in many European countries argued
that some integration was required. Jelle Zijlstra, the minister of economic affairs of the Netherlands, asserted in the early 1950s that credible tariff removal required "common policies on taxes, wages, prices and
employment policy" (Milward 1992: 188). Similarly, the Belgian government believed that policy harmonization was required to equalize costs
and that without it a customs union would not be feasible, as countries
would impose new forms of protectionist policies. Thus, in the late
1940s the Belgian coal mining industry argued that a common market
could only be accepted if German wage and social security costs were
raised to Belgian levels.[12] French standards on such questions as equal
pay for men and women and the length of the workweek were initially
higher than in other EEC countries, and French officials persistently demanded policy harmonization in the social area as a precondition for
trade liberalization (Sapir 1995).

Such pressure to harmonize social standards generally stems, on the
one hand, from pressure by interest groups that fear the erosion of their
rents—hardly a valid rationale for policy integration—and, on the other,
from concern that domestic policies may be used to reimpose protection.
Addressing the latter often does not require policy integration; the national treatment principle will constrain most efforts to substitute domestic policy for trade policy. The main exception concerns regulatory
regimes that block competition on a nondiscriminatory basis, as discussed above, in "Policy Integration to Increase Competition." Policy
integration has the potential to increase the welfare gains from RIA
membership, but there is no justification for making integration a condition for eliminating tariffs.

While governments may seek to agree on common regulatory principles to govern the behavior of public entities or restrict the use of
domestic policies, this is best done directly and should not be made
a precondition for trade liberalization. A linkage strategy that seeks to
use trade policy to induce policy reform in a partner country will be
costly, given the welfare losses from protection, and for small countries,
which have no market power or leverage, it will be ineffective. For
small countries, foreign economic policies are best regarded as part of
their "environment"; they may not be ideal from the small country's
point of view, but this does not eliminate the gains that can be obtained
from trading.

Compensation and Enforcement

Policy integration can be used as a mechanism to compensate members for trade liberalization or to manage the integration of markets for "sensitive" sectors where trade liberalization is simply not politically feasible. It can also enhance the enforceability of free trade commitments. Thus, the inclusion of policy integration initiatives in RIAs may be driven by domestic political constraints that would otherwise impede international cooperation in a policy area, or by a perception that the credibility of efforts to liberalize trade and investment is enhanced by including policy integration in an agreement.

Political and Credibility Gains from Cooperation on Domestic Policies. Policy integration may be an explicit RIA goal, with preferential trade liberalization as a subsidiary goal designed to pay off powerful interests that would otherwise oppose it. Conversely, policy integration may be included in an RIA to bolster free trade politically. The EU's history suggests that Europe was not able to make much progress toward internal trade liberalization until "it was discovered . . . that further progress depended on . . . some policy of 'positive' integration . . . because the removal of discriminatory [trade] policies threatened to undermine just as many entrenched interests as [policy integration] would have done" (Milward 1984: 421).

Conceptually, this type of situation is straightforward. Although there are potential national gains from policy integration or trade reform, there are likely to be some groups that lose from it or that are powerful enough to insist on a payoff for accepting it. Environmental groups in countries contemplating an RIA may insist that their concerns be addressed, or labor groups may insist that their interests be protected (as, for example, in the case of NAFTA). Such favors, in the form of transfers or exceptions, may be opposed by those who must pay for them, whereas issue linkage—putting further (regulatory) issues on the table—might increase the total gains from integration, assuage any losers, and mobilize additional support for liberalization and integration.

In practice, however, identifying feasible or actual issue linkages is not simple. National negotiating positions are driven by complex patterns of lobbying and interest group politics, which are seldom apparent to outsiders, and the explanations offered for the tradeoffs made between governments are better viewed as part of the political process of selling the outcome than as accurate accounts of motivations. But the nature of the tradeoffs is clear in enough instances for us to be sure that this is an important dimension of the negotiation of RIAs. In Europe, for example, the formation of the ECSC and the creation of the Common Agricultural Policy (CAP), both examples of deep integration, were clearly driven by the perception that merely liberalizing trade policies in these sectors was politically not feasible.

For a developing country, placing policy integration in an RIA context may help overcome political opposition to reform in general by reducing uncertainty, offering compensation, or making outside pressures for reform more effective. For example, Tunisia's decision to pursue a binding reciprocal agreement with the EU was substantially driven by a view that it would aid the general reform process (Mustafa Nabli, former minister of planning of Tunisia, personal communication, 1998).

Policy Integration as an Aid to Enforcement of Trade Agreements. Policy integration can help prevent backsliding on trade liberalization commitments, and the threat of reversal of a trade liberalization may help enforce policy integration commitments. Border policies can easily be monitored without policy integration, but integration can reduce conflicts over the legitimacy of policies that have trade-impeding effects. In addition to transparency and information, which can be aided by institutions established to undertake policy integration, enforcement requires a credible threat that sanctions will be imposed if a rule is violated. Policy integration can help here by empowering institutions to enforce commitments and make their decisions binding on RIA members. This can reduce uncertainty over enforcement and result in benefits by lessening the need for hedging and "insurance."

It may be difficult or costly to retaliate against a violation of a negotiated discipline within a single-subject agreement. For example, if one member claims that its partner's domestic standards are inadequately enforced and imposes its own duplicative certification requirements, it makes little sense for the partner to retaliate by doing the same. The threat of a wider breakdown of cooperation may be more effective. An important point is that policy integration may allow for credible threats of noncooperation in areas of interest to a partner without threatening trade relationships.

Policy integration can also help in enforcing trade liberalization commitments by removing a government's ability to use domestic policy instruments as a substitute for trade policy. Similarly, mutual recognition or harmonization of regulatory regimes may help reduce trading risks by lowering (or, ideally, eliminating) the possibility of being confronted with allegations of dumping or subsidization and by creating alternative ways of dealing with such disputes if they arise. The extent to which governments perceive a need to pursue policy integration as insurance against opportunistic or nationalistic use of domestic policy instruments will depend on many factors, including past use of specific policies, the level of trust, the willingness to accept regulatory competition, and the type of RIA involved. Where to draw the line is largely a political decision, and RIAs differ markedly in their use of policy integration to constrain trade and domestic policy.

The arguments just made do not imply that "anything goes" in policy integration. They recognize the complexity and sui generis nature of RIA formation. But they are simultaneously an injunction to the policymaker to be explicit about issue linkages and cross-issue tradeoffs and how they contribute to the general good. The EU's experience with the CAP illustrates that the economic cost of inappropriate deep integration can be high.

Local versus Regional versus Global Cooperation

There are two dimensions to the geographic question: the set of countries involved in establishing a norm, and the range of countries to which the norm applies. On the former, there is a tradeoff between matching local requirements and tastes and reaping the efficiency benefits of global standards. On the latter, nondiscrimination—that is, global application—is always better, if it is feasible

Global Standards: The Preferred Route. Developing countries should pursue outward-looking strategies based on global standards and best practices to the greatest extent possible, rather than develop local or regional norms. This not only saves resources that would be used in developing the standards but also reduces the chances of standards being used as a means of segmenting markets and stifling competition. An additional benefit is that such standards are typically relatively light; they usually rely mainly on market forces and so help avoid laying the heavy hand of officialdom on commercial activities. These injunctions are especially important if there are network externalities or economies of scale, for then openness to the largest possible set of actors carries the greatest rewards.

Sometimes, formal agreements between states are needed to facilitate trade, and an existing RIA provides a natural framework for negotiating such agreements. But the rules that are adopted should be regional only to the extent that this is unavoidable. The case for unavoidability applies where, although the need for intercountry coordination is pressing, global standards are not appropriate—perhaps because local tastes are idiosyncratic—or have not yet been developed. If regional coordination is required, it should, where possible, take the form of competition between regulatory regimes rather than harmonization, as this allows for differences in preferences and economic conditions. If harmonization is deemed necessary, it should be limited to the adoption of minimum standards that comply with international norms, if these exist (see, for example, Kanbur, Keen, and van Wijnbergen 1995).

It is sometimes argued that global fora are too unwieldy to use for developing standards. In fact, multilateral cooperation between states in standard setting and prudential regulation predates the rise of regionalism, and it continues to be the dominant form of intergovernmental cooperation because in many spheres the world is the optimal level for such cooperation (box 6.6). Also, despite sometimes fiercely regional rhetoric, many of the standards and norms embodied in RIAs are international; for example, the EU has adopted the recommendations of the Bank for International Settlements (BIS) on banking and relies on disciplines negotiated in the WTO for government procurement. The more that international norms are used by RIAs, the less likely it is that policy integration will lead to detrimental outcomes. This is because these norms are set through a process of consensus and tend to be minimum standards. RIAs could help expand the use of such norms and become instruments through which they can be enforced.

Less Discrimination Means More Benefits from Policy Integration.
Policy integration based on international standards is likely to have the maximum effect on competition and hence on economic welfare within an RIA, and it is less likely to be detrimental to nonmembers of RIAs.[13] Even if policy integration is specific to an RIA, it may enhance global welfare if it is applied on a nondiscriminatory basis to all traders. Measures to simplify customs procedures and documentary requirements reduce transactions costs on imports from all origins. Similarly, if in the context of an RIA a government commits to a privatization program that limits domestic subsidies or applies competition law more strictly, this may benefit third countries as well as partners. Thus, nonmembers of the RIA are likely to gain from openness, just as they do from lower MFN tariffs. Conversely, regional policies applied discriminatorily are quite likely to impose costs on foreigners, just as discriminatory tariffs can (see chapter 8).

Mutual recognition or harmonization-based policy integration—in or out of an RIA—can result in effective discrimination against outsiders.

Box 6.6 Multilateral Policy Integration and the Enforcement Role of RIAs

More than 30 intergovernmental organizations emerged between 1860 and 1914. (The table lists a number of them.) Most of them covered infrastructure, including postal services (1863), marine signaling (1864), technical railway standards (1883), ocean telegraphy (1897), and aerial navigation (1910). Multilateral institutions allowed the emergence of a Europe-wide market for industrial goods. International interconnection norms agreed under the auspices of the International Telegraph Union eliminated the requirement that telegrams be printed out at each border post, walked across the border, and retyped. The Universal Radiotelegraph Union aimed at preventing a global radio monopoly by requiring interconnection across different technologies.

International railway unions promoted networks by standardizing rolling stock, allowing companies to use each other's rolling stock, and enforcing a single bill of lading so that one document could be used for all trans-European shipments. This took place roughly a century before the EU's adoption of a single customs document. All continental European countries except Russia and Spain adopted the same rail gauge, drove on the left, and aligned signals, brakes, and timetables (Pollard 1974: 50–51). This standardization was largely driven by the private sector; business can often achieve cooperation more readily than governments. The Rail Union (Central Office for International Railway Transport) of 1890 played a significant role in dismantling protectionism in the late 19th century by prohibiting transit duties on goods shipped by rail, and the Brussels Tariff Union made the remaining restrictions transparent by publishing lists of tariffs in five languages.

Intergovernmental organizations proliferated after World War II with, for example, the formation of the GATT (now the WTO), the United Nations system, the International Civil Aviation Organization (ICAO), and the Organisation for European Economic Co-operation, which became the OECD. By developing norms and practices to facilitate the expansion of international markets and manage conflicts between jurisdictions, these bodies help foster economic growth. The hallmark of such organizations is that governments cooperate in developing standards, ranging from technical requirements for maritime transport (the International Maritime Organization), to customs procedures (the World Customs Organization), to labor rights and working conditions (the International Labour Organisation), to capital adequacy standards for banks (the Bank for International Settlements). The resulting standards are often adopted by RIAs.

RIAs differ from the global standards institutions by offering enforcement mechanisms. Resolving interstate conflicts has always figured on the agenda of international conferences and organizations but has often been ineffective. In the early 20th century a number of proposals were made to develop international instruments for the extension of binding arbitration to intellectual property, the principle of equality of foreigners in taxation (national treatment), civil and commercial procedure, customs tariffs, the right of foreigners to hold property, the regulation of companies, and claims for damages. These were opposed by countries that sought to retain their national sovereignty (Murphy 1994: 104). Of the bodies mentioned above, only the United Nations and the WTO have binding dispute settlement mechanisms.

Trade-Related Intergovernmental Organizations Established before 1914

Objective	Organization and date of creation
Infrastructure and related "software"	International Telegraph Union (1865)
	Universal Postal Union (1874)
	International Railway Congress Association (1884)
	Central Office for International Railway Transport (1890)
	Diplomatic Conference on International Maritime Law (1905)
	Universal Radiotelegraph Union (1906)
	Permanent International Association of Road Congresses (International Automobile Convention) (1909)

(Box continues on next page.)

Box 6.6 *(continued)*

Trade-Related Intergovernmental Organizations Established before 1914 (continued)

Standards	International Bureau of Weights and Measures (1875)
	Metric Union (1877)
	International Bureau of Analytical Chemistry of Human and Animal Food (1912)
Intellectual	International Union for the Protection of Industrial Property (1883)
property	International Union for the Protection of Literary and Artistic Works (1886)
Trade	Brussels Tariff Union (International Union for the Publication of Customs Tariffs) (1890)
	Hague Conference on Private International Law (1893)
	International Bureau of Commercial Statistics (1913)
Dispute	Permanent Court of Arbitration (1899)
settlement	International Court of Prize (1907; never ratified)

Source: Adapted from Murphy (1994): 48–49.

What matters, then, is whether outsiders can be "recognized" in turn. The principles of open access and conditional MFN can be applied to third parties seeking to join the "club." If a country meets the minimum conditions for membership in any particular product or standard, it should be able to participate in a policy integration initiative.[14]

Introducing such a transitivity rule in the WTO could help expand the reach of MRAs: if countries A and B and countries B and C each had MRAs, A and C would automatically accept each other's norms and products. Thus, subject to conditions ensuring that the original mutual recognitions were genuine (for example, that if A could not agree to the extension to C, it would have to suspend the agreement with B), it would be possible to move toward broader, even global, standards regimes. The more open RIAs are to efforts by nonmembers to participate in their policy integration dimensions, and the more they rely on international standards, the less worrisome policy integration in RIAs will be.

But participation in the most important dimension of MRAs—acceptance of conformity assessment—may be difficult for developing countries. Neither the United States nor the EU has concluded MRAs with developing countries. Special efforts may be required to ensure that regional policy integration does not perpetuate or increase this discrimination. One option would be to seek agreement from partner countries that conformity assessment by internationally established certification entities will be accepted and that greater reliance will be placed on the private sector and the market mechanism (self-certification). It is of particular importance to keep policy integration free of the preferential dimensions of the RIAs. Such contamination is not unknown; for example, the EU tried to include restrictive preferential rules of origin in MRAs with the United States, but U.S. industry put up successful resistance (Wilson 1999). Developing countries may find it useful to seek WTO disciplines that ban such attempts.

POLICY INTEGRATION TO DATE: MORE PROMISE THAN REALITY

RIAs differ in the extent to which they have pursued policy integration. Many embody only the minimum required to implement an FTA or a customs union, while others have gone far toward full integration of domestic policies. Determining the extent to which RIAs have a policy integration agenda can only be done case by case and must to some extent be a subjective exercise. This section provides an overview of the status of and prospects for policy integration in RIAs.

Coverage

The coverage of policy integration varies enormously across RIAs. On balance, few RIAs have gone far down the policy integration track, and most do not go much, if at all, beyond the WTO.

Cooperation on Product Standards Rarely Goes beyond WTO Rules. Most RIAs that include disciplines on product standards use international standards as their norms (as do WTO standards agreements). Some have adopted foreign standards unilaterally; for example, CARICOM members generally use British standards (Page 1998).

Australia and New Zealand have gone farthest on standards—in some respects, beyond the EU. A joint accreditation system for conformity assessment was created in 1991 to harmonize auditing and certification systems and criteria with international standards. In 1995 this was complemented by an agreement to create the Australia New Zealand Food Standards Council. The 1997 Trans-Tasman Mutual Recognition Agreement, along EU lines, covers both goods and services. Goods sold legally in one country can be sold in the other, and persons licensed to practice an occupation in one country are automatically licensed in the other.[15]

In NAFTA, each party has agreed to accredit or otherwise recognize testing and certification performed by partner country bodies. The Group of Three and MERCOSUR provide for MRAs in this area but have not yet made significant progress. Other RIA pacts do not address certification and conformity assessment.

Services Liberalization: A Recent Phenomenon. Outside the EU, efforts to liberalize international services transactions within RIAs became prominent only in the late 1980s and early 1990s—in CUSTFA and, later, NAFTA, and in the CER. RIAs have not led the WTO by much, if at all; services were introduced in the GATT agenda in 1986. The EU began to make substantial progress only in the mid-1980s, with the launch of the Single Market Programme. Even though national treatment applied formally to member state services providers, European services markets in fact remained highly segmented until the late 1980s. Doctors, pharmacists, lawyers, accountants, and other professionals had to retake certification examinations to practice in a different country. Liberalization of financial services was impeded because many members continued to restrict capital movements. Much of the SMP aimed at integrating EU services markets, and many of the directives issued by the European Commission related to services industries. For example, in 1989 the Second Banking Directive made home countries responsible for prudential supervision (setting and enforcing liquidity and solvency standards) and allowed credit institutions authorized in one state to establish branches and provide banking services anywhere in the EU. Directives were also developed for investment services, mutual funds, insurance, road and air transport, telecommunications, professional (accounting, legal, and medical) services, and mutual recognition of diplomas in pharmacy and other "regulated" professions.

The NAFTA and the CER have comprehensive coverage of services activities, using a negative list; that is, all services sectors are covered unless specifically exempted. A NAFTA Professional Services Annex sets out procedures for developing standards for professional practice, requires the abolition of citizenship and permanent residency requirements in licensing and certifying professional service providers, and establishes work programs to liberalize licensing for foreign legal consultants and engineers.

The Andean Pact, the CACM, and the SADC have done little to liberalize services. In SACU and CARICOM certain services sectors have been integrated more for historical than for deliberate policy reasons. In CARICOM national treatment applies to banking, health, education, tourism, and transport services, and many of these services are provided jointly. The Group of Three is similar to NAFTA, but sectoral coverage is narrower. (Transport remains the subject of negotiation.) In MERCO-

SUR free circulation of services is a long-term objective, to be achieved by 2007. Progress has been slow, however; members are still negotiating a framework agreement. ASEAN members have until recently restricted services liberalization to their commitments under the General Agreement on Trade in Services (GATS). In 1997 they agreed in principle to full liberalization (on a preferential basis) of most services by 2020. The FTAs between the EU and Mediterranean countries do not include services; those with Central and Eastern European countries do. Except in the EU, either the multilateral GATS process is leading liberalization of services or the GATS commitments of RIA members do not differ significantly from RIA commitments (Hoekman and Sauvé 1994; Page 1998).

Competition and Industrial Policy Disciplines. The EU imposes far-reaching disciplines on member state regulatory policies to underpin the realization of a single market. Common rules apply to subsidies, monopolies, government procurement practices, and antitrust. These are complemented by detailed European legislation relating to the achievement of the Internal Market. The goal of these competition provisions is to ensure a "level playing field" or "equal competitive opportunities" in European markets for suppliers from all member states. All of the EU provisions relating to competition and industrial policies are also found in the EEA.

A commitment to apply common disciplines in areas such as antitrust, subsidies, and state monopolies is also a central dimension of the EU-centered RIAs. Increasingly, the EU appears to be requiring its partners in Eastern and Central Europe and the Mediterranean to adopt its internal market rules and to introduce national legislation that is consistent with its norms (independent of any consideration of trade effects). Enforcement of competition rules is largely left to national bodies, and dispute settlement provisions are largely political in nature, residing with the Association Councils, which may make recommendations when disputes arise but may not issue binding instructions.

The CER agreement between Australia and New Zealand is similar to the EU in its coverage of competition and industrial policies. In 1988 a Protocol on Acceleration of Free Trade in Goods stipulated that nationals of one state could be investigated by the competition authorities of the other and could be required to respond to requests for information. Each nation amended its antitrust legislation to extend it to Australian or New Zealand firms with market power in either the national market or the combined market. Courts are empowered to sit in either country; orders can be served in either; and judgments by each country's courts or authorities are enforceable in the other. Unlike the situation in the EU, the application of antitrust remedies remains strictly national. The CER also includes subsidy disciplines stronger than those of the WTO. Industry-specific subsidies are banned, and export subsidies were prohibited in 1987.

Other RIAs have less, or nothing, on competition policy, although many RIAs have rules on subsidies. Export subsidies are frequently prohibited, as in the Andean Pact, the CACM, CARICOM, MERCOSUR, and the Group of Three. MERCOSUR members have begun harmonizing their competition laws and creating a mechanism for coordinated action to prevent anticompetitive practices from affecting intra-area trade (Rowat, Lubrano, and Porrata 1997). A December 1996 protocol prohibits concerted practices that restrict or distort competition and affect trade between member states. The protocol gives MERCOSUR institutions the power to enforce these rules, although implementation remains the responsibility of national competition agencies.[16] The 1996 Canada-Chile FTA requires each member to adopt or maintain measures to proscribe anticompetitive business conditions, and it also requires competition authorities to consult and cooperate.

Persistence of Contingent Protection. A number of RIAs, including the EU, the EEA, the CER, and the Canada-Chile FTA, ban the use of instruments of contingent protection such as antidumping and countervailing duties. The CER abolished antidumping on trade between Australia and New Zealand in 1990, following a decision that national competition regimes should be applied to such trade. As in the EU, elimination of antidumping was linked to the transition path toward complete free trade.

Antidumping remains applicable to intra-MERCOSUR trade.[17] There is no explicit requirement or commitment that antidumping on intrabloc trade will be eliminated, but the arguments for maintaining it on internal trade have been subject to periodic inconclusive reviews.

The Canada-Chile FTA specifies that antidumping on products ceases to be applicable on intra-FTA trade as tariffs on those products are eliminated or by January 1, 2003, at the latest. The abolition does not extend to countervailing duties. A committee has been set up to define subsidy disciplines further and to eliminate the need for countervailing duties. Elimination of antidumping occurred without agreement on the application of common competition rules for trade. The explicit exception for maintaining countervailing duties suggests that subsidy and industrial policies were a greater cause for concern than private anticompetitive practices.

Antidumping and countervailing duties remain applicable to imports from the Central and Eastern European and Mediterranean countries that have signed FTAs with the EU and to the customs union between the EU and Turkey (Togan 1997). Notwithstanding the agreement to adopt EU-consistent competition disciplines, the Europe Agreements do not specify that antidumping will be phased out or eliminated. The EU insists that application of competition laws and principles is not enough; what is necessary (but not sufficient) is that all of the Internal Market directives also be applied.[18] The EU RIAs illustrate that there is no presumption that pursuing harmonization in competition policies will lead to the elimination of contingent trade policies on intraregional trade.

Given that the substantive case for antidumping duties is so weak in the first place, it is difficult to identify economic conditions under which RIAs should abolish them. A number of observations are pertinent, however:

1. Explicit linkages between abolishing antidumping and adopting common antitrust rules are by no means the norm.
2. Antidumping may be used as a tool to extract concessions from potential partners (as in the Europe and Euro-Mediterranean Agreements).
3. If an RIA aims at a single market, there can be no role for antidumping. Although common antitrust disciplines may be adopted as part of deeper integration efforts, their dominant aim is usually integration per se rather than abolition of antidumping internally.
4. Much depends on the extent to which governments can be prevented from intervening directly in domestic industries. This seems to be one of the main concerns underlying the EU's unwillingness to give up its right to impose antidumping duties on imports from the European transition economies and the Mediterranean countries. The fact that NAFTA did little to impose disciplines on subsidies may be an important element in U.S. unwillingness to give up antidumping. The Canada-Chile FTA is also noteworthy in this connection in that countervailing duties remain applicable.

Environmental and Social Policies. The EU (as is often the case when it comes to policy integration) is in the vanguard of cooperation on environmental policy. In part, this reflects efforts by "high standards" countries such as Denmark, Germany, and the Netherlands to export their norms to all members. It has taken decades for the environment to become an EU competence, and many years for the European Commission to begin to affect environmental policy in less "green" member states.

Environmental regulations are much less prominent in other RIAs. NAFTA includes a number of supplemental agreements, including one on the environment, that are largely aimed not at harmonization but at ensuring that national laws and regulations are enforced. A committee can levy fines or recommend trade sanctions if a NAFTA signatory does not apply its national law.

The EU has adopted a number of social policy directives. The Treaty of Rome supports harmonization of social policies, although (except for a requirement that men and women be treated equally) there are no deadlines, targets, or criteria. The Social Chapter of the Maastricht Treaty sets out a list of basic rights and freedoms for workers (and for citizens in general), but these do not apply in all member countries. Most other RIAs do not contain disciplines on social policies, or if they do, they have never been implemented or developed. MERCOSUR has a working group discussing the issue. NAFTA's North American Agreement on Labor Cooperation provides a forum for exchanging information and monitoring labor conditions, but, as with the environmental side agreement, only the failure to enforce relevant national laws can be challenged.

Depth of Integration: A Function of Political Objective

Most RIAs are commercial instruments—their primary objective is to facilitate trade. Over time, some RIAs have pursued elements of domestic policy integration, driven by the potential for gains from cooperation in particular areas and by concerns that governments might use domestic policies as a substitute for trade policies. Such efforts are by their very nature limited and partial. They are also paralleled, in both intent and outcome, by initiatives in the WTO. It is useful to distinguish them from initiatives in RIAs that have as their objective economic integration or union, which are discussed in this subsection.

The RIA that has gone furthest in integrating domestic policies—the EU—is an agreement between states seeking to achieve economic union. Cooperation consequently extends far beyond liberalization of trade in products and factors. The EU has created supranational institutions with mandates to make policy in specific areas, the power to initiate rule-setting proposals, and a significant degree of autonomy—as manifested in secretariats staffed by career professionals that are formally independent of member governments and have their own sources of funding. Once adopted, the rules that are developed have direct effect in national law, thus allowing citizens to invoke EU rules in national courts. In areas where the EU has competence, rules are often set by majority vote. Enforcement of EU rules is binding, with ultimate enforcement power vested in the supranational European Court of Justice.

Next to the EU, the CER has achieved the most in integrating domestic policies. It has adopted elements from the EU—the Australia New Zealand Food Standards Council works under majority voting rules—but does not rely on supranational institutions. Instead, integration depends on national implementation of laws and regulations on a nondiscriminatory basis; regular review and expansion of the agreement; and extensive mechanisms for consultations and transparency. The institutional structure is light. The CER is an important example for developing countries because it illustrates that deep integration can be achieved without the supranational structure found in the EU. But this model may be difficult to emulate; the high degrees of similarity and trust between the two partner countries seem to be a vital ingredient in its success.

Most other RIAs do not come close to the EU or CER levels of policy integration. Most do not have supranational institutions responsible for implementing their agreements but rely instead on secretariats, staffed by delegations from member states, that lack initiation powers or autonomy. Rule-making is based on consensus and unanimity, whether formal or informal. Enforcement mechanisms are often diplomatic and restricted to governments

In fact, the enforcement mechanisms of many RIAs reveal their fundamental "shallowness," relying as they do on either diplomatic conflict resolution or nonbinding panel processes. WTO procedures are often stronger than those in RIAs. Even where an RIA's panel-based dispute resolution is stronger than that of the WTO, the latter plays a significant role de facto. For example, the arbitration of investor-state disputes in NAFTA is binding and is directly accessible by investors, whereas only governments have access to the WTO—yet in many cases NAFTA members have preferred to use WTO dispute settlement procedures. Canada and the United States have generally used the WTO to deal with disputes other than antidumping. Even for antidumping, where panel decisions are binding in national law, the substantive requirements they impose are those of the WTO.

Prospects for Policy Integration in RIAs

Although, to date, little has been achieved in the way of policy integration in most RIAs, integration is under discussion in connection with a number of existing and prospective agreements. Two major regional initiatives now under negotiation—the Asia-Pacific Economic Cooperation (APEC) initiative and the Free Trade Area of the Americas (FTAA)—illustrate the issues and challenges. Among them are ensuring that policy integration efforts include the abolition of instruments of contingent protection; focusing on trade facilitation and the reduction of redundant red tape; agreeing to binding and enforceable commitments; and applying as many rules as possible on a nondiscriminatory basis.

APEC and the Goal of Nondiscriminatory Liberalization. APEC has created a large number of bodies to explore possible coordination in areas relevant to the organization's goal of free trade. Services, competition policy, investment regimes, standards and conformity assessment, customs procedures, intellectual property rights, and government procurement are all under discussion, although contingent protection is not. The process for pursuing liberalization and integration is unique in that it relies on unilateral "individual action plans" in each area that are to be implemented on a nondiscriminatory basis. The plans submitted by the 18 members take up thousands of pages. Given that implementation of commitments can take many years (the free trade objective is to be realized by developed country members in 2010 and by developing country members in 2020), many of the plans are no more than statements of intent. Commitments are not legally enforceable, and countries are not bound by any agreement. The focus instead is on developing nonbinding principles relating to the application of domestic policies such as competition law and standards.

The nonbinding nature of APEC-based policy integration suggests that the WTO may well be the primary vehicle for locking in whatever unilateral reforms are implemented by members. APEC activities have largely been instruments for communication, information exchange, and technical assistance. Although this can be beneficial in providing focal points and identifying best practices, insofar as policy integration requires formal agreements between governments it would appear that the APEC process is inherently limited to what can be achieved by applying the national treatment and MFN principles. These principles can give rise to major economic benefits and should certainly be pursued, but policy integration that requires formal instruments of cooperation such as

MRAs must be based on binding, enforceable agreements so that violations can be contested. Since the objective of APEC members is to apply liberalization and policy reforms on a nondiscriminatory basis, the WTO is the natural forum in which to embed such agreements—in the process, ensuring that they are open to all WTO members. The WTO is also the best institution for locking in country-specific liberalization commitments, as its dispute settlement mechanism is substantially stronger than the diplomatic processes envisaged for APEC.

A weakness of the APEC discussions is the absence of serious efforts to limit the reach of contingent protection. One of the strengths of the initiative is the emphasis on policy integration—often based on identification and unilateral adoption of best practices—with the aim of facilitating trade by reducing transactions costs associated with customs and with testing and certification procedures. Another strength, at least according to current plans, is that APEC will not have trade preferences for intramember trade; the intention is that all its trade liberalization will be MFN. Bergsten (1997), however, argues that APEC will need at least the threat of preferences and discrimination if it is to prosper and to include the United States. Thus, this strength is more of a challenge than a fact.

The FTAA: No Serious Negotiations as Yet. As with APEC, the FTAA has a large number of working groups exploring possible modalities for cooperation on domestic regulatory policies. Free intraregional trade in merchandise is to be attained by 2005. It remains to be seen what emerges as regards services liberalization and policy integration more generally, for although there has been a great deal of preliminary and procedural analysis, substantive negotiations have yet to begin. A likely difference from APEC is that commitments and agreements will be binding and subject to enforcement procedures.

The negotiating agenda of the FTAA is very broad and extends beyond what is currently covered by the WTO. In this respect there is substantial potential for members to achieve deeper integration. A key challenge—indeed, a litmus test—will be whether agreement can be achieved to go significantly beyond the WTO by establishing free trade and investment in services and the right of establishment as general principles, and the extent to which initial liberalization commitments will go farther than governments have committed to under the GATS. Another indicator of the depth of integration will be whether contingent protection will be applicable to intra-FTAA trade. A working group on subsidies, antidumping measures, and countervailing duties has been engaged in information collection and exchange, with a particular emphasis on eliminating remaining agricultural export subsidies and other trade-distorting measures affecting agriculture. The terms of reference of the group make no mention of developing recommendations for disciplining the use of contingent protection.

CONCLUSION

This chapter has explored the role of policy coordination in developing country RIAs, drawing mainly on EU experience, which offers by far the most detailed example to hand. The conclusion that emerges is that although policy integration offers scope for considerable gains, great political and technical efforts are required to achieve it. Developing country governments should not casually assume that policy integration will automatically generate big welfare gains: unless they invest heavily in it, policy integration will evade them. We have also emphasized that governments should exploit the many opportunities to reduce transactions costs and market segmentation that multilateral organizations and unilateral action offer.

NOTES

1. Schiff and Winters (2002a) discuss nonregulatory cooperation.

2. The principle of positive comity requires that a government body take into account the interests of another country in the application of national law.

3. Poland, for example, is said to have maintained a "non-transparent system of certification and product approvals that is not harmonized with international standards, nor does it accept manufacturer self-certification. Due to the need to gain separate certification, foreign exports meeting international standards might not obtain Polish approval" (Wilson 1999: 37). One standards-related trade dispute between the EU and Poland involved allegations that a Polish ban on imports of gelatin on the basis of health concerns reflected a desire to protect local producers (*Financial Times,* February 19, 1998).

4. This discussion draws on Hoekman and Braga (1997).

5. Indeed, firms may have entered Portugal's market precisely to take advantage of the regulated prices.

6. See Greenwold and Cox (1993) and Francois, Palmeter, and Nelson (1997) for descriptions and analyses of U.S. procurement practices.

7. Research suggests that predation is very much the exception, not the rule, in antidumping cases. In more than 90 percent of actual antidumping actions, an antitrust authority would not have intervened on grounds of competition, let alone predation (Schöne 1996; Messerlin 1997). The consensus among most

economists is that antidumping as practiced today has, de facto, nothing to do with predation.

8. Among the examples of non-trade-related policy areas in which cooperation can overcome problems created by externalities are shared natural resources, such as the environment and watercourses, and common infrastructure projects, such as power generation and transborder transport schemes (corridors). Schiff and Winters (2002a) discuss these cases in greater detail.

9. Schiff and Winters (2002a) examine the issue of regional spillovers in areas such as the environment, natural resources, infrastructure, and energy; and whether RIAs can help in reaching a cooperative solution.

10. The focus here should be on policies, not outcomes. An RIA may lead to industries' shifting production facilities to a partner country where environmental policies are less stringent, but as long as environmental policies in the partner countries are appropriate for local conditions and national preferences, this is desirable. Of course, for a variety of reasons, policies might not be optimal, and in these cases shifting the location of production might be either costly or beneficial.

11. Holmes controls for the possibility that the data reflect the passage of closed-shop legislation as a reaction to a concentration of industry, rather than vice versa, by focusing on the border areas of each state. Along either side of the border, other conditions affecting location are likely to be very similar, while the amount of industry in the border areas is sufficiently small not to reflect the importance of industry to the state's overall level of activity.

12. The discussion of proposals for a European customs union in the early 1950s included virtually every question that came to be addressed in the Maastricht treaty: a common European currency, monetary policy, freedom of labor, mutual recognition of professional qualifications, a common company law, a free capital market, and common workplace and product safety standards (Milward 1992: 191).

13. These statements must be qualified if there is imperfect competition in the affected sectors, for then the RIA may be able to benefit at the expense of nonmembers by its choice of standard.

14. In this context, the "club" is *not* the RIA; it is defined relative to one standard or product, not the whole range of products covered by the RIA. If the latter definition applied, the proposal would merely amount to requiring RIAs to be open to any country that can negotiate suitable entry conditions, which, as we argue in chapter 8, is not a satisfactory or realistic way of achieving nondiscrimination in the world economy.

15. This MRA was originally concluded among the states of Australia in 1992; essentially, what was done was to extend it to New Zealand.

16. Since MERCOSUR institutions operate by consensus, a national competition authority will have the option of refusing to implement a decision. The protocol must be ratified by the parliaments of member states before it becomes effective. Uruguay and Paraguay have yet to create the necessary institutions.

17. Antidumping has been used actively by some members of MERCOSUR. Argentina initiated 33 antidumping cases on imports from Brazil during the period 1992–96, making Brazil the number one target for such actions (Tavares de Araujo and Tineo 1998).

18. The EU is requiring its future members to adapt national competition rules to EU standards more strictly than has been the norm for existing member states (P. Holmes 1996: 5). Pittman (1998) documents that the Central and Eastern European countries have already gone far down the harmonization road.

CHAPTER 7

Regional Integration as Politics

Countries sometimes form trade blocs for noneconomic reasons, such as national security, peace, and assistance in developing political and social institutions. These are public goods that are unlikely to be adequately provided in the absence of some form of intervention, such as an RIA. Political objectives can be important for RIAs—sometimes overwhelmingly so—but it is still desirable that they be achieved efficiently and that policymakers pay heed to their economic cost. However, no economic analysis of an RIA is complete without taking the potential welfare benefits of political objectives into account. This chapter examines some of the political objectives of regionalism, discusses their economic implications, and assesses whether trade preferences are necessary for achieving these goals. It is not a review of the political science of regionalism but, rather, an assessment of how political objectives should shape our economic appraisal of regionalism.

Political benefits such as peace and security can sometimes swamp the simple material considerations that usually determine economic policy. Moreover, since such benefits are typically shared by only a limited number of countries—usually, neighbors—it makes sense to seek them on a regional basis rather than multilaterally. Thus, this issue forms a relatively more important part of the analysis of RIAs than of some other international issues.

The following section explains how, under some circumstances, the formation of an RIA may be an effective way of dealing with security tensions between neighboring countries. The argument is, essentially, that mutual trade fosters peace between countries and regionalism

188 REGIONAL INTEGRATION AND DEVELOPMENT

fosters trade. We show that for an RIA designed to enhance security, the optimum external tariff (on imports from nonmembers) declines over time and as integration deepens.

We next briefly discuss the use of RIAs to reduce and manage pressures for migration. Although such objectives have been frankly admitted to in practice—for example, in NAFTA and in the Europe Agreements between the EU and the countries of Central and Eastern Europe—their effectiveness in this regard is far from certain.

Joining an RIA with democratic countries can help a developing country achieve or uphold democracy if the RIA imposes on its members "club rules" such as democracy and civil rights. As is discussed in the third section of the chapter, this assistance is likely to be more effective if the other members have large economies; larger partners are generally able to impose greater costs on (or withdraw greater benefits from) recalcitrants than can smaller ones. The size of the developing country and its proximity to its democratic partners also matter. A partner country is likely to be far more concerned about possible spillovers from events in a nearby, sizable developing country than about those in a small, distant one or resulting from "a quarrel in a faraway country between people of whom we know nothing."[1]

The final section examines the connection between economic integration and political integration—in particular, whether increased regional integration is likely to weaken or strengthen the nation-state. It argues that resource pooling and collective action can increase the effectiveness of the state in small or even medium-size nations in dealing with economic problems such as pollution, guarding against third-country security threats, and enhancing international influence by lowering negotiation costs and increasing bargaining power in dealings with the rest of the world. Cooperation of this kind, however, does not usually require trade preferences.

REGIONAL INTEGRATION AS A MEANS OF REDUCING FRICTIONS BETWEEN ANTAGONISTIC NEIGHBORS

The idea that trade can be an important force for creating and maintaining peaceful relations between countries dates at least from the 18th century (see box 7.1) and is probably a good deal older. Since forming an RIA almost always increases trade between the partners, there seems to be a good chance that the pacific effects of trade would extend to this particular form of trade relationship.[2] In fact, this is true only when the RIA is between relatively evenly balanced partners whose governments genuinely wish to improve security and when the benefits from the RIA are distributed in a relatively equal way.

Box 7.1 Trade and Peace: The Political Lineup Follows the Economic Lineup

The notion of using international trade to defuse tension and bring nations together dates back at least to the publication in 1795 of *Perpetual Peace* by Immanuel Kant (1992: 157). In the 19th century British politician Richard Cobden persistently advocated that Britain trade freely with her neighbors to convince them of the advantages of free trade and to lock them more fully into the community of nations. Cordell Hull, U.S. secretary of state from 1933 to 1944, and one of the architects of the postwar international trading order, advocated this view throughout his public life. He declared that "if we could increase commercial exchanges among nations over lowered trade and tariff barriers and remove unnatural obstructions to trade, we would go a long way toward eliminating war itself" (Hull 1948: 84). Of World War II, he wrote, "Yes, war did come, despite the trade agreements. But it is a fact that war did not break out between the United States and any country with which we had been able to negotiate a trade agreement. . . . With very few exceptions, the countries with which we signed trade agreements joined together in resisting the Axis. The political lineup followed the economic lineup" (365).

Diplomatic considerations were at the heart of the 1860 Anglo-French (Cobden-Chevalier) commercial treaty (Irwin 1993: 95, 96). France was worried about offending protectionist interests, while Britain was somewhat reluctant to pursue an agreement that would violate its policy of unilateral free trade. Nevertheless, both governments saw a commercial treaty as a way of defusing tensions and improving diplomatic relations and decided to sign it. In 1889 the Italian economist Vilfredo Pareto argued that customs unions were "a means to better political relations and eventual pacification" (Machlup 1977: 41).

As early as 1943, French statesman Jean Monnet, one of the founding fathers of the European Economic Community (EEC), wrote, "There will be no peace in Europe if the states reconstitute themselves on a basis of national sovereignty with its policies of prestige and economic protection . . . the constitution of large armies will again be necessary . . . Europe will once again be recreated in fear . . . unless the States of Europe join in a Federation or a 'European entity' that results in a common economic unit" (Monnet, "Notes de réflexion," August 5, 1943).

Monnet and compatriot Robert Schuman, the other architect of the EEC, explicitly argued that a goal of the European Coal and Steel Community (ECSC), the precursor of the EEC, was to make Franco-German war not only "unthinkable, but materially impossible" (Swann 1992: 6). The preamble to the 1951 Paris Treaty establishing the ECSC "resolved to substitute for age-old rivalries the merging of their essential interests, [and] to create, by establishing an economic community, the basis for a broader and deeper community among peoples long divided by bloody conflicts." Walter Hallstein, who had been a president of the EC Commission, later put it succinctly: "We are not in business at all, we are in politics" (Swann 1992: ix).

Another potential approach to achieving peace in Europe would have been to deal with defense matters directly. But by 1956, such attempts as the European Political and Defence Communities had failed. Monnet and Schuman understood that, given the extent of mistrust after the war, the indirect approach of economic integration was the only one likely to be acceptable to all parties at the time.

Trade as a Promoter of Peace

Increasing international trade might improve security in three related ways:

1. More trade means greater economic interdependence between the countries involved. This increases the stake each country has in the welfare of its neighbor and makes war more costly. It also in-

creases the number of people who have an economic interest in peaceable relations and so helps strengthen political pressures against going to war.

2. More trade means more interaction between the peoples and governments of the two countries, more familiarity with the neighbor's goods and services, and greater understanding of their cultural, political, and social institutions. All this is likely to increase trust.

3. Secure trading relations will reduce the likelihood of war by increasing security of access to the partner's supplies of strategic raw materials and reducing the threat of trade embargo. This argument is especially important in a world of high trade barriers where access to other sources is difficult—the situation in Europe around 1950, when Jean Monnet and other French leaders were concerned that the German coal barons in the Ruhr would have too much control over French industry (Duchêne 1994). The post–World War I solution of direct control of German resources had been discredited and was not an option. Monnet instead pushed for the creation of the ECSC so that Germany could rebuild its industry without being a threat to France. This sectoral approach to security was later expanded to the integration of general trade relations, with the creation of the EEC.

Economists have examined some of the implications of uncertain access to strategic raw materials. Arad and Hillman (1979) show how fear of being cut off from foreign sources of defense equipment can cause countries to overinvest in their own defense industries. Hillman and Long (1983) discuss the optimal exploitation of a mineral resource if the alternative foreign supply is uncertain. In both cases an RIA or a global institution that ensured partner supplies would be both politically and economically advantageous.

A fourth possible strategic benefit of trade is that the greater trust generated by increased trade may, in time, pay a peace dividend as defense spending falls.

In all these cases one can envisage a virtuous cycle whereby increasing trade permits closer integration, first through more thorough trade liberalization and then through policy or deep integration that binds the parties closer together and facilitates yet further growth in trade, and so on (see box 7.2, below).

Although direct evidence of the effect of trade on the likelihood of conflict between any pair of countries is limited, numerous studies have confirmed Chan's (1984) conclusion that conflict between countries is

---

Box 7.2 Modeling Trade and Security Externalities

If increased trade between two countries reduces tensions between them because of increased trust and economic dependency, what can economic analysis say about the type of intervention that can capture this security externality? Schiff and Winters (1998) examine this issue within a formal three-country model, with two small, antagonistic countries and a large "rest of the world."

The model shows that, absent security externalities, nondiscriminatory free trade is the optimal policy for the two small countries. If, however, increased mutual imports provide additional security for small countries, it is worth subsidizing them by lowering their price relative to other goods. This could be accomplished directly, but, given the fiscal objections to subsidies and their liability to capture, it is more frequently done by creating an RIA that taxes imports from the rest of the world, raises their prices, and therefore lowers the relative prices of intrabloc imports. The arrangement is optimal (welfare is maximized) when external tariffs are set so that the marginal benefit from security—including a "peace dividend" from reduced defense expenditures—equals the marginal cost of trade diversion. Under these circumstances, the net welfare impact of forming an RIA is positive and is not ambiguous, as it would be in the absence of security effects.

Strictly, to be equivalent to an import subsidy, the RIA should be accompanied by taxes on domestic sales to raise their prices relative to member imports, but even if this is not done, there will be security benefits from the trade preferences (although then the optimal tariffs are lower). The case for an RIA is strengthened if security is related to both imports from and exports to the potentially antagonistic partner, and there may be yet further benefits because in this case full optimization requires that countries cooperate.

Over time, the optimal tariff on imports from nonmembers is likely to fall in such a security-inspired RIA. As antagonism between the two countries diminishes, due to increased intrabloc trade, the subsidy on intrabloc trade (or the optimal external tariff) falls. Thus, if security is the main motivation for forming the RIA, the RIA's external trade policy should become increasingly open over time. This is precisely what took place in the EC/EU: average tariffs on manufacturing products fell from about 13 percent in 1958 to about 3 percent after the Uruguay Round.

Are trade preferences the only way to obtain security benefits? Since deep integration can also lower trading costs and increase trade flows, it can enhance security even in the absence of trade preferences (and if external trade barriers are present, their optimal level falls following deep integration). But it seems likely that countries will engage in deep integration—which implies giving up a degree of sovereignty—only with countries they already trust. If trust is initially low, trade preferences may be the only available instrument until the degree of trust has increased. This, in fact, increases the warranted level of the external tariff in the early stages of an RIA, for preferences not only boost trade directly but also, by creating conditions for future deep integration, promise further security and economic gains later.

---

less prevalent if both are democratic. Polachek (1992, 1996) explains this finding through the effect of democracy on international trade. He estimates that democratic countries trade more with each other than do other countries and, using detailed data from the Conflict and Peace Data Bank, finds trade to have a significant and negative impact on conflict. Polachek estimates that a 6 percent increase in trade lowers his measure of conflict by about 1 percent. A key feature of these results is that

Polachek tested for causality and found that an increase in trade between partners caused a reduction in conflict but that reduced conflict did not increase trade.[3]

We are not saying that trade always promotes peace or that trade is sufficient for peace. Clearly, trade partners do fight, and sometimes over trade issues, as discussed below. On the whole, however, there is persuasive evidence that trade will generally tend to foster peaceable, if not friendly, relations between countries.

RIAs as Promoters of Peace

So far, we have been discussing the effect on conflict of trade in general—implicitly, nondiscriminatory trade. It is widely held, however, that discriminatory trade has the same effect. Although this argument seems highly plausible under certain conditions, it is not always the case.

Political scientists have researched the use of trade diplomacy within a regional context and have concluded that trade relations, including RIAs and, especially, deeper arrangements, might assist political relations between member countries by developing means for avoidance and management of intramural conflict. The negotiations between leaders of neighboring countries that are required to form and operate an RIA tend to generate trust between them. This helps them identify with each other, understand each others' problems, and interpret each others' actions. Trade talks allow political or economic elites to form coalitions for subsequent collaboration and consensual action.[4] Wallace (1994: 4) argues that the "most striking phenomenon of formal European integration has been the interpenetration of national administrations, with ministers and officials from different governments in close and continuous contact."

The main motivation for creating the ECSC in 1951 and the EEC in 1957 was to reduce the threat of war in Europe, especially war between France and Germany. Similar motives are found in the creation of ASEAN—to reduce tensions between Indonesia and Malaysia (De Rosa 1995)—and of APEC and the CACM, which include potential political or military opponents (Page 1998). Anwar (1994), in assessing ASEAN's role as promoter of regional peace, notes that intraregional conflicts occurred among the five founding members before ASEAN was founded but not afterward. Srinivasan (1994: 7) argues that greater economic interdependence among South Asian countries would help defuse tensions among them, stating that "promoting freer movement of goods, services, people and capital in the region might also facilitate the resolution of political and territorial disputes."

Security also seems to have played an important role in the Southern Cone of South America. The Argentine and Brazilian militaries long justified their claims to resources for defense partly on the potential threats from each other. In the mid-1980s the two countries signed nuclear cooperation agreements and economic agreements covering steel and automobiles in the expectation that this would help reduce tensions between them by curtailing the power of the military and strengthening their fragile democracies. The creation of MERCOSUR in 1991 reinforced this process and bound smaller neighbors into it.

Rubens Ricupero, secretary-general of the United Nations Conference on Trade and Development (UNCTAD) and former finance minister of Brazil, confirms the importance of MERCOSUR's security aspects:

> Both countries were emerging from a period of military governments during which considerable tension had characterized the bilateral relationship, centered on a long-standing controversy about competing hydroelectric projects in international rivers of the Plata Basin. Both militaries had also continued to pursue their secret nuclear programs. It was essential to start with agreements in the economic area in order to create a more positive external environment that rendered it possible to contain the military nuclear programs and to replace rivalry by integration. This effort was developed along successive stages and eventually led to signature by the two governments of Brazil and Argentina. (Personal communication, 1998)

Thus, as with the ECSC and the EC, the indirect path to enhancing security through economic integration was deemed an essential first step.

Africa provides what may be a related example. In 1986, 11 of 15 members of ECOWAS ratified a mutual defense protocol that authorizes military intervention by the community in conflicts between members or if conflict in a member country is instigated from outside and is likely to endanger peace and security in the entire community (*Oxford Analytica Daily Brief*, September 5, 1997). One interpretation of this initiative is that by creating institutions spanning the linguistic divide—an almost unique achievement in West Africa—ECOWAS enabled neighbors to develop cooperative behavior that eventually allowed them to address mutual security concerns. In fact, in this view, ECOWAS has gone farther than either MERCOSUR or the EU, for it uses an actual defense pact to bolster security, while the others use only economic integration.

In cases where security is an issue and is amenable to trade-related policy, creating an RIA may be the optimal approach (see box 7.2). Under such circumstances, we can also infer that the optimal level of protection that RIA members maintain against imports from nonmembers will fall over time as trade grows and also following policy integration. This last observation can be used as a test for identifying countries' unobservable motivations for creating an RIA: if security were the main motive, tariffs would fall, and therefore if tariffs do not fall, we know that the efficient pursuit of security was not the main objective of the RIA, regardless of the rhetoric surrounding its creation. This observation can also serve as a policy prescription for "security-inspired" RIAs.

RIAs Are Not Always Effective Routes to Peace

In the EU and MERCOSUR, integration helped enhance security by internalizing security externalities associated with intrabloc trade. The main reason for the success of these RIAs in achieving this goal is that the members were actually looking for arrangements to solve a security problem, not an economic one, and that defense pacts were not feasible, given low trust at the time. Thus, their objectives were political rather than economic, and member countries structured the RIAs in such a way as to attain those objectives. Among other things, economic gains and losses were shared in ways that member countries perceived as fair.[5] Many other RIAs, however, are motivated by economics. In these cases an asymmetric distribution of benefits and costs may result in frictions among member countries. In other words, the pursuit of economic gain may result in security losses if the gains for one member come essentially at the expense of other members.[6]

Thus, the finding that trade enhances security does not allow us to conclude that policies which promote trade within a region will always improve the prospects for regional peace. Indeed, they may have precisely the opposite effect. Policy-induced integration promotes trade at a price. The tariff preferences that induce regional trade can create powerful income transfers within the region and can lead to the concentration of industry in a single location. The countries or regions which lose income or industry can be so resentful that separatist movements arise and the overall risk of conflict is increased. In such cases, disintegration, as happened with East and West Pakistan, may be the outcome.

A clear example of how integration can trigger conflict was the American Civil War. The United States constituted a customs union in which the North produced manufactures that were sold in the South, while the southern states produced cotton that was exported to Europe. Tariffs nearly triggered civil war in 1828, when Congress, dominated by northern interests, sharply raised the U.S. import duty on manufactures. The effect of what was known in the South as the "Tariff of Abominations" was to increase the price that northern manufacturers could charge in the South, generating a massive income transfer from the South to the North. South Carolina refused to collect the duties and threatened to secede unless the tariff was rescinded. The federal government sent in troops, but Congress backed down before fighting developed. In 1860 northern interests tried again, and this time Congress would not back down. This, perhaps as much as slavery, was the issue that led the southern states to try to quit the Union (Adams 1993).

Another example is the East African Community (EAC). Here, Kenya was the equivalent of the northern states in the American case. Tanzania and Uganda complained about the income transfers that the common external tariff on manufactures created. They also feared that there would be an increasing agglomeration of manufacturing in Nairobi, which had a head start on industrialization compared with the smaller industrial centers of Dar es Salaam in Tanzania and Jinga in Uganda. Arguments about compensation for the income transfers led to the collapse of the EAC, the closing of borders, and the confiscation of Community assets in 1978. This atmosphere of hostility contributed to conflict between Tanzania and Uganda in 1979.

In the light of these examples, in which the trade policy used to promote regional integration was so unfair that it actually worsened intraregional security, the success of the EEC looks even more remarkable. Among the favorable factors was, first of all, a genuine desire for security, perhaps traceable to Europe's extraordinarily bloody history, which saw three Franco-German conflicts in a century, and to the failure of a number of other efforts at integration such as the European Political and Defence Communities. It also helped that the key players, France and Germany, were relatively evenly balanced. Had they not been, an alternative solution to the security problem—hegemonic domination—would have been more likely than the reliance on mutual benefits that characterizes the RIA route.

Furthermore, reflecting the genuine wish for reconciliation, the European Community has always pursued regional integration in ways that avoid transfers large enough to trigger conflict. This was partly a matter of negotiating style and partly of design (Winters 1997b). The style was consensual: negotiators were always looking for compromise and conciliation. When a country signaled that a Community policy would cause it major political or economic problems, it was accommodated, either by being offered compensation, as with the British budget rebate negotiated by Prime Minister Margaret Thatcher, or through a very gradual adjustment process, as with application of the rules on labor mobility to new members Portugal and Spain. The key design feature was that the Community's external tariffs were generally low and declining, so that the income transfers arising from exploitation of consumers in one nation by producers in another were relatively small.

The one exception was agriculture, which has been highly protected, has generated large income transfers between countries, and has been a source of some internal political conflict. In grand terms, however, even agriculture was part of the inspired peace bargain. The Common Agricultural Policy arose because France wanted access to German markets at the high prices that German farmers also desired. The conflict over agriculture has not often been between France and Germany but between these two countries and other members, especially the United Kingdom.

The economic costs of forming a security-enhancing RIA are important, even if the objective is as apparently noneconomic as securing peace. Before deciding to form such an RIA, policymakers should be convinced that trade will enhance trust significantly—that contact will help, not harm, general relations, and that it will create no new frictions. They should also ask whether an RIA is the most efficient mechanism for internalizing security externalities. Should they choose to form an RIA for security reasons, they should ensure that tariffs are not set higher than is absolutely necessary to capture the security externalities that exist, and they need to realize that these tariffs should decline over time and following deeper measures of integration.

RIAs AND SOCIAL AND POLITICAL PRESSURES: POTENTIALLY HELPFUL, BUT NOT A PANACEA

The formation of an RIA is sometimes seen as a means of preventing or reducing the spread of civil disturbances or civil war from neighboring nations or of controlling migratory flows. The EU has been concerned with such threats from North Africa, and this has been one motivation behind the Euro-Mediterranean Agreements. The hope is that these agreements, including their associated aid protocols, will improve the economic situation in the North African partner countries and help contain the problems. Similarly, both the United States and Mexico have been concerned about the possibility of occasional social strife and violence in Mexico spreading northward, and both hoped that NAFTA, by facilitating access to U.S. markets, would help improve Mexico's economic situation and reduce social tensions. Implicit in this hope is that NAFTA will increase Mexican economic welfare.

Closely related is the manifest desire of rich countries to stem large-scale migration from poorer countries even if it does not immediately threaten political and social stability. This too has played a role in the formation of RIAs, including NAFTA and the EU's Europe Agreements with the countries of Central and Eastern Europe (OECD 1995). In the case of NAFTA, Presidents Salinas and (George H. W.) Bush argued that helping Mexico export more goods would help it export fewer people, thereby reducing migration pressures. The recent Euro-Mediterranean agreements also provide evidence of such motivation.

Whether RIAs do help solve migration problems depends on whether trade and migration are complements or substitutes. Standard trade theory holds that they are substitutes, so that increased trade integration is likely to reduce income or wage differentials and decrease labor migration flows. More recent analysis, however, and some empirical results have shown that North-South trade and migration may well be complements, so that integration may not lower migration, especially of unskilled labor.

Four main arguments lead in this direction. First, it may plausibly be argued that migration entails a fixed cost and that developing country capital markets are highly imperfect (López and Schiff 1998). If so, very poor people may not be able to afford migration, and a policy that increased their incomes could relax their capital constraint and allow them to move. Second, the costs of migration decrease as more information about the destination country becomes available. Since, for the reasons discussed above, this seems a likely effect of an RIA, migration to the new partners could increase. Third, even if an RIA is welfare improving overall—which, we have argued, cannot be taken for granted—it may not benefit unskilled workers, who are the real bêtes noires of the potential countries of immigration. For example, since the mid-1980s, unskilled workers have fared poorly in Mexico, with declines in their real income of 10 to 15 percent (Hanson and Harrison 1999). To the extent that this deterioration is attributable to NAFTA, the incentives for these people to emigrate, if not their ability to do so, is increased by integration. Finally, the changes in the production structure induced by an RIA will cause some people to migrate internally within member countries, and evidence suggests that once people have been shaken loose from their "homelands," their propensities to migrate internationally increase. That is, having once uprooted and moved from, say, rural areas to Mexico City or to areas bordering the United States, it is a small step to move farther, to the United States itself (Sewastynowicz 1986; Morrison and Zabin 1994).

Migration remains an issue even within common markets in which free mobility of labor is ostensibly an objective. The EU set a 13-year transition period before Portugal and Spain were permitted completely free access to other members' labor markets. Similarly, it is widely accepted that fear of migration is one of the reasons behind the reluctance of the EU to consider Turkish membership seriously. Even among long-standing members of the EU, migration has not been made easy, and labor mobility is much lower in Europe than in the United States (Blanchard and Katz 1992). In part, this is cultural, but it also reflects multiple policy frictions, such as pension transferability, housing systems, and health provision, that make effective migration complicated or worse.

THE ROLE OF REGIONAL INTEGRATION IN STRENGTHENING DEMOCRACY AND POLITICAL INSTITUTIONS

RIAs can be useful tools for improving political institutions. Trade blocs with strong club rules can help anchor democratic reforms in member countries. Membership in an RIA can increase the likelihood of achieving or upholding democracy, especially if the bloc includes large democratic developed countries. Newer or less politically advanced countries may gain from joining an RIA that includes at least one large developed country if accession is part of a strategy of pursuing political, economic, or social reforms (or preventing backsliding), when such moves would not be feasible without the conditionality embodied in the RIA's club rules. Those rules often include democracy and human rights.

MERCOSUR put its—at the time, informal—democracy rule into practice in April 1996, when the commander of Paraguay's armed forces was said to be contemplating a military coup. The bloc's four presidents (with backing from the United States and the Organization of American States) reportedly quelled the rumored coup with a strong joint statement that democracy was a condition of membership in the bloc. Two months later MERCOSUR amended its charter to formally exclude any country that "abandons the full exercise of republican institutions."[7] In forming FTAs with MERCOSUR, Bolivia and Chile accepted democracy as a condition for membership (see box 7.3).

Box 7.3 Democracy in MERCOSUR

The Presidential Declaration on the Democratic Commitment in MERCOSUR, signed in San Luis, Argentina, on June 25, 1996, made democracy a condition of membership for the four member countries, Argentina, Brazil, Paraguay, and Uruguay. This condition was extended to the FTAs between MERCOSUR and Bolivia and Chile in the Protocol of Ushuaia, signed on July 24, 1998.

How credible is the "democratic commitment"? Are member countries likely to act on it and punish countries that deviate from democratic principles? One indication of the credibility of the commitment is provided by the specifics of the Protocol of Ushuaia, which sets forth the full validity of democratic institutions as an indispensable condition for the existence of the MERCOSUR agreements and establishes procedures for consulting on violations. If there is rupture of the democratic order in one state, the other countries are to consult among themselves and with the affected state. If these consultations prove ineffective, the other countries will decide on the nature and extent of the measures to be applied. The sanctions listed range from suspension of the right to participate in the organs of the various agreements up to suspension from MERCOSUR. These measures are to be adopted by consensus and communicated to the affected state, which does not participate in the decisionmaking process. The sanctions are to end once it has been verified that democratic order has been fully reestablished.

MERCOSUR and the associated countries have reduced ambiguity about the "democratic commitment" to a minimum. Punishment seems very likely, and the market of MERCOSUR plus Bolivia and Chile is important enough to the member countries that they are likely to consider the threat of retaliation seriously. Thus, the threat is likely to be effective.

It is generally thought that the framers of MERCOSUR borrowed the democracy idea and language from the 1957 Treaty of Rome that established the EEC. But although it seems understood that only democracies are eligible for (new) membership, the Treaty of Rome does not mention democracy (although it does mention peace and liberty).

Why is there a strong statement on democracy in MERCOSUR and not in the EEC? All EEC member countries had been democratic for more than a decade in 1957, and the United States acted as a sort of guarantor. MERCOSUR member countries, by contrast, were emerging from long periods of military rule, there was no external guarantee, and preserving and consolidating fragile democracies was an important objective of the governments involved.

The EEC had no formal democracy requirement, although by convention and practice it was understood from the mid-1960s that such a condition existed, at least for new members. Bhalla and Bhalla (1997: 159) argue that it was generally understood that "the acceptance of the poorer economies of Greece, Spain and Portugal was motivated largely by the desire to help these restored democracies remain democratic by bolstering them politically and economically." Similarly, the Europe Agreements with accession candidates in Central and Eastern Europe and the Baltic area are designed to "facilitate" the transition countries' "full integration into the community of democratic nations" (title 1, art. 2). Latvia, a candidate for EU accession, is reviewing its citizenship policies for its Russian minority to meet EU concerns about human rights (*Washington Post,*

July 24, 1998). The EU agreements with Mediterranean countries also include respect for human rights and the rule of law, as does the Cotonou Agreement between the EU and the ACP countries. In the 1992 Treaty on European Union, explicit reference is made to democracy, although not in any operational form.

Conditions regarding democracy and human rights will be truly effective only if the penalties for violating them are severe and their enforcement credible. As with economic policies (chapter 4), it is difficult to pin down exactly what inspires credibility, but for developing countries an explicit statement of the club rule seems necessary, and an explicit and plausible plan for its enforcement highly desirable (see box 7.3). In the absence of such conditions, it is difficult to see how the objective will be achieved—and, in particular, how it will be achieved without the need to resort to the sort of explicit political pressure that MERCOSUR had to exert in the case of Paraguay.

The enforceability of club rules depends both on the value of belonging to the bloc and on the credibility of the threat of action. First, new members who, in joining a large bloc, obtain significant benefits—including access to a large market and greater bargaining power with the rest of the world—are unlikely to break the rules (or backslide) and so risk losing these benefits. Admittedly, parties that pose threats to democracy may not be moved by such considerations, but ordinary economic agents will be, and so the condition will increase the difficulty of building support for insurrection. Second, the credibility of the threat of action is likely to be greater if violation of club rules by new members entails a large cost to the other members. That cost may be direct and economic or (perhaps more likely) indirect and political, such as a demonstration effect.

The effectiveness of club rules is likely to vary with the nature of the membership. RIAs between small low-income countries, which typically trade very little with each other, are less able to impose significant costs on recalcitrants by ejecting them. Choosing large, important partners improves the chances that club rules will be enforced. Because a country is likely to be more concerned about the social and political conditions of a nearby than of a far-off country, enforcement of club rules is likely to be more effective in RIAs between neighbors than in those between distant partners.

Two other circumstances will affect the credibility of enforcement. First, it seems unlikely that nondemocracies, or countries where democracy is very fragile, will prove stern disciplinarians even if a democracy rule exists. Second, the enforcer has to see enforcement as an important issue in itself. It is also important that there be no competing issues that are more vital to the enforcer. While the Cold War was in progress, Western powers were far more concerned to ensure that client countries were securely anticommunist than with the details of their governance structures. Imposing democracy rules was just not an element of policy.

We have noted the importance of proximity. The question of distance is relevant to one current debate. The EU's Cotonou Agreement with the ACP states has the goal of eventually replacing the Lomé Conventions with a series of regional economic partnership agreements (EPAs) with groups of ACP countries (McQueen 1998). It includes, as an "essential element," the developing partners' respect for human rights and democracy, as well as injunctions to manage their economies properly (Council of the European Union 1998). Some commentators (for example, Winters 2001; Schiff and Winters 2002a, 2002b) argue that the EU's interest in enforcing good economic policy in the ACP countries, let alone "good" political practice, is very doubtful. The ACP countries are too small and distant to affect any EU interest materially, and the various EU members frequently have different views on any particular case. In addition, disciplining former colonies for pursuing economic or political policies that are not approved in European capitals looks like an international public relations nightmare. On this view, EPAs will generate no additional credibility for the ACP countries. A contrary view, at least on economic credibility, is set forth by Collier and others (1997), who see the EU as the stern external agent of restraint that developing countries require in order to convince the world that they are reliable and will succeed economically. The argument is essentially that the EU is so important to the ACP countries that they would never flout it. Thus, the EU can do its partners some good at almost no cost to itself.

An interesting feature of the club rules–democracy argument for RIAs is that it is one case where there is clearly no multilateral substitute. Multilateral trade arrangements cannot propose and enforce these sorts of rules, which are simply not part of the mandate of organizations such as the WTO. Other international organizations such as the United Nations or regional and multilateral development institutions may be able to persuade member countries to abide by some rules, but so far, these do not include democracy or other constraints on political regimes. It would appear that positive spillover effects in the political arena are only possible in large regional arrangements that include club rules.

REGIONALISM AND THE NATION-STATE

Joining an RIA necessarily requires surrendering some immediate control over policymaking and losing some political autonomy, if only over tariffs on partners' exports. (So, of course, does membership in the WTO.) Some RIAs, however, go deeper than this and create institutions for joint decisionmaking. For example, as the EU's integration has deepened, decisionmaking has increasingly moved away from national capitals to Brussels, and much of the current debate is shaped by the belief that some form of political unification must eventually follow the creation of an integrated economic unit (box 7.4).[8] But such integration need not result in the suppression of the nation as an organizational framework or in the loss of effective sovereignty. On the contrary, by pooling sovereignty, members of an RIA may be able to preserve and enlarge it and thus strengthen the concept of national identity and integrity. Nation-states can strengthen themselves by creating a united front against external pressures or by joining forces in international negotiations. Setting aside considerations of coalition building and policy spillovers, however, such cooperation does not strictly require an RIA in the sense of trade preferences.

Box 7.4 Trade Preferences Do Not Inevitably Lead to Political Integration

Although few customs unions aim explicitly at political union, many have gone far beyond simple preferential trading arrangements to achieve a degree of political integration. Economic integration has often been a precursor to and facilitator of closer political association (as in the EEC) or even state formation, as in the *Zollverein,* founded in 1834, which contributed to the creation in 1871 of the German nation-state. Similarly, Moldavia and Wallachia formed a customs union in 1847 before uniting as Romania in 1878.

But economic integration is not needed for political integration. In the past—and today in some developing countries—nations had internal trade barriers, which meant that they were politically, but not economically, integrated. In the Middle Ages customs collectors were frequently stationed not just at the boundaries but in the interior of political units—at important market centers, junctions of trade routes, or mountain passes. England and Scotland became united under a single monarch in 1603, but attempts to reach agreement on commercial union failed until the Act of Union in 1707 (Irwin 1993). Although politically unified under the king for centuries, France remained divided—even after several reforms—by 1,600 internal tolls and tariffs until the French Revolution enabled their abolition in 1790. Each Swiss canton retained tariff autonomy until 1848. More recently, Hong Kong (China) and mainland China have achieved political unity without full economic integration, as internal trade barriers and dual customs jurisdictions persist.

Not only is economic integration not necessary for political integration but it can also decrease regional political unity. Common external tariffs or rules of origins may operate as irritants and as a stimulant to separatist movements. Such was the case with Western Australia in the Australian Commonwealth, the Prairie Provinces in Canada, and the North and the South in the antebellum United States.

Regional Integration to Deal with Outside Threats and Regional Hegemons

The normal approach to external security threats is for countries to form alliances independent of any trade preferences. It is possible, however, to start with a trade pact, based on "hopes that economic union between the weak would ripen into political union, and that by the political union of the weak a power might be established strong enough to defend against aggression from outside" (Viner 1950: 92). Nations that feared being absorbed forcibly by larger states have united to forestall such coercion.

Thus, the Austrian emperor proposed (but eventually aborted) an economic union with Spain and Bavaria as a defensive scheme against France in 1665 (Viner 1950: 93). More recently, the Gulf Cooperation Council (GCC) was created in 1981 partly in response to the potential threat of regional powers such as the Islamic Republic of Iran and Iraq (Schiff and Winters 1998), and ASEAN was partially motivated by a perceived need to stem the threatened spread of Communism in Southeast Asia. A major motive of Central and Eastern European countries in applying for membership to the EU is as protection from a perceived threat from Russia.

The Southern African Development Coordination Conference (SADCC) was initially formed in 1980 to provide a united front against, and reduce dependence on, South Africa. After apartheid ended, South Africa was invited to join the group, now the Southern African Development Community (SADC). The difference was that whereas SADCC involved cooperation on trade matters in general but not mutual trade preferences per se, SADC is developing a trade protocol based on preferences.

Regional Integration and Negotiations with the Outside World

Regional cooperation (which may, but need not, involve trade preferences) can strengthen the voices of small nations. These countries often face severe disadvantages in dealing with the rest of the world because of their low bargaining power and high negotiation costs. Bilateral and multilateral negotiations often require substantial financial resources, time, and expert knowledge, which are limited in small countries. As the world has become more integrated and the number of issues to be dealt with in the international arena has grown, the incentive for small countries to cooperate with their neighbors has grown, as well.

Small countries can substantially reduce their negotiation costs and at the same time increase their market and negotiating power by pooling their resources and acting together to articulate shared interests. This is more likely to come about (Andriamananjara and Schiff 2001):

- If their interests are similar (so that intrabloc negotiation costs are low)
- If the cost of international negotiations is high (creating greater incentives to cooperate), and
- If a large number of issues needs to be dealt with (which both increases the incentives and makes it easier to construct packages in which every party can gain).

Establishing a regional grouping typically involves "logrolling": "I'll vote for your issue if you vote for mine." By trading support for each other's preferred issues, countries can get more than they could obtain unilaterally (Andriamananjara and Schiff 2001). Even so, such coalition formation is neither easy nor common. Members will usually have to sacrifice some preferred positions even before the international negotiation process begins as the coalition settles on priorities. These steps can be politically difficult, especially if the group is large and the countries differ widely. The coalition also needs to devise ways of responding to offers and setbacks in negotiations, for it is quite certain that they will not achieve all that they hope for initially. Setting up a secretariat and formulating suitable institutional rules for decisionmaking may help in these processes but require significant time and resources up front.

Relatively shallow but highly successful examples of cooperation of this kind are the Scandinavian and ASEAN groups in the WTO. These blocs pool their resources to attend meetings, providing regular briefings for each other. If they agree on an issue (and they put some effort into discovering beforehand whether they do or not), the representatives may speak for the group; if not, individual countries look after their own interests.

At a deeper level, small Caribbean nations increased their bargaining power by establishing CARICOM in 1973 to pool their negotiation resources and formulate common policy stances (see box 7.5). This allowed the member states to reduce their negotiation costs and exert greater influence outside the region than would have been possible had they acted independently. The region acquired bargaining power at the very highest level of North-South politics. Representatives of CARICOM countries took the lead in formulating and articulating the positions of the ACP group in negotiating the Lomé Conventions. By pooling their support, the CARICOM nations succeeded in getting their nationals elected to key international positions such as Commonwealth secretary-general and ACP secretary-general. In the process, they ensured that the

Box 7.5 CARICOM and International Negotiations

All Caribbean states face problems of political and economic viability because of their extremely small size. CARICOM, created in 1973, has as members Antigua and Barbuda, The Bahamas, Barbados, Belize, Dominica, Grenada, Jamaica, Montserrat, St. Kitts and Nevis, St. Lucia, St. Vincent and the Grenadines, and Trinidad and Tobago. The members have populations ranging from 10,000 to 2.55 million and GDPs of from $0.24 billion to $6.3 billion.

CARICOM was intended to give the region a more powerful voice and presence to defend its interests in international affairs (Byron 1994; IADB 1995). The group has three main areas of activity: economic integration; cooperation in noneconomic areas (health, education, and transport) and in operation of common services; and coordination of the foreign policies of the member states. CARICOM has been particularly active in negotiating preferential access to European and North American markets, negotiating for consistent and remunerative commodity prices, obtaining larger flows of concessionary finance for the region, and raising the region's profile in multilateral institutions (Byron 1994). It has been involved in negotiations between the ACP countries and the EU and with the GATT/WTO, the proposed Free Trade Area of the Americas, the United Nations Conference on Trade and Development (UNCTAD), and the United Nations Convention on the Law of the Sea (UNCLOS). It has taken part in commissions or joint councils with Canada, Cuba, Japan, Mexico, the United States, the Organization of American States, and the Group of Three. A single microstate would not have had the human, physical, or financial capacity to conduct fruitful negotiations unilaterally in so many areas.

region's interests in commodity trade and development cooperation were taken into account. They also consolidated multilateral links with other parts of the developing world, established themselves as full participants in the activities of the United Nations (U.N.), despite that organization's earlier ambivalence on the issue of microstate membership, and focused on getting U.N. organs to address the development needs of small island developing states. Finally, they succeeded in collectively negotiating a whole range of preferential market access agreements—for example, CARIBCAN with Canada, the Caribbean Basin Initiative with the United States, and the Lomé Conventions and (along with other developing nations) the generalized system of preferences (GSP) with the EU. Despite its relatively limited trade and investment impact, CARICOM has been successful in serving as a political instrument in joint negotiations on trade and investment with larger countries and regional trading blocs.

The existence of a visible regional and supranational authority may attract more foreign assistance (or even foreign direct investment) because it is easier for the donor community to deal with the group as an entity than with each country individually. Regarding the SADCC, Inotai (1991) observes: "More recently, common activities emerged in order to attract higher volumes of external financial resources. By 1988, SADCC could ensure external financing for 20 industrial projects, and is now working on getting additional resources for 11 more projects." The SADCC's successor, the SADC, now acts as a regional coordinating mechanism with the donor community. For instance, in February 1996 the U.S. Department of Commerce signed a memorandum of understanding with the SADC that outlines six areas for cooperation in advancing commercial development in southern Africa.

As for other RIAs, in ASEAN Japanese aid has played an important role in assisting regional industrial projects, including automobile assembly and parts production (Bhalla and Bhalla 1997). Similarly, following its advocacy of regionalism as a principle, the European Union has actively assisted subregional integration—for example, in Central Europe, the Mediterranean, and the CACM.

Finally, the objective of strengthening negotiating and bargaining power is not confined to the formation of blocs by small countries. Whalley (1998b) argues that this idea was shared by the countries involved in the creation of the EEC in the late 1950s, which felt that together they would have much greater leverage in negotiations with the United States than they would individually. Similar arguments were made in the United Kingdom in favor of joining the EEC. Whalley asserts that the goal of increasing negotiating power, especially vis-à-vis NAFTA, was also present in the formation of MERCOSUR.

Having discussed the appeal and efficacy of RIAs in the political arena, we turn to the issue of market power as part of the discussion, in chapter 8, of the effects of regional integration on global trade liberalization.

NOTES

1. British Prime Minister Neville Chamberlain's infamous phrase about the German invasion of Czechoslovakia in 1938 (Taylor 1979).

2. Recall that the worry about RIAs is not that they reduce trade but that the extra trade they bring about reduces economic welfare.

3. Although these tests are informative, it should be noted that they rely on a limited, temporal notion of causality: A causes B if observing the current and past outcomes of A helps predict the current value of B.

4. Others take the view that friendly nations or allies, rather than enemies, tend to form RIAs—that the order of causation is from friendship to regional integration. Mansfield (1993) argues that countries will lower barriers only with allies (not with adversaries) because increased trade will raise incomes, which can enable higher defense expenditures, which in turn only makes sense if the

countries are allies. The fact that an RIA might be as likely to reduce income as to increase it counts against this view as a general theory.

5. One cause of perceptions of unfairness can clearly be short-to-medium-term fluctuations in exchange rates. As noted in chapter 1, for reasons of space we decided not to deal with macroeconomics and to limit the analysis to real phenomena.

6. Of course, tension arising from the redistribution of rents is not specific to RIAs. For instance, Schiff (1998) argues that if moving all the way to free trade results in such a redistribution of rents across ethnic groups that it raises tensions among those groups (destroys social capital), it may be harmful economically.

7. Presidential Declaration on the Democratic Commitment in MERCOSUR, San Luis, Argentina, June 25, 1996; Talbott (1996); "Survey on MERCOSUR," *The Economist,* October 12, 1996.

8. As president of the European Commission, Jacques Delors stated that one consequence of the Single European Act would be that four-fifths of those decisions then taken in national capitals would eventually be made in Brussels (Milward 1992: 2). The increasing number of lobbying groups setting up in Brussels seems to support the view of the EU's increasing importance in decisionmaking.

CHAPTER 8

Trade Blocs and the Rest of the World

RIAs are, by nature, exclusive clubs. Every country in the world is excluded from nearly every RIA in the world, and every RIA excludes nearly every country. Discrimination against excluded countries is real and causes significant trade diversion, for which we present new empirical evidence in this chapter. Trade diversion can harm excluded countries (in shorthand, the rest of the world, ROW), particularly where they face large trade blocs. The extent of the harm depends on how much the RIA diverts trade and on the structure of the ROW economy in the sectors in which trading patterns are affected. As a rule, trade blocs harm nonmembers least if they are less trade diverting, liberalize their external trade, and boost global competition by increasing member efficiency and growth.

The other main issue in the intersection between RIAs and the rest of the world is whether RIAs are stepping stones toward globally freer trade, or millstones around the neck of progress toward that goal. Many arguments have been advanced for the benign view—that regionalism stimulates global trade negotiations, that it makes negotiations simpler, that "open regionalism" liberalizes trade, or that blocs can advance farther and faster than global negotiations. In truth, however, the world of multiple trade blocs is still too new to allow a definitive answer to this question, and much of the evidence shows that advances in multilateral trade negotiations have led, not followed, the formation of trade blocs. Moreover, there are strong analytical reasons to suggest that regionalism is more likely to undermine than to support full free trade and that it may increase the chances of trade wars.

The WTO's rules and practices on regionalism impose some discipline on the worst kind of trade blocs but cannot, in the end, prevent members from creating RIAs that harm themselves or others. Moreover, the rules do not fully apply to developing countries and are not enforced very actively anyway. We cannot identify rule changes that are both feasible and desirable, but we do urge that current rules be clarified and enforced. We also suggest that more attention be paid to assessing the economic effects rather than just the legal standing of proposed RIAs.

TRADE DISCRIMINATION: STILL SIGNIFICANT

Trade discrimination against excluded countries commonly causes significant trade diversion. Although this diversion is not inevitably harmful to the rest of the world, it will be injurious under two common circumstances: when nonmembers tax their international trade (for example, by imposing tariffs), and when nonmembers' export prices fall as a result of falling demand. Merely examining the value of ROW exports to the RIA is not sufficient to identify harm; one really needs to consider the evolution of ROW imports and the prices paid for them relative to the prices of exports—the terms of trade. In addition, the difference between the value of a unit of exports and the resources required to produce it have to be examined.

One might think that after five decades of tariff cuts and two decades of reform of nontariff barriers, trade restrictions would be so low as to hardly matter. But although tariffs of 30 percent are less distortionary than tariffs of 60 percent, trade barriers are still high enough to impart a significant bias to international trade. Preferential reductions in these tariffs—through RIAs—will further distort trade and probably impose costs; even a discriminatory tariff of 5 percent can have significant effects on import sourcing if goods are highly substitutable. If discrimination extends to areas such as standards testing and enforcement, or to public procurement, trade diversion is likely to be even more significant.

The degree of discrimination arising from an RIA is related to the height of the "normal," nonpreferential trade barrier—the most-favored-nation (MFN) barrier—and to the proportion of trading partners or of trade covered by MFN status.[1] Only about 14 percent of EU members' imports pay tariffs.[2] These imports, which are clearly discriminated against, include some goods from developing countries outside the ACP group and from non-European industrial countries. Even for manufactures, the least restricted sector, tariffs range up to 22 percent for motor vehicles, 18.2 percent for footwear, and 13.4 for clothing. Tariff peaks facing nonpreferred exporters are even higher in the United States—up to 25 percent for motor vehicles, 57 percent for footwear, and 35.3 percent for apparel—and in Japan (10.2, 48.8, and 17.8 percent, respectively, for these goods).

Developing country tariffs also remain high enough to distort the tradeoff between home and imported supplies and between preferred and nonpreferred sources of imports. Table 8.1 presents average and maximum tariffs for selected developing countries and the common external tariffs of some current or planned customs unions. These data show significant discrimination against suppliers who do not receive exemptions.

Table 8.1 Tariff Averages and Peaks in Selected Developing Countries and Customs Unions
(percent)

Country or customs union and date of tariff data	Average	Maximum
Brazil (1997)	12.2	70
Mexico (1997)	13.4	260
Venezuela (1997)	12.0	35
Kenya (1994)	35.1	62
Senegal (1996)	27.0	124
India (1997)	30.1	260
Indonesia (1996)	13.0	200
Thailand (1996)	22.8	100
Andean Pact (CET)	12.8[a]	—
MERCOSUR (CET, 2006)	12.0	63
SACU (1997)	8.7	78
UDEAC (CET, 1995)	18.6	30
UEMOA (1996)	13.2b	—

— Not available.
Note: CET, common external tariff; MERCOSUR, Common Market of the South; SACU, Southern African Customs Union; UDEAC, Union douanière et économique de l'Afrique Centrale (renamed CEMAC); UEMOA, West African Economic and Monetary Union.
a. Weighted tariff from Echavarria (1998).
b. The detailed CET is still under negotiation. The reported figure is an estimate from International Monetary Fund (IMF) sources.

TRADE DIVERSION AND EXCLUDED COUNTRIES

The cost of trade diversion has been a recurring theme of this book, usually from the viewpoint of partner countries. Here we examine whether trade diversion could be large enough to harm excluded countries seriously. Strictly, trade diversion refers only to the social cost incurred by the importing countries as high-cost supplies displace low-cost ones. But nonmember countries can also lose welfare if their exports are displaced, which can happen not only because of policy distortions but also because member costs have fallen as a result of, say, efficiency-enhancing deep integration. In this section (and here only), we interpret diversion as including these latter effects, although, as argued briefly below, such effects should not be subject to international control or redress.

Evidence of Trade Diversion

It used to be fashionable to argue that RIAs did not actually raise trade barriers and caused only very limited trade diversion. In the most studied case, that of the EEC and its associated arrangements, trade diversion in manufactures was generally held to be slight (Balassa 1974; Truman 1975; Winters 1987; Sapir 1992). More recent evidence, however, suggests that diversion can be significant even when regional integration is accompanied by external liberalization.

Bayoumi and Eichengreen (1997) find that the formation of the EEC reduced the annual growth of member trade with other developed countries by 1.7 percentage points, with the main attenuation occurring over 1959–61, just as preferences were starting to bite. Cumulating the decline in growth over 1957–73, and noting that total EEC imports from the rest of the world were $83.1 billion in 1973, puts lost ROW exports at $24 billion in that year. The formation of EFTA had similar, if smaller, effects. Frankel and Wei (1998) find that by 1990 trade diversion had largely erased the EEC's tendency to trade unusually heavily with the rest of the world, while Sapir (1997) finds that over 1960–72, "EFTA exports to the EC suffer[ed] from their nonpreferential status," as did other European nonmember countries' exports in later periods. Our own analysis, which focuses on 1980–96, finds evidence of trade diversion from the deepening of the EC and EFTA and possibly from the formation of NAFTA and MERCOSUR (Yeats 1998; Soloaga and Winters 2001; see also the discussion in chapter 2).

NAFTA is too recent, and its experience too confounded by the 1994 devaluation of the peso, to allow the firm identification of trade diversion, but there is indicative evidence at the sectoral level. Mexico increased tariffs on non-NAFTA imports of clothing from 20 to 35 percent in March 1995, just as it was reducing those on NAFTA imports. U.S. exports to Mexico increased in value by 47 percent between 1994 and 1996, while those from the rest of the world fell by 66 percent. The explanation for a large part of this change is probably not the tariff per se but the combination of the devaluation, which made assembly in Mexico very competitive, and NAFTA's rules of origin, which strongly encouraged Mexican manufacturers to use U.S. clothing parts. In the U.S. market, imports of clothing and finished textiles from Mexico increased by 91 percent and those from Canada by 93 percent over 1993–96 as these imports were exempted from higher tariffs and from import quotas. Meanwhile, imports from Asia fell. The U.S. International Trade Commission (USITC 1997) views these changes as evidence of trade diversion.

Loss of Exports to Trade Diversion

Previous chapters have shown that trade diversion is directly harmful to RIA members that suffer it. Diversion also has an immediate and direct effect on the exports of the rest of the world: they fall. This is frequently taken as sufficient evidence of harm, for in the traditions of trade diplomacy and the GATT, exports are "good," and imports are "bad." If we are interested in economic welfare, however, we cannot draw this conclusion so readily. Indeed, if everything else, including imports, were held constant, a reduction in a country's exports would improve its economic welfare because the goods—or the resources used to produce them—could be redirected to the domestic market.

In fact, of course, we cannot hold everything else constant: the ROW's loss of exports reduces its ability to buy imports. The losses its consumers face as they cut back on imports must be balanced against their gains from consuming the resources that were to be exported. There are three situations in which these components will not be perfectly offsetting:

1. Because of market distortions, a dollar spent on imports may confer more welfare than can be produced by diverting to local consumption the resources required to produce a dollar's worth of exports.
2. Lower demand from within the RIA may drive down the price of ROW exports, so that the rest of the world loses purchasing power and welfare because each remaining unit of exports buys fewer imports. It is the change in the relative prices of ROW ex-

ports and imports—the terms of trade—that matters, not the loss of exports per se, and it is this that should be the focus of investigation.[3]

3.   If the loss of exports is nonmarginal, some of the benefits of specialization itself will be lost.

If a unit of exports generates more welfare than would alternative uses of the resources taken to produce it, losing exports becomes costly. For each unit of exports lost, real income will fall by the difference between the value of the exports—that is, the imports that they buy—and their value in the domestic economy.[4] This will happen if exporting generates supernormal profits because export markets are imperfectly competitive. Those profits will be lost on any trade that is diverted and cannot be replaced by alternative sales at the same price. Industries with economies of scale are in a similar position. If the creation of an RIA causes industry in the rest of the world to lose scale economies, the cost of all its output increases, imposing costs on other consumers of its output and reducing its profit margins. This is the story behind predictions (for example, by Haaland and Norman 1992) that EFTA would lose significantly from the EU's Single Market Programme.

A major potential wedge between the value and the cost of exports is export taxes. Under perfect competition, the price of a unit of exports equals the returns to the factors used in producing it (including entrepreneurship), plus any taxes imposed. If the export is lost and not replaced, only the former is recouped. Explicit export taxes are relatively rare these days, but implicit taxes abound.[5] Most important, import taxes (tariffs) actually tax exports.[6] If an RIA cuts an excluded country's total exports, this eventually implies a decrease in imports, and if these imports are worth more than they cost (because they pay taxes), welfare is lost as they fall. Similar arguments apply to other implicit export taxes, such as excise taxes on inputs, excessive fees for international communications services, and an overvalued currency. With average tariffs exceeding 10 percent in most developing countries, real income losses equivalent to over 10 percent of the value of the diverted trade will be common. Trade diversion can also cause losses if exports generate positive externalities. Most relevant, probably, are exports of manufactures, which many observers believe have spillover effects through their role in training managers and workers, increasing marketing experience and reputation within markets, and improving technological know-how in general. The evidence in favor of such externalities is mixed (Aitken, Hanson, and Harrison 1997), but if they do exist, exports are worth more than the revenue they generate, and their loss is socially harmful.

A related argument views production and employment as valuable in themselves and holds that trade diversion reduces them. To be true, this requires both that the diverted exports cannot be replaced by other exports and that the resources released as total exports fall cannot be reemployed. Under these circumstances, trade diversion causes losses, but one questions why the resources cannot be employed elsewhere. Setting aside transitional unemployment as workers seek new jobs, which is real enough but limited in duration, it is not clear why aggregate employment depends on the level of exports. And if it does, is the problem the trade diversion caused by the RIA, or labor market rigidities in the rest of the world?

The Effect of Large RIAs on Nonmembers' Terms of Trade

The effect of an RIA on the prices at which ROW firms can sell their products depends largely on its size. Small RIAs will rarely matter, as they almost never affect the prices at which trade occurs. But some RIAs, such as the EU or, potentially, the FTAA, are large enough to affect world prices. Their behavior has implications for all the players in the market (positive for buyers if the price falls, and negative for sellers), whether or not they deal with the RIA itself. The significance of price changes is that they affect not only marginal trade but also the whole volume of existing trade (see chapter 2). If a shock means that exporters have to drop their prices to sell the last 1 percent of exports to member countries, this is a small misfortune if only that 1 percent carries the lower price. But if exporters cannot discriminate between buyers, they have to drop their price on all sales—a pure loss on the first 99 percent.

It is more common, perhaps, for goods to be differentiated by place of production and for different markets to be segmented. Here, exporters face downward-sloping demand curves in each of their markets: they have to reduce prices to sell more units. Lower demand from the RIA market exerts downward pressure on the prices of their sales in the RIA, leading to exports being reoriented toward other markets and to resources being switched to producing other goods. If the RIA takes a large proportion of the output of the affected goods, and if the goods account for a large share of total output, the price reductions could be significant for suppliers in the rest of the world. The effect will be greatest for these suppliers' sales in the RIA and next greatest in other markets for the affected exports, but it will be felt in markets for all other goods. Whichever of these applies, factors of production in the exporting country earn less; that is, their income falls.

Despite being central to the theoretical literature for more than a century, the terms-of-trade effects of commercial policies have been almost entirely neglected by empirical economists. They have, however, been identified by analysts using computable general equilibrium (CGE) models—for example, Gasiorek, Smith, and Venables (1992) and Scollay and Gilbert (2001). The latter model many of the proposed RIAs in the Asia-Pacific region and find that nonmembers typically lose, as shown in table 8.2.

Turning to genuine empirical work exploring actual outcomes, among 20th century publications we cannot identify even one empirical ex post study of regional integration that focuses on price effects.[7] Recent research by the World Bank has started to fill this lacuna, as described next.

Livestock Trade in South America. An example of "large market" effects with small export volumes is sales of live cattle in South America (Gupta and Schiff 1997). Cattle are not easily transported within developing countries and are subject to rigorous veterinary regulations in most developed countries. Consequently, Latin America represents a natural regional market. In 1966–68, before the formation of the Andean Pact in 1969, Peru imported mainly from Argentina but also from Colombia (table 8.3) and accounted for about 30 percent of Argentine cattle exports. By 1970, the situation was reversed, with the RIA member supplier, Colombia, displacing the nonmember, Argentina.

Although quantities do not necessarily indicate welfare effects, these shifts also led to price changes. Before the formation of the Andean Pact,

Table 8.2 Estimates of Potential Welfare Effects of Selected Asia-Pacific RIAs
(percentage of real GDP)

RIA	Welfare effect for members	Welfare effect for nonmembers	Welfare effect for world
FTAA	0.08	−0.02	0.01
APEC preferences	0.58	−0.12	0.27
Japan, Republic of Korea, and China	0.50	−0.03	0.09
Japan and Chile	−0.03	0.00	−0.01
Japan and Canada	−0.02	−0.01	−0.01
AFTA and CER (Australia and New Zealand)	0.44	−0.01	0.00

Note: AFTA, ASEAN Free Trade Area; APEC, Asia-Pacific Economic Cooperation; ASEAN, Association of Southeast Asian Nations; CER, Closer Economic Relations agreement; FTAA, Free Trade Area of the Americas.
Source: Scollay and Gilbert (2001).

Table 8.3 Peru's Cattle Imports before and after Formation of the Andean Pact

Item	1966–68 ("before")	1970–72 ("after")
Imports (thousands of metric tons)		
From Argentina	32	1
From Colombia	7	27
Premium on exports to Peru (percent)		
By Argentina	7	4
By Colombia	−3	2

Source: Gupta and Schiff (1997).

Argentine exporters' prices were 7 percent higher per unit in Peru than elsewhere. After that, the premium fell to 4 percent. For Colombia, the change in premiums on sales to Peru was in the opposite direction. In all, the loss to Argentina amounted to perhaps $700,000. This is not huge, even at 1966 prices (unless you are an Argentine cattle exporter), but it illustrates that even a small RIA can have negative effects on neighbors in segmented markets.

Brazil and MERCOSUR. Brazil's membership in MERCOSUR has been accompanied by a significant decline in the relative prices of imports from nonpartner countries (Chang and Winters 2002). Figure 8.1 reports the relative price of Brazil's imports from Argentina versus prices of imports from the United States, averaged (unweighted) over the 323 products that Brazil imported from both countries in every year during the period 1990–96. Although both price averages fell, presumably because of macroeconomic conditions in Brazil, U.S. prices fell by much more, as MERCOSUR came into operation. Formal econometric esti-

Figure 8.1 Average Prices of Brazil's Imports from Argentina Relative to Prices of Imports from the United States, 323 Commodities, 1990–96

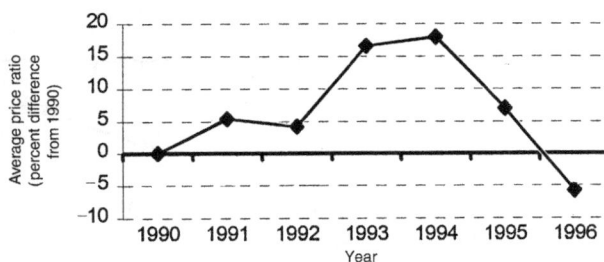

Source: Chang and Winters (2002).

mates suggest that these changes in relative price are substantially the results of differences in tariffs on the two suppliers. Similar results appear for comparisons between Argentine and developing country export prices (for Chile, Korea, and Mexico), although the sets of goods exported by Argentina and each of the other exporters are much smaller, making the estimates less precise.

Theory suggests that MERCOSUR will increase Argentine (member) prices and decrease U.S. (nonmember) prices. The results above are consistent with this view but do not prove it. The researchers therefore also compared nonmembers' export prices to the Brazilian (MERCOSUR) market with those to non-MERCOSUR markets. If exporters can charge different prices in different markets, export prices to non-MERCOSUR markets (which are numerous and are collectively much more important than MERCOSUR markets) can be taken as a norm. Changes in the relative prices of exports to Brazil and elsewhere then reflect factors specific to Brazil, including MERCOSUR membership. Figure 8.2 plots the prices of U.S. exports to Brazil and to the non-MERCOSUR world averaged over the set of products exported to both markets in all years. It clearly demonstrates that whereas non-MERCOSUR prices rose, those to Brazil declined sharply as MERCOSUR preferences were phased in. Figure 8.3 reports the same information for Korean exporters.

The figures are startling, but of course, other things may have happened to Brazil besides its entrance into MERCOSUR. Chang and

Figure 8.2 Average Prices of U.S. Exports to Brazil Relative to Prices of U.S. Exports to the Rest of the World, 1,356 Commodities, 1991–96

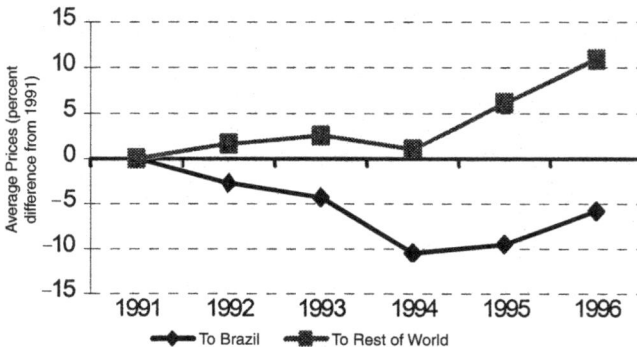

Source: Chang and Winters (2002).

Figure 8.3 Average Prices of Exports from the Republic of Korea to Brazil Relative to Prices of Korea's Exports to the Rest of the World, 99 Commodities, 1990–96

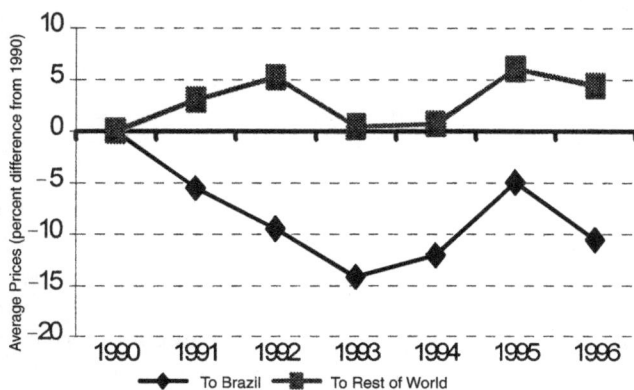

Source: Chang and Winters (2002).

Winters find, however, that even after allowing for costs, exchange rates, inflation, and MFN tariffs, the relative prices of nonmember exports to Brazil and elsewhere are significantly related to Brazil's tariffs on MER-COSUR members. For products that Argentina also exports to Brazil, U.S. suppliers appeared to reduce their export prices to Brazil relative to non-MERCOSUR markets by slightly over one-fifth of the reduction in internal tariffs, and other exporters reduced their prices a bit more.

Schiff and Chang (forthcoming) find similar but stronger price effects. Using the same data, they distinguish between products that Argentina exports to Brazil and those it does not. For the former, they confirm Chang and Winters' results qualitatively, using somewhat different criteria to define market presence. For the latter—goods that Argentina does not currently supply—they distinguish between goods that Argentina does not export at all and goods that it exports to markets other than Brazil and for which Argentina thus represents "potential competition" to U.S. exporters in Brazil's market. In the first case MERCOSUR has no effect on U.S. export prices, whereas in the second Schiff and Chang find results similar to those of Chang and Winters. It is worth noting that the price changes recorded here benefit Brazil and, almost certainly, Argentina at the expense of excluded countries. Whether the gains outweigh the losses globally depends on details of the model that the papers do not explore directly—specifically, the nature of costs and competition. The theoretical model used to motivate the empirical estimates would suggest overall gains, but other underpinnings for the same estimates suggest the contrary. In other words, even the threat of entry by the preferred partner imposes costs on nonmembers. Both studies find that Brazil's MFN liberalization raises relative prices of excluded countries in Brazil's market. Chang and Winters, however, find these effects much weaker than the adverse preferential ones.

EFTA and the EC. Finally, box 8.1 illustrates, using the case of EFTA and the EC, the main problems that small economies can have if their principal market joins or deepens an RIA.

One of the main fears of excluded countries is that a newly formed or deepened RIA will absorb investment that they might otherwise have received. Regional integration frequently leads to temporary investment booms within an RIA, and if there is a finite set of investment opportu-

---

Box 8.1 Trade Diversion and Investment Switching in Europe

In the late 1980s the five continental EFTA countries were heavily dependent on the EC market. On average, they exported 35 percent of their GDP, and 53 percent of their exports went to the EC. Thus, roughly 18 percent of their income was generated directly from sales to the EC.

The EC's Single Market Programme (SMP) was designed to integrate EC markets and, by increasing competition and exploiting economies of scale, raise the efficiency of EC producers. This was a direct threat to EFTA producers, especially in the sectors where the EC market was most fragmented and imperfectly competitive and so offered the most room for improvement in the skill-intensive engineering sectors. Because these sectors were also imperfectly competitive in EFTA, they were the ones that generated the largest labor rents and profits in EFTA members. Estimates (probably rather conservative) suggested that EFTA output in some of these sectors would fall by over 5 percent and gross domestic product (GDP) by nearly 0.5 percent as the SMP was implemented (Haaland and Norman 1992).

Shifts in investment around this time made these predictions look only too plausible. More or less as the SMP was announced, every EFTA country suffered a decline in FDI inflows and an increase in outflows. These changes reversed themselves only as countries embraced the European Economic Area (EEA) or full accession to the EC (Baldwin, Forslid, and Haaland 1996).

Although analysts reckoned that many excluded countries would benefit from the SMP as EC demand for their exports increased and EC export prices fell (Gasiorek, Smith, and Venables 1992), in EFTA these benefits were swamped by production losses. The solution for the EFTA countries was to join the SMP so that they too could benefit from the large, more efficient market. It was predicted that this move would turn the GDP loss of 0.5 percent into a gain of nearly 3 percent. Because the countries did join the EEA and eventually sought full accession, the costs of their being excluded could not be observed. Yet the fact that they did move closer to the EC, and the observed shifts in investment flows, suggest that the threats were perceived to be serious (Haaland and Norman 1992).

nities or a finite volume of investable funds, it is not unreasonable to fear some switching between recipients. We have not, however, found hard evidence that investment or FDI inflows have fallen in excluded countries as a result of RIA creation.

The effect of the EC's Single Market Programme on EFTA provides probably the strongest test of losses attributable to investment switching. The expected shock was large, and since investment is forward looking, actual investment is likely to respond to these expectations. FDI fell in every EFTA country after the SMP was announced and recovered only as these countries signed onto the EEA or committed to accession to the EU (Baldwin, Forslid, and Haaland 1996). Unfortunately, although the study by Baldwin, Forslid, and Haaland is suggestive, it offered no formal ex post analysis of the situation, and so it is possible that the decrease in FDI reflected cyclical factors rather than a structural effect.

THE ROAD TO MULTILATERALISM: ARE RIAs STEPPING STONES, OR MILLSTONES?

In this section, we shift the focus from the immediate consequences of regionalism for nonmember welfare to whether regionalism sets up forces that encourage or discourage evolution toward globally freer trade. Given the difficulties in understanding the dynamics of any reform, it is hardly surprising that there are as yet no categorical answers (see box 8.2). Chapter 3 showed that RIAs can be set up in ways that promote liberalism internally. The systemic aspects considered here are less optimistically balanced. Most of the plausible systemic arguments suggest that regionalism will tend to undermine multilateralism, and those authors who do not come to this conclusion nevertheless tend toward the implication that even if regionalism helps reduce levels of protection, it does so in ways that increase the chances of fragmenting the world economy into warring blocs.

The stakes in the bet as to whether RIAs are stepping stones to multilateral trade liberalization or millstones around its neck are huge.[8] Opening trade and increasing competition have been part of virtually every sustained economic growth experience, and the unprecedented postwar growth of world output and income was clearly allied to these factors. Moreover, systemic effects affect everybody, even bystanders. This is particularly important for small- and medium-size economies, which depend heavily on international trade and are the principal beneficiaries of an orderly and nondiscriminatory trading regime.

8.2 Stepping Stones, or Millstones? A Summary

At first blush, regionalism looks like an important step on the road to global free trade. The recent explosion of RIAs (see figure 1.1 in chapter 1) has, after all, gone hand-in-hand with the greatest multilateral trade liberalization in history. But despite the large number of RIAs in the world, most are too recent, too incomplete, or too idiosyncratic to support conclusions about a world of many RIAs, and there is little empirical evidence about the effects of regionalism on the world trading system.

Even though regionalism and nondiscriminatory trade liberalization have progressed together over the past decade, especially in Latin America, the little evidence we have suggests that multilateral opening has led the way and trade blocs have followed. Many countries reformed their trade well before they joined RIAs: Argentina, Brazil, Mexico, and Turkey are salient examples (Foroutan 1998). Many members of RIAs in Africa, and some in Latin America, have not reformed. And many countries have reformed without joining RIAs, among them Chile in the 1970s and 1980s, Indonesia, and Korea.

There is also some question as to the degree of openness that trade blocs foster. Relatively few RIAs advance significantly beyond the WTO obligations their members have taken on in difficult areas such as agriculture, services, and controlling antidumping actions.

The perception that the existence of trade blocs makes global liberalization easier to achieve because it reduces the number of negotiating parties is also open to question. Blocs may well find it just as difficult to achieve internal agreement, and their combined size will make it easier for them to resist global pressures to liberalize, as well as give them the power to force others to liberalize. We need only recall the difficulty the EU had in negotiating in previous GATT rounds and its long obstinacy about opening up its agricultural markets.

Although economists have built many theoretical models of RIAs and the world trading system, few have generated testable predictions about observable phenomena, and still less about measurable ones. Moreover, even if there were testable predictions, there is very little to test them on. Few RIAs have been sufficiently effective and long-lived to warrant drawing empirical conclusions from their experience, and a world of multiple RIAs is a recent development. This has two implications. First, although we need to make all the use of empirical information that we can, ultimately we have to rely heavily on a priori reasoning. Second, the question about regionalism and multilateral trade concerns the future, not the past. The four decades ending in 1986 saw remarkable progress in liberalizing trade in industrial goods multilaterally, but there was little effective regionalism. In the past decade and a half, in addition to continuing progress on industrial goods, a start has been made on agriculture and services, and a huge reversal has occurred in developing country rhetoric about and practice of trade policy. This has been accompanied by a growth of regionalism but, at least in a temporal sense, could not have been caused by it.[9] The question for this section is precisely what this burst of regionalism, and any continuation of it, imply for future multilateral trade liberalization.[10]

Regionalism affects the progress of multilateral trade liberalization by several routes: by altering the internal incentives for trade liberalization, by affecting the way in which RIA members interact, and by changing the interactions between RIAs and the rest of the world. Chapter 3 dealt with the first two, noting, among other things, the danger of producer lobbies driving RIAs toward trade diversion and the beneficial dynamic that trade-creating RIAs might have in reducing protection. Here we examine the interactions between members and nonmembers, discussing specifically domino regionalism, multilateral trade negotiations, and "open regionalism."

Essentially, there are three arguments. The first is that the behavior of the major blocs—the EU, NAFTA, and APEC—will affect the multilateral system in ways that are basically exogenous for developing countries. All that the latter can do is to seek to influence that behavior, perhaps via international institutions, and to prepare for its consequences. The second is that RIAs (including those involving developing countries) may affect the behavior of developing countries themselves, altering their own propensities for nondiscriminatory liberalization and their willingness to support and protect the multilateral system. If enough developing countries are affected, this too will have systemic effects, in which case developing countries must themselves take some direct responsibility for the consequences of regionalism. The third is that regionalism could affect the processes of multilateralism as well as the outcomes (see "Negotiating Power of RIAs," below).

It might seem that asking whether regionalism could reverse multilateral trade liberalization is merely an intellectual indulgence. After all, do not the WTO rules governing RIAs expressly forbid RIAs to increase trade barriers? But this view is too simplistic, for several reasons.

For many developing countries, there is a wide gulf between their actual (applied) tariffs and the maxima committed to in their formal bindings in the WTO. For example, when Mexico nearly doubled tariffs on 503 import items from non-NAFTA sources in 1995, it did so without violating any bindings. WTO rules are ambiguous and poorly enforced. A determined government can make trade policy more restrictive in ways more or less immune to WTO disciplines—say, through antidumping actions or health regulations. In a world edging toward general trade liberalization, any deceleration in that process is equivalent to an increase in protection relative to the original path.

Multilateralism as a Process

This chapter is mainly concerned with outcomes: progress toward multilateral free trade. But one also needs to ask about multilateral processes and behavior—the "ism" part. "Multilateralism" is a much-used but little-defined, term. In one attempt at precision, Ruggie (1992) sees it as a deep organizing principle of postwar international life, with three defining characteristics:

- *Indivisibility*—the system is a whole in that the actions of one party affect all parties and each party acknowledges its allegiance to the whole.
- *Generalized rules of conduct*—interactions between parties are governed by widely recognized general principles rather than ad hoc or particularistic interests.
- *Diffuse reciprocity*—all parties expect to gain from the system but do not demand precise reciprocity in every separate transaction.

The translation of these principles into concrete form in the international trading system is straightforward. The system is *indivisible* in that it permits an extremely dense and far-reaching network of trade links and intergovernmental contacts, and it is viewed as having an existence separate from all the individual trade links between participants. Moreover, its separate existence is seen as valuable. The trading system's most obvious *generalized norm* is nondiscrimination, one element of which (MFN) immediately and automatically extends bilateral agreements to all members. *Reciprocity* is *diffuse* in that governments do accept individual actions that appear not to be in their immediate interests, but it is generally accepted that, overall, every country has to gain from the system.

Under these criteria, regionalism clearly undermines multilateralism, as it defies MFN. It is also divisive, since it exacerbates tendencies for parties to focus more strongly on some links than on others. One argument in defense of regionalism is that it is subject to generalized rules that all have agreed and that indivisibility should not preclude some links being stronger than others. The first point merely recognizes that the world trading system is imperfectly multilateral; the second, in practice, depends on whether governments shift their focus from general to particular trade relations. Since RIAs certainly shift the focus to some degree, regionalism does corrode the multilateralism of the global trading system, if only mildly at present.

Because the multilateralism of the trading system is part of a broader multilateral order encompassing areas such as security, money, and the environment, it is conceivable that regionalism could have a wider effect on multilateralism. At present this does not seem to be a problem, but if trading frictions between, or about, trading blocs grow more strident, more than just trade could be at stake, as was seen in the breakup of the EAC in the 1970s.

Negotiating Power of RIAs

Many RIAs explicitly aim to increase the negotiating power of their members on the world scene. In customs unions, which have a common trade policy, the scope for enhancing negotiating power by coordinating the positions of several countries is obvious. Coordination in trade negotiations is open to any set of countries, of course, but having a formal RIA makes it easier and more credible. We argue that this coordination could slow multilateral liberalization or even lead to increases in protection.

In 1991 Paul Krugman famously suggested that the worst number of (equal-sized) RIAs for world welfare was three. With fewer, larger blocs, more trade is tariff free (which is beneficial). There is, however, more trade diversion, and blocs have greater bargaining power and so raise their tariffs against each other (both of which are harmful). Obviously, a single bloc is best because that means global free trade, but for small numbers of blocs, diversion and competitive tariff setting outweigh the benefits of intrabloc free trade.

Krugman's result has turned out to be very fragile. He analyzed only customs unions, but most RIAs are FTAs, in which members maintain their own external tariff regimes. FTA members have two good reasons for lowering their tariffs on nonmembers as the FTA expands: to reduce trade diversion, and to compete to capture tariff revenue and boost their competitiveness by reducing tariffs relative to their partners (see the discussion in chapter 3).

Furthermore, countries interact more or less continuously on trade issues, and each interaction influences those that come after it. This opens the possibility that current cooperation can be maintained by the threat of future punishment. In this context, a trade agreement is sustainable if, for each party, the value of the stream of benefits expected to arise from keeping the agreement exceeds that of the stream arising from breaking it. Breaking the agreement would entail choosing a policy that maximizes immediate welfare but with a period of punishment ensuing. The trade-off depends on three sets of factors:

- The rate at which the future is discounted. Cheating (raising one's tariff) means high immediate payoffs followed by lower payoffs during the punishment phase. The higher the rate of discount (that is, the lower the relative weight placed on the future), the more likely a country is to cheat.
- The probabilities that cheating will be punished (and how, and for how long) and that cooperation will be rewarded (that the other party will not cheat and that the agreement will not be overturned by some exogenous shock).
- Trading arrangements, such as RIAs, that affect the volumes and patterns of trade. The lower is the tariff in a trade agreement, the greater are the (immediate) benefits of cheating (raising one's own tariffs unilaterally) and the stronger (more costly) is the punishment needed to make the agreement sustainable. Stronger punishment allows more cooperative behavior—that is, lower tariffs in the agreement.

This framework allows us to ask directly and simply whether, by changing the various incentives, regionalism fosters lower or higher tariffs on the rest of the world.

Regionalism and Tariff Levels

Bond and Syropoulos (1996) suggest that, starting from worldwide free trade, introducing RIAs and allowing them to expand creates two countervailing forces: the incentive to cheat grows, but so does the welfare loss in the resulting trade war. In their model, the former dominates, with the result that it is more difficult to maintain free trade in a bloc-ridden world and that the minimum tariff which can be supported by this kind of cooperation increases as bloc size increases. In short, regionalism increases the pressures for protectionism.

The discount rate is crucial in the operation of these so-called trigger strategies because it trades off the immediate benefits of cheating against the eventual costs of a trade war. This raises the question of the time scale over which these games are played. In terms of individual tariffs and tariff wars, the period required for retaliation is so short that there are hardly any gains to cheating. Thus, discipline seems virtually complete, and the model suggests that nothing much affects the cooperative outcome.

It is, however, more plausible to view regimes as the instruments, the GATT rounds as the natural periodicity, and policies such as the zeal with which antidumping policies are applied and the use of health and technical regulations as the weapons. Then the periods required to recognize defection and retaliate become much longer. The important effect of regionalism is not on the "tactics" of trade policy but on the "strategy." RIAs

Box 8.3 Regionalism and Protection

Theory cannot determine whether RIAs will increase their protection against nonmembers. Foroutan (1998) attempts to settle the matter through direct empirical observation of the behavior of blocs. While most empirical work necessarily considers particular case studies, her study takes a cross-developing country approach.

Because nearly every country is in or is discussing an RIA, it is difficult to devise a comparator group for members of RIAs. Foroutan exploits the fact that in the past not every country was a member, and not every bloc affected trade significantly. She classifies RIAs according to whether they are "effective," defined as having a material effect on the share of intrabloc trade in the group's total trade. Comparing members of effective and ineffective blocs sheds some light on the consequences of RIAs for external trade policy.

The attribution is necessarily rough and ready, but effective RIAs among developing countries (up to 1995) are defined as including the CACM (1960–75 and again since 1990), the Andean Pact (since 1990), MERCOSUR, UEMOA, and SACU. Among the individual countries affected by their RIA memberships are Cameroon, Israel, Kenya, Mexico, and Zimbabwe. Foroutan then compares these developing countries with those that were not in effective RIAs, using three dimensions: average applied tariffs and nontariff barrier (NTB) coverage; Uruguay Round concessions; and openness. The samples differ across the three exercises because of data availability; the table below shows results for average tariffs and for openness.

Average applied tariffs and NTB coverage

The Latin American RIAs now have some of the lowest average tariffs and NTB coverage among developing countries and have achieved the greatest liberalization of any group since the mid-1980s. Except for Chile, the small "non-RIA" group has made much less progress. In Africa, until 1994, neither RIA nor non-RIA countries had displayed much tariff liberalization (NTB data are not available); the latest available data yield a mean average tariff that is almost the same for the two groups. South Asia has liberalized but remains highly protected, East Asia has always been relatively liberal but now has higher average tariffs than reforming Latin America, and the Middle East and North Africa region shows no reform and fairly high average protection. The most liberal group in the study is that consisting of members of North-South RIAs: Israel, Mexico, and Turkey.

Uruguay Round concessions

Here, the only feasible comparison is between the Latin America RIA group and all non-RIA countries. The RIA group cut its bound tariff by more and bound more of its tariffs in the Uruguay Round than did the non-RIA group, but it also completed the round with significantly higher bound tariffs.

Openness

The measure of openness used was (nonfuel imports + exports)/GDP, and the non-RIA group displayed the greatest average increases in openness between 1980–84 and 1990–94. The Latin America–RIA countries show some increase, but not to the levels achieved in the 1970s.

Strong trade reform appears to be mostly associated with RIA membership. Is it possible to conclude that trade reform is a result of RIA membership? There are five reasons for withholding that judgment at present.

1. A more detailed examination shows that much of the trade reform preceded RIA membership, as happened in Argentina, Brazil, Mexico, and Turkey.
2. At the country level, many RIA members have not reformed (examples are members of the CACM in its early period and African RIA members), whereas plenty of non-RIA countries, including

(Continued on next page.)

Box 8.3 *(continued)*

Chile, Indonesia, and Korea, have done so. General tendencies notwithstanding, reform clearly involves much more than RIA membership alone.

　3. Many of our hypotheses about the effects of RIAs on protection operate only over fairly long time periods, whereas the data cover mostly rather recent integration.
　4. The general results depend very heavily on the Latin American experience. But since other forces may well have been at work in that region, we must be cautious about attributing too much to regionalism.
　5. The results on actual openness tend in the opposite direction from those on policies.

Foroutan's results certainly refute the simple hypothesis that RIAs necessarily and immediately lead to protectionism, and they are consistent with the idea that regionalism helps lock in previous MFN liberalization. As with so much of this debate, the jury is not so much "still out" as "still listening" while sufficient evidence is accumulated. Better than waiting for the evidence to come in, however, would be for RIAs to arrange their policies and institutions to ensure that they actually deliver their liberal promise rather than the opposite.

Average Tariffs in Developing Country RIA Members and Other Countries
(percent)

Group	Average tariff				Openness[a]			
	RIA Countries		Non-RIA Countries		RIA Countries		Non-RIA Countries	
	1981–85	1990–94	1981–85	1990–94	1980–84	1990–94	1980–84	1990–94
Countries in North-South RIAs	20.6	10.2			19	22		
Latin America	31.0	13.8	25.8	15.4	26	30	174	107
Sub-Saharan Africa	35.6	31.0	30.7	24.4	47	45	40	48
South Asia			59.9	41.8			22	30
East Asia			20.5	15.0			43	68
Middle East and North Africa			26.3	26.6			40	43

Note: Blanks denote not applicable.
[a] (Exports + nonfuel imports)/GDP.
Source: Foroutan (1998).

will tend to reduce the incentive to take a world view of the broad trends of trade policy because intrabloc trade comes to be seen as a substitute for trade with the rest of the world. The danger is that countries in RIAs will be less willing to sustain liberal regimes. Box 8.3, which explores the issue empirically, suggests not that regionalism is accompanied by an immediate descent into protectionism or a retreat from it but, rather, that multilateral liberalization has tended to lead regional liberalization.

　Bond, Syropoulos, and Winters (2001) use a similar framework to examine the deepening of an existing regional arrangement. They observe that as the bloc deepens, its trade with the rest of the world tends to decline. The excluded countries then find the original agreement unattractive and will initiate tariff increases unless the bloc reduces its tariffs. The bloc will almost certainly prefer lowering its external tariff to getting into a trade war, and so a new, lower tariff equilibrium is usually feasible. It is important to note, however, that at this new equilibrium the rest of the world could be worse off than it was before the deepening. It cannot prevent the bloc from deepening its integration, and even though it finds the new equilibrium the best alternative from among the new set of feasible outcomes, this does not imply anything relative to the starting point.

Has Regionalism Spurred Multilateral Negotiations?

Many commentators argue that the creation of the EEC in 1957 led to these kinds of endogenous tariff adjustment. Thus, for example, they suggest that the formation of the EEC led directly to the Dillon and Kennedy Rounds of GATT negotiations as the United States sought to mitigate the EEC's potential for diverting trade (Lawrence 1991; Sapir 1993; WTO 1995). Although this scenario is perfectly conceivable, the argument is not straightforward.

1. It seems unlikely that multilateral negotiations would have ceased completely had the EEC not been created, especially given the global reach of the United States during the 1960s. Thus, at most, the EEC affected the timing and extent, but not the existence, of the rounds.
2. Agriculture played an important role in the formation of the EEC, and the EEC was probably more successful in resisting that sector's liberalization in the multilateral trade negotiations than its members would have been individually. As a result, future liberalization probably became more, not less, difficult.
3. Suppose that the hypothesis were true and that the creation of the EEC did lead to negotiations. The logic of the argument is essentially coercive: EEC members did something that their trading partners considered harmful and then offered to mitigate it in return for concessions. Coercion may be warranted, and the outcome may have been beneficial, but this is a dangerous game. It depends critically on the willingness of the partners to fold, by negotiating, rather than to fight by raising tariffs, and to respond multilaterally rather than regionally. In economists' models such as we have just explored, we can work out the incentive to fold, but in the real world it is not so easy.

4. Even if coercion worked for the EEC, it probably would not for smaller RIAs of developing countries.

It has also been argued that regionalism was behind the Tokyo Round. Winham (1986) reports that both the first EEC enlargement (including free trade with EFTA) and the restrictiveness of the CAP were factors in the U.S. desire for a round. The former observation seems no more compelling than those about the creation of the EEC, while the latter is distinctly two-edged: to attribute the Tokyo Round to regionalism requires, first, that the CAP induced negotiations and, second, that regionalism increased trade restrictions in agriculture. For this to be advantageous in its net effect on multilateral progress again requires a negotiating structure in which might and countervailing power are the critical forces behind liberalization.

Finally, consider the Uruguay Round. The WTO (1995) says, "there is little doubt that . . . the spread of regionalism [was a] major factor in eliciting the concessions needed to conclude" the round. There was, indeed, a perception that the failure of the round would lead to regional fragmentation. This almost certainly encouraged the spread of "defensive" regionalism during the early 1990s, but whether that trend pressured the two major parties in the round to agree is not clear. After all, they were the prime "regionalists," and they would certainly not have been the principal casualties of fragmentation. Some senior EU negotiators have said that the 1993 Seattle APEC summit induced the EU finally to concede on agriculture and to conclude the Uruguay Round (Bergsten 1997). Again, this may be true, but there are strong counterarguments. For example, APEC was not advertised as a discriminatory RIA, and any discrimination would have been far in the future. Furthermore, the principal necessary condition for the EU to complete the round was agricultural reform, which was initiated in 1990 and completed in 1992 (Hathaway and Ingco 1996).

These arguments do not inform developing country trade policy directly: no single developing country exerts enough leverage to affect global trade talks. Developing countries, however, have a vital interest in the world trading system and may be able to influence developed country behavior indirectly via diplomacy or WTO rules—especially if they act together. One alarming possibility is that regionalism might undermine U.S. or EU willingness to participate actively in the multilateral system.[11] Over the past three decades the United States and the EU have been major players, monitoring both smaller countries' policies and each other's. A loss of interest by either would upset this delicate balance and reduce the WTO's overall effectiveness.

Domino Regionalism

Above, we implicitly assumed that nonmember countries could respond to an RIA only through MFN negotiations. A second response, however, is to join the RIA or create a new one—what has been termed "domino regionalism" (Baldwin 1995, 1997). The idea is that one act of regional integration can stimulate the next because the larger a bloc is, the greater the costs to excluded countries of not belonging to it.[12] Baldwin (1995) coined the phrase to describe the process by which, after three decades of resistance, three Scandinavian countries decided in the late 1980s to seek EU membership. Although these countries were still uncomfortable with the EU politically, the economic pressures from the Single Market Programme were overwhelming, and as one Scandinavian country joined, the pressures on the next increased. Similarly, Canada sought to turn U.S.-Mexican trade talks into an expansion of CUSFTA, which eventually became NAFTA; several Latin American and Caribbean countries later sought accession to NAFTA; Bolivia and Chile have FTA associations with MERCOSUR; Mediterranean and Eastern European countries are racing to conclude association agreements with the EU; and a number of late entrants are seeking membership in the Cross-Border Initiative in Africa. And when multilateral progress loses momentum, domino regionalism receives a further boost. For example, in the wake of the largely sterile Seattle WTO ministerial conference in 1999, Singapore, a former paragon of nondiscrimination, sought agreements with New Zealand and the United States.

The spread of regionalism is not evidence of its virtue. In a regionalized world a country may be better off inside than outside an RIA, but this tells us nothing about whether it prefers a regionalized to a nonregionalized world. To give a graphic illustration, if there is gang warfare in your neighborhood, it may be best to belong to a gang but that does not make gangs a good thing.

A further problem with the view that domino effects necessarily render regionalism benign is that it takes two to tango. Even if excluded countries seek access to an RIA, the existing members may not wish to let them in, at least not without significant down payments (see Andriamananjara and Schiff 2001). RIAs tend to turn the terms of trade against nonmembers, so the optimal bloc size, looking from the inside out, is smaller than the whole world: there needs to be somebody outside to exploit.

Even voluntary regionalism can make everyone worse off. A simple illustrative model of such effects is shown in figure 8.4. Frankel, Stein, and Wei (1997) divide a world of many countries into four continents, with

Figure 8.4 Domino Regionalism: Changes in Welfare as RIAs Form

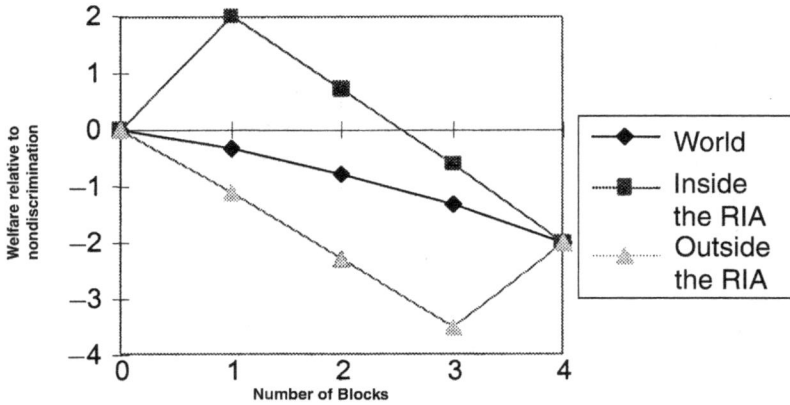

Source: Frankel, Stein, and Wei (1997).

zero trading costs between countries within the same continent and positive costs between continents. At the start, each continent has an MFN trade policy. Any one continent can then improve its welfare by forming an FTA: overseas producers will have to lower their prices to mitigate their loss of competitiveness and will, as a result, suffer either a decline in income or the loss of part of the FTA market. Next, a second continent benefits by creating an RIA, converting a loss of welfare into gain, and then the third does the same, converting larger losses into smaller ones. Even the fourth continent gains by creating an RIA, although by then all continents are worse off than under MFN policies. World welfare falls at every stage, but no continent has the incentive to undo the regionalism individually.[13]

Could such processes lead all the way to global free trade? Almost certainly not, because insiders benefit by turning the terms of trade against outsiders and so seek to prevent unlimited expansion of their blocs. If several blocs of roughly equal size formed, it is possible (but not certain) that they would subsequently negotiate with each other to achieve global free trade. In most models, however, it is more likely that multiple blocs will be of different sizes and that the final steps toward free trade will be vetoed by the larger blocs (Nordstrom 1995; Campa and Sorenson 1996). Only if RIAs were somehow obliged to accept any country that wished to join would evolution to global free trade be likely, and even then, in the course of achieving it, countries might suffer lower welfare than they had under MFN tariffs. Thus, the speed and security of the convergence to global free trade would be critical considerations to take into account in advocating such "open access," even if it were feasible—which it is not (see box 8.4).[14] Insider resistance to expansion certainly

Box 8.4 Is Open Access the Key to Benign Regionalism?

Both in theoretical models (for example, Yi 1996) and in policy discussions (Bhagwati 1991; Serra and others 1997), and as long ago as the preparatory meetings for the London Monetary and Economic Conference of 1933, it has been suggested that the key to ensuring that RIAs lead to multilateralism is "open access." That is, any country willing to abide by an RIA's rules should be guaranteed admission. To date no RIA has offered such unconditional access. Most have restricted geographic domains, and even within these domains it is existing members who determine whether applicants meet the conditions. A simple rule of, say, internal free trade or "national treatment for investors" may be objectively assessable, although even then the transition period needs to be negotiated, but anything more—dispute settlement, excluded sectors, a common antidumping policy, and so on—certainly requires negotiation and threatens candidates with delay and veto.

Where an RIA involves few conditions (as is the case with the Cross-Border Initiative in eastern and southern Africa, which does not rigorously enforce either internal preferences or external tariff harmonization), there is little incentive to exclude geographically eligible countries. Indeed, there is perhaps some incentive to include them, in an attempt to enhance the bloc's negotiating power in world trade talks and vis-à-vis international institutions. The result is expansion to include a wide range of different economies.

NAFTA, which has as its principal rules completely free trade in goods and open investment, might on that account have automatic entry, but it does not. Accession is not restricted geographically but is "subject to terms and conditions as may be agreed . . ." This resistance, however, probably has more to do with avoiding adjustment in the United States than with the need to negotiate issues such as quotas for professional migration or dispute settlement. MERCOSUR is happy to accept new members, but because fairly deep integration is planned, detailed negotiation is required. Association with MERCOSUR, the status chosen by Chile, is easier but does not offer full integration, and even it required several years of talks.

The EU stands ready to sign association agreements with many neighboring countries and with all of the middle-income members of the Africa, Caribbean, and Pacific group—but only on its own terms concerning such issues as rules of origin, excluded sectors, and the use of antidumping duties. Full membership in the EU is anything but open access. The United Kingdom had to apply three times; it will take Turkey at least 30 years to get in; and there is no timetable for countries such as Ukraine and Georgia. Negotiations are tortuous even when accession is agreed in principle. The EU's White Paper on Eastern European Accession is hundreds of pages long; each candidate faces a formidable list of demands and requirements prior to membership and is subject to annual reports on its progress. In several cases these countries are required to adopt policies from which some existing members are exempt—for example, the social chapter of the Maastricht Treaty.

In all the cases listed here, accession may be better for nonmembers than staying outside and suffering discrimination, but it may not be better than MFN trade. Thus, since the expansion of RIAs all the way to global free trade is far from ensured, one cannot necessarily view successful accessions as stepping stones to multilateralism. Moreover, negotiated accession can lead to asymmetric agreements in which benefits to developing country candidates are reduced and may be appropriated by existing members through side conditions on issues such as the environment, labor regulations, and rules of origin. Since the more complex aspects of RIAs, especially those with budgetary implications, must be negotiated, access can never be automatic and unconditional. Hence, it seems rather naive to believe that in practice the WTO could write or enforce general rules for open access. Although relatively open access—as in APEC, which has the slogan of "open regionalism"—might seem less threatening and exploitative than closed access (as in NAFTA), one cannot rely on this route to deliver benign regionalism.

occurs in the real world, although probably less for consciously exploitative reasons than out of a general resistance to change and a fear of budgetary consequences. Consider, for example, how long it took the EU even
to admit the possibility of Turkish accession, or how tortuous the process
of accession has become for the countries of Central and Eastern Europe.
Similarly, NAFTA has rejected overtures from many countries, and
APEC had a moratorium on accession from 1993 to 1996.

Most formal analysis of domino regionalism assumes countries of
equal size that are identical in every respect except for the goods in which
they have comparative advantage. Thus, the only significant characteristic of an RIA is its size, rather than which countries are members, and
there is no issue about how to share the benefits of integration. Once we
break free of this assumption, the compatibility of different partners and
struggles over distribution start to matter, and they greatly complicate
the process and analysis of RIA enlargement.

Given the different interests of excluded and member countries, what
does the evidence show about the domino effect? Table 8.4 provides a
summary. The "Strong expansion" column lists nine RIAs that have expanded over time while maintaining the nature of the RIA or strengthening it. Among these are the EU; APEC; CUSFTA, in its expansion to
NAFTA; and other RIAs in Sub-Saharan Africa, Asia, Central and Eastern Europe, and the Caribbean. The "Intermediate expansion" list of
RIAs that have expanded through a weaker form of integration contains
two customs unions, the EU and MERCOSUR, that expanded by forming FTAs—in the case of the EU, with Mediterranean countries and with
Central and Eastern European countries and for MERCOSUR, with

Table 8.4 Domino Regionalism: Strong, Intermediate, and No Expansion

Strong expansion	Intermediate expansion	No expansion
EU (formerly EC): 1957, Belgium, France, Germany, Italy, Luxembourg, Netherlands; 1973, Denmark, Ireland, United Kingdom; 1981, Greece; 1986, Portugal, Spain; 1995, Austria, Finland, Sweden; inclusion of some of the Central and Eastern European countries and some Mediterranean island countries planned	Euro-Mediterranean Agreement: FTAs between EU and Mediterranean countries	Andean Pact, Arab Common Market, CACM, CBI, CEPGL, COMESA, EAC, ECOWAS, G3, GCC, IOC, SAARC, SACU
CUSFTA: 1989, Canada, United States; 1994, expansion to NAFTA through inclusion of Mexico; possible expansion to FTAA	FTAs between EU and Mexico, EU and Chile, and so on	
APEC: 1989, Australia, Brunei Darussalam, Canada, Indonesia, Japan, Republic of Korea, Malaysia, New Zealand, Philippines, Singapore, Thailand, United	FTAs between MERCOSUR and Chile, and between MERCOSUR and Bolivia	

Table 8.4 *(continued)*

Strong expansion	Intermediate expansion	No expansion
States; 1991, China, Hong Kong (China), Taiwan (China); 1993, Mexico, Papua New Guinea; 1994, Chile; 1998, Peru, Russian Federation, Vietnam		
CARICOM: 1973, Antigua and Barbuda, Barbados, Jamaica, St. Kitts and Nevis, Trinidad and Tobago; 1974, Belize, Dominica, Grenada, Montserrat, St. Lucia, St. Vincent and the Grenadines; 1983, The Bahamas (part of the Caribbean Community but not of the Common Market)		
CEMAC (originally UDEAC): 1966, Cameroon, Central African Republic, Chad, Republic of Congo, Gabon; 1989, Equatorial Guinea		
SADC: 1980, Angola, Botswana, Lesotho, Malawi, Mozambique, Swaziland, Tanzania, Zambia, Zimbabwe; 1990, Namibia; 1994, South Africa; 1995, Mauritius; 1998, Democratic Republic of the Congo, Seychelles		
UEMOA: 1994, Benin, Burkina Faso, Côte d'Ivoire, Mali, Niger, Senegal, Togo; 1997, Guinea-Bissau		
CEFTA: 1993, Czech Republic, Hungary, Poland, Slovak Republic; 1996, Slovenia; 1997, Romania; 1999, Bulgaria		
AFTA: 1992, Indonesia, Malaysia, Philippines, Singapore, Thailand; 1994, Brunei Darussalam; 1995, Vietnam; 1997, Lao People's Democratic Republic, Myanmar; 1999, Cambodia		

Note: AFTA, ASEAN Free Trade Area; APEC, Asia-Pacific Economic Cooperation; ASEAN, Association of Southeast Asian Nations; CACM, Central American Common Market; CARICOM, Caribbean Community and Common Market; CBI, Cross-Border Initiative (Africa); CEFTA, Central European Free Trade Area; CEMAC, Economic and Monetary Community of Central Africa; CEPGL, Economic Community of the Countries of the Great Lakes; COMESA, Common Market for Eastern and Southern Africa; CUSFTA, Canada–United States Free Trade Agreement; EAC, East African Cooperation; EC, European Community; ECOWAS, Economic Community of West African States; EU, European Union; FTA, free trade area; FTAA, Free Trade Area of the Americas; G3, Group of Three (Colombia, Mexico, and Venezuela); GCC, Gulf Cooperation Council; IOC, Indian Ocean Commission; MERCOSUR, Common Market of the South; NAFTA, North American Free Trade Agreement; SAARC, South Asian Association for Regional Cooperation; SACU, Southern African Customs Union; SADC, Southern African Development Community; UDEAC, Union douanère et économique de l'Afrique Centrale; UEMOA, West African Economic and Monetary Union.
Source: Authors' compilation.

Chile and Bolivia. Note that MERCOSUR differs from other RIAs in that its members wanted to expand by accepting Chile as a member but Chile preferred to maintain an independent trade policy and form an FTA with MERCOSUR. Finally, there are 13 RIAs in the "No expansion" column.

Although the number of RIAs that have expanded is approximately the same as the number of those that have not, when the size of RIAs is considered, the expanding RIAs strongly dominate. This is exactly what theory would predict: it is the economic power of the bloc—to stimulate efficiency at home and to discriminate against outsiders—that encourages entry. Finally, we reemphasize that through expansion of RIAs a domino effect is not necessarily a good thing.

Regionalism as Insurance

The main incentive for domino regionalism is to avoid being outside a bloc when nearly everyone else is inside, either because one's terms of trade would suffer or out of fear of a trade war that would close markets that were not contractually bound open. This "insurance motive" was seen in the spread of RIAs in the 1920s and 1930s (Eichengreen and Frankel 1995). Throughout that period, France pursued an active regional policy toward its own colonies and in Eastern Europe as a counter to British and German influence. As Germany reasserted itself, it adopted regional means, starting with a proposed customs union with Austria in 1931, which the other powers blocked only by exercising their powers over the German financial system. Germany then gradually built an even tighter web of regional trading arrangements (Irwin 1993). Britain had granted some preferences to its colonies from 1919 on, and in 1932 it deepened and widened these as it introduced higher tariffs on other partners. The United States, which had increased tariffs strongly for essentially domestic reasons under the 1929 Smoot-Hawley Act, tried to recapture bilateral markets in the Reciprocal Trade Agreements Act of 1934. The lesson of this period is that regionalism grew up remarkably quickly to fracture a relatively evenhanded, if somewhat sclerotic, trading regime.

The process of breaking into regional blocs is potentially explosive (Oye 1992). Not only is there an incentive for each country to join a bloc even if the result is that eventually everyone is worse off, but there is an incentive to join early. The costs of remaining outside escalate as the bloc grows, and if existing members use accession negotiations to extract an "entrance fee," that also rises (see box 8.4).[15]

The term "insurance motive" highlights another possible problem with developing countries' seeking to defend their market access by signing RIAs. The more uncertain the world, the higher are insurance premiums, and the costs of errors are lower if one is insured. In other words, large powers may gain from saber rattling—by maintaining tariffs or hostile antidumping regimes—while small countries are deciding whether to join them, and after joining, the small countries will be less concerned to preserve a global system than previously. As saber rattling is effective only if there is some chance of coercion, this makes regionalism of this kind look quite hostile to multilateralism.[16] Box 8.5 explores

---

Box 8.5 Insurance Policies

Signing an RIA may offer assured access to partner markets in two senses: first, through avoidance of day-to-day harassment from antidumping or countervailing duties and other administrative means of protection and, second, as a haven if total trade war breaks out. Mercifully, the latter is a very low-probability event at present, and it is difficult to forecast what form it would take. Some recent results from Whalley (1998a), however, give a feel for the orders of magnitude at stake.

Whalley uses a CGE model of the world economy disaggregated into seven countries or regions. Six of these potentially fight trade wars, while the other area (the rest of the world) remains completely passive. Trade wars have different outcomes according to which countries or regions have combined to form customs unions. Using actual 1986 values as a base, Whalley explores trade wars in which each country or bloc fixes its tariffs to maximize its own welfare, taking rivals' tariffs as given. (Of course, this ignores WTO strictures on raising tariffs, but the insurance is intended for just such a breakdown.) The only constraint is that if an RIA exists before war breaks out, it remains in operation afterward. The table presents the implications of four possible configurations of customs unions measured relative to 1986 actual values.

The precise numerical results should not be taken seriously, for they are subject to a host of uncertainties, but the broad pattern is informative. In trade wars large economies (such as the United States and the EC) suffer least or even gain. Others suffer heavily, especially if they are highly dependent on a large bloc that becomes very restrictive, as is the case with Canada and Other Western Europe in the table. Entering the bloc basically solves the problem: compare Canada in columns 1 and 2, Mexico in columns 2 and 3, and Other Western Europe in columns 3 and 4. As one small country protects itself, the burdens on others increase, as happens with Japan and the rest of the world.

With losses of this size, the incentives to seek accession if the danger of a trade war increases are huge. The Other Western Europe group has a turnaround of 43.6 percent of GDP from joining a North American–European customs union. Even a small perceived increase in the probability of a trade war would be sufficient to persuade it to bear trade diversion and other costs of entry to avoid the worse outcome.

The table refers to customs unions, and hence the blocs coordinate their external trade policies and can exploit, in so small a model, a great deal of market power to raise their tariffs. If the RIAs were FTAs, the costs of being excluded would be rather lower and would not rise monotonically as the FTA expanded (because a large FTA tends to reduce its external tariffs to lessen the costs of trade diversion). The basic idea that being outside is very costly holds true, however.

(Box continued on next page.)

Box 8.5 *(continued)*

Losses of Economic Welfare from Trade Wars, for Economies Inside and Outside Customs Unions
(equivalent variations as a percentage of GDP)

Trade War with:	No customs union	Canada-U.S. customs union	North American customs union	North American-European customs union
United States	1.2	0.5	−0.4	0.5
Canada	−25.5	0.9	0.4	−0.7
Mexico		−8.5	0.1	−0.3
Japan		−5.2	−5.2	−5.4
EC (12 members)	−8.5	3.4	3.4	2.5
Other Western Europe	−5.2	−33.1	−33.5	10.1
Rest of World	−10.6	−10.9	−11.1	−13.4
World total	−6.0	−5.8	−5.8	−6.2

Source: Whalley (1998a).

the high incentives for "insurance regionalism" in the current world. Such problems do not look very serious at present, for developed countries have many other nonexploitative relationships with developing countries and may not find "insurance premiums" worth pursuing in this way. But insurance is for worst-case scenarios, and our point is that developing countries should not complacently assume that regionalism will preserve them if a crisis arises.

One can observe the same sort of phenomena in today's world, albeit in a much attenuated form. One of the reasons that New Zealand Prime Minister Helen Clark cited for her country's seeking a regional arrangement with Singapore was a fear of being left outside as the world split up into blocs, into none of which New Zealand fitted naturally. This fear was arguably stimulated by the stasis in APEC (which accounts for a very large proportion of New Zealand's trade) and "the failure of world leaders to agree on an agenda for a new wave of trade liberalization" (*Far Eastern Economic Review*, August 17, 2000).

RIAs as Negotiating Partners: Do They Promote Free Trade?

If RIAs make trade negotiations easier, perhaps they can help the world evolve toward freer trade. Coordinated coalitions may, as noted above, have greater negotiating power than their members individually, and such coalitions may facilitate progress just by reducing the number of players represented in a negotiation (Krugman 1993; Kahler 1995). But this result is not guaranteed. For example, a negotiation between one dominant partner and a competitive fringe of small countries might be easier and proceed farther than if the fringe coalesced into a significant counterforce, but if the blocs are genuinely unified, it is probably reasonable to expect negotiations to be easier with fewer partners.

Unfortunately, this condition is rarely met, so any gains from having fewer players in the last stage of a negotiation are offset by the complexity of agreeing joint positions in the first phase. This tradeoff is examined in Andriamananjara and Schiff (2001). The difficulties of achieving a European position on agriculture and cultural protection in the Uruguay Round are well known, and formulating EEC positions in the Tokyo Round proved complex (Winham 1986). Moreover, two-stage negotiations need not be more liberal than one-stage ones (Basevi, Delbono, and Mariotti 1994). To be sure, Germany and the United Kingdom pressured France to agree to the agricultural deal in the Uruguay Round, but they had to make potentially trade-restricting concessions on "commercial defense instruments" (antidumping) to clinch the deal. The negotiating power of African countries would not be greatly enhanced by cooperation, and the benefits are not likely to outweigh the costs of combining their different interests into a single negotiating position (Wang and Winters 1998).

The customs unions that attend the next round of global trade talks will need to establish procedures for determining their negotiating positions. SACU's previous practice of delegating all responsibility to South Africa begins to look less tenable as divisions emerge between members, and MERCOSUR has yet to devise really robust internal decisionmaking capacity. Thus, at least in the foreseeable future, RIAs do not seem likely to facilitate even traditional trade negotiations. Moreover, if RIAs are being extended or new ones are being created, the process can swamp developing countries' limited negotiating capacity (box 8.6).

As the WTO has extended its reach, it has embraced subjects in which most central customs union authorities have no mandate to negotiate. Mixing national and customs union responsibilities seems unlikely to simplify matters, and it is not realistic to expect member countries to surrender sovereignty on sensitive issues to regional bodies just because trade negotiations are in train.

Do RIAs Make It Easier to Tackle Tough Issues?

It is frequently claimed that a strength of the regional approach to liberalization is that handling tough cases is easier (Kahler 1995). That is, there are areas in which regional liberalization or harmonization between like-minded countries is feasible when multilateral progress is not.

Box 8.6 The Overburdened Negotiator

Reserves of administrative skill, political capital, and imagination are finite; if they are devoted to an RIA, they are not available for multilateral objectives. These arguments were advanced—somewhat implausibly—to explain EU and U.S. behavior during the Uruguay Round, but they must be several times more important for developing countries.

Negotiating an RIA, especially with a major power that has its own objectives, will absorb a huge proportion of the policymaking skills of a developing country. Such skills are typically so scarce that many developing countries have the same negotiator dealing with both the EU in Brussels and the WTO in Geneva. In fact, the governments of a number of smaller European countries have asked the WTO to postpone its trade policy review exercises for their countries because they are wholly absorbed in negotiating association agreements with the EU.

Moreover, flying to Brussels or Washington to undertake regional negotiations is altogether more gratifying than working quietly at home to reduce arbitrary tariff peaks or improve customs administration. This is one reason why policymakers and private sector groups are prepared to grasp the painful nettles of reform that RIA negotiations call for and to stick to the agreements they make. But the process can be harmful if the RIA does not deliver benefits commensurate with the opportunity costs of negotiation.

The importance of developing country capacity constraints is illustrated in the recent discussion of multilateral trade policy, where lack of capacity has become a prominent theme. For example, the WTO's Doha Ministerial Declaration, a 5,000-word document, contains 19 references to capacity building and 21 to technical assistance for developing countries (see Winters 2002).

This seems most likely for activities that are highly restricted (such as agriculture, trade subject to antidumping measures, and some services) and for areas that are highly technical or sensitive (standards, competition policy, and services regulation). For example, NAFTA and the Group of Three have tackled investment; Brazil has accepted free trade in information technology goods within MERCOSUR but refused to sign the global Information Technology Agreement (ITA) in 1997; and Chile and Canada have eschewed antidumping actions on mutual trade but not in relation to third countries.[17]

Until recently, however, even RIAs of developed countries, let alone those between developing ones, had not advanced much farther with liberalization than the multilateral system (Hoekman and Leidy 1993). Agriculture frequently remained restricted (for example, in EFTA); transport, culture, and other "sensitive" services were excluded (CUSFTA); and government procurement was ignored de facto, if not de jure (EEC). The EU, especially in its Single Market Programme, has advanced beyond the GATT on a broad front, but this took 30 years to initiate and is, to date, unique. More recently, there have been other advances, such as NAFTA's plans to ultimately liberalize agriculture and procurement. But overall, RIAs have not led multilateral liberalization to the extent that is sometimes supposed.

There is also the question of whether regionalism *is* actually more effective than multilateralism in liberalizing deeply. Has global liberalization actually been ruled out, or, if RIAs were not an option, would a little more time and effort yield global progress? Having got the ball rolling, will RIAs later slow it down, for the reasons discussed above? On a prescriptive note, to the extent that RIAs are justified by their ability to open up otherwise closed sectors, it is important to ensure that the subsequent switch from regionalism to the multilateral track can be managed effectively. The necessity for, and the means of achieving, this switch should be written into the initial terms of RIAs.

An extension of the "tough cases" argument is that RIAs help develop blueprints for subsequent multilateral negotiations (Bergsten 1996; Lawrence 1996). For example, the EU pioneered "bulk" mutual recognition for industrial standards and services harmonization, and NAFTA's investment chapter may inform a multilateral negotiation (if there is one). On the other hand, the EEC suggested the CAP as a model for agriculture in the Kennedy Round. (See Preeg 1970: 152.)

But the major powers could also seek to use RIAs to reinforce their initial positions in future multilateral negotiations. If they have greater politico-economic power within their own regions than in the world in general, it is easy to imagine their building up coalitions for their own policies before taking issues into a multilateral round. Arguably, the United States used approaches by potential partners in the Americas and Asia to broaden the negotiating agenda for its relations with Europe (Ostry 1998), while Europe did the same with the EEA and its Europe Agreements.

The benefits of developing regional blueprints depend heavily on whether they are liberalizing (Bhagwati 1993) and on whether they are otherwise well suited to developing countries' needs and capacities. Major powers already use the carrot of access to the generalized system of preferences (GSP) to promote environmental and labor conditions in developing countries; the EU looks for action in such areas and on intellectual property in the Europe Agreements; and the United States has used NAFTA as a tool for enforcing Mexican labor and environmental standards. By negotiating singly with the major powers, developing countries are essentially placed in competition with each other and lose a good deal of their (small) reserves of negotiating power. The deals they can achieve could be much less favorable than those that might emerge from multilateral talks under the WTO, and they may be less open and liberal, as well.

Moreover, there are dangers in such tactics. First, even if the major powers' aspirations are inherently desirable, building up rival teams can make final negotiations more, rather than less, difficult. Second, when only one regional bloc is advocating a policy, other countries might sufficiently resent the pressure to adopt it that they pull back. De facto rejection by developing countries of the OECD draft Multilateral Agreement on Investment in 1998 contained at least elements of this reaction. Third, the time it takes to build regional coalitions can delay multilateral talks. Fourth, coalitions rooted in formal RIAs are here to stay: multilateral processes may fail, but the blocs remain. This is quite different from a negotiating coalition, which dissolves if it fails to gain its objectives.

To be sure, progress is required in "new" areas such as standards, but, as was noted in chapter 6, it is frequently better pursued independent of tariff preferences. Thus, while we may well learn from RIAs how to tackle particular aspects of liberalization, this is not a convincing reason for pursuing regionalism per se.

Open Regionalism: Little More Than a Slogan

Open regionalism was the idea of the 1990s. Crafted to describe APEC's original aspirations and to convey their complete consistency with multilateral objectives, the accolade has been applied to many blocs at some point in their history. Unfortunately, it is difficult to pin down exactly what "open" means.

Before trying to clothe the concept of "open regionalism" with meaning, we should remove its fig leaves. First, although there is a presumption that greater openness makes RIAs more benign, nothing can guarantee that they do not hurt the rest of the world. Second, the main reason for pursuing "open regionalism" is to benefit the members themselves, but none of the definitions that have been proposed absolutely guarantees such an outcome.

Srinivasan (1998) has called "open regionalism" an oxymoron, and that is surely true at the limit of its range: a perfectly open economy could not discriminate in the way that regionalism in the trade sense requires. Once we come in from the edge, however, it does make sense to ask whether some RIAs are more open than others.

Writing about APEC, the group for which the term was coined, Bergsten (1997) offers five definitions of "open regionalism":

1. *"Open access,"* whereby any country willing to abide by an RIA's rules may join that RIA. Bergsten argues that, strictly interpreted, this is not realistic because RIAs have restricted geographic domains, but easy access for countries within their domains would be one acceptable definition. Bergsten defines the EU as open in this respect.

2. *Unconditional MFN (or concerted unilateralism)*. This was the definition of early APEC advocates, who saw the coalition as a means of encouraging countries to liberalize together and so provide for each other some of the terms of trade and political-economy benefits of a full GATT round. Although some members of APEC still adhere to this aspiration, Bergsten is doubtless correct in saying that it is quite unacceptable in the United States, where reciprocity is seen as an essential part of liberalization.[18] It would, of course, also not be regionalism as defined in this book.

3. *Conditional MFN,* whereby intra-APEC liberalization would be extended to any country that reciprocated. Given APEC's size, no country would be likely to reject the offer of an FTA, Bergsten says, but it might take time for others to come on board, and in the interim there would be trade discrimination. There might also be resentment at APEC's making take-it-or-leave-it offers. Conditional MFN is very similar to open access but requires an operational definition of reciprocity. Bergsten suggests using conditional MFN as a threat and indeed says APEC has already implicitly done so—as a means of obtaining (nearly) global deals such as the ITA, which was initiated by APEC in 1996.

4. *Global liberalization* through traditional unilateral and multilateral trade liberalization on an MFN basis. It is possible that APEC could lead a movement to remove all trade barriers by its own internal free trade deadline of 2010 for developed countries and 2020 for developing countries.

5. *Trade facilitation,* under which APEC countries would reduce border frictions and pursue policy integration, but with a focus on elements that operate multilaterally.

APEC has yet really to decide among these alternatives, as there has not yet been any "APEC liberalization." Members have certainly not introduced any discriminatory trade policies (with the minor exception of the APEC business visa), but neither have they moved beyond implementing their Uruguay Round obligations and, for developing members, their own unilateral reforms.

For the future, Bergsten recommends a combination of points 2 through 5 to make clear that APEC's objective is global liberalization, that it will achieve internal liberalization by 2020, that it (or at least its larger members) will discriminate in a WTO-consistent fashion if other countries do not reciprocate, and that it welcomes proposals by other countries on sectors and timetables for liberalization (in other words, that APEC wishes to negotiate, rather then dictate terms for, its extension to the rest of the world). Although perhaps more positive in its approach and timetable, this manifesto is not very different from the EEC's 1957 statement that "by establishing a customs union between themselves, member states aim to contribute, in the common interest, to the harmonious development of world trade, the progressive abolition of restrictions on international trade and the lowering of customs barriers" (Treaty of Rome, art. 110, sec. 1).

Other commentators have taken up the cry of "open regionalism." Echavarria (1998) sees "open regionalism" in the Andean Pact in the sense that it lowered tariffs relative to the 1980s. Brazil's foreign minister, Luiz Felipe Lampreia, speaking to the U.N. General Assembly in September 1996, proclaimed "open regionalism" in MERCOSUR because of the tariff reductions and the group's enlargement. The U.S. Council of Economic Advisers defined U.S. policy as laying the foundation for "open, overlapping plurilateral trade agreements as stepping stones to global free trade" (CEA 1995), while Pelkmans and Brenton (1999) see recent EU policy as "open regionalism" in the sense of "GATT compatibility" and as having gone "some way" toward "open regionalism" in the nonpreferential sense. Former WTO director-general Renato Ruggiero declared, "The answer [to marrying regionalism and multilateralism] is . . . 'open regionalism,'" which he defined as "in practice . . . the MFN principle" (quoted in Srinivasan 1998).

Openness is an important component of development and a valid objective for all developing countries; if countries feel they must have regionalism, let it be genuinely open. But "open regionalism" is a slogan rather than an analytical term. It is defined in so many different ways that it conveys no information about an RIA other than that its members are embarrassed to be thought of as protectionist. In particular, a claim of "open regionalism" should confer on a bloc no presumption of economic value and no immunity from analysis to see if it is acting in either its own or in other countries' interests.

REGIONALISM AND THE WTO

The analysis thus far suggests that international policy toward regionalism should aim at:

- Encouraging RIAs to achieve trade creation and avoid trade diversion, both for the sake of members and to minimize harm to excluded countries;
- Permitting deep integration, including nation building, between members;

- Preserving the effects of previous liberalizations and providing credibility for any liberalizations that form part of the RIA; and
- Supporting a liberalizing dynamic within member countries and in the world trading system as a whole.

The instrument we have for international policy on trade blocs is the WTO. This section explores how it manages regionalism and whether its rules could be reformed to help it do better.[19]

GATT, and All That

RIAs are an officially sanctioned, but conditional, exception to the GATT's rules on nondiscrimination. The conditions imposed on RIA formation doubtless constrain and mold the pattern of regionalism in the world, but they are not adequate, and are not well enough enforced, to ensure that regionalism is economically beneficial for either its members or excluded countries. And although improved adherence to current rules is desirable, no feasible reform can guarantee that only beneficial RIAs are created. The responsibility for good outcomes falls on governments themselves; apart from a complete ban, they cannot tie their own or each other's hands sufficiently tightly in the WTO to preclude the possibility of harmful RIAs being formed.

The world trading system works pragmatically and consensually. The GATT was created in 1947 as a temporary body to assist countries in trade liberalization. Its role was to codify and record a series of tariff reductions that its members wished to make and to provide a structure to give credibility to those reductions. To discourage the reversal or nullification of tariff cuts, it restricted the use of policies that impose duties on trade on an ad hoc basis (such as antidumping duties and emergency protection) and of equivalent policies, such as internal taxes on imports. It also defined some important mechanics for the trading system—for example, the valuation of trade for customs purposes.

A key concept of the GATT—indeed, the cornerstone of the present world trading system—is nondiscrimination between different sources of the same imported good. Nondiscrimination is achieved by requiring members to accord each other MFN treatment except in specified circumstances. With an assurance of nondiscrimination, when A negotiates a reduction in one of B's tariffs, A knows that the commercial value of its effort will not be undermined by B's then offering C an even lower tariff. This, in turn, makes A more willing to "buy" the concession by reducing one of its own tariffs on B and so encourages trade liberalization.

Over 50 years of operation, the GATT operated in a low-key, consensual, member-driven fashion. It did not "adjudicate" trade disputes; rather, it had a dispute settlement process that was less concerned with law than with solving disputes in a way that preserved the previously negotiated balance of benefits, maintained consensus, and allowed the liberalizing bandwagon to continue to roll. The WTO, which was created in 1995 to oversee the GATT and certain other agreements, is more legalistic but still focuses on pragmatic and mutually acceptable solutions to problems. The WTO administers a set of rules for behavior, not a set of outcomes; it is concerned with members' meeting agreed obligations and being accorded agreed rights rather than with economic outcomes per se. The WTO/GATT has undoubtedly been a force for economic good, but its role has not been defined in those terms.

The GATT traditionally did not intrude into domestic politics. It had no ability to force member countries to liberalize if they did not wish to, and it was extremely light-handed in its requirements about the shape of domestic legislation. The WTO is more far-reaching. Its greater breadth and its "single undertaking"—under which members must subscribe to (virtually) all its rules instead of treating some as optional extras, as had been the case—constrains governments more tightly. Nevertheless, the WTO, like the GATT, can be effective only if it proceeds more or less by consensus.

Given this background, the WTO can enhance the economic well-being of developing countries in four ways:

1. If sufficient members wish, it can organize periodic rounds of tariff negotiations that offer opportunities and incentives to members to reduce their barriers to trade.

2. It provides guidelines for domestic policy—directly in some cases, but, more importantly, indirectly, by shaping the terms of the debate. Governments resisting pressures to protect particular groups are immeasurably strengthened if they can point to prohibitions in the WTO agreements. Similarly, lobbyists are strengthened if the WTO explicitly permits the policies they want, even if only conditionally. "After 145 countries have debated and confirmed the legitimacy of policy X," they say, "what right has the government to deny us its benefits?" (The answer is, "almost every right," for the WTO defines minimum standards of behavior, not norms—but it is a hard case to make.)[20]

3. It can protect the rights of WTO members against certain rules violations by other members. It cannot, however, guarantee members against harm.[21]

4. It provides a forum and a mechanism for governments to manage the spillovers from members' trade policies to their partners. Bagwell and Staiger (1998) show how the GATT traditions of reciprocity and nondiscrimination combine to minimize such spillovers—reciprocity, because two members offering mutual tariff concessions are likely to generate (at least partially) offsetting terms-of-trade effects, and nondiscrimination, because it prevents aggressive coalitions from forming.

These four potential benefits provide a yardstick for assessing the WTO's current rules about RIAs and exploring whether they can be improved.

The Rules for RIAs: Useful, but Not Infallible

Article XXIV of the GATT specifies the conditions under which countries may violate the MFN clause by forming RIAs. It imposes three principal restrictions (see the annex to this volume). An RIA:

- Must not, "on the whole," raise protection against excluded countries;
- Must reduce internal tariffs to zero and remove "other restrictive regulations of commerce" other than those permitted by other GATT articles; and
- Must cover "substantially all trade."

The GATT's logic is essentially mercantilist—stressing the rights of trading partners to market access—rather than economic, with a focus on the economic costs and benefits of policy. From the mercantilist perspective, the first two conditions make sense. The rule against increasing protection against excluded countries preserves the sanctity of tariff bindings by ensuring that forming an RIA does not provide a wholesale way of dissolving previous bindings. It is supplemented by the requirement that compensation is due to individual partners for tariff increases induced by the RIA if other reductions to keep the average constant do not maintain a fair balance of concessions. Together with the 1994 Uruguay Round Understanding on the Interpretation of Article XXIV, which deals with how to measure tariff barriers for RIAs, these provisions offer reasonable assurances about the barriers facing nonmembers.

The condition on reducing internal tariffs to zero helps defend the MFN clause by making it subject to an "all-or-nothing" exception. If countries were free to negotiate different levels of preference with each trading partner, binding and nondiscrimination would be fatally undermined. No member could be sure that it would receive the benefits it expected from negotiating and reciprocating a partner's tariff reduction. Also, if a customs union is a first step toward nation building, it is inappropriate that an international trade treaty should stand in the way of such progress. Thus, internal free trade, such as is (usually) achieved within a single country, would seem to be an acceptable derogation of MFN, whereas preferences would not be. The third condition reinforces this interpretation by requiring a serious degree of commitment to an RIA in terms of sectoral coverage.

Article XXIV also makes sense when viewed as a guide to economic policy. The requirement not to raise the average level of protection against excluded countries' exports not only honors those countries' market access rights but also closes one otherwise available route to increased protectionism. This is desirable on any account, but in the context of RIAs, the danger and costs of trade diversion will be greater if members can increase their external tariffs. The second and third conditions—no internal tariffs, and substantial coverage—are important in heading off pressure to use tariffs to fine-tune political favoritism toward domestic industries or partner countries; they help prevent governments from restricting RIAs to swaps of trade-diverting concessions and so avoiding politically more painful trade creation. These rules essentially require a serious commitment to integration of member markets as a condition for proceeding.

Article XXIV is generally an aid to better RIAs, but it is certainly not sufficient for good economic policy. Even if the conditions were applied without exception, they would not preclude harmful RIAs. RIAs that are wholly GATT-compatible can nevertheless be predominantly trade diverting; excluded countries can suffer terms-of-trade declines; protection can increase; and institutions can arise that make liberal policies less likely.

Moreover, there are major difficulties in interpreting the WTO conditions on regionalism. Despite the Uruguay Round Understanding, there is no agreement about what "substantially all trade" means—even about whether it refers to the proportion of actual trade covered or to the inclusion of all major sectors of the economy. Similarly, the treatment of nontariff barriers in assessing the overall level of trade restriction is not defined, nor is that of rules of origin. The requirement that "other restrictive regulations of commerce" be removed between members is ambiguously worded: several exceptions to this requirement are identified explicitly, but other barriers, including antidumping duties and emergency protection, are not. Complete integration between members of an RIA would abolish all these barriers, and so their continuation—as, for example, in NAFTA and the Euro-Med Agreements—suggests an unwillingness to proceed very far in that direction.

Perhaps because of its ambiguities, Article XXIV has been notoriously weakly enforced. RIAs have to be notified to the GATT, and until 1996 each was then reviewed by an ad hoc working party to see if it was in conformity with Article XXIV. According to the WTO (1995: 16), of 69 working parties reporting up to and including 1994, only 6 were able to agree that an RIA met the requirements of Article XXIV, and only 2 of the 6 RIAs—CARICOM and the customs union of the Czech and Slovak Republics—are still operative. The remaining working parties did not conclude that the agreements were not in conformity; they merely left the matter undetermined.

This agnosticism is essentially the product of the GATT's consensual nature. The first major test of Article XXIV was the Treaty of Rome, which established the EEC. The political pressure to permit it was enormous: EEC countries would almost certainly have put the EEC before the GATT in the event of conflict, and the United States strongly supported the treaty. The treaty, however, clearly violated Article XXIV, and so the only feasible solution was not to push the review to conclusion.[22] Given a start like this—along with the EEC's willingness to support more or less any RIA in the GATT, the need for working parties to reach consensus, and the GATT's inability to make an adverse determination without the acquiescence of the party at fault—it is hardly surprising that future reviews proved little more demanding.[23] Nor have matters improved with the establishment of a single Committee on Regional Trading Agreements (CRTA, discussed below) to conduct the reviews. The inability to rule on conformity does not mean that the rules have had no effect, for we do not know the extent to which they have influenced the structure of RIAs that have come forward or which potential arrangements they have deterred.[24] It is not an encouraging record, however, either from the point of view of enforcing current rules or from that of rewriting the rules to increase their ability to distinguish good from bad RIAs.

Finally, Articles XXIV.10 and XXV of the GATT can be used to grant waivers to make otherwise inadmissible policies GATT-legal. This was done for the ECSC (1952) and the United States–Canada Auto Pact (1965). Under the WTO, waivers are still feasible but are time limited.

Weaker Rules for Developing Countries. As if all this were not enough, a further complication for developing countries is the Enabling Clause of 1979, which significantly relaxes the conditions for creating

RIAs that include only developing countries. It drops the conditions on the coverage of trade and allows developing countries to reduce tariffs on mutual trade in any way they wish and to employ nontariff measures "in accordance with criteria which may be prescribed by the" GATT members. It then supplements the first condition with the nonoperational requirement that the RIA not constitute a barrier to MFN tariff reductions or cause "undue difficulties" for other contracting parties.

In practice, developing countries have had virtual carte blanche. Twelve preferential arrangements have been notified under the Enabling Clause, including the LAIA, ASEAN, and the GCC. Internal preferences of 25 and 50 percent figured in ASEAN's trading plans, in many of the arrangements concluded under the LAIA, and in the GCC. There is little sign that internal preferences have undermined MFN agreements with other trading partners, but until recently, these countries did not make many MFN agreements. Indeed, until the late 1980s, the Latin American and African countries' frequent use of regional arrangements and their weak participation in the multilateral rounds might suggest a substitution of one form of liberalization for another. More worrying were the sectoral agreements that abounded in Latin America. Nogués and Quintanilla (1993) argue that there is little doubt that the 17 agreements that Argentina and Brazil had signed by 1986 generated significant trade diversion.

The Enabling Clause further dilutes the weak discipline that Article XXIV imposes. Even if Article XXIV does not actually stop many harmful practices, it does at least avoid automatically giving them the respectability of legal cover. Thus, while the GATT knowingly and willingly permitted LAFTA (1960) and the initial notification of ASEAN (1977) to violate Article XXIV (Finger 1993b), at least it required continuing consultation with partners and left open the possibility of challenge in the dispute settlement process. The Enabling Clause offers more cover in various areas and thus erodes even this discipline.[25]

Loopholes in Rules on Services. Article XXIV and the Enabling Clause of the GATT refer to trade in goods. The equivalent for services is Article V of the GATS, which is modeled closely on them (see the annex to this volume). The requirement not to raise barriers to third countries is rather tighter: it is applied sector by sector rather than "on the whole," and third-country suppliers already engaged in "substantive business" in an RIA's territory before the RIA is concluded must receive RIA treatment. The "substantially all trade" ambiguity is only slightly abated, with an explicit note that "substantially" is to be "understood in terms of number of sectors, volume of trade and modes of supply." For covered sectors, "substantially all discrimination" is to be removed, but since the requirement is defined as consisting of "elimination of existing discriminatory measures, and/*or* prohibition of new or more discriminatory measures" (emphasis added), it need amount to very little.[26] Developing countries receive "flexibility" on "substantially all discrimination" and exemption from the need to give RIA treatment to third-country firms with "substantial business" in member countries.

Proposals for Improving the Rules on RIAs: "Feasible" and "Desirable" Do Not Overlap

The WTO rules on RIAs are not exactly broken, but they are creaky, and it is worth asking what might be done about them. We focus here on their economic content and benefits and on the feasibility of reform. We also require that any reforms be clear and operational, removing ambiguity rather than adding to it. Feasibility, which depends on the attitudes of member countries and the need to remain within the GATT's basic pragmatic and consensual framework, seems to us more of a constraint than devising economically sensible rules.[27] Few countries within RIAs appear to seek tighter discipline, least of all the EU and the United States. The EU is intent on enlargement—extending its Mediterranean agreements and implementing the Cotonou Agreement—while the United States is heavily engaged in the FTAA negotiations. Neither the EU nor the United States submitted proposals to the 1999 Seattle ministerial conference of the WTO, and while they accepted the issue as part of the Doha Development Agenda, neither has sought to advance the topic.[28]

An RIA that does not reduce external barriers almost inevitably causes trade diversion. One counter to this would be to require RIA members to liberalize, both to reduce diversion and to induce external trade creation with nonmembers. Finger (1993b) views these reductions as a "price" to be negotiated to persuade nonmembers to forgo their MFN rights. How far the parties are prepared to go in a negotiation, however, is determined by the prevailing rules and enforcement mechanisms, which define the outcome should negotiations fail. Unfortunately, these provisions currently give nonmembers almost no negotiating power. Other authors have therefore made more concrete proposals.

Greater Liberalization by RIAs. Bhagwati (1993) suggests a requirement that for each tariff heading, a customs union's common external tariff be bound at the minimum tariff for that heading among all members. This does not guarantee the elimination of trade diversion (suppose that the tariffs of three members were 98, 99, and 100 percent), but it would clearly reduce it. It would impose a high (mercantilist) price on RIA formation that only "serious" integrators would pay, and it would, overall, be trade liberalizing. As a reform it is admirably clear, and if feasible, it would be desirable economically. Its demanding nature, however, makes it very unlikely to succeed in the present circumstances.

Serra and others (1997) propose that members of FTAs be required to bind their tariffs at the actual applied rates on the eve of the RIA. Apart from what this might do to pre-FTA applied rates, the suggestion is random in its liberalizing effect, which reduces its moral force. Bhagwati, by contrast, would just ban FTAs. Like his proposal on customs unions, this is consistent with seeking to restrict RIAs to those that are committed to far-reaching integration, but it too faces severe feasibility constraints, especially since some FTAs proceed quite far in other directions and have become the more popular form of regional integration.

Conditions for Rules of Origin. Tied up with the FTA question is that of rules of origin. Serra and others (1997) suggest requiring that they be no more restrictive than before the RIA. This is laudable, but, in practice it is difficult to determine, ad hoc in nature, open to manipulation, and potentially very complex in the face of technological changes. A better course would be a requirement precluding the manipulation of such rules for protectionist purposes—requiring, for example, that countries adhere to a single set of rules of origin agreed internationally, or that a country's preferential rules be the same as its nonpreferential ones. R. Wonnacott (1996) suggests a number of milder reforms in this direction: that rules of origin be banned where tariffs differ between members by less than, say, 2 percentage points; that for each commodity they be banned for the FTA member with the lowest tariff, and so on. These rules might be acceptable but would only scratch the surface.

Exports—The Wrong Criterion. One proposal envisions mounting ex post reviews to determine whether nonmember exports have fallen since an RIA was created and, if they have, demanding changes in policies (McMillan 1993). Although it is frequently taken seriously (see, for instance, Frankel, Stein, and Wei 1997), the proposal is wrong in virtually every respect. Exports are the wrong criterion (welfare is related to imports, not exports); quantitative targets are the wrong way to formulate trade policy (they create more rents and market power than do tariffs); economic modeling is still too imprecise to permit identification of causes with any credibility; and ex post adjustment after five years is no basis for the policy predictability sought by investors.

More Vigorous Enforcement of Existing Rules. Two arguably more feasible proposals entail enforcing current rules more rigorously. Even they, however, currently encounter fierce opposition and will require great political commitment by many WTO members to be implemented. To be acceptable to the major powers, they will certainly need to be accompanied by a grandfather clause to assure current RIAs that they will not be undermined by new interpretations.

1. A precise definition and enforcement of "substantially all trade" would be a useful innovation. A quantitative indicator would be clear, but it would need to be high, given that the kinds of trade restrictions countries wish to maintain typically constrain existing trade quite fiercely already. The frequently cited 80 percent, which dates from consideration of the Treaty of Rome, is not adequate. Even 90 percent, which seems to inform current EU-MERCOSUR talks, is not indicative of serious integrationary intent. We would advocate 95 percent after 10 years and 98 percent after 15.

2. Similarly, a more constraining view of "other restrictive regulations of commerce"—to ensure that these regulations cover the effects of rules of origin on excluded countries and that obvious barriers such as safeguards actions and antidumping duties are abolished internally—would be useful. The latter requirement would increase the degree of trade creation, as safeguard and antidumping policies are explicitly aimed at preserving domestic output levels. Thus, these requirements would raise the political bar for "serious" regionalism.

More Radical Reforms. There are three major proposals for creating a "liberal dynamic":

1. *Time limits.* Srinivasan (1998) proposes that RIAs be permitted only temporarily; all RIA concessions would have to be extended to all countries within, say, five years. This is effectively a ban on RIAs and certainly precludes any gains they might offer in terms of deep integration or nation building. It is not a serious contender.

2. *"Open access."* Beginning at least with the U.S. submission to the preparatory committee of the 1933 London Monetary and Economic Conference, scholars and policymakers have argued that

requiring RIAs to admit any country willing to accept their rules both reduces the RIAs' adverse effects on excluded countries and establishes a liberal dynamic (Viner 1950). While this may be true if admission can be guaranteed, virtually every RIA extant has geographic restrictions on membership and also has features that require negotiation and so vitiate the promise of "open access" (see box 8.4).

3. *Prohibition.* Bagwell and Staiger (1998) assert that FTAs necessarily undermine the ability of the WTO to address the spillovers from one country's trade policy to another's welfare through reciprocal tariff negotiations. This might lead to fewer such negotiations or to worse outcomes in those that occur. The implication is that, as in Bhagwati's view, FTAs should be banned. (The case against customs unions in this dimension is weaker, especially if the partners have "similar" trade policy objectives.)

Procedural Fixes: The CRTA. The Committee on Regional Trading Agreements (CRTA), which reports to the WTO's General Council, was established in February 1996 to increase the transparency, efficiency, and consistency of the WTO's treatment of RIAs. It was seen as a means of ensuring more rigorous review of new RIAs, since a single group would review all of them, using the same criteria and with more searching notification and information requirements. The CRTA would also undertake periodic reviews of existing RIAs and could resolve some of the systemic issues that remained after the Uruguay Round. The more thorough review was seen as a route to better compliance with WTO requirements, while the consideration of conceptual issues was a step toward refining the rules and codifying them more precisely.

Unfortunately, the CRTA has still not got into its stride after six years. Its assessments of particular cases have been stymied by the lack of clear systemic rules, and its discussion of rules has been stalemated on exactly the same "substantially all" and "other regulations" issues as bedeviled the Uruguay Round discussions. By December 2000, the CRTA had initiated consideration of 86 RIAs (including 32 inherited from previous working parties). It had completed factual analysis of 62 of these but had been unable "to conclude any examination referred to it" (report by the chairman of the CRTA to the WTO General Council, December 2000).

The CRTA is the key to improved near-term management of RIAs by the WTO. Although RIAs are open to dispute if third countries feel aggrieved (at least until the CRTA has formally certified their WTO-conformity), the rules on "serious" intent to integrate are not really vulnerable to the dispute process. Members do not normally bring internal disputes to the WTO, and third countries are unlikely to press RIAs to include more sectors if they expect this extension to increase trade diversion.[29] Similarly, why would a third country seek to free RIA members from the threat of each other's antidumping legislation? Hence if issues concerning the coverage of sectors or the depth of integration are missed at the outset, they are missed forever.

Recently, however, an RIA did figure in the WTO's dispute settlement process. As part of the EU-Turkey customs union, Turkey imposed quotas on imports of certain textiles and clothing so that the EU's quotas (under the Multifibre Arrangement) would not be undermined by deflected trade. India complained and won a ruling against the quotas on the grounds that they were not fundamental to the customs union. The dispute panel stated that alternative means should be found to meet Turkey's objectives. These might include levying tariffs (for which India could demand compensation), phasing out the EU restrictions, or using rules of origin to control the movement of third-country goods from Turkey to the EU. The ruling suggests a willingness to subordinate Article XXIV to other parts of the GATT, which could have significant implications for new customs unions or for expansions.

The WTO's rules on regionalism are far from perfect, but it is impossible to devise rules that reliably sort beneficial from harmful RIAs. If that process is to be followed at all, it will have to be done case by case by the CRTA. But the CRTA faces a serious timing problem. Unless agreements are submitted to the WTO early in the process of negotiation—when they would be very provisional—reviews will generally be too late to influence their initial form or to affect public debate. If the reviews then call for changes that would upset carefully negotiated compromises, they will be resisted and resented by members, which is bad news for a consensual organization. Thus, considerable political courage will be called for to enforce CRTA findings until the requirements are sufficiently understood and respected by members to be met ab initio. This process of review and response would be aided by detailed economic studies of RIAs, extending well beyond the legalities of GATT Article XXIV and GATS Article V. But both immediately and ultimately, the responsibility for good RIAs lies with governments themselves.

Conclusion: Rules Are Not the Answer

Rules are not the answer, or even a large part of the answer, for ensuring that regionalism will be beneficial. Rather, the need is for understanding.

In the end, subject only to imperfect constraints on the effects on excluded countries, governments will act in what they believe to be their best interests, and rules can help illuminate these interests by informing the parties to the debate about received opinion and norms. But on topics that are as case specific and sui generis as RIAs, advocates will always be able to find plausible exceptions to norms, and no set of rules seems likely to be very effective at distinguishing beneficial from harmful RIAs. Thus, it seems unlikely that great efforts to rewrite the WTO's rules on RIAs will be adequately rewarded.

None of the fundamental reforms to GATT Article XXIV and GATS Article V proposed to date seems likely to command enough political support to make any progress, and none of the minor ones seems worth the effort. Accordingly, we offer the following recommendations:

- Extend the disciplines of Article XXIV and Article V to RIAs between developing countries.
- Enforce these disciplines rigorously in the CRTA, especially those on the coverage and depth of liberalization.
- Use the dispute settlement procedure to enforce third countries' right not to face increases in protection, whether the increases are direct, or indirect through the use of tools such as rules of origin.

Even these steps will require major expenditure of political capital by many countries. We therefore suggest that continuing studies of particular RIAs be conducted, not just with respect to Article XXIV and Article V disciplines but also in terms of the RIAs' overall effects on economic performance. This will help policymakers and the public understand what they can and cannot expect from regional integration.

NOTES

1. The term "most-favored-nation" arises from the long-standing trade diplomacy practice of guaranteeing a partner treatment at least as good as is granted to the most favored partner. If this extends to all partners, all are treated equally in a nondiscriminatory fashion. Universal MFN is the cornerstone of the GATT, the treaty that has governed trade relations since 1947. But the term "most favored" is now ironic. Almost no country pays tariffs above MFN levels, and most pay less via the generalized system of preferences (GSP), other unilateral preferences, or formal RIAs. Only 10 countries pay MFN tariffs on all their exports to the EU. All others, except for the Democratic People's Republic of Korea, which pays above MFN levels, receive some sort of preference (Winters 2000).

2. The 14 percent figure is what is left after allowing for imports from EU members, RIA partners, trade under the GSP, and goods with zero MFN tariffs. This is about 40 percent of the EU's imports from non-EU sources (Sapir 1998).

3. It is also possible that by improving efficiency or generating economies of scale, the RIA will drive down the prices of its exports (ROW imports). Then the rest of the world benefits from the RIA, as Gasiorek, Smith, and Venables (1992) predicted for the EU's Single Market Programme and Flores (1997) for MERCOSUR.

4. This result, of course, refers to total exports; if exports diverted from the RIA can be sold elsewhere at the same price, no damage is done.

5. In any case, one feels uneasy criticizing an RIA because it reduces an exporter's ability to levy taxes on members' imports.

6. Import taxes allow domestic producers to raise their prices and thus bid resources away from exporters. Alternatively, trade may be thought of as the process of swapping exports for imports: if the government requires 10 percent of the imports to be turned over to it as tax, the effect is the same as if it required 10 percent of the exports to be turned over. Trade is discouraged, and both exports and imports fall.

7. The common approach to measuring the effects of RIAs on nonmembers is to consider changes in ROW exports; this, as we have argued above, is at best an indirect approach to measuring the welfare of the rest of the world.

8. Loosely, multilateral trade liberalization means that nearly all countries reduce barriers on imports from nearly all partners.

9. Some theorists have argued, albeit in very particular models, that regionalism has sprung from the success of multilateralism. For example, Ethier (1998) assumes that as the world economy liberalizes, the incentive for any individual developing country to liberalize also increases. He sees RIAs as the preferred modality for this liberalization because, in comparison with nondiscriminatory opening, they appear to allow greater confidence that FDI inflows will follow reform. Freund (1998) argues that as MFN tariffs come down, RIAs become easier to sustain (in a sense defined in the section "Regionalism and Tariff Levels" in this chapter), and trade diversion becomes less costly relative to the benefits of increased competition.

10. On a broad historical canvas, of course, regionalism, which goes back to at least 1815, predates multilateralism. But the current trading system based on the GATT arose in 1947 from other forces and preceded significant regional arrangements between independent powers by at least several years.

11. Levy (1995) shows theoretically how acquiring fringes of FTA partners could weaken EU and U.S. interest in mutual negotiations.

12. The concept, although not the name, goes back at least to Hufbauer (1989).

13. Frankel, Stein, and Wei's model is not at all robust; small asymmetries in size or changes in parameter values can change the results. It is adequate, nevertheless, for demonstrating formally the interaction between RIAs.

14. In November 2001, at the 14th Pacific Economic Co-operation Council meeting in Hong Kong, Jim Sutton, trade negotiations minister of New Zealand and a champion of open regionalism, said it was inconceivable that any bloc would grant totally automatic right of entry to countries willing to abide by its rules.

15. In the 1930s it was not only terms of trade disadvantages that worried politicians but also simple mercantilist effects, as countries sought to reduce imports competitively. Suppose that the United Kingdom aimed to reduce its imports by £1 million. Under MFN rules, each of n equal partners might expect to lose $£(1/n)$ million in exports. But if m partners were exempt because they had an RIA with Britain, each remaining partner would face losses of $£1/(n - m)$ million. If the "entrance fee" absorbed nearly all the benefit of accession, the fee would increase from $1/n$ for the first to $1/(n - 1)$ for the second, and so on. The incentive to be first is obvious.

16. For any individual facing given risks, having insurance is better than not, but abolishing the risk and the insurance it necessitates would be better.

17. Oye (1992) argues that the 1930s also fit this pattern. He asserts that regional arrangements such as U.S. bilateral arrangements under the Reciprocal Trade Agreements Act were politically feasible because they almost guaranteed export expansion in partner markets in return for import liberalization. In this way they started to relax restrictions that were immune to multilateral efforts.

18. It now seems likely that Japan would also be unwilling to pursue unilateral approaches (Scollay and Gilbert 2001).

19. The rules of international commerce are embodied in three main agreements: the General Agreement on Tariffs and Trade (GATT), the General Agreement on Trade in Services (GATS), and the Agreement on Trade-Related Aspects of Intellectual Property Rights (TRIPs). They are administered by the WTO, two of whose principal tools are the Trade Policy Review Mechanism (TPRM) and the Understanding on Dispute Settlement. The WTO has 145 members. The principal nonmember economies, which are seeking accession, are Russia, Saudi Arabia, and Ukraine; the countries of Eastern Europe and Central Asia constitute the other main group of current candidates.

20. The parallel is that the law permits me to smoke, subject to some conditions. That does not make smoking good for me, nor does it help me stop my kids from smoking.

21. For example, if a country is harmed by another's breaking into its export markets, there is—properly—no redress under the GATT.

22. For example, in reviewing the treaty, the head of the GATT secretariat expressed "the view, with which he thought there was no disagreement, that the incidence of the common tariff was higher than that of the rates actually applied by the member states at the time of entry into force of the Treaty of Rome" (GATT document C/M/8, para. 6; cited in GATT 1994: 750).

23. Under GATT procedures, finding a party in violation of its obligations re-

quired unanimity (and therefore the consent of the violating party). This is not true of the WTO.

24. Within the GATT, there was a feeling that the article had influenced the structure of U.S.-Canadian and U.S.-Israeli agreements (personal communication from a senior GATT staff member, 1999). We can also identify cases in which WTO rules, or their equivalent, have prevented RIAs. For example, in 1932 the United Kingdom and the United States refused to waive their MFN rights, preventing the implementation of the Ouchy Convention, a forerunner of the Benelux customs union (Viner 1950). Similarly, negotiators of the draft Multilateral Agreement on Investment (MAI) found no way of preventing some concessions on services among members from also applying to nonmembers via the GATS MFN clause, and they therefore held back such concessions. GATS Article V permits regional arrangements, but the MAI was far too narrowly defined to qualify as one.

25. There is also an unresolved dispute about whether Article XXIV can be applied to an arrangement notified under the Enabling Clause, as the United States demanded with respect to MERCOSUR.

26. Together, these requirements seem to impose no discipline on the sectors that are excluded from the RIA, although these sectors may still be covered by the members' GATS obligations.

27. Schott (1989) offered an early analysis of these sorts of points.

28. WTO document JOB (99)/4797/Rev.2.

29. The United States and its partners still use the WTO dispute settlement procedure, but there has never been a formal GATT dispute between the EU and any country with which it has a formal RIA.

CHAPTER 9

Rules of Thumb for Regionalism

Experience shows that sound international trade policy is a fundamental requirement for economic development. Under almost any circumstances, sound policy includes maintenance of open borders for trade in goods and services and for foreign direct investment. This openness is best achieved by reducing barriers to trade and investment evenhandedly on all partners, through nonpreferential trade liberalization. Experience shows, too, that unilateral trade liberalization is desirable whether or not trading partners reduce their barriers in return. But political pressures can push governments toward regionalism (preferential trade liberalization), and so in some circumstances RIAs may be appropriate solutions to national policy needs. For example, RIAs may confer credibility on policy regimes, help to solve political problems, or increase competition.

Both when RIAs are desirable for some positive purpose and when they arise for essentially political reasons, there are strong returns to ensuring that they are set up with economic efficiency in mind. Even if their objective is ostensibly noneconomic (say, enhancing national security), it is important to minimize the economic price paid for such gains. Unfortunately, it is impossible to devise universal policy guidelines for application to every single RIA because so much depends on the circumstances of each case. We can, however, derive a number of concrete and fairly robust rules of thumb that have wide application and provide a useful benchmark against which to measure specific plans. In what follows, these rules of thumb are listed under the eight central messages that emerge from the analysis in the foregoing chapters.

Message 1: Use RIAs as a way of fostering competition.

If a developing country government wishes to participate in a RIA, it should use it as a procompetitive instrument. Governments should ask whether the RIA will foster greater competition in domestic markets and should focus on incorporating provisions that will help achieve this outcome.

To increase the likelihood that this criterion is satisfied:

1. Minimize the extent of discrimination against nonmembers by using the opportunity provided by the RIA to lower protection against the rest of the world—unilaterally, if necessary. This is of particular importance for small countries.

2. Resist pressure from sectoral lobbies to favor trade-diverting RIAs. Minimize exceptions to the coverage of regional free trade, and include services.

3. Go beyond the abolition of formal trade barriers and reduce the "invisible" barriers associated with the enforcement of regulatory and procedural requirements.

4. Include formal commitments granting the right of establishment and national treatment to foreign direct investors, including those in services markets.

Message 2: North-South dominates South-South.

Not all partners are equal. RIAs with high-income countries are more likely to generate significant economic gains than are those with poorer ones.

1. Developing country governments that want to take part in RIAs should generally seek to form them with large, rich neighboring countries or blocs. By virtue of their size and (usually) efficiency, such partners are more likely to increase domestic competition and to be better sources of trade and of FDI-related technology transfers. Provided that the partners are genuinely interested in the performance of the developing country, richer partners will generate more policy and political credibility than poorer ones.

2. If rich partners are already providing largely duty-free access, a North-South RIA may give rise to large transfers to northern producers, which will directly reduce the developing partner's welfare. Care should be taken to ensure that corresponding benefits

such as credibility, financial transfers, and access to the partner's more sensitive markets are locked in before committing to the RIA.

3. To lessen the size of any resource transfers, governments should reduce the average level of tariffs and other trade barriers that are maintained against nonmembers.

4. RIAs between small economies are likely to be trade diverting. If they are pursued, particular attention should be paid to securing the benefits of creating larger "home" (regional) markets by increasing intrabloc competition. Attention should also be given to lowering protection against the rest of the world in order to obtain the benefits of greater extrabloc competition.

5. RIAs between poor economies could cause divergence in income between partners, which could harm some partners (typically, the less developed and poorer ones) absolutely and heighten political tensions between members. These effects could be mitigated by reducing trade barriers against nonmembers and by including provisions for compensation for tariff revenue losses.

Message 3: Credibility gains require explicitness.

RIAs can enhance the credibility of economic and political reform programs, but generally only if they explicitly include provisions and mechanisms that directly affect the policies of interest.

Governments engaging in RIAs are advised to:

1. Fully specify the transition path to regional free trade (what will be reduced or eliminated, and when) and minimize the probability of reversals of liberalization by prohibiting the application of instruments of contingent protection.

2. Sign RIAs with partners large enough to enforce agreements and close enough to wish to do so, and incorporate explicit language in the RIA that requires action on the part of partner countries in instances of noncompliance or backsliding.

3. Include binding dispute settlement mechanisms that are not diplomatic in nature or conditional on foreign policy considerations.

4. Keep in mind that economic credibility will be achieved only if the RIA represents good policy in its own right. No RIA will stimulate investment if the fundamentals, such as secure property rights and good macroeconomic policies, are not in place.

Message 4: Only efficient RIAs are likely to help politically.

RIAs can help solve political problems; but if they are economically wasteful or divisive, they could have opposite effects.

1. Trade preferences may be useful for achieving political objectives such as national security, but the optimal level of such preferences declines over time.
2. Cooperation with others can help reinforce national sovereignty where individual governments are too small to address problems alone. This can apply both to technical matters and to pooling national efforts in international negotiating or regulatory fora. Because the optimal groupings for cooperation and pursuit of shared interests will vary by issue, one cannot assume that every RIA will automatically deliver these benefits.

Message 5: Regional cooperation does not generally require trade preferences.

The existence of widespread intercountry spillovers calls for cooperation between developing countries in areas other than trade policy, such as regulatory reform and infrastructure provision. Usually, however, these goals should be pursued independent of trade discrimination.

1. Governments should adopt good practices unilaterally through the simplification of administrative requirements and recognition of foreign regulatory regimes where this does not conflict with the ability to achieve public interest objectives. Although the politics may be easier if several countries reform in concert, strong reformers should avoid being tied indissolubly to slower ones.
2. If regional product standards or regulations for producers are required to offset market failures, international norms should be adopted if these exist or can be developed. If regional norms are necessary, they should be nondiscriminatory and open to all countries, wherever possible.
3. Where harmonization is necessary, partners should define minimum, rather than universal, standards within an RIA and should ensure that regulations are appropriate to all members' levels of development and administrative capabilities.
4. Trade preferences might aid policy integration or regional cooperation by putting more issues on the table or by providing an institutional framework for cooperation. Multilateral negotiations or

unilateral adoption of international norms may, however, be more effective.

Message 6: Beware of transactions costs in operating RIAs.

Governments should consider carefully the transactions and implementation costs associated with different types of RIAs.
1. FTAs require costly rules of origin. Their costs can be reduced by adopting the same rules as apply to nonpreferential trade and by using the "change in tariff heading" approach instead of criteria based on local content or value added.
2. Customs unions may be preferable to FTAs, but only if internal borders are actually abolished (frequently, they remain) and the common external tariff is low.
3. Customs unions' institutions for setting common trade policy should be designed to reduce protectionist biases by, for example, ensuring that a single political body is responsible for both the gains and the losses generated by trade barriers.

Message 7: RIAs may have positive or negative fiscal implications.

The fiscal dimensions of RIAs are important for countries where trade taxes generate a significant share of government revenue.
1. In economies with less-developed tax systems, trade taxes can offer a relatively effective and uncorrupt means of raising revenue. Trade taxes are not, however, a permanent solution to revenue needs. The RIA should be used as an opportunity to develop and reform domestic tax structures. Policymakers should ensure that reasonably nondistortionary domestic taxes can compensate for any decline in tariff revenues.
2. Customs unions may also ease collection costs by reducing the scope for smuggling.

Message 8: Do not rely on the WTO to ensure that RIAs are beneficial.

Countries should not rely on the WTO to ensure that RIAs are beneficial to members and outsiders. The WTO forbids some destructive forms of regionalism, but its main contribution toward constraining the potentially negative implications of regionalism for nonmembers is as an instrument for pursuing global liberalization on an MFN basis.

1.   Governments should monitor what happens after an RIA is implemented and use this information as the basis for notification and negotiation in the WTO. Surveillance efforts should include price as well as quantity effects on a commodity-by-commodity basis.

2.   RIAs—the country's own and those of others—should be assessed on the basis of national development objectives and criteria, not according to whether they satisfy the relevant WTO articles.

3.   The WTO review procedures and dispute settlement process should be more vigorously used to enforce the existing rules and contest the negative effects of protectionist dimensions of RIAs, including rules of origin and the application of contingent protection.

4.   The differences between the WTO's rules for developing and developed country RIAs should be eliminated. In particular, the rules requiring nearly complete commodity coverage and no increases in average protection levels should apply to all countries.

Appendix. Selected WTO Provisions on Regional Integration Arrangements

GATT ARTICLE XXIV

4. The contracting parties . . . also recognize that the purpose of a customs union or of a free trade area should be to facilitate trade between the constituent territories and not to raise barriers to trade.

5. (a) With respect to a customs union . . . the duties and other regulations of commerce imposed at the institution . . . shall not on the whole be higher or more restrictive than the general incidence of the duties and regulations of commerce applicable in the constituent territories prior to the formation of such union . . .

   (b) With respect to a free-trade area . . . the duties and other regulations of commerce maintained in each of the constituent territories and applicable at the formation of such free-trade area . . . shall not be higher or more restrictive than the corresponding duties and other regulations of commerce existing in the same constituent territories prior to the formation of the free-trade area . . .

   (c) Any interim agreement . . . shall include a plan and schedule for the formation of such a customs union or of such a free-trade area within a reasonable length of time.

7. (a) Any contracting party deciding to enter into a customs union or a free-trade area, . . . shall promptly notify the CONTRACTING PARTIES and shall make available to them such information . . .

8. (a) A customs union shall be understood to mean the substitution of a single customs territory for two or more customs territories, so that: (i) duties and other restrictive regulations of commerce (except, where necessary, those permitted under Articles XI, XII, XIII, XIV, XV and XX) are eliminated with respect to . . . substantially all the trade in products originating in such territories . . .

8. (b) A free trade area shall be understood to mean a group of two or more customs territories in which the duties and other restrictive regulations of commerce (except, where necessary, those permitted under Articles XI, XII, XIII, XIV, XV and XX)

are eliminated on substantially all the trade between the constituent territories in products originating in such territories.

THE ENABLING CLAUSE (THE DECISION ON DIFFERENTIAL AND MORE FAVORABLE TREATMENT, RECIPROCITY AND FULLER PARTICIPATION OF DEVELOPING COUNTRIES)

1. Notwithstanding the provisions of Article I of the General Agreement, contracting parties may accord differential and more favorable treatment to developing countries, without according such treatment to other contracting parties.
2. The provisions of paragraph 1 apply to the following: . . . (c) Regional or global arrangements entered into amongst less-developed contracting parties for the mutual reduction or elimination of tariffs and, in accordance with criteria or conditions which may be prescribed by the CONTRACTING PARTIES, for the mutual reduction or elimination of non-tariff measures, on products imported from one another; . . .

THE URUGUAY ROUND UNDERSTANDING ON THE INTERPRETATION OF ARTICLE XXIV

2. The evaluation . . . of the duties and other regulations of commerce . . . shall . . . be based upon an overall assessment of weighted average tariff rates and of customs duties collected. . . . For this purpose, the duties and charges to be taken into consideration shall be the applied rates of duty. It is recognized that for the purpose of the overall assessment of the incidence of other regulations of commerce for which quantification and aggregation are difficult, the examination of individual measures, regulations, products covered and trade flows affected may be required.
3. The "reasonable length of time" referred to in Article XXIV 5(c) should exceed 10 years only in exceptional cases. . . .

GATS ARTICLE V

1. This Agreement shall not prevent any of its Members from being a party to or entering into an agreement liberalizing trade in

services between or among the parties to such an agreement, provided that such an agreement:

(a) has substantial sectoral coverage,[1] and

(b) provides for the absence or elimination of substantially all discrimination, in the sense of Article XVII, between or among the parties, in the sectors covered under subparagraph (a), . . .

3. (a) Where developing countries are parties to an agreement of the type referred to in paragraph 1, flexibility shall be provided for regarding the conditions set out in paragraph 1, particularly with reference to subparagraph (b) thereof, in accordance with the level of development of the countries concerned, both overall and in individual sectors and subsectors . . .

4. Any agreement referred to in paragraph 1 shall be designed to facilitate trade between the parties to the agreement and shall not in respect of any Member outside the agreement raise the overall level of barriers to trade in services within the respective sectors or subsectors compared to the level applicable prior to such an agreement.

NOTES

1. [*The following note is in the original GATS text.*] This condition is understood in terms of number of sectors, volume of trade affected and modes of supply. In order to meet this condition, agreements should not provide for the *a priori* exclusion of any mode of supply.

Bibliography

The word *processed* denotes informally reproduced works that may not be commonly available through libraries. Web addresses for works available online as full texts are provided, if known, at the end of the entry. Abstracts of CEPR Discussion Papers may be accessed at <http://www.cepr.org/pubs/new-dps/dp_papers.htm>.

Acemoglu, Daron, Simon Johnson, and James A. Robinson. 2001. "The Colonial Origins of Comparative Development: An Empirical Investigation." *American Economic Review* 91 (5): 1369–1401.

Adams, Charles. 1993. *For Good and Evil: The Impact of Taxes on the Course of Civilization.* Lanham, Md.: Madison Books.

Aitken, Brian J., and Ann E. Harrison. 1999. "Do Domestic Firms Benefit from Direct Foreign Investment? Evidence from Venezuela." *American Economic Review* 89 (3): 605–18.

Aitken, Brian J., Gordon H. Hanson, and Ann E. Harrison. 1997. "Spillovers, Foreign Investment, and Export Behavior." *Journal of International Economics* 43 (1–2, August): 103–32.

Aitken, N. D. 1973. "The Effect of the EEC and EFTA on European Trade: A Temporal Cross-Section Analysis." *American Economic Review* 63 (5): 881–92.

Aitken, N. D., and W. R. Lowry. 1973. "A Cross-Sectional Study of the Effects of LAFTA and CACM on Latin American Trade." *Journal of Common Market Studies* 11 (4, June): 326–36.

Aitken, N. D., and R. S. Obutelewicz. 1976. "A Cross-Sectional Study of EEC Trade with the Association of African Countries." *Review of Economics and Statistics* 58 (4, November): 425–33.

Alburo, Florian A., Carlos C. Bautista, and Maria Socorro H. Gochoco. 1992. "Pacific Direct Investment Flows into ASEAN." *ASEAN Economic Bulletin* (March).

Alogoskoufis, G. 1995. "The Two Faces of Janus: Institutions, Policy Regimes and Macroeconomic Performance in Greece." *Economic Policy: A European Forum* (April): 147–84.

Amjadi, Azita, and L. Alan Winters. 1999. "Transport Costs and 'Natural' Integration in Mercosur." *Journal of Economic Integration* 14 (4, December): 497–521.

Anderson, Kym, and Hete Norheim. 1993. "History, Geography and Regional Economic Integration." In Kym Anderson and Richard Blackhurst, eds.,

Regional Integration and the Global Trading System, 19–51. New York: St. Martin's Press.

Anderson, Svein S., and Kjell A. Eliassen. 1993. *Making Policy in Europe: The Europeification of National Policy-Making.* London: Sage Publications.

Andriamananjara, Soamiely, and Maurice Schiff. 2001. "Regional Cooperation among Microstates." *Review of International Economics* 9 (1, February): 42–51.

Anwar, Dewi Fortuna. 1994. *Indonesia in ASEAN: Foreign Policy and Regionalism.* New York: St. Martin's Press.

Arad, Ruth W., and Arye L. Hillman. 1979. "Embargo Threat, Learning and Departure from Comparative Advantage." *Journal of International Economics* 9 (May): 265–75.

Bagwell, Kyle, and Robert W. Staiger. 1998. "Will Preferential Trading Arrangements Undermine the Multilateral Trading System?" *Economic Journal* 108 (July): 1162–82.

———. 1999. "An Economic Theory of GATT." *American Economic Review* 89 (1, March): 215–48.

Balassa, Bela. 1974. "Trade Creation and Trade Diversion in the European Common Market: An Appraisal of the Evidence." *Manchester School of Economic and Social Studies* 42: 93–135.

———. 1989. "Tariff Reductions and Trade in Manufactures among the Industrial Countries." In Bela Balassa, *Comparative Advantage, Trade Policy and Economic Development,* 131–39. London: Harvester Wheatsheaf.

Balasubramanyam, Venkataraman N., Mohammed A. Salisu, and David Sapsford. 1996. "Foreign Direct Investment and Growth in EP and IS Countries." *Economic Journal* 106 (January): 92–105.

Baldwin, Richard E. 1989. "The Growth Effects of 1992." *Economic Policy: A European Forum* 4 (October): 248–81.

———. 1992. "Measurable Dynamic Gains from Trade." *Journal of Political Economy* 100 (1, February): 162–74.

———. 1993. "On the Measurement of Dynamic Effects of Integration." *Empirica–Austrian Economic Papers* 20 (2): 129–45.

———. 1994. *Towards an Integrated Europe.* London: Centre for Economic Policy Research.

———. 1995. "A Domino Theory of Regionalism." In Richard E. Baldwin, Pertti Haaparanta, and Jaakko Kiander, eds., *Expanding Membership of the European Union.* Cambridge, U.K.: Cambridge University Press.

———. 1997. "The Causes of Regionalism." *World Economy* 20 (7): 865–88.

Baldwin, Richard E., and Rikard Forslid. 1996. "Trade Liberalization and Endogenous Growth: A q-Theory Approach." NBER Working Paper 5549. National Bureau of Economic Research, Cambridge, Mass. Available at <http://papers.nber.org/papers/w5549>.

Baldwin, Richard E., and Elena Seghezza. 1996. "Testing for Trade-Induced Investment-Led Growth." CEPR Discussion Paper 1331. Centre for Economic Policy Research, London.

Baldwin, Richard E., and Anthony J. Venables. 1995. "Regional Economic Integration." In Gene Grossman and Kenneth Rogoff, eds., *Handbook of International Economics*, vol. 3: 1597–1644. Amsterdam: North-Holland.

Baldwin, Richard E., Rikard Forslid, and Jan I. Haaland. 1996. "Investment Creation and Diversion in Europe." *World Economy* 19 (6, November): 635–59.

Baldwin, Richard E., Joseph F. Francois, and Richard Portes. 1997. "The Costs and Benefits of Eastern Enlargement: The Impact on the EU and Central Europe." *Economic Policy: A European Forum* 24 (April): 125–76.

Bandyopadhyay, Subhayu, and Howard J. Wall. 1999. "Customs Union or Free Trade Area? The Role of Political Asymmetries." *Review of International Economics* 7 (4): 665–72.

Barrett, Scott. 1994 "Conflict and Cooperation in Managing International Water Resources." Policy Research Working Paper 1303. World Bank, Policy Research Department, Public Economics Division, Washington, D.C. Processed.

Barros, Pedro. 1995. "Conduct Effects of Gradual Entry Liberalization in Insurance." *Journal of Regulatory Economics* 8: 45–60.

Basevi, Georgio, Flavio Delbono, and Mario Mariotti. 1994. "Bargaining with a Composite Player: An Application to the Uruguay Round of GATT Negotiations." *Journal of International and Comparative Economics* 3: 161–74.

Bayoumi, Tamim, and Barry Eichengreen. 1997. "Is Regionalism Simply a Diversion? Evidence from the Evolution of the EC and EFTA." In Taketoshi Ito and Anne O. Krueger, eds., *Regionalism versus Multilateral Trade Arrangements.* NBER–East Asia Seminar on Economics, vol. 6. Chicago: University of Chicago Press.

Ben-David, Dan. 1993. "Equalizing Exchange: Trade Liberalization and Economic Convergence." *Quarterly Journal of Economics* 108 (3, August): 653–79.

——————. 1994. "Income Disparity among Countries and the Effects of Freer Trade." In Luigi L. Pasinetti and Robert M. Solow, eds., *Economic Growth and the Structure of Long-Term Development*, 45–64. London: Macmillan.

——————. 1996. "Trade and Convergence among Countries." *Journal of International Economics* 40: 297–98.

—————. 1998. "Convergence Clubs and Subsistence Economies." *Journal of Development Economics* 55: 155–57.

Bergsten, C. Fred. 1996. "Globalizing Free Trade." *Foreign Affairs* 75 (May–June): 105–20.

—————. 1997. "Open Regionalism." *World Economy* 20: 545–65.

Bernal, Richard L. 1998. *The Integration of Small Economies in the Free Trade Area of the Americas.* Policy Papers on the Americas 9. CSIS Americas Program. Washington, D.C.: Center for Strategic and International Studies.

Bhagwati, Jagdish. 1987. "VERs and Quid Pro Quo DFI and VIEs: Political-Economy-Theoretic Analysis." *International Economic Journal* 1: 1–4.

—————. 1991. *The World Trading System at Risk.* Princeton, N.J.: Princeton University Press.

—————. 1993. "Regionalism and Multilateralism: An Overview." In Jaime de Melo and Arvind Panagariya, eds., *New Dimensions in Regional Integration,* 22–57. New York: Cambridge University Press.

Bhagwati, Jagdish, and Arvind Panagariya. 1996. "Preferential Trading Areas and Multilateralism: Strangers, Friends, or Foes?" In Jagdish N. Bhagwati and Arvind Panagariya, eds., *The Economics of Preferential Trading Agreements.* Washington, D.C.: AEI Press.

Bhagwati, Jagdish, and T. N. Srinivasan. 1996. "Does Environmental Diversity Detract from the Case for Free Trade?" In Jagdish Bhagwati and Robert E. Hudec, eds., *Fair Trade and Harmonization: Prerequisites for Free Trade?* Cambridge, Mass.: MIT Press.

—————. 1999. "Outward-Orientation and Development: Are Revisionists Right?" Yale University Economic Growth Center Discussion Paper 806. New Haven, Conn.

Bhalla, A. S., and P. Bhalla. 1997. *Regional Blocs: Building Blocks or Stumbling Blocks?* New York: St. Martin's Press.

Bilal, Sanoussi. 1998. "Why Regionalism May Increase the Demand for Trade Protection." *Journal of Economic Integration* 13: 30–61.

Blanchard, Oliver Jean, and Lawrence F. Katz. 1992. "Regional Evolutions." *Brookings Papers on Economic Activity* 1: 1–61.

Blomström, Magnus, and Ari Kokko. 1997. "Regional Integration and Foreign Direct Investment: A Conceptual Framework and Three Cases." Policy Research Working Paper 1750. World Bank, International Trade Division, Washington, D.C. Available at <http://econ.worldbank.org/resource.php?type=5>.

—————. 1998. "Foreign Investment as a Vehicle for International Technology Transfer." In Giorgio Barba Navaretti, Partha Dasgupta, Karl G.

Maler, and Domenico Siniscalco, eds., *Creation and Transfer of Knowledge: Institutions and Incentives*. Heidelberg and Berlin: Springer Verlag.

Bond, Eric W. 1997. "Competition Policy in Customs Unions: Theory and an Example from U.S. History." Pennsylvania State University, University Park. Processed.

Bond, Eric W., and Constantinos Syropoulos. 1996. "The Size of Trading Blocs: Market Power and World Welfare Effects." *Journal of International Economics* 40: 411–37.

Bond, Eric W., Constantinos Syropoulos, and L. Alan Winters. 2001. "Deepening of Regional Integration and Multilateral Trade Agreements." *Journal of International Economics* 53 (2, April): 335–61.

Brada, Josef C., and Jose A. Mendez. 1988. "An Estimate of the Dynamic Effects of Economic Integration." *Review of Economic and Statistics* 70 (February): 163–68.

Byron, Jessica. 1994. "CARICOM in the Post–Cold War Era: Regional Solutions or Continued Regional Contradictions?" Working Paper Series 178. Institute of Social Studies, The Hague.

Campa, J. M., and T. L. Sorenson. 1996. "Are Trade Blocs Conducive to Free Trade?" *Scandinavian Journal of Economics* 98 (2): 263–73.

Catinat, Michael, and Alexander Italianer. 1988. "Completing the Internal Market: Primary Microeconomic Effects and Their Implementation in Macroeconometric Models." Commission of the European Communities, Brussels.

CEA (Council of Economic Advisers). 1995. *Council of Economic Advisers Annual Report*. Washington, D.C.

CEC (Commission of the European Communities). 1988. "The Economics of 1992." *European Economy* 35. Luxembourg.

————. 1996. *European Economy*. Luxembourg.

Cecchini, Paolo, with Michael Catinat and Alexis Jacquemin. 1988. *The European Challenge, 1992: The Benefits of a Single Market*. Aldershot, Hants, U.K.; Brookfield, Vt.: Gower.

Chan, Steve. 1984. "Mirror, Mirror on the Wall . . . Are the Freer Countries More Pacific?" *Journal of Conflict Resolution* 28: 617–48.

Chang, Won, and L. Alan Winters. 2002. "How Regional Blocs Affect Excluded Countries: The Price Effects of MERCOSUR." *American Economic Review* 92 (4, September): 889–904.

Coe, David T., and Elhanan Helpman. 1995. "International R&D Spillovers." *European Economic Review* 39: 859–87.

Coe, David T., and Alexander W. Hoffmaister. 1999. "Are There International R&D Spillovers among Randomly Matched Trade Partners? A Response to

Keller." IMF Working Paper WP/99/18. International Monetary Fund, Washington, D.C. Available at <http://www.imf.org/external/pubind.htm>.

Coe, David T., Elhanan Helpman, and Alexander W. Hoffmaister. 1997. "North-South R&D Spillovers." *Economic Journal* 107 (January): 134–49.

Collier, Paul. 1996. "The Role of the African State in Building Agencies of Restraint." In Mats Lundahl and Benno J. Ndulu, eds., *New Directions in Development Economics: Growth, Environmental Concerns, and Government in the 1990s*, 282–98. Studies in Development Economics, vol. 3. London and New York: Routledge.

Collier, Paul, Patrick Guillaumont, Sylviane Guillaumont, and Jan Willem Gunning. 1997. "The Future of Lomé: Europe's Role." *World Economy* 20 (3): 285–306.

Cooper, C. A., and B. F. Massell. 1965. "Toward a General Theory of Customs Unions for Developing Countries." *Journal of Political Economy* 73: 256–83.

Cordoba, J. 1996. "Rules of Origin in Free Trade Agreements." World Bank, Latin America and the Caribbean Department, Washington, D.C. Processed.

Council of the European Union. 1998. "Negotiating Directives for the Negotiation of a Development Partnership Agreement with the ACP Countries." Information Note 10017/98. European Union, Brussels.

Daniel, Timothy P., and Andrew N. Kleit. 1995. "Disentangling Regulatory Policy: The Effects of State Regulations on Trucking Rates." *Journal of Regulatory Economics* 8: 267–84.

Dee, Philippa, Alexis Hardin, and Michael Schuele. 1998. "APEC Early Voluntary Sectoral Liberalization." Productivity Commission Staff Research Paper. AusInfo, Canberra.

de Melo, Jaime, Claudio Montenegro, and Arvind Panagariya. 1993. "L'intégration régionale hier et aujourd'hui." *Revue d'Economie du Développement* 1 (1–2, February): 1–49. Also published as "Regional Integration, Old and New." Policy Research Working Paper 985. World Bank, Country Economics Department, Washington, D.C., 1992, processed.

de Melo, Jaime, Arvind Panagariya, and Dani Rodrik. 1993. "Regional Integration: An Analytical and Empirical Overview." In Jaime de Melo and Arvind Panagariya, eds., *New Dimensions in Regional Integration*. New York: Cambridge University Press.

DeRosa, Dean A. 1995. *Regional Trading Arrangements Among Developing Countries: The ASEAN Example*. Research Report 103. International Food Policy Research Institute.

Dickens, W. T., and L. F. Katz. 1987. "Inter-Industry Wage Differences and Industry Characteristics." In Kevin Lang and Jonathan S. Levin, eds., *Unem-*

ployment and the Structure of Labor Markets, 48–89. Oxford, U.K.: Blackwell.

Di Leva, Charles. 1998. "International Environmental Law and Development." *Georgetown International Environmental Law Review* 10 (2): 501–49.

Dinar, Ariel, and Aaron Wolf. 1997. "Economic and Political Considerations in Regional Cooperation Models." *Agricultural and Resource Economics Review* 26 (1, April): 7–22.

Dissou, Yasid. 2002. "Dynamic Effects in Senegal of Regional Trade." *Review of International Economics* 10 (1): 177–99.

Dixit, Avinash. 1984. "International Trade Policies for Oligopolistic Industries." *Economic Journal* 94: 1–16.

————. 1988. "Anti-Dumping and Countervailing Duties under Oligopoly." *European Economic Review* 32: 55–68.

Djankov, Simeon, and Bernard Hoekman. 1997. "Trade Reorientation and Productivity Growth in Bulgarian Enterprises." Policy Research Working Paper 1707. World Bank, International Economics Department, International Trade Division, Washington, D.C. Available at <http://econ.worldbank.org/resource.php?type=5>.

————. 2000. "Foreign Investment and Productivity Growth in Czech Enterprises." *World Bank Economic Review* 14 (1): 49–64.

Dollar, David. 1992. "Outward-Oriented Developing Economies Really Do Grow More Rapidly: Evidence from 95 LDCs, 1976–1985." *Economic Development and Cultural Change* 40 (April): 523–44.

Doyle, Michael. 1986. *Empires.* Ithaca, N.Y.: Cornell University Press.

Duchêne, François. 1994. *Jean Monnet: The First Statesman of Interdependence.* New York: Norton.

Echavarria, Juan José. 1997. "Trade Flows in the Andean Pact Countries: Unilateral Liberalization or Regional Preferences?" In Shahid Javed Burki, Guillermo E. Perry, and Sara Calvo, eds., "Trade: Towards Open Regionalism. Annual World Bank Conference on Development in Latin America and the Caribbean 1997." World Bank, Washington, D.C.

————. 1998. "Trade Flows in the Andean Countries: Unilateral Liberalization or Regional Preferences?" Organization of American States, Trade Unit, Washington, D.C. Processed.

Edwards, Sebastian. 1993. "Openness, Trade Liberalization, and Growth in Developing Countries." *Journal of Economic Literature* 31 (3, September): 1358–93.

————. 1998. "Openness, Productivity and Growth: What Do We Really Know?" *Economic Journal* 108 (447, March): 383–98.

Eichengreen, Barry, and J. Frankel. 1995. "Economic Regionalism: Evidence from Two 20th Century Episodes." *North American Journal of Economics and Finance* 6: 89–106.

Emerson, Michael. 1988. *The Economics of 1992: The E.C. Commission's Assessment of the Economic Effects of Completing the Internal Market.* Oxford, U.K.: Oxford University Press.

Engerman, Stanley L., and Kenneth L. Sokoloff. 1997. "Factor Endowments, Institutions, and Differential Paths of Growth among New World Economies." In Stephen Haber, ed., *How Latin America Fell Behind,* 260–304. Stanford, Calif.: Stanford University Press.

Ethier, W. J. 1998. "Regionalism in a Multilateral World." *Journal of Political Economy* 106 (6, December): 1214–45.

European Commission. 1996. "Economic Evaluation of the Internal Market." *European Economy.* Reports and Studies 4. Luxembourg.

———. 1997. *The Single Market Review.* Subseries III: *The Dismantling of Barriers.* Vol. 3: *Customs and Fiscal Formalities at Frontiers.* Luxembourg.

———. 1998. *The Single Market Review.* Subseries IV: *Impact on Trade and Investment.* Vol. 4 (1): *Foreign Direct Investment.* Luxembourg.

Evenett, Simon J., and Bernard Hoekman. 1999. "Government Procurement Discrimination and International Trade." World Bank, Development Research Group, Trade, Washington, D.C. Processed.

Fernandez, Raquel, and Jonathan Portes. 1998. "Returns to Regionalism: An Analysis of Nontraditional Gains from Regional Trade Agreements." *World Bank Economic Review* 12 (2, May): 197–220.

Finger, J. Michael, ed. 1993a. *Antidumping: How It Works and Who Gets Hurt.* Ann Arbor: University of Michigan Press.

———. 1993b. "GATT's Influence on Regional Arrangements." In Jaime de Melo and Arvind Panagariya, eds., *New Dimensions in Regional Integration.* New York: Cambridge University Press.

Flores, R. 1997. "The Gains from MERCOSUR: A General Equilibrium, Imperfect Competition Evaluation." *Journal of Policy Modeling* 19 (1, February): 1–18.

Foroutan, Faezeh. 1996. "Turkey, 1976–85: Foreign Trade, Industrial Productivity, and Competition." In Mark J. Roberts and James R. Tybout, *Industrial Evolution in Developing Countries: Micro Patterns of Turnover, Productivity, and Market Structure,* 314–37. New York: Oxford University Press.

———. 1998. "Does Membership in a Regional Preferential Trade Arrangement Make a Country More or Less Protectionist?" *World Economy* 21 (May): 305–36.

Francois, Joseph F. 1997. "External Bindings and the Credibility of Reform." In Ahmed Galal and Bernard Hoekman, eds., *Regional Partners in Global Markets: Limits and Possibilities of the Euro-Med Agreements*. London: Centre for Economic Policy Research.

Francois, Joseph F., and C. R. Shiells, eds. 1994. *Modeling Trade Policy: Applied General Equilibrium Assessments in North American Free Trade*. Cambridge, U.K.: Cambridge University Press.

Francois, Joseph F., David Palmeter, and Douglas Nelson. 1997. "Government Procurement in the U.S.: A Post–Uruguay Round Analysis." In Bernard Hoekman and Petros Mavroidis, eds., *Law and Policy in Public Purchasing: The WTO Agreement on Government Procurement*. Ann Arbor: University of Michigan Press.

Frankel, Jeffrey A., ed. 1998. *The Regionalization of the World Economy*. Chicago: University of Chicago Press.

Frankel, Jeffrey A., and David Romer. 1999. "Does Trade Cause Growth?" *American Economic Review* 89 (3, June): 379–99.

Frankel, Jeffrey A., and Andrew K. Rose. 2000. "Estimating the Effect of Currency Unions on Trade and Output." NBER Working Paper 7857. National Bureau of Economic Research, Cambridge, Mass. Available at <http://papers.nber.org/papers/w7857>.

Frankel, Jeffrey A., and Shang-Jin Wei. 1998. "Regionalization of World Trade and Currencies: Economics and Politics." In Jeffrey A. Frankel, ed., *The Regionalization of the World Economy*. Chicago: University of Chicago Press.

Frankel, Jeffrey A., Ernesto Stein, and Shang-Jin Wei. 1997. *Regional Trading Blocs in the World Economic System*. Washington, D.C.: Institute for International Economics.

Freund, Caroline L. 1998. "Multilateralism and the Endogenous Formation of PTAs." International Finance Discussion Paper 614. Board of Governors of the Federal Reserve System, Washington, D.C.

Fujita, Masahisa, Paul Krugman, and Anthony J. Venables. 1999. *The Spatial Economy: Cities, Regions, and International Trade*. Cambridge, Mass.: MIT Press.

Fukase, Emiko, and Will Martin. 2000. *Free Trade Membership as a Stepping Stone to Development: The Case of ASEAN*. World Bank Discussion Paper 421. Washington, D.C.

Fuleihan, Basil. 1997. "The Impact of EU Association on Lebanon's Fiscal Position." In Wassim Shahin and Kamal Shehadi, eds., *Pathways to Integration: Lebanon and the Euro-Mediterranean Partnership*, ch. 6. Beirut: Lebanese Center for Policy Studies.

Gasiorek, Michael, Alasdair Smith, and Anthony J. Venables. 1992. "'1992': Trade and Welfare—A General Equilibrium Model." In L. Alan Winters, ed., *Trade Flows and Trade Policy after 1992*. Cambridge, U.K.: Cambridge University Press.

Gatsios, Konstantine, and Larry Karp. 1991. "Delegation Games in Customs Unions." *Review of Economic Studies* 58 (2): 391–97.

———. 1995. "Delegation in a General Equilibrium Model of Customs Unions." *European Economic Review* 39 (2): 319–33.

GATT (General Agreement on Tariffs and Trade). 1994. *Analytical Index: Guide to GATT Law and Practice*. 6th ed. Geneva.

Graham, Edward M., and J. David Richardson, eds. 1997. *Global Competition Policy*. Washington, D.C.: Institute for International Economics.

Greenwold, S., and A. Cox. 1993. "The Legal and Structural Obstacles to Free Trade in the United States Procurement Market." *Public Procurement Law Review* 2: 237–52.

Grossman, Gene M., and Elhanan Helpman. 1995. "The Politics of Free-Trade Agreements." *American Economic Review* 85 (4): 667–90.

Gupta, Anju, and Maurice Schiff. 1997. "Outsiders and Regional Trade Agreements among Small Countries." Policy Research Working Paper 1847. World Bank, Development Research Group, Washington, D.C. Available at <http://econ.worldbank.org/resource.php?type=5>.

Haaland, Jan I., and Victor D. Norman. 1992. "Global Production Effects of European Integration." In L. Alan Winters, ed., *Trade Flows and Trade Policy after 1992*. Cambridge, U.K.: Cambridge University Press.

Haddad, Mona, and Ann Harrison. 1993. "Are There Positive Spillovers from Direct Foreign Investment? Evidence from Panel Data for Morocco." *Journal of Development Economics* 42 (1, October): 51–74.

Hall, R. E., and C. I. Jones. 1999. "Why Do Some Countries Produce So Much More Output per Worker Than Others?" *Quarterly Journal of Economics* 114 (1): 83–116.

Hamilton, C. B. 1988. "Restrictiveness and International Transmission of the 'New' Protectionism." In Robert E. Baldwin, Carl B. Hamilton, and André Sapir, eds., *Issues in U.S.-EC Trade Relations*. Chicago: University of Chicago Press.

Hansen, Niles M. 1969. "Regional Development and the Rural Poor." *Journal of Human Resources* 4 (2, spring): 205–14.

Hanson, Gordon H. 1996. "Economic Integration, Intraindustry Trade and Frontier Regions." *European Economic Review* 40 (April): 941–49.

———. 1997. "Increasing Returns, Trade and the Regional Structure of Wages." *Economic Journal* 107: 113–33.

————. 1998. "Regional Adjustment to Trade Liberalisation." *Regional Science and Urban Economics* 28: 419–44.

Hanson, Gordon H., and Ann Harrison. 1999. "Trade Liberalisation and Wage Inequality in Mexico." *Industrial and Labor Relations Review* 52 (2): 271–88.

Harrison, Ann. 1994. "Productivity, Imperfect Competition and Trade Reform: Theory and Evidence." *Journal of International Economics* 36 (1–2, February): 53–73.

————. 1996. "Determinants and Effects of Direct Foreign Investment in Côte d'Ivoire, Morocco, and Venezuela." In Mark J. Roberts and James R. Tybout, eds., *Industrial Evolution in Developing Countries: Micro Patterns of Turnover, Productivity, and Market Structure*, 163–86. New York: Oxford University Press.

Harrison, Glenn W., Thomas F. Rutherford, and David G. Tarr. 1996. "Increased Competition and Completion of the Market in the European Union: Static and Steady State Effects." *Journal of Economic Integration* 11 (3, September): 332–65.

————. 1997. "Trade Policy Options for Chile: A Quantitative Evaluation." Policy Research Working Paper 1783. World Bank, Development Research Group, Trade, Washington, D.C. Available at <http://econ.worldbank.org/resource.php?type=5>.

————. 2002. "Trade Policy Options for Chile: The Importance of Market Access." *World Bank Economic Review* 16 (1): 49–79.

Hathaway, Dale E., and Merlinda D. Ingco. 1996. "Agricultural Liberalisation and the Uruguay Round." In Will Martin and L. Alan Winters, eds., *The Uruguay Round and the Developing Countries*. Cambridge, U.K.: Cambridge University Press.

Hathaway, Oona A. 1998. "Positive Feedback: The Impact of Trade Liberalization on Industry Demands for Protection." *International Organization* 52 (summer): 575–612.

Henderson, David. 1999. *The MAI Affair: A Story and Its Lessons*. London: Royal Institute for International Affairs.

Henrekson, Magnus, Johan Torstensson, and Rasha Torstensson. 1997. "Growth Effects of European Integration." *European Economic Review* 41 (8, August): 1537–57.

Herin, Jan. 1986. "Rules of Origin and Differences between Tariff Levels in EFTA and in the EC." EFTA Occasional Paper 13. Geneva.

Hillman, Arye L., and Ngo Van Long. 1983. "Pricing and Depletion of an Exhaustible Resource When There Is Anticipation of Trade Disruption." *Quarterly Journal of Economics* 98 (May): 215–33.

Hindley, Brian, and Patrick Messerlin. 1993. "Guarantees of Market Access and Regionalism." In Kym Anderson and Richard Blackhurst, eds., *Regional Integration and the Global Trading System*. New York: St. Martin's Press.

Hinojosa-Ojeda, Raúl A., Jeffrey D. Lewis, and Sherman Robinson. 1995. "Regional Integration Options for Central America and the Caribbean after NAFTA." *North American Journal of Economics and Finance* 6 (2, fall): 121–48.

Hirschman, Albert O. 1958. *The Strategy of Economic Development*. New Haven, Conn.: Yale University Press.

Hoekman, Bernard. 2000. "The Next Round of Services Negotiations: Identifying Priorities and Options." *Federal Reserve Bank of St. Louis Review* 82 (4, July–August): 31–48.

Hoekman, Bernard, and Carlos A. Primo Braga. 1997 "Protection and Trade in Services: A Survey." *Open Economies Review* 8: 285–308.

Hoekman, Bernard, and Simeon Djankov. 1997. "Effective Protection and Investment Incentives in Egypt and Jordan: Implications of Free Trade with Europe." *World Development* 25: 281–91.

Hoekman, Bernard, and D. Konan. 1999. "Deep Integration, Nondiscrimination, and Euro-Mediterranean Free Trade." In Jürgen von Hagen and Mika Widgren, eds., *Regionalism in Europe*. Boston: Kluwer Academic.

Hoekman, Bernard, and Michael P. Leidy. 1993. "Holes and Loopholes in Integration Agreements: History and Prospects." In Kym Anderson and Richard Blackhurst, eds., *Regional Integration and the Global Trading System*, 218–45. New York: St. Martin's Press.

Hoekman, Bernard, and Petros Mavroidis, eds. 1997. *Law and Policy in Public Purchasing: The WTO Agreement on Government Procurement*. Ann Arbor: University of Michigan Press.

Hoekman, Bernard, and Pierre Sauvé. 1994. "Regional and Multilateral Liberalization of Trade in Services: Complements or Substitutes?" *Journal of Common Market Studies* 32: 283–317.

Holmes, Peter. 1996. "Competition Policy and Integration: Levelling or Tilting the Playing Field." Global Economic Institutions Working Paper 21. London: Centre for Economic Policy Research.

Holmes, Peter, and Alasdair Smith. 1997. "Dynamic Effects of Regional Integration." In *Regionalism and Development: Report of the European Commission and World Bank Seminar (June 2, 1997)*. European Commission Studies Series 1. Brussels.

Holmes, Thomas. 1998. "The Effect of State Policies on the Location of Manufacturing: Evidence from State Borders." *Journal of Political Economy* 106: 667–705.

Horn, Henrik, and James Levinsohn. 1996. "Merger Policies and Trade Liberalization." NBER Working Paper 6077. National Bureau of Economic Research, Cambridge, Mass. Available at <http://papers.nber.org/papers/w6077>.

Horn, Henrik, Harald Lang, and Stefan Lundgren. 1995. "Managerial Effort Incentives, X-Inefficiency and International Trade." *European Economic Review* 39 (1, January): 117–38.

Hsieh, Chang-Tai. 2001. "Comment on 'Trade Policy and Economic Growth: A Skeptic's Guide to the Cross-National Evidence,' by Rodriguez and Rodrik." In Ben S. Bernanke and Kenneth Rogoff, eds., *NBER Macroeconomics Annual 2000*, 325–30. Cambridge, Mass.: MIT Press.

Hufbauer, G. C. 1989. *The Free Trade Debate: Reports of the Twentieth Century Fund Task Force on the Future of American Trade Policy*. New York: Priority Press.

Hull, Cordell. 1948. *The Memoirs of Cordell Hull*. New York: Macmillan.

Hunter, Linda, James R. Markusen, and Thomas F. Rutherford. 1992. "U.S.-Mexico Free Trade and the North American Auto Industry: Effects on the Spatial Organisation of Production of Finished Autos." *World Economy* 15 (1, January): 65–81.

IADB (Inter-American Development Bank). 1995. "Economic Integration in the Americas: Periodic Note on Integration." Washington, D.C. Available at <http://www.iadb.org/int/intpub/nota/homepage.htm>.

Inotai, András. 1991. "Regional Integration among Developing Countries, Revisited." Policy Research Working Paper 643. World Bank, Country Economics Department, Washington, D.C. Processed.

Irwin, Douglas A. 1993. "Multilateral and Bilateral Trade Policies in the World Trading System: A Historical Perspective." In Jaime de Melo and Arvind Panagariya, eds., *New Dimensions in Regional Integration*. New York: Cambridge University Press.

Jacquemin, Alexis, and André Sapir. 1991. "Competition and Imports in the European Market." In L. Alan Winters and Anthony J. Venables, eds., *European Integration: Trade and Industry*. Cambridge, U.K.: Cambridge University Press.

Johnson, H. G. 1965. "An Economic Theory of Protectionism: Tariff Bargaining and the Formation of Customs Unions." *Journal of Political Economy* 73: 256–83.

Jones, Charles I. 2001. "Comment on 'Trade Policy and Economic Growth: A Skeptic's Guide to the Cross-National Evidence,' by Rodriguez and Rodrik." In Ben S. Bernanke and Kenneth Rogoff, eds., *NBER Macroeconomics Annual 2000*, 330–38. Cambridge, Mass.: MIT Press.

Jones, Maldwyn A. 1983. *The Limits of Liberty*. East Kilbride, Scotland: Thomson.

Kahler, Miles. 1995. *International Institutions and the Political Economy of Integration*. Washington, D.C.: Brookings Institution Press.

Kanbur, R., M. Keen, and S. van Wijnbergen. 1995. "Industrial Competitiveness, Environmental Regulation and Direct Foreign Investment." In Ian Goldin and L. Alan Winters, eds., *The Economics of Sustainable Development*, 289–302. Cambridge, U.K.: Cambridge University Press.

Kant, Immanuel. [1795] 1992. *Perpetual Peace: A Philosophical Essay*. Bristol, U.K.: Thoemmes.

Karras, Georgios. 1997. "Economic Integration and Convergence: Lessons from Asia, Europe and Latin America." *Journal of Economic Integration* 12 (4): 419–32.

Kawai, Masahiro, and Shujiro Urata. 1996. "Trade Imbalances and Japanese Foreign Direct Investment: Bilateral and Triangular Issues." Discussion Paper Series F-52. Institute of Social Science, University of Tokyo.

Keller, Wolfgang. 1998. "Are International R&D Spillovers Trade-Related? Analyzing Spillovers among Randomly Matched Trade Partners." *European Economic Review* 42 (8, September): 1469–81.

————. 2002. "Geographic Localization of International Technology Diffusion." *American Economic Review* 92 (1, March): 120–42.

Kemp, M. C., and H. Wan, Jr. 1976. "An Elementary Proposition Concerning the Formation of Customs Unions." *Journal of International Economics* 6: 95–97.

Kokko, Ari. 1996. "Productivity Spillovers from Competition between Local Firms and Foreign Affiliates." *Journal of International Development* 8 (4, July–August): 517–30.

Konan, Denise E., and Keith E. Maskus. 2000. "Joint Trade Liberalization and Tax Reform in a Small Open Economy: The Case of Egypt." *Journal of Development Economics* 61 (2): 365–92.

Krishna, Pravin. 1998. "Regionalism and Multilateralism: A Political Economy Approach." *Quarterly Journal of Economics* 113 (1, February): 227–51.

————. Forthcoming a. "Are Regional Trading Partners 'Natural'?" *Journal of Political Economy*.

————. Forthcoming b. "Comment on 'Regionalism and Economic Development' by Anthony Venables." In R. Devlin, A. Estevadeordal, and S. Evenett, eds., *Regional Integration and Trade in the Development Agenda*. Brookings Institution and Inter-American Development Bank Conference, May 31–June 1, 2001. Washington, D.C.: Brookings Institution Press.

Krishna, Pravin, and Devashish Mitra. 1998. "Trade Liberalization, Market Discipline and Productivity Growth: New Evidence from India." *Journal of Development Economics* 56 (2, August): 447–62.

Krueger, Anne O. 1997. "Political Economy of Mexico's Entry into NAFTA." In Takatoshi Ito and Anne O. Krueger, eds., *Regionalism versus Multilateral Trade Arrangements*. Chicago: University of Chicago Press.

Krugman, Paul R. 1991. "Is Bilateralism Bad?" In Elhanan Helpman and Assaf Razin, eds., *International Trade and Trade Policy*. Cambridge, Mass.: MIT Press.

————. 1993. "Regionalism versus Multilateralism: Analytical Notes." In Jaime de Melo and Arvind Panagariya, eds., *New Dimensions in Regional Integration,* 58–78. New York: Cambridge University Press.

Krugman, Paul R., and Raul Livas Elizondo. 1996. "Trade Policy and the Third World Metropolis." *Journal of Development Economics* 49: 137–50.

Krugman, Paul, and Anthony J. Venables. 1990. "Integration and the Competitiveness of Peripheral Industry." CEPR Discussion Paper 363. Centre for Economic Policy Research, London.

————. 1996. "Integration, Specialization, and Adjustment." *European Economic Review* 40 (3–5): 959–67.

Kugler, Maurice. 2001. "Sectoral Diffusion of Spillovers from Foreign Direct Investment." Department of Economics Working Paper. University of Southampton, U.K.

Lawrence, Robert Z. 1991. "Emerging Regional Arrangements: Building Blocs or Stumbling Blocks?" In Richard O'Brien, ed., *Finance and the International Economy 5: The AMEX Bank Review Prize Essays,* 23–35. New York: Oxford University Press.

————. 1996. *Regionalism, Multilateralism, and Deeper Integration*. Washington, D.C.: Brookings Institution Press.

Lawrence, Robert Z., and Robert E. Litan. 1990. "The World Trading System after the Uruguay Round." *Boston University International Law Journal* 8 (2, fall): 247–76.

Lecomte, Henri Bernard Solignac. 1998. "Options for Future ACP-EU Trade Relations." ECDPM Working Paper 60. European Centre for Development Policy Management, Maastricht, the Netherlands.

Levinsohn, James. 1993. "Testing the Imports-as-Market-Discipline Hypothesis." *Journal of International Economics* 35 (1–2, August): 1–22.

Levy, Philip. 1995. "Free Trade Agreements and Inter-Bloc Tariffs." January. Yale University, New Haven, Conn. Processed.

————. 1997. "A Political Economy Analysis of Free-Trade Agreements." *American Economic Review* 87 (4): 506–19.

López, Ramón E., and Maurice Schiff. 1998. "Migration and the Skill-Composition of the Labor Force: The Impact of Trade Liberalization in LDCs." *Canadian Journal of Economics* 31 (2): 318–36.

Lucas, Robert E. 1988. "On the Mechanics of Economic Development." *Journal of Monetary Economics* 22 (July): 3–42.

Lumenga-Neso, Olivier, Marcelo Olarreaga, and Maurice Schiff. 2001. "On 'Indirect' Trade-Related Research and Development Spillovers." Policy Research Working Paper 2580. World Bank, Development Research Group, Trade, Washington, D.C. Available at <http://econ.worldbank.org/resource.php?type=5>.

Machlup, Fritz. 1977. *A History of Thought on Economic Integration.* New York: Columbia University Press.

Magee, Stephen P., and Hak-loh Lee. 1997. "Tariff Creation and Tariff Diversion in a Customs Union: The Endogenous External Tariff of the EEC, 1968–1983." Nota Di Lavoro 38 (97): 1–39. Fondazione Eni Enrico Mattei, Milan.

Mansfield, Edward D. 1993. "Effects of International Politics on Regionalism in International Trade." In Kym Anderson and Richard Blackhurst, eds., *Regional Integration and the Global Trading System.* New York: St. Martin's Press.

Marshall, Alfred. 1920. *Principles of Economics.* London: Macmillan.

Martin, Will. 1996. "Assessing the Implications for Lebanon of Free Trade with the European Union." World Bank, Washington, D.C. Processed.

McKibbin, Warwick J. 1994. "Dynamic Adjustment to Regional Integration: Europe 1992 and NAFTA." *Journal of the Japanese and International Economy* 8: 422–53.

McMillan, John. 1993. "Does Regional Integration Foster Open Trade? Economic Theory and GATT's Article XXIV." In Kym Anderson and Richard Blackhurst, eds., *Regional Integration and the Global Trading System,* 292–310. New York: St. Martin's Press.

McQueen, Matthew. 1998. "Lomé versus Free Trade Agreements: The Dilemma Facing the ACP Countries." *World Economy* 21 (4, June): 421–44.

Messerlin, Patrick A. 1983. "Bureaucracies and the Political Economy of Protection: Reflections of a Continental European." *Weltwirtschaftliches Archiv* 117: 468–96.

————. 1997. "Competition Policy and Anti-Dumping Reform." In Jeffrey J. Schott, ed., *The World Trading System: Challenges Ahead.* Washington, D.C.: Institute for International Economics.

————. 1998. "Technical Regulations and Industry Standards in the EU." World Bank, Washington, D.C. Processed.

—————. 2001. *Measuring the Costs of Protection in Europe: European Commercial Policy in the 2000s.* Washington, D.C.: Institute for International Economics.

Midelfart Knarvik, Karen Helene, Henry G. Overman, Stephen Redding, and Anthony J. Venables. 1999. "The Location of Industry in Europe." *Economic Papers* 142. European Commission, Brussels.

Milward, A. S. 1984. *The Reconstruction of Europe, 1945–51.* Berkeley: University of California Press.

—————. 1992. *The European Rescue of the Nation-State.* Berkeley: University of California Press.

Milward, Alan S., and S. B. Saul. 1973. *The Economic Development of Continental Europe, 1780–1870.* Totowa, N.J.: Rowman and Littlefield.

Mohieldin, M. 1997. "The Egypt-EU Partnership Agreement and Liberalization of Services." In Ahmed Galal and Bernard Hoekman, eds., *Regional Partners in Global Markets: Limits and Possibilities of the Euro-Med Agreements.* London: Centre for Economic Policy Research.

Morrison, A. R., and C. A. Zabin. 1994. "Two-Step Mexican Migration to the United States: The Role of Mexican Export Agriculture." Tulane University, Department of Economics, New Orleans, La. Processed.

Motta, Massimo, and George Norman. 1996. "Does Economic Integration Cause Foreign Direct Investment?" *International Economic Review* 37 (4, November): 757–83.

Moukarbel, Iskandar. 1997. "Impact of the Free Trade Agreement with the European Union Countries on the Lebanese Economy." In Wassim Shahin and Kamal Shehadi, eds., *Pathways to Integration: Lebanon and the Euro-Mediterranean Partnership*, ch. 7. Beirut: Lebanese Center for Policy Studies.

Murphy, Craig. 1994. *International Organization and Industrial Change: Global Governance since 1850.* New York: Oxford University Press.

Neven, Damien J. 1996. "Regulatory Reform and the Internal Market." In Organisation for Economic Co-operation and Development, *Regulatory Reform and International Market Openness.* Paris.

Ng, Francis, and L. Alan Winters. 1998. "Tariff Reform in Senegal: A Simple Numerical Analysis." World Bank, Development Research Department, Washington, D.C.

Nishimizu, Mieko, and John M. Page, Jr. 1982. "Total Factor Productivity Growth, Technological Progress, and Technical Efficiency Change: Dimensions of Productivity Change in Yugoslavia, 1965–78." *Economic Journal* 92 (368, December): 920–36.

Nogués, Julio, and R. Quintanilla. 1993. "Latin America's Integration and the Multilateral Trading System." In Jaime de Melo and Arvind Panagariya, eds.,

New Dimensions in Regional Integration, 278–313. New York: Cambridge University Press.

Nordstrom, H. 1995. "Customs Unions, Regional Trading Blocs and Welfare." In Richard Baldwin, Pertti Haaparanta, and Jaakko Kiander, eds., *Expanding Membership of the European Union,* 54–78. Cambridge, U.K.: Cambridge University Press.

North, Douglass C. 1990. *Institutions, Institutional Change and Economic Performance.* Cambridge, U.K.: Cambridge University Press.

OECD (Organisation for Economic Co-operation and Development). 1995. *Regional Integration and the Multilateral Trading System: Synergy and Divergence.* Paris.

Olarreaga, Marcelo, and Isidro Soloaga. 1998. "Endogenous Tariff Formation: The Case of Mercosur." *World Bank Economic Review* 12 (2, May): 297–320.

Olson, Mancur, Jr. 1996. "Big Bills Left on the Sidewalk: Why Some Nations Are Rich and Others Poor." *Journal of Economic Perspectives* 10 (2): 3–24.

Ordover, J. A., and R. D. Willig. 1986. "Perspectives on Mergers and World Competition." In Ronald E. Grieson, ed., *Antitrust and Regulation.* Lexington, Mass.: Lexington Books.

Ostry, Sylvia. 1998. Presentation to the First Academic Colloquium of the Americas, San José, Costa Rica.

Oye, Kenneth. 1992. *Economic Discrimination and Political Exchange: World Political Economy in the 1930s and 1980s.* Princeton, N.J.: Princeton University Press.

Page, Sheila. 1996. "Intensity Measures for Regional Groups." Prepared for the European Association of Development Research and Training Institutes (EADI) Ninth General Conference, September 11–14, Vienna.

————. 1998. "Regions and Developing Countries." Overseas Development Institute, London. Processed.

Palmeter, N. David. 1993. "Pacific Regional Trade Liberalization and Rules of Origin." *Journal of World Trade* 27 (5, October): 49–62.

Panagariya, Arvind. 1997. "The Meade Model of Preferential Trading: History, Analytics and Policy Implications." In Benjamin J. Cohen, ed., *International Trade and Finance: New Frontiers for Research,* 57–88. Cambridge, U.K.: Cambridge University Press.

Panagariya, Arvind, and R. Findlay. 1996. "A Political-Economy Analysis of Free-Trade Areas and Customs Unions." In Robert C. Feenstra, Gene M. Grossman, and Douglas A. Irwin, eds., *The Political Economy of Trade Policy: Papers in Honor of Jagdish Bhagwati.* Cambridge, Mass.; London: MIT Press. Reprinted 1999 in Jagdish Bhagwati, Pravin Krishna, and Arvind

Panagariya, eds., *Trading Blocs: Alternative Approaches to Analyzing Preferential Trade Agreements*, 335–56. Cambridge, Mass.: MIT Press.

Panagariya, Arvind, and Pravin Krishna. 2002. "On Necessarily Welfare-Enhancing Free Trade Areas." *Journal of International Economics* 57 (2): 353–67.

Pelkmans, J. 1990. "Regulation and the Single Market: An Economic Perspective." In Horst Siebert, ed., *The Completion of the Internal Market*. Tübingen, Germany: J. C. B. Mohr.

Pelkmans, J., and P. Brenton. 1999. "Bilateral Trade Agreement with the EU: Driving Forces and Effects." In Olga Memedovic, Arie Kuyvenhoven, and Willem T. M. Molle, eds., *Multilateralism and Regionalism in the Post–Uruguay Round Era: What Role for the EU?* 87–120. Boston, Mass.: Kluwer Academic.

Perroni, Carlo, and John Whalley. 1994. "The New Regionalism: Trade Liberalization or Insurance?" NBER Working Paper 4626. National Bureau of Economic Research, Cambridge, Mass. Available at <http://papers.nber.org/papers/w4626>.

Pittman, Russell. 1998. "Competition Law in Central and Eastern Europe: Five Years Later." *Antitrust Bulletin* 43 (1): 174–228.

Polachek, Solomon W. 1992. "Conflict and Trade: An Economics Approach to Political Interactions." In Walter Isard and Charles H. Anderton, eds., *Economics of Arms Reduction and the Peace Process: Contributions from Peace Economics and Peace Science*, 89–120. Amsterdam: North-Holland.

—————. 1996. "Why Democracies Cooperate More and Fight Less: The Relationship between International Trade and Cooperation." *Review of International Economics* 5 (3): 295–309.

Pollard, Sidney. 1974. *European Economic Integration, 1815–1970*. London: Thames and Hudson.

Porter, Michael. 1998. *On Competition*. Cambridge, Mass.: Harvard Business School Press.

Preeg, Ernest H. 1970. *Traders and Diplomats; An Analysis of the Kennedy Round of Negotiations under the General Agreement on Tariffs and Trade*. Washington, D.C.: Brookings Institution.

Puga, Diego, and Anthony J. Venables. 1997. "Preferential Trading Arrangements and Industrial Location." *Journal of International Economics* 43 (3–4): 347–68.

—————. 1998. "Trading Arrangements and Industrial Development." *World Bank Economic Review* 12 (2): 221–50.

Richardson, Martin. 1994. "Why a Free Trade Area? The Tariff Also Rises." *Economics and Politics* 6 (1): 79–96.

————. 1995. "Tariff Revenue Competition in a Free Trade Area." *European Economic Review* 39: 1429–37.

Ricupero, Rubens. 1998. "What Policy Makers Should Know about Regionalism." Keynote address, World Bank conference on regionalism, Geneva, May.

Roberts, Mark J., and James R. Tybout. 1996. *Industrial Evolution in Developing Countries: Micro Patterns of Turnover, Productivity, and Market Structure.* New York: Oxford University Press.

Robinson, Sherman, and Karen Thierfelder. 1999. "Trade Liberalization and Regional Integration: The Search for Large Numbers." TMD Discussion Paper 34. International Food Policy Research Institute, Trade and Macroeconomics Division, Washington, D.C.

Robson, Peter. 1987. *Integration, Développement et Equité.* Paris: Economica.

————. 1998. *Economics of International Integration.* 4th ed. London: Routledge.

Rodriguez, Francisco, and Dani Rodrik. 2001. "Trade Policy and Economic Growth: A Skeptic's Guide to the Cross-National Evidence." In Ben S. Bernanke and Kenneth Rogoff, eds., *NBER Macroeconomics Annual 2000.* Cambridge, Mass.: MIT Press.

Rodrik, Dani. 1988. "Imperfect Competition, Scale Economies, and Trade Policy in Developing Countries." In *Trade Policy Issues and Empirical Analysis,* 109–37. National Bureau of Economic Research Conference Report series. Chicago: University of Chicago Press.

Roemer, J. E. 1977. "The Effect of Sphere of Influence and Economic Distance on the Commodity Composition of Trade in Manufactures." *Review of Economic Statistics* 59: 318–27.

Romer, Paul M. 1986. "Increasing Returns and Long-Run Growth." *Journal of Political Economy* 94 (5): 1002–37.

————. 1990. "Endogenous Technical Change." *Journal of Political Economy* 98: S71–S102.

Rowat, Malcolm, Michele Lubrano, and Rafael Porrata. 1997. *Competition Policy and MERCOSUR.* World Bank Technical Paper 385. Washington, D.C.

Ruggie, John G. 1992. "Multilateralism: The Anatomy of an Institution." *International Organization* 45 (3, summer): 561–98.

Rutherford, Thomas F., Elisabet E. Rutstrom, and David Tarr. 2000. "A Free Trade Agreement between the European Union and a Representative Arab Mediterranean Country: A Quantitative Assessment." In Bernard Hoekman and Jamel Zarrouk, eds., *Catching Up with the Competition: Trade Opportunities and Challenges for Arab Countries.* Ann Arbor: University of Michigan Press.

Sachs, Jeffrey D., and Andrew Warner. 1995a. "Economic Reform and the Process of Global Integration." *Brookings Papers on Economic Activity* 1: 1–95.

—————. 1995b. "Natural Resource Abundance and Economic Growth." NBER Working Paper 5398. National Bureau of Economic Research, Cambridge, Mass. Available at <http://papers.nber.org/papers/w5398>.

Sapir, André. 1992. "Regional Integration in Europe." *Economic Journal* 102 (415): 1491–506.

—————. 1993. "The European Community: A Case of Successful Integration? A Comment." In Jaime de Melo and Arvind Panagariya, eds., *New Dimensions in Regional Integration*. New York: Cambridge University Press.

—————. 1995. "The Interaction between Labour Standards and International Trade Policy." *World Economy* 18 (6): 791–803.

—————. 1997. "Domino Effects in West European Trade, 1960–92." CEPR Discussion Paper 1576. Centre for Economic Policy Research, London.

—————. 1998. "The Political Economy of EC Regionalism." *European Economic Review* 42: 717–32.

Scharpf, Fritz W. 1988. "The Joint Decision Trap: Lessons from German Federalism and European Integration." *Public Administration* 66 (autumn): 239–78.

Schattschneider, E. E. 1935. *Politics, Pressures and the Tariff*. New York: Arno Press.

Schiff, Maurice. 1997. "Small is Beautiful: Preferential Trade Agreements and the Impact of Country Size, Market Share, and Smuggling." *Journal of Economic Integration* 12 (3, September): 359–87.

—————. 1998. "Ethnic Diversity and Economic Reform in Sub-Saharan Africa." *Journal of African Economies* 7 (3): 348–61.

—————. 2001. "Will the Real Natural Trading Partner Please Stand up?" *Journal of Economic Integration* 16 (2, June): 245–62.

Schiff, Maurice, and Won Chang. Forthcoming. "Market Presence, Contestability, and the Terms-of-Trade Effect of Regional Integration." *Journal of International Economics*.

Schiff, Maurice, and Yanling Wang. 2002a. "Education, Governance, and Trade-Related Technology Spillovers in Latin America." World Bank, Development Research Group, Trade, Washington, D.C. Processed.

—————. 2002b. "Regional Integration and Trade-Related Technology Diffusion: The Case of NAFTA." World Bank, Development Research Group, Trade, Washington, D.C. Processed.

————. 2002c. "Technology Diffusion and Productivity Gains: Mexico and Poland's Trade with CUSFTA and the EU." World Bank, Washington, D.C.

Schiff, Maurice, and L. Alan Winters. 1998. "Regional Integration as Diplomacy." *World Bank Economic Review* 12 (2, May): 271–95.

————. 2002a. "Regional Cooperation and the Role of International Organizations and Regional Integration." Policy Research Working Paper 2872. World Bank, Development Research Group, Trade, Washington, D.C. Available at <http://econ.worldbank.org/resource.php?type=5>.

————. 2002b. "Regionalism and Development: The Implications of World Bank Research for ACP and Latin American Countries." *Journal of World Trade* 36 (3, June): 479–99.

Schiff, Maurice, Yanling Wang, and Marcelo Olarreaga. 2002. "Trade-Related Technology Diffusion and the Dynamics of North-South and South-South Integration." Policy Research Working Paper 2861. World Bank, Development Research Group, Trade, Washington, D.C. Available at <http://econ.worldbank.org/resource.php?type=5>.

Schöne, Rainer. 1996. "Alternatives to Anti-Dumping from an Antitrust Perspective." Ph.D. dissertation. University of St. Gallen, Switzerland.

Schott, Jeffrey, ed. 1989. *Free Trade Areas and U.S. Trade Policy*. Washington, D.C.: Institute for International Economics.

Scollay, Robert, and John P. Gilbert. 2001. *New Regional Trading Arrangements in the Asia Pacific?* Policy Analyses in International Economics 64. Washington, D.C.: Institute for International Economics.

Serra, Jaime, José Córdoba, Gene Grossman, Carla Hills, John Jackson, Julius Katz, Pedro Noyola, and Michael Wilson. 1997. *Reflections on Regionalism: Report of the Study Group on International Trade*. New York: Carnegie Endowment for International Peace.

Sewastynowicz, James. 1986. "Two-Step Migration and Upward Mobility on the Frontier: The Safety Valve Effect in Pejibaye, Costa Rica." *Economic Development and Cultural Change* 34 (July): 731–53.

Shepsle, Kenneth A., and Barry A. Weingast. 1981. "Political Preferences for the Pork Barrel: A Generalization." *American Journal of Political Science* 25 (February): 96–111.

Smarzynska, Beata K. 2000. "Technological Leadership and Foreign Investors' Choice of Entry Mode." Policy Research Working Paper 2314. World Bank, Development Research Group, Trade, Washington, D.C. Available at <http://econ.worldbank.org/resource.php?type=5>.

————. 2002. "Composition of Foreign Direct Investment and Protection of Intellectual Property Rights: Evidence from Transition Economies." Policy Research Working Paper 2786. World Bank, Development Research Group,

Trade, Washington, D.C. Available at <http://econ.worldbank.org/resource.php?type=5>.

Smith, Alasdair, and Anthony J. Venables. 1988. "Completing the Internal Market in the European Community: Some Industry Simulations." *European Economic Review* 32: 1501–25.

Soloaga, Isidro, and L. Alan Winters. 2001. "Regionalism in the Nineties: What Effect on Trade?" Policy Research Working Paper 2156. World Bank, Washington, D.C. Available at <http://econ.worldbank.org/resource.php?type=5>. Also issued as CEPR Discussion Paper 2183, Centre for Economic Policy Research, London, 1999.

Solow, Robert M. 1956. "A Contribution to the Theory of Economic Growth." *Quarterly Journal of Economics* 70 (1): 65–94.

Srinivasan, T. N. 1994. "Regional Trading Arrangements and Beyond: Exploring Some Options for South Asia: Theory, Empirics and Policy." Report IDP-142. World Bank, South Asia Region, Washington, D.C.

————. 1997. "The Common External Tariff of a Customs Union: Alternative Approaches." *Japan and the World Economy* 9: 447–65.

————. 1998. "Regionalism and the WTO: Is Nondiscrimination Passé?" In Anne O. Krueger, ed., *The WTO as an International Organization*. Chicago: University of Chicago Press.

Stephenson, S. 1996. "The Economic Impact of Rules of Origin in the Asia-Pacific Region." Prepared for the Eighth Trade Policy Forum of the Pacific Economic Co-operation Council, Seoul, September.

Summers, Lawrence H. 1991. "Regionalism and the World Trading System." In *Policy Implications of Trade and Currency Zones: A Symposium Sponsored by the Federal Reserve Bank of Kansas City, Jackson Hole, Wyoming, August 22–24, 1991, 295–302*. Kansas City, Mo.: Federal Reserve Bank of Kansas City.

Swann, Dennis. 1992. *The Economics of the Common Market*. Harmondsworth, Middlesex, U.K.: Penguin.

Talbott, Strobe. 1996. "Democracy and the National Interest." *Foreign Affairs* 75: 47–63.

Tavares de Araujo, José, and Luis Tineo. 1998. "The Harmonization of Competition Policies among Mercosur Countries." *Antitrust Bulletin* 43 (1): 45–70.

Taylor, Telford. 1979. *Munich: The Price of Peace*. New York: Vintage.

Teljeur, E. 1998. "Free Trade: Does South Africa Gain?" *Trade and Industry Monitor* 6: 1–6. Trade and Industry Secretariat, South Africa.

Tinbergen, Jan. 1954. *International Economic Integration*. Amsterdam: Elsevier.

Togan, Subidey. 1997. "Opening Up the Turkish Economy in the Context of the Customs Union with EU." *Journal of Economic Integration* 12: 157–79.

Torrent, Ramon. 2002. "Regional Integration Instruments and Dimensions: An Analytical Framework." In Robert Devlin and Antoni Estevadeordal, eds., *New Frontiers in Trade and Regional Integration*, ch. 8. Washington, D.C.: Inter-American Development Bank.

Truman, E. M. 1975. "The Effects of European Economic Integration on the Production and Trade of Manufactured Products." In Bela Balassa, ed., *European Economic Integration*, 3–40. Amsterdam: North Holland.

Tybout, James. 2000. "Manufacturing Firms in Developing Countries: How Well Do They Do, and Why?" *Journal of Economic Literature* 38 (1, March): 11–44.

Tybout, James R., and M. Daniel Westbrook. 1995. "Trade Liberalization and the Dimensions of Efficiency Change in Mexican Manufacturing Industries." *Journal of International Economics* 39 (1–2, August): 53–78.

Tybout, James, Jaime de Melo, and Vittorio Corbo. 1991. "The Effects of Trade Reforms on Scale and Technical Efficiency: New Evidence from Chile." *Journal of International Economics* 31 (3–4, November): 231–50.

Unter, Brian. 1998. "Maximizing Custom Benefits—A Global Model for Regulatory Reform." Prepared for the U.S.-China Standards, Testing, and Certification Workshop, Information Technology Industry Council, Washington, D.C., February 17–18.

USITC (U.S. International Trade Commission). 1997. *The Impact of the North American Free Trade Agreement on the U.S. Economy and Industries: A Three-Year Review*. USITC Publication 3045. Washington, D.C.

Vamvakidis, Athanasios. 1998. "Regional Integration and Economic Growth." *World Bank Economic Review* 12 (2, May): 251–70.

————. 1999. "Regional Trade Agreements or Broad Liberalisation: Which Path Leads to Faster Growth? Time Series Evidence." *IMF Staff Papers* 46 (1, March). Available at <http://www.imf.org/external/pubind.htm>.

Venables, A. 2000. "Les accords d'intégration régionale: facteurs de convergence ou de divergence?" (Regional integration agreements: Forces for convergence or divergence?). *Revue d'Economie du Développement* (June): 227–46.

————. 2002. "Winners and Losers from Regional Integration Agreements." London School of Economics, Department of Economics. Processed.

Verdoorn, P. J. 1960. "The Intra-Bloc Trade of Benelux." In E. A. G. Robinson, ed., *Economic Consequences of the Size of Nations*. London: Macmillan.

Viner, Jacob. 1950. *The Customs Union Issue*. New York: Carnegie Endowment for International Peace.

Vogel, David. 1995. *Trading Up: Consumer and Environmental Regulation in a Global Economy*. Cambridge, Mass.: Harvard University Press.

Wallace, William. 1994. *Regional Integration: The West European Experience.* Washington, D.C.: Brookings Institution Press.

Wang, Z. K., and L. Alan Winters. 1998. "Africa's Role in Multilateral Trade Negotiations: Past and Future." *Journal of African Economies* 7: 1–33.

Whalley, John. 1998a. "The Interface between Environmental and Trade Policies." In Alan M. Rugman and John J. Kiron, with Julie A. Soloway, eds., *Trade and the Environment: Economic, Legal and Policy Perspectives,* 72–81. Elgar Reference Collection. International Library of Critical Writings in Economics, vol. 87. Cheltenham, U.K.: Elgar.

————. 1998b. "Why Do Countries Seek Regional Trade Agreements?" In Jeffrey A. Frankel, ed., *The Regionalization of the World Economy,* ch. 3. Chicago: University of Chicago Press.

Willmore, L. N. 1974. "The Pattern of Trade and Specialisation in the Central American Common Market." *Journal of Economic Studies* 1: 113–34.

————. 1976. "Trade Creation, Trade Diversion and Effective Protection in the Central American Common Market." *Journal of Development Studies* 12: 396–14.

Wilson, John S. 1996. "Eliminating Barriers to Trade in Telecommunications and Information Technology Goods and Services: Next Steps in Multilateral and Regional Liberalization Efforts." In Organisation for Economic Co-operation and Development, *Regulatory Reform and International Market Openness.* Paris.

————. 1999. "Product Standards and International Trade." World Bank, Washington, D.C. Available at <www1.worldbank.org/wbiep/trade/Standards/papers.htm>.

Winham, Gilbert R. 1986. *International Trade and the Tokyo Round Negotiation.* Princeton, N.J.: Princeton University Press.

Winters, L. Alan. 1987. "Britain in Europe: A Survey of Quantitative Trade Studies." *Journal of Common Market Studies* 25: 315–35.

————. 1992a. "Integration, Trade Policy and European Footwear Trade." In L. Alan Winters, ed., *Trade Flows and Trade Policy after "1992,"* 175–209. Cambridge, U.K.: Cambridge University Press.

————, ed. 1992b. *Trade Flows and Trade Policy after "1992."* Cambridge, U.K.: Cambridge University Press.

————. 1993. "The European Community: A Case of Successful Integration." In Jaime de Melo and Arvind Panagariya, eds., *New Dimensions in Regional Integration.* New York: Cambridge University Press.

————. 1994. "The EC and Protection: The Political Economy." *European Economic Review* 38: 596–603.

————. 1997a. "Lebanon's Euro-Mediterranean Agreement: Possible Dynamic Benefits." In Wassim Shahin and Kamal Shehadi, eds., *Pathways to Integration: Lebanon and the Euro-Mediterranean Partnership,* ch. 3. Beirut: Lebanese Center for Policy Studies.

————. 1997b. "What Can European Experience Teach Developing Countries about Integration?" *World Economy* 20: 889–912.

————. 2000. "The EU's Preferential Trade Agreements: Objectives and Outcomes." In Pitou van Dijck and Gerrit Faber, eds., *The External Economic Dimension of the European Union,* 195–222. The Hague: Kluwer Law International.

————. 2001. "Post-Lomé Trading Arrangements: The Multilateral Alternative." In Jürgen von Hagen and Mika Widgren, eds., *Regionalism in Europe.* Boston: Kluwer Academic.

————. 2002. "Doha and the World Poverty Targets." Prepared for Annual Bank Conference on Development Economics, World Bank, Washington, D.C., April 25, 2002. Available at <http://econ.worldbank.org/view.php?type=5&confid=2579&id=14983>.

Winters, L. Alan, and Won Chang. 2000. "Regional Integration and Import Prices: An Empirical Investigation." *Journal of International Economics* 51 (2): 363–77.

Wolff, Edward N., and M. Ishaq Nadiri. 1993. "Spillover Effects, Linkage Structure, and Research and Development." *Structural Change and Economic Dynamics* 4 (December): 315–31.

Wonnacott, Paul, and Mark Lutz. 1989. "Is There a Case For Free Trade Areas?" In Jeffrey Schott, ed., *Free Trade Areas and U.S. Trade Policy,* 59–84. Washington, D.C.: Institute for International Economics.

Wonnacott, Paul, and Ronald Wonnacott. 1981. "Is Unilateral Tariff Reduction Preferable to a Customs Union? The Curious Case of the Missing Foreign Tariffs." *American Economic Review* 71 (4): 704–14.

Wonnacott, Ronald J. 1996. "Free Trade Agreements: For Better or Worse?" *American Economic Review* 86 (2, May): 62–66.

World Bank. 2000. *Trade Blocs.* Policy Research Report. New York: Oxford University Press.

————. Various years. *World Development Indicators.* Washington, D.C.

WTO (World Trade Organization). 1995. *Regionalism and the World Trading System.* Geneva: WTO Secretariat.

————. *Annual Report, 1996.* Geneva.

————. 1998. "WTO Trade Facilitation Symposium, 9–10 March 1998, Report by the Secretariat." Document G/C/W/115. Geneva.

Yannopoulos, George N. 1990. "Foreign Direct Investment and European Integration: The Evidence from the Formative Years of the European Community." *Journal of Common Market Studies* 28 (3, March): 235–59.

Yeats, Alexander J. 1998. "Does Mercosur's Trade Performance Raise Concerns about the Effects of Regional Trade Arrangements?" *World Bank Economic Review* 12 (1, January): 1–28.

Yi, Sang-Seung. 1996. "Endogenous Formation of Customs Unions under Imperfect Competition: Open Regionalism Is Good." *Journal of International Economics* 41 (August): 153–77.

Index

insurance motive, 236–238
integration of domestic policies, *see* policy integration
intellectual property rights (IPR) protections, 134–135
Intergovernmental Authority on Development (IGAD), 76
intergovernmental organizations, trade-related, 172–173, 258n19, *see also* World Trade Organization (WTO)
International Centre for Settlement of Investment Disputes (ICSID), 105
International Monetary Fund (IMF), 111
international norms, adoption of, 170–174
interventionism, 5
intraindustry trade, 46–47
investment, 17–18, 101–103
  BITs, 17, 104–105
  capital, rate of return on, 114
  credibility provided by RIAs, 107–113
  FDI, *see* foreign direct investment
  general policy reforms more important than RIAs, 102–103
  growth and industrial location, 103, 115–117
  lower transaction costs, RIAs leading to, 114
  multilateral agreements, 106–107, 113
  North-South agreements
    FDI, 119, 120–121
    growth, effect on, 116
    reform credibility, 108, 111–112
    South-South agreements, vs., 17, 102, 116–117
    stimulus to invest, 114, 115
  policies on, 101–102, 103–107
  policy integration, 150
  public planning projects, failure of, 103–104, 121n1
  reform of bad policy and incentives for good policy, RIAs providing, 108–112
  South-South agreements, 17, 102, 116–117

  stimulus to investment, RIAs as, 113–117
  trade diversion and excluded countries, 220–221
  treatment of investment in current RIAs, 105–106
IOC, *see* Indian Ocean Commission
IPR, *see* intellectual property rights) protections
Iran, Islamic Republic of, 203
Iraq, 203
Ireland, 26
Israel, 71, 259n24
Italy, 4, 26

J
Jamaica, 27
Japan
  ASEAN aid, 206
  estimated potential welfare effects of RIAs on, 216
  FDI, 117–119, 120
  FTAs, 6
  insurance motive, 238
  RIAs, selected list of, 27
  services trade restrictions, 160

K
Kant, Immanuel, 189
Kenya
  agglomeration and location of industries, 142
  collapse of East African Community, 121n1, 195
  comparative advantage, 69–71
  excluded countries, trade discrimination against, 211
  multiple memberships, 78
  public investment planning, failure of, 121n1
  RIAs, selected list of, 27, 28
knowledge capital and spillovers, 126–127
  agglomeration and location of industries, 137
  endogenous (self-generated) growth theory, 125, 126, 132–133

www.ingramcontent.com/pod-product-compliance
Lightning Source LLC
Chambersburg PA
CBHW020335270326
41926CB00007B/192